# PROTECTING THE PAST

## Edited by
## George S. Smith
## John E. Ehrenhard

CRC Press

Boca Raton  Ann Arbor  Boston  London

**Library of Congress Cataloging-in-Publication Data**

Protecting the past / edited by George S. Smith and John E. Ehrenhard.
     p.  cm.
  Includes bibilographical references and index.
  ISBN 0-8493-8877-5
  1. Cultural property. Protection of--United States 2. United
States--Antiquities--Collection and preservation. 3. Indians of
North America--Antiquities--Collection and preservation.
  4. Antiquities--Thefts.  I. Smith, GeorgeS. II Ehrenhard, John E.
E159.5.P76   1991
363.6'9--dc20

                       91-22870
                       CIP

This book represents information obtained from authentic and highly regarded sources. Reprinted material is quoted with permission, and sources are indicated. A wide variety of references are listed. Every reasonable effort has been made to give reliable data and information, but the author and the publisher cannot assume responsibility for the validity of all materials or for the consequences of their use.

Direct all inquiries to CRC Press, Inc., 2000 Corporate Blvd., N. W., Boca Raton, Florida, 33431.

Photo on cover is entitled "Lightning" courtesy of K. Kitagawa.

# PREFACE A

## Jeremy A. Sabloff

*"Words, words, mere words, no matter from the heart"*
*William Shakespeare, Twelfth Night*

For years archaeologists have lamented the looting and destruction of archaeological sites and materials. The efforts of a number of dedicated individuals, including both professional and avocational archaeologists, Native Americans, and elected officials, as well as small organizations such as the American Society for Conservation Archaeology, have resulted in some important laws and regulations that help to protect archaeological resources, on both the national and local levels. But in spite of all this assiduous work, looting and destruction continue unabated. Clearly, relatively small-scale attempts to change widespread practices, no matter how well intentioned or how skillfully argued, are simply not sufficient to bring these practices to a halt. Isolated victories over the forces of depredation are legion, but overall, the defenders of the archaeological record appear to be losing the war.

Fortunately, in recent years archaeologists have come to realize that they must change their tactics if they are to turn the tide in the preservation conflict. Informed by the successes of other preservationists, such as those concerned with the general environment, they have begun to adopt the successful tactics of group efforts and public outreach. Federal archaeologists, state historic preservation officers, state archaeologists, and the Society for American Archaeology, the largest association of professional archaeologists concerned with the archaeology of the Americas, have seen that if they speak in concert within their own spheres and work together more broadly on the preservation of the archaeological record, their chances of success increase.

Moreover, archaeologists have perceived that their undertakings in the realm of new legal means to combat looting will be of no avail without a well-planned campaign of public education. Telling the general populace, on one hand, and legislators, on the other, that ravagement of archaeological sites was bad and should be stopped was not as self-evident to their listeners as it was to them. Rhetoric alone obviously was insufficient. Archaeologists realized that exhortation had to be combined with clear, well-reasoned justifications.

Such a strategic shift, which is still underway, has not been as simple and easy as it would appear it should be. Over the years, archaeologists have become too accustomed to speaking to their colleagues who do not need to be persuaded about the unfortunate consequences of site destruction. They are not used to regularly dealing with people who disagree with their premises, or with others who are completely indifferent to the problems discussed and do not see them as moral issues. In addition, many of their colleagues have looked down at attempts to communicate with nonscholarly audiences. However, these problems are not insurmountable and, in the past few years, have happily begun to recede.

*Protecting the Past: Readings in Archaeological Resource Protection* is a superb example of the new strategy in outreach and discusses some of the recent successes in concerted action, many of the promising programs to counter looting that are currently being implemented or contemplated, and a few of the most difficult problems that still must be surmounted. I am certain that this highly ambitious book will have a very positive influence in such efforts, and I wish to congratulate and thank the editors and authors for putting together such an exciting, useful volume.

# PREFACE B

## Pete V. Domenici
## United States Senator

With unfortunate frequency, thieves break into some noted art museum and steal works of art. News of the heist is relayed around the world through television, radio, newspapers, and magazines. Invariably, the theft is described as "sensational," and commentators bemoan the loss of these treasured cultural objects.

The loss of these paintings and other artworks certainly is a tremendous loss not only to the museum from which they are stolen, but also to the public. No longer will the public be able to study and enjoy these works that are part of our shared cultural heritage. The public and the media are justifiably concerned about this cultural thievery.

Yet, where is the concern of the public and the media about the cultural thievery that is being committed every week across our land? On public lands across our nation, pothunters and other archaeological looters are digging through ancient Indian pueblos, historic Spanish shipwrecks, and the graves of Civil War soldiers and Native Americans, then stealing artifacts for a collection or sale.

A 1987 General Accounting Office (GAO) study found that approximately 44,000 of the 136,000 archaeological sites in the Four Corners States of New Mexico, Arizona, Colorado, and Utah have been looted. In a 5 1/2-year period ending in 1986, the Bureau of Land Management (BLM), the Forest Service, and the National Park Service documented 1222 looting incidents in the four states.

The stolen artifacts include woven baskets with intricate designs, turquoise ornaments, metates for grinding corn, bows and arrows, clothing made with feathers from domesticated turkeys, and, most importantly, pottery. The prehistoric peoples of the Four Corners States developed distinctive ceramics that are notable for the detailed geometric and pictorial designs with which they are decorated. They are more than just interesting artifacts; they are works of art.

Like an art heist, the theft of archaeological artifacts also deprives the public of the opportunity to study and enjoy objects that are part of our shared cultural heritage.

For example, a nationally significant archaeological site in New Mexico was recently looted. The site, which was in the process of being nominated for inclusion on the National Register of Historic Places, contains the ruins of a prehistoric pueblo associated with the Casas Grandes culture. The 20-acre site encompasses several plazas and as many as 250 rooms that were used by Native American people from 1200 to 1400 A.D.

Pothunters dug through the ruins, unearthing artifacts. In the process, they disturbed the site and scattered the artifacts that they did not want to steal. The looting not only led to the loss of cultural artifacts, but also destroyed valuable scientific information that could have been helpful in analyzing the culture of the people who lived there.

The media did not relay word of this tragic theft to the world. Where is the hue and cry about the theft of archaeological artifacts? Where are the reporters and the cameras alerting the public to this loss? Where are the commentators explaining the impact of this loss on our society?

Archaeological resources located on federal land have been protected since 1906, when Congress enacted the Antiquities Act. The Antiquities Act provides that qualified institutions may be issued permits for the excavation of archaeological sites. It also provides criminal penalties for unauthorized excavations. In the late 1970s the courts invalidated a crucial section of the Antiquities Act, thus creating the need for stronger legislation.

In 1979, I wrote the Archaeological Resources Protection Act (ARPA). ARPA toughened the laws protecting archaeological resources on federal lands by imposing severe criminal penalties for unauthorized excavation, damage, destruction, or removal of archaeological resources. It provides fines of up to $100,000 and 5 years in jail for criminal violations. It also allows federal land managers to impose civil penalties for violations and to grant rewards for information on violations.

In 1988 I authored amendments to ARPA that lowered the felony threshold for ARPA offenses, made attempted looting of archaeological artifacts on federal land a crime, directed federal land management agencies to develop plans for archaeological surveys of their lands, required the agencies to prepare a schedule for surveying those areas that are likely to contain the most important archaeological resources, and mandated that federal agencies develop processes for reporting suspected incidents of looting of archaeological resources on their lands.

Unfortunately, despite the effective mechanisms of ARPA, archaeological looting continues. A major reason for continued looting is the inadequate funding for federal cultural resource management to prevent looting.

We have made progress on funding for cultural resource management in recent years. In fiscal year 1981, $38.6 million was appropriated for cultural resource management by the Bureau of Land Management, the Forest Service, and the National Park Service. In fiscal year 1990, Congress appropriated $85.2 million. In real terms, funding for the cultural resource management programs of these three agencies increased 65% from 1981 to 1990.

Unfortunately, much remains to be done. The Federal Government efforts to protect archaeological resources on the lands under its control remain inadequate. Our nation's archaeological heritage continues to be stolen and sold as quaint curios.

Just as we are outraged by the theft of masterpieces from museums, we must also be outraged by the theft of our nation's archaeological artifacts. The failure to protect our nation's archaeological resources constitutes a breach of faith by the Federal Government. As the trustee of these lands for the American people, the Federal Government has an obligation to assure th these resources are not destroyed or stolen by those who have no respect for the past.

# PREFACE C

## Constance B. Harriman

Archaeological resources possess an aura of mystery, almost of magic: a bit of pottery, a drawing on a lonely canyon wall, a carved ornament — the owners long since vanished. Historian Barbara Tuchman expressed it well: "The unrecorded past is none other than our old friend, the tree in the primeval forest which fell without being heard." Our archaeological resources are our key to that unrecorded past.

We hold in our own hands a sherd of pottery perhaps untouched by other human hands for a thousand years. From a hundred different facts about it, we can begin to reach into the past. We try to reconstruct the lives of people who had hopes, dreams, and fears probably very similar to our own. And in doing so, we gain an understanding of ourselves.

But half of the facts about the pottery sherd may be forever lost by such a simple action as its mere careless removal from the exact spot where it was discarded long ago. The thief of the saleable artifacts that lay near it has no regard for the information so casually tossed aside. These thieves are not just stealing a piece of pottery or a bit of carved ornament. They are stealing from each one of us an irreplaceable part of our own human inheritance.

The authors, editors, and publisher of this volume are to be commended for providing such a timely and relevant set of articles on the topic of archaeological site protection. The articles provide up-to-date details on the problem; examples of efforts to fight looting; and descriptions of organizational, legal, and informational tools that can be used in our fight to protect the nation's archaeological resources. Taken in hand with the Society for American Archaeology's (SAA) recently released action plan to fight looting, *Save the Past for the Future: Actions for the '90s,* this volume should be of use and interest to many readers.

As the Assistant Secretary of the Interior for Fish and Wildlife and Parks, I was responsible for cultural and natural resource preservation policy development and implementation through programs managed by the Fish and Wildlife Service and the National Park Service. One of the major issues I faced, and in which I continue to be keenly interested, is the management and protection of our *cultural* heritage, because lands managed by federal agencies contain hundreds of thousands of archaeological and historic sites that bear witness to our history.

In recent years many of us in the conservation community have become increasingly alarmed at the rate at which our archaeological resources are being irretrievably lost. Thousands of archaeological sites and historic structures on federal, state, and private lands are being damaged by acts of vandalism, looting for personal or commercial gain, natural deterioration, and modern development. Federal land managers must continuously make difficult decisions on how best to attack these problems within budget and work force constraints. Because we are unable to protect in perpetuity *all* our archaeological sites, federal agencies are forced to choose and prioritize the sites that will receive protection.

It is imperative that archaeologists and archaeological organizations, such as the SAA, become more directly involved with federal land managers. Government agencies and private groups need to work together as partners to decide how they can best achieve their common interests in archaeological preservation. If they do not work together in partnership and cooperative approaches to protecting our irreplaceable and historic resources, the future of the archaeological manifestations of our country's heritage will be seriously in peril.

Paralleling the SAA *Save the Past for the Future* effort, Secretary of the Interior Manuel Lujan recently announced a new national strategy for archaeology programs in the Federal Government. On March 20, 1990, he issued a directive on protection of archaeological resources. His directive urges program managers to place greater emphasis on *four* program areas. Department of Interior land managers are to

1.  Emphasize public education activities for citizen participation in archaeological projects
2.  Explore ways federal and other public agencies can cooperate to prevent resource destruction and to discourage looting
3.  Improve the exchange of information between federal agencies about archaeological reports and investigations they undertake
4.  Survey public lands to locate and evaluate sites and implement programs to address the monumental challenge of curating federal collections and data

Both Secretary Lujan and I believe that all federal agencies should focus more attention on these four program areas. I urge archaeologists as well as federal land managers to immediately undertake all of these important activities.

I believe that the SAA's *Actions for the '90s* and Interior's initiative will enhance the preservation of America's rich archaeological heritage. Given the magnitude of the challenges before us and their urgency, we must work together — public agencies, archaeologists and their professional organizations, and the American public — to improve archaeological preservation in the years ahead.

# ACKNOWLEDGMENTS

We owe our thanks to many people. First and foremost are the individual authors who contributed their time and expertise to this volume. Without their cooperation, dedication, and friendship this book would not have been possible. Neither would this book have materialized without Pat Kelly of The Telford Press. It was his unsolicited inquiry to the Interagency Archeological Services Division that got this project started. That telephone call, seeking to know whether or not we would be interested in preparing a book on archeological resource protection, ultimately led to the coordination of a number of groups which were all in some way independently working on archaeological site protection projects. In particular, we would like to acknowledge the Interagency Working Group on the Public Awareness of Federal Archeology (chaired by the Archeological Assistance Division, National Park Service), the Society for American Archaeology Anti-Looting Project, the Taos Anti-Looting Conference participants, and the Center for Ancient Studies, University of Minnesota (who are responsible the excellent series entitled "Presenting the Past"). We are indebted to Drs. Bennie C. Keel and Charles R. McGimsey III for reviewing all the articles. These two men have worked tirelessly to protect the past and their insight and comments were most valuable. We would like to thank the National Park Service, Southeast Region and the Southeast Archeological Center for their moral support and encouragement in the early going. We are especially grateful to the staff of our respective divisions for carrying the workload while we worked on the book. Without their cooperation this volume would not have been completed on schedule.

Individual author acknowledgements are included at the end of some of the articles. This brings up an important point, that in any endeavor of this nature many more people than those acknowledged actually contribute to its successful completion. To those too numerous to name, the editors and the authors acknowledge your contributions. To all involved, it has been our honor and pleasure to work with such a diverse and professional group.

Last but not least a special note of appreciation to those men and women who in some way protected the past for all of us. Without their appreciation for the past and their desire to protect it little would be left and our understanding of the past and the discipline of archaeology would be considerably diminished.

**George S. Smith**
**John E. Ehrenhard**

# LIST OF CONTRIBUTORS

**Roger Anyon**
Director
Zuni Archaeology Program
Zuni, New Mexico

**Jean M. Auel**
Author
Sherwood, Oregon

**Judith A. Bense**
Associate Professor and Director
Institute of West Florida Archaeology
University of West Florida
Pensacola, Florida

**David S. Brose**
Chief Curator of Archaeology
Cleveland Museum of Natural History
Cleveland, Ohio

**Annetta L. Cheek**
Federal Preservation Officer
Office of Surface Mining Reclamation and
Enforcement
Washington D. C.

**Hester A. Davis**
State Archaeologist
Arkansas Archaeological Survey
Fayetteville, Arkansas

**Tom Des Jean**
Archaeologist
Big South Fork National River and
  Recreation Area
National Park Service
Oneida, Tennessee

**Pete V. Domenici**
Senator, New Mexico
Washington D. C.

**John E. Ehrenhard**
Chief
Interagency Archeological Services
  Division
National Park Service
Atlanta, Georgia

**Walter W. Enloe**
Director
Global Education
College of Education
University of Minnesota
Minneapolis, Minnesota

**John M. Fowler**
Deputy Executive Director and
  General Counsel
Advisory Council on Historic Preservation
Washington D. C.

**Edward Friedman**
Archaeologist
Bureau of Reclamation
Denver, Colorado

**Elizabeth Grant**
Attorney at Law
Federal Trade Commission
Washington D. C.

**Constance Harriman**
Former Assistant Secretary
Fish and Wildlife and Parks
Washington D. C.

**Nancy W. Hawkins**
Archaeologist
State Historic Preservation Office
Baton Rouge, Louisiana

**Teresa L. Hoffman**
Deputy State Historic Preservation Officer
Arizona State Parks
Phoenix, Arizona

**Sherry Hutt**
Judge
Maricopa County Superior Court
Phoenix, Arizona

**John H. Jameson Jr**.
Archaeologist
Interagency Archeological Services
  Division
National Park Service
Atlanta, Georgia

**W. James Judge**
Professor
Department of Anthropology
Fort Lewis College
Durango, Colorado

**Betsy Kearns**
Co-Director
Historical Perspectives, Inc.
Riverside, Connecticut

**Bennie C. Keel**
Archaeologist
Southeast Archeological Center
National Park Service
Tallahassee, Florida

**Thomas F. King**
Consultant in Historic Preservation
Silver Spring, Maryland

**Cece Kirkorian**
Co-Director
Historical Perspectives, Inc.
Riverside, Connecticut

**Marc Kodack**
Archaeologist
Environmental Resources Branch
Corps of Engineers
Savannah, Georgia

**Patricia C. Knoll**
Archaeologist
Archeological Assistance Division
National Park Service
Washington D. C.

**Ruthann Knudson**
Archaeologist
Archeological Assistance Division
National Park Service
Washington D. C.

**Shereen Lerner**
State Historic Preservation Officer
Arizona State Parks
Phoenix, Arizona

**Andrew R. Mason**
Graduate Student
Department of Anthropology and
  Sociology
University of British Columbia
Vancouver, British Columbia, Canada

**Martin E. McAllister**
Archaeologist
Archaeological Resource Investigations
Rolla, Missouri

**Charles R. McGimsey III**
Professor Emeritus
Department of Anthropology
University of Arkansas
Fayetteville, Arkansas

**Francis P. McManamon**
Departmental Consulting Archaeologist
National Park Service
Washington, D. C.

**Nan McNutt**
President
McNutt and Associates
Petersburg, Alaska

**Phyllis Mauch Messenger**
Associate to the Director/Director of
  Outreach
Institute of International Studies
University of Minnesota
Minneapolis, Minnesota

**Mark Michel**
President
The Archaeological Conservancy
Santa Fe, New Mexico

**Jerald T. Milanich**
Curator of Archaeology
Florida Museum of Natural History
Gainesville, Florida

**Paul R. Nickens**
Research Archaeologist
Department of the Army, Waterways
  Experiment Station, Corps of Engineers
Vicksburg, Mississippi

**Loretta Neumann**
President
CEHP, Inc.
Washington D. C.

**David L. Pokotylo**
Assistant Professor and Curator of
  Archaeology
Museum of Anthropology
University of British Columbia
Vancouver, British Columbia, Canada

**Kathleen M. Reinburg**
Vice President
CEHP, Inc.
Washington D. C.

**Kristine Olson Rogers**
Professor of Law and Associate Dean
  for Academic Affairs
Northwestern School of Law
Lewis and Clark College
Portland, Oregon

**A. E. (Gene) Rogge**
Director
Southwest Cultural Resources Services
Dames & Moore
Phoenix, Arizona

**Jeremy A. Sabloff**
Professor
Department of Anthropology
University of Pittsburgh
Pittsburgh, Pennsylvania

**Lynell Schalk**
Special Agent in Charge
Bureau of Land Management
Portland, Oregon

**Harvey M. Shields**
Director
Office of Research
U. S. Travel and Tourism Administration
Department of Commerce
Washington D. C.

**Karolyn E. Smardz**
Administrator
Archeological Resource Center
Toronto Board of Education
Toronto, Ontario, Canada

**George S. Smith**
Chief
Investigation and Evaluation Branch
Southeast Archeological Center
National Park Service
Tallahassee, Florida

**Richard C. Waldbauer**
Archaeologist
Archeological Assistance Division
National Park Service
Washington D. C.

**Peter S. Wells**
Director
Center for Ancient Studies
University of Minnesota
Minneapolis, Minnesota

# TABLE OF CONTENTS

# FORWARD

# PROTECTING THE PAST: CULTURAL RESOURCE MANAGEMENT — A PERSONAL PERSPECTIVE

## Charles R. McGimsey III

To be technical, it perhaps could be stated that cultural resource management (CRM) was born with the politicizing that preceded and was essential to the ultimate passage of the Antiquities Act of 1906. (For a fascinating account of this process, see Lee, 1970.) But as a coherent, identified concept applicable specifically to archaeology, it crystallized in the minds of a few archaeologists at the Airlie House conference in 1974 and was given formal birth, or at least was christened, with the publication of that report (McGimsey and Davis 1977). At least the Airlie House conferees thought that this was the case, for they specifically stated, "We soon realized we had an opportunity to legitimize and christen, through an official naming ceremony, what had actually been born over the past few years — the whole idea of cultural resource management" (McGimsey and Davis 1977:25).

Obviously, the concept of "managing" archaeological resources rather than simply investigating them did not spring full blown and without precedent in the minds of the Airlie participants. The principal value of the Airlie House conferences, as it was designed and intended to be, was the drawing together and crystallization of a wide range of previous thinking on a series of six specific topics relevant then (and now) to archaeology. One of the sets of discussions at Airlie House was specifically directed toward the management of archaeological resources (McGimsey and Davis 1977:25–63). I don't recall any discussions at the time as to whether we were really talking about "archaeological resource management." The Airlie discussions, by their very nature, were wide ranging and broadly based, and I think all of the participants, perhaps because of their anthropological background, were really thinking about and concerned with all cultural resources, not just archaeological ones. I do remember a discussion at a 1984 board meeting of the Society of Professional Archaeologists (SOPA) where it was suggested that the SOPA emphasis should really be titled archaeological resource management rather than cultural resource management, and indeed, they have so changed that title, but the idea never has achieved broad-scale acceptance, and perhaps it shouldn't. We all should be, and no doubt like to think that we are, interested in managing the full scope of cultural resources even if, as archaeologists, our primary area of concern is with the archaeological ones.

The Antiquitites Act of 1906 was followed, in an episodic fashion, by other efforts to legislate the management of the resource base (see Fowler, Friedman, Cheek, Neumann, and Rogers, this volume, for further discussion of historic preservation legislation). The establishment of the National Park Service (NPS) in 1916 and the Historic Sites Act of 1935 established a policy of public concern and resulted in management plans for some specific areas in federal ownership, but nothing developed that could be said to be a national consciousness of the need to protect and manage cultural resources. The archaeological profession itself, until well after World War II, tended to be a mirror of these times — more concerned with exploration and investigation than management.

This is not a criticism. At the time, the major concern, and correctly so, was to determine what was out there, archaeologically speaking, rather than with the disappearance of the resource base. There was so much that had not yet been discovered or understood that it was impossible to develop any realistic parameters regarding uniqueness or scarcity. There certainly was a sense of what was being lost through looters and other destructive forces, but an attempt to manage this archaeological resource base was simply not a realistic goal for the small number of professional archaeologists active in the U.S. prior to World War II.

The archaeological activity that took place during the Depression of the 1930s and into the early 1940s resulted in the recovery of massive amounts of archaeological data (much still undigested), but could not, in any realistic sense of the term, be described as management. It was primarily a channeling of available human resources toward archaeological targets of opportunity. That is not to say, of course, that considerable thought did not go into specific programs and projects.

Shortly after the conclusion of World War II, the U.S. Army Corps of Engineers established its ambitious program of damming and controlling part of the Missouri River Basin and, since then, most of the river systems in the U.S. As the Corps program got underway, Julian Steward challenged his Smithsonian archaeological colleagues to develop a program or course of action to deal with the archaeological consequences of this construction activity. The end result was the River Basin Salvage (RBS) program initiated by the Smithsonian, but soon transferred to the National Park Service and its Interagency Archeological Services (IAS). Though still geographically constrained, the areas inundated were so extensive and the funding, relatively speaking, so massive that some measure of cultural resource management inevitably came into play.

A major force throughout this era and beyond, the Committee on the Recovery of Archeological Remains (CRAR, as it became known) was an informally organized group of (largely) professional archaeologists and was sponsored by various scientific societies, but latterly it became essentially self-perpetuating. It served as an advisory body to the NPS Interagency Archeological Services, but it rapidly became also the chief legislative champion of archaeology and the archaeological conscience before Congress. More than once it saved the archaeological appropriation of the RBS and IAS programs.

CRAR also served as a major communication link among the rather considerable number of federal agencies involved with archaeology in the 20-year period of 1948 to 1968. It held annual meetings in Washington, D.C. (the travel expenses of which were paid by the NPS/IAS). The first day of the usual 2-day meeting was an informal no-holds-barred discussion with NPS personnel, many of whom were brought in from across the country. This give-and-take session discussed what the Federal Government felt the profession was doing right and wrong and, in turn, what the profession felt was right and wrong about the federal program. No outsiders (except those invited) were welcomed at these free-wheeling, essentially confidential sessions. The second day was much more formal and was usually held in one of the Department of Interior meeting rooms. CRAR sat as a panel and heard more or less formal reports (that it had requested) from all federal agencies active in archaeology, as to what that agency was doing and what problems it had had or foresaw. Thus, everyone concerned on the federal level was aware of what was happening archaeologically, and there was ample opportunity for interchange among the agencies and between them and the CRAR as representative of the profession.

CRAR fulfilled a vital but little known or heralded function during a critical period of archaeological development in this country. It died in 1977 largely as a result of a Carter Administration decision against advisory committees, unfortunately just at a time when the profession and the government were most in need of it. As a latter day member, I would like some day to more fully document this organization and the associated period of archaeological development. Certainly somebody should.

The real period of gestation leading to the conceptualization and birth of full blown programs of cultural resource management was, in my opinion, the 10 years from 1968 through 1977. No one person can be fully aware of the many rivulets that have become the present river of concepts identified under the rubric of cultural resource management. What follows is primarily a history of my own awareness of the process.

We need to set the stage. When I came to Arkansas in the fall of 1957 as an instructor in anthropology and assistant curator of the University Museum, I was the only archaeologist in the state. I knew little about southeastern archaeology and nothing about the archaeology of Arkansas. I had a commitment of $1000 to run a field school (a far better research budget than most states at the time, I was to find). So when Pinky Harrington of the NPS showed up on my doorstep a few months after my arrival to ask if I was interested in a contract to survey a reservoir (Greers Ferry) in north central Arkansas, I was delighted at the chance to learn by experience something of the local scene. Having been ensconced at the university for a few months, I presented myself to the dean (probably only the second or third time I had seen him) and asked for the spring semester off to do research. At the time I thought nothing of this request or of its being granted, though in retrospect I am both appalled at my innocence (gall?) and astonished at the dean's acquiescence.

My "research design" as proposed and accepted by the NPS (or perhaps it was vice versa) was simplicity itself. "I would find out as much as I could about what was present in the area, with the funds the NPS said it had available." That decided, in February 1958, I went to Greers Ferry, inquired around for an amateur, and asked him to show me an Indian mound. I had never seen one. The reader must bear in mind that except for a 20-page unpublished report on a brief season of survey at Table Rock Reservoir, some distance to the north of me, there was no archaeological literature for the entire north central part of the state (and very little for the rest).

That same year, the Arkansas General Assembly requested that I recommend what the state should do with regard to preserving its archaeological resources. As a good burgeoning bureaucrat, I conducted a poll of the other states. I found that for the vast majority of the states, my rather poor situation (fiscally and in terms of relevant literature) was anything but unique. The point of all this is that at that time the profession was not yet ready to manage anything.

To manage a resource you need have, at a minimum (1) some conception as to the nature and extent of the resource to be managed, (2) a plan, and (3) a fairly broad base of support for such a plan among the parties affecting the resource. In Arkansas and in almost all other states, none of these elements were yet present.

It was 1968 before I or my colleagues in the Mississippi Alluvial Valley began to look away from our immediate research projects and make any assessment of what was going on in the real world and how it might affect our archaeological resource base. In the case of Arkansas and Missouri, we were dragged out of our respective holes and asked to look about by John Corbett, then chief of the IAS (and a man who, in my opinion, has received too little recognition for his foresight and for his ability to hold together and develop the IAS during a critical period for the profession).

He asked, with disarming and feigned innocence, if either Carl Chapman or I had any idea what the Soil Conservation Service (SCS) program of land leveling was doing to the archaeological resources in our respective states. Neither of us did. John offered a little NPS money to help us find out.

We, like most archaeologists at the time, had been concerned chiefly with doing the best, most perceptive, scientific job we could on the targets of opportunity presented to us (which for many were river basin projects funded by NPS). We had little drive and generally less incentive to worry about the "larger picture" or being concerned with developing a program for managing the resources in an entire region, area, or state. And even if we had, few of us had adequate data with which to accomplish it.

For my part I had devoted much of my time between 1957 and 1968 to facilitating the development of public support for, and legislative adaption of, a statewide program in archaeology: an essential step toward management, no doubt, but I don't recall that I conceived of it in those terms at that time. I worked largely behind dams because that was where the money was and, frankly, devoted little more than hand-wringing attention to the rest. In that, I do not feel that I was unique.

It was an entirely new idea to me when Corbett suggested to Chapman and me that we should determine what effects land leveling and other agricultural practices were having on our state archaeology. And the most cursory look was a revelation. We discovered, for instance, that in Arkansas the SCS planned to level all levelable land in the next 20 years (they haven't quite), with a subsequent loss of perhaps four fifths of the sites in eastern Arkansas, the homeland of the Mississippi culture (Ford, Rolingson, and Medford 1972).

Things began happening thick and fast. In 1967 the Arkansas Legislature had finally established the statewide Arkansas Archeological Survey. In 1968, using the tag end of the Survey's first year appropriation, Hester Davis, Jimmy Griffin, and I initiated a series of conferences that resulted in the short-lived, but significant, MAVAP (Mississippi Alluvial Valley Archeological Program) organization.

We convened a series of three meetings: one each in Greenville, MS, the bootheel of Missouri, and in East St. Louis, IL, attended by some 50 archaeologists — most of those doing active research in the valley at that time. From this came one of the first regional research designs in the U.S. (McGimsey, Davis, and Griffin 1968); the booklet *Stewards of the Past* (60,000 copies of which were subsequently distributed by state organizations nationwide); the impetus of what became, five years later, the Moss-Bennett legislation; and a stark realization on the part of all of us that we were indeed facing a situation of crisis proportions (Davis 1972a). We decided we had jolly well better start developing some plans.

It was at this same time, too, that I had completed a second national survey of state- and federally supported archaeological programs (again at the request of the Arkansas General Assembly), the result of which was largely completed by late 1970 (McGimsey 1972).

In short, in the span of a few short years I had gone from a scientific life concerned with my own particular research projects of the moment to being almost forced to concentrate on archaeological resources in the broadest possible context. My situation was by no means unique. It was the beginning of a time of transition and turmoil that would soon touch all but the most provincial archaeologists (geographically or intellectually).

In some ways my situation during the early and mid seventies was unique. The solid and well-funded program provided to me by the state of Arkansas meant that during the 5 years (1969 to 1974) of Moss-Bennett's development, rewriting, and ultimate passage, I was more available than most to go to Washington.

It happened also that during this period I was on the Executive Committee of the Society for American Archaeology (SAA) (from 1971 to 1972) and was president-elect and president from

---

*   Over a 5-year period, I was out of the state around one third of the time each year. Needless to say, this was made possible, without seriously hurting the Arkansas Archaeological Survey program, only because of the superb staff of that organization. With respect to the caliber of support I was provided, I have no hesitation in saying that my situation was (and remains) unique.

1973 to 1975. I was also asked to join the CRAR in 1971 and served until its demise. I was getting heavily involved nationally.

For one reason or another, I traveled nationwide during much of the mid seventies, talking, listening, and, whenever possible, endeavoring to arouse both the profession and the general public to the situation faced by all concerning the rapid disappearance of our cultural resource base. In 1971 I was employed by the NPS to spend 6 weeks touring the country, talking to all but one or two NPS archaeologists nationwide as well as to regional directors and park superintendents for whom they worked. On the basis of this, I made an extensive report on the condition of the national archaeological program and recommended changes in organization and direction, some of which were actually implemented. I used my year as president-elect of SAA to attend and talk at almost all the regional archaeological meetings that year (1973/74). I used the opportunity of being the Archaeological Institute of America (AIA) Norton Lecturer (1975) to discuss the rapidly developing situation with those normally classical scholars, nationwide.

What I am trying to convey here is not the extent of my own activity but the tenor of the time. It was a time of intense and extensive communication within the profession and between it and many of its publics — to a degree unprecedented at any time before. There were meetings, conferences, and discussions all over the country, covering topics (management, ethics, etc.) that had rarely been covered before with such intensity.

It was a time when the 35 or so archaeologists with the NPS were almost the only archaeologists employed by the Federal Government; when archaeologists employed by private businesses or self-employed archaeologists were concepts not even dreamed about. It was a time when new approaches and responsibilities of the discipline of archaeology were brought into focus. It was a time when CRM, the conservation ethic, and regional planning all came to the fore as major forces, changing both the profession and the discipline forever.

Obviously, people other than I had been active (physically and mentally) during this period, as well (remember, this is a personal perspective, not an all-encompassing history). The two external instances that most impressed themselves on my own consciousness and thinking were Lipe's seminal paper on conservation archaeology (Lipe 1974, but first formulated in 1971 and first presented in 1972), and the 1974 Denver CRM Conference (Lipe and Lindsay 1974).

The Denver conference was an extraordinary one, with a high sense of need and a challenge to address vital problems intensely felt by all of the participants. There was a sense of commonality of problem and dedication to developing approaches to solutions, exceeded, in my experience, only by the six Airlie House seminars. This excitement bubbled over into after-hours discussions; one result, which took place in an adjacent bar, was the foundation of the American Society for Conservation Archaeology.

This whole period was one of extraordinary activity and intellectual interchange among professionals (and, increasingly by the mid 1970s, by an ever expanding number of federal agencies), both regionally and nationally.

One of the major results of this sometimes near-frantic activity and reassessment during the mid 1970s was a crystallization of the need for broad-scale regional approaches, for coordinated attacks (e.g., Southwest Archaeological Research Group, SARG), and, above all, for plans for managing and preserving the resource base as a total entity, not simply piecemeal as targets of opportunity arose. The stage was set for the birth of CRM.

The development of archaeological knowledge in the 1970s and 1980s has been considerable. Our knowledge of the archaeological data base has increased manyfold over that of the 1950s and early 1960s. Much of this increase has come about primarily through the operation of CRM practices. This data is still often piecemeal and undigested, but it is a part of the record and will be increasingly available in the near future as researchers learn to utilize the capability of computerized data bases.

I believe one of the important, but often overlooked, aspects of the Moss-Bennett process was that during the 5 years it was in the making, there was an unusual amount of interchange not just among members of the profession, but among the federal agencies themselves, as witnessed by the large numbers of meetings and conferences mentioned above. By the time Moss-Bennett became law, virtually every involved federal agency was fully aware of the legislation and was already gearing up to handle its responsibilities thereunder.

The profession too was geared up. Unlike the situation that prevailed in the 1950s or even the early 1960s, nearly everyone in the profession was now very aware of, if not actively involved with, the crisis with regard to the archaeological resource base, and of the need for long-range planning and active, coherent, consistent management policies and programs. The general public, as well, had increasingly been made aware by such articles as that by Davis in *Science* (Davis 1972a), lectures such as my Norton series, the increased awareness of archaeology by the National Trust, and continued, indeed increased, active input by the profession into the legislative process nationally, and to only a slightly lesser extent, locally.

By the end of the 1970s there was a wide-spread support base within and outside the archaeological profession (though not all archaeologists thought, or think, CRM is a good idea; but that is another story). In addition, partly through local initiative, but owing much of its drive to NPS initiative via grants for state plans (to Massachusetts and Arkansas initially) and its Resource Preservation Planning Process (RP3), there are a growing number of local, state, and regional data bases and, to a lesser extent, actual plans for the management of archaeological resources. In the Mississippi Valley, the early 1968 MAVAP effort was supplemented in the early 1970s by a series of regional summaries done under Hester Davis' direction (Davis 1970, 1972b, 1975). In this same area the latest and most comprehensive regional summary and management plan is the one recently completed by the Arkansas Archeological Survey (as lead agency) for the Southwestern Division of the Corps of Engineers. This 14-volume summary (if that is not an oxymoron) encompasses the area from the Mississippi River to the Arizona/New Mexico border and from southern Kansas to the Gulf — roughly one fourth of the contiguous U.S. During this period, too, the federal planning process has been considerably strengthened by additional legislation and procedures.

In short, to a very large extent we now have all the basic elements necessary to begin management and protection of the resource base. Our knowledge of the data base now is such that in most areas we have a reasonable handle on what is probably out there — if not yet (if ever) a full grasp of the details. We have a broad base of support, or at least awareness among the profession, federal agencies, and at least some elements of the public. And, increasingly, we have state plans available and in place, or under development. Continued development and implementation is the challenge of the 1990s.

The Airlie House meetings on the management of archaeological resources, held in July to September 1974, and the subsequent 2 years during which the report was widely circulated and updated as a result of a rapidly changing federal situation, served, in many ways, to summarize and crystallize this period of activity. They provided a focus and a base for the future development of CRM, such that in retrospect, I believe the judgment of the authors was correct, that the report would more or less officially christen, through an official naming ceremony, what had been born over the past few years — the whole concept of cultural resource management.

The present volume endeavors to explore the many paths taken by this healthy and ever-growing child of the 1970s and to suggest paths for management and protection to follow in the 1990s and beyond. Protecting the past has come of age.

## REFERENCES CITED

**Davis, H. A., Ed.** (1970) *Archaeological and Historical Resources of the Red River Basin*, Arkansas Archaeological Survey Research Series No. 1.

**Davis, H. A.** (1972a) The crises in American archeology, *Science* 175(4019), 267–282.

**Davis, H. A.** (1972b) An inventory and assessment of the archaeological and historical resource of the Lower Mississippi Alluvial Valley to January 1971. Report submitted to Southeast Region, National Park Service.

**Ford, J. L., Rolingson, M. A., and Medford, L. D.** (1972) *Site Destruction due to Agricultural Practices*, Arkansas Archaeological Survey Research Series No. 3.

**Lee, R. F.** (1970) *The Antiquities Act of 1970*, Office of History and Historic Architecture, Eastern Center, Washington, D.C.

**Lipe, W. D.** (1974) A conservation model for American archaeology, *Kiva*, 39(3,4).

**Lipe, W. D. and Lindsay, A. J., Jr.** (1974) *Proc. 1974 Cultural Resource Management Conf.*, Museum of Northern Arizona Technical Series No. 14.

**McGimsey, C. R., III** (1972) *Public Archeology*, Seminar Press, New York.

**McGimsey, C. R., III and Davis, H. A.** (1977) *The Management of Archaeological Resources. The Airlie House Report*, Special publication of the Society for American Archaeology

**McGimsey, C. R., III, Davis, H. A., and Griffin, J. B.** (1968) *A Preliminary Evaluation of the Status of Archeology in the Mississippi Alluvial Valley*, Arkansas Archaeological Survey, limited distribution.

# PROTECTING THE PAST

# INTRODUCTION

### George S. Smith and John E. Ehrenhard

*"While it will always be true that archeologists need to communicate effectively among themselves, it now is abundantly clear that unless they also communicate effectively with the general public, and with those making decisions affecting the cultural resource base, all else will be wasted effort"* (McGimsey and Davis 1977:89).

## PURPOSE

We are witnessing a tremendous increase in the commercialization of the human prehistoric and historic record. Archaeological sites are being looted and vandalized to the extent that if something is not done in the near future to curb this destruction, there will be little of our collective past left for future generations. The destruction of archaeological resources has not subsided even though the Federal Government and many state and local governments have passed laws protecting archaeological sites. Current estimates of the extent of the looting and vandalism vary widely. In a report prepared by the Government Accounting Office for Congress, entitled "Problems Protecting and Preserving Federal Archeological Resources" (1987), it was reported that 32% of the known sites on public lands in the Four Corners area of the Southwest (New Mexico, Arizona, Utah, and Colorado) had been looted. In the investigative report prepared for Congress (1988), entitled "The Destruction of America's Archaeological Heritage: Looting and Vandalism of Indian Archaeological Sites in the Four Corners States of the Southwest", it was estimated that the percentage of looted sites in this part of the country could be as high as 90%. Estimates for the rest of the country are probably not much different. Even with these estimates, the problem is critically understated by the fact that the Federal Government reports that approximately 90% of the lands they manage have not been adequately examined to identify and evaluate the archaeological resources they contain (Keel, McManamon, and Smith 1989). In other words, the percentages discussed above reflect the looting of known sites on public lands and do not take into consideration the looting of sites that may not be identified and monitored by land-managing agencies. Sites on private property are not faring much better. In the report prepared by the National Park Service, entitled "1988 Historic Preservation Assessment Needs", it was reported that as much as 50% of all private and public sites nationwide have been looted.

Protecting the remaining portion of our collective archaeological heritage is one of the major challenges confronting the archaeological community in this decade. This sentiment was firmly voiced at the 54th annual meeting of the Society for American Archaeology during a landmark plenary session entitled "Our Vanishing Past — The Willful Destruction of a Nation's Heritage." Throughout this session, noted scholars, politicians, and concerned individuals from varied walks of life discussed the extent and impact of looting and vandalism and how we can combat the problem through more effective law enforcement, legislation, training, and education. This book, in part, was written in response to the challenges set forth in this historic session, as well as to recommendations from the Interagency Working Group on the Public Awareness of Federal Archaeology, the Society for American Archaeology Antilooting Project, and the

University of Minnesota "Presenting the Past to the Public" conference series, and to direction provided by recent amendments to the Archaeological Resources Protection Act.

Over the past two decades there has been considerable activity regarding archaeological site protection. Unfortunately, little has been printed or widely disseminated beyond those immediately involved. A notable exception was the *Airlie House Report* (McGimsey and Davis 1977), which was one of the early documents that dealt specifically with the protection and management of cultural resources in the U.S. The purpose of *Protecting The Past* is to present some of the current and ongoing work regarding archaeological resource protection, in a topically organized format. This book is written for a diverse audience in an effort to reach the people who can most effectively help decrease the amount of archaeological resource crime taking place in America. This audience consists of professional and avocational archaeologists, law enforcement personnel, attorneys, judges, politicians, educators, and, by far the most influential group, the public. The challenge is to coordinate and focus the efforts of these diverse groups into a national program aimed at protecting the past for the future.

As stewards of our unwritten past, we must continually strive to increase the amount of archaeological information that is available to the public. One of the challenges of doing this is to disseminate information concerning various archaeological resource protection issues. We must increase public awareness, understanding, appreciation, and protection of the fragile and dwindling archaeological resources. To do that, we must also educate ourselves (those charged with keeping our legacy alive) on the issues.

We hope that the following presentations will stimulate discussion and action and inspire dynamic strategies for protecting archaeological sites and decreasing archaeological crime. *Protecting the Past* is a testament of our collective resolve to win.

## ORGANIZATION AND CONTENT

The topics and articles contained in this book have been specifically selected to address a variety of archaeological resource protection issues. The authors chosen were selected because of their topical expertise and active involvement in archaeological resource protection activities. As a result, a wide variety of perspectives are presented by authors from many diverse fields, including not only archaeology and law enforcement, but law, politics, education, museology, and marketing. The papers are organized into six chapters that are designed to address specific issues. Concluding remarks are presented in the **Epilogue**. An appendix contains policy statements by professional organizations regarding the protection of archaeological sites.

The **Preface** contains comments from the past president of the Society for American Archaeology (Sabloff), a U.S. senator who is and has been a leader in archaeological resource protection (Domenici), and the former Department of Interior Assistant Secretary for Fish and Wildlife and Parks (Harriman), regarding the need to protect the nation's archaeological resources. Their comments clearly point out the extent of the problem and the need for a coordinated effort to protect the nation's archaeological resources.

The **Forward** presents a personal overview of the development of archaeological resource protection in the U.S., focusing mainly on activities in the 1960s and 1970s (McGimsey). These two decades saw a tremendous increase in the number of archaeological sites impacted by large construction projects, as well as the number of professionals involved in archaeology, and an increased concern for protecting archaeological resources. It was during this important period that the method and theory of cultural resource management crystallized.

The first chapter in the book is **Archaeology and the Public**. The concept of archaeological resources as part of the Public Trust is discussed (Knudson), as is the much-quoted but little-studied public attitude regarding archaeology and archaeological site protection (Pokotylo).

The second chapter, **Archaeology and the Law**, discusses the following topics: the legal structure for archaeological resource protection in the U.S. and its basis in the principles of federalism (Fowler); the development of historic preservation law and the political and social climate in which it developed from the late 1700s up to and including passage of the Archeological and Historic Preservation Act of 1974 (Friedman); the passage of the Archaeological Resources Protection Act of 1979 and the 1988 amendments to it (Cheek); the workings of Congress and how laws, including those to protect archaeological sites, are made (Neumann); the development of state and tribal laws and public education programs to protect archaeological sites (Rogers and Grant); and the cooperative efforts between archaeologists, law enforcement personnel, and attorneys, necessary to successfully protect archaeological resources (Hutt).

The types of archaeological data lost when sites are looted, the effect this has on interpreting the past (Nickens), and the extent and magnitude of the looting problem on federal, Indian, and private lands (King, McAllister) are discussed in the chapter on **Archaeological Site Destruction**.

The chapter on **Protecting Archaeological Sites through Education** contains articles on saving sites through education (Lerner); involving the media in site protection (Milanich); community involvement in Florida and how it has increased public awareness and appreciation for archaeological resources, resulting in increased site protection (Bense); writing archaeology for the public and the benefits for site protection (Auel); implementing anthropology and archaeology into precollege classrooms to instill the preservation ethic in the next generation (Rogge); a city wide archaeology program in Canada and how it has increased public awareness and appreciation for archaeological resources (Smartz); a national model for teaching conservation archaeology to children (McNutt); including archaeology in the existing school curriculum and the positive effect on site protection in Louisiana (Hawkins); the archaeologist as global educator teaching respect for other cultures, past and present (Messenger and Enloe); the use of marketing techniques to understand the problem of looting and effectively target archaeological resource protection programs (Shields); how avocational archaeology groups are assisting in protecting the past (Davis); details of a conference series on presenting the past to the public (Wells); the role of museums in protecting the past (Brose); sources of information on educational aspects of archaeological projects and information on prosecuted archaeological looting cases (Knoll); and sources of available training in archaeological resource protection (Waldbauer).

Examples of successful programs are discussed in the chapter entitled **Archaeological Site Protection Programs**. Articles include an example of a very successful Bureau of Land Management program to protect archaeological sites in Oregon (Schalk); efforts by American Indians to protect archaeological sites (Anyon); a National Park Service archaeological site monitoring program in Kentucky and Tennessee (Des Jean); the use of signs to inform the public about archaeological resource protection and the need to protect sites (Jameson and Kodack); how sites can be protected at the local level (Kearns and Kirkorian); protecting sites by involving the public in site protection efforts (Hoffman); the Federal Governments efforts to protect the nation's archaeological resources (McManamon); the Society for American Archaeology efforts to protect the past (Reinburg); the results and recommendation of the Society for American Archaeology Antilooting workshop (Judge); and how the Archaeological Conservancy is saving sites (Michel).

The final chapter **The Future of Protecting the Past** outlines what has been done, what is being done, and what remains to be done if archaeological resources are to be preserved for future generations (Keel). Concluding remarks are presented in the **Epilog**.

## REFERENCES CITED

General Accounting Office (1987) Problems protecting and preserving federal archeology resources, GAO/RCED-88-3, General Accounting Office, Washington, D.C.

House Committee on Interior and Insular Affairs (1988) The destruction of America's archaeological heritage: looting and vandalism of Indian archaeological sites in the Four Corners states of the Southwest, Committee Print No. 6, U.S. Government Printing Office, Washington, D.C.

**Keel, B. C., McManamon, F. P., and Smith, G. S.** (1989) Federal archeology: the current program, National Park Service, Department of the Interior, Washington, D.C. (20402-9325: S/N 024-005-010-572).

**McGimsey, C. R., III and Davis, H. A.** (1977) *The Management of Archaeological Resources: The Airlie House Report,* special publication of the Society for American Archaeology.

# *Chapter 1*

## *ARCHAEOLOGY AND THE PUBLIC*

"One thing hastens into being, another hastens out of it. Even while a thing is in the act of coming into existence, some part of it has already ceased to be. Flux and change are forever renewing the fabric of the universe, just as the ceaseless sweep of time is forever renewing the face of the eternity. In such a running river, where there is no firm foothold, what is there for a man to value among all the many things that are racing past him?" (Marcus Aurelius, Meditations, 6:15)

# THE ARCHAEOLOGICAL PUBLIC TRUST IN CONTEXT

## Ruthann Knudson

## INTRODUCTION

We all have a right to our past, and our past is the worldwide record of the human experience. Each human being has an inalienable right to use the intellectual and spiritual values inherent in archaeological materials to understand and/or believe one is secure in her or his place in the physical and social world. This is a basic tenet of Euroamerican society, which is derived from the Western Judeo-Christian value system. This article is a discussion of rights and responsibilities for the stewardship of the past, based on that ethic, in the context of multiple cultural values and contemporary corporate cultures.

The idea of having the security of knowledge of one's place (both at the individual and societal levels) is not restricted to Western Judeo-Christian thought (cf. Frazer 1890; Malinowski 1955), but merits identification as the basis of this author's ethical system.

A second ethical tenet asserts that there should be a search for the common ground among conflicting values when resolving conflicts over the treatment of values differentially significant to different value systems.

A public trust is an individual or group responsibility to protect other people's rights to these heritage values and to the things (artifacts, ecofacts, sites) that embody these values. Because things and ideas are involved, they can be considered property — common property held in a common trust.

This article describes the ethical context in which archaeological site protection is assumed to be a public good.

## PHILOSOPHY, LANGUAGE, AND CULTURE

The readings in this volume about archaeological resource protection, as well as other discussions of the topic, are based on assumptions that are most frequently kept implicit — answers to the questions: what are archaeological resources, and why do they merit protection? Explicitly addressing these assumptions involves philosophical statement and analysis of the principles underlying archaeology, which have been set forth in previous discussions (Green 1983; Knudson 1983, 1991; Lipe 1974; McGimsey 1983; Wildesen 1983).

In the late 20th century, the human community consists of diverse cultures and languages that form the structure of local, regional, tribal, national, and international communications that are involved in archaeological management conflict resolutions. This cultural diversity supports miscommunication based on perceptions, verbalisms, and expectations (cf. Habermas 1989). This article uses terms and concepts in general U.S. media-oriented English language, relying on standard dictionary definitions (Neufeldt and Guralnik 1988).

In the dictionary, "archaeology" is restricted to the scientific study of past cultures. "Culture" is the system of ideas, beliefs, institutions, technologies, arts, and languages held and passed along by a group of people. While the distinctiveness of the groups characterized by different cultural systems is generally recognized on a major linguistic scale (e.g., Navajo vs. Chinese vs. French), there are also finer scales of corporate cultural systems (Deal and Kennedy 1982) that are significant to archaeological management (e.g., federal land manager vs. natural resource developer vs. general public consumer). "Cultural relativity" defines the value of each culture only in relationship to other cultures; i.e., no cultural system is of absolute value as compared with any other. This concept is used as a basic anthropological principle and is not intended to lead into postprocessual archaeological paradigms (Shanks and Tilley 1987).

"Science" is systematized knowledge (intellectual ideas) derived from observation and study to determine principles. "Humanistic values" are a system of thought or action based on human interests or ideals, and "spiritual values" relate to the beliefs of the soul (generally by a group of people), those things that are sacred or devotional; these are in contrast to scientific values. "Resources" are things that are ready for use, and "use" means putting something into action or (physical, intellectual, or spiritual) service. "Property" is the right to possess (ownership), use, or dispose of something. The term is used to refer to the rights to things or to knowledge, whether knowledge of scientific or intellectual research ideas (Nelken 1984) or of sacred places where knowledge is part of the inherent sacred nature of the place (e.g., Kelley and Francis 1990). A "trust" is the firm belief in the integrity and/or reliability of someone, or a more legalistic fiduciary responsibility to protect someone else's property. "Protection" is to shield from injury, damage, or loss, or to guard and/or defend.

While the dictionary definition of "archaeological materials/remains/resources" focuses on their scientific use, general (professional and lay) definitions of these terms include all things from the human past and all of their scientific, humanistic, and spiritual values. Many of the humanistic values are ascribed to ancient resources, based on their derived scientific information, but are no less important components. There is clearly a major scientific component to the remains of a 10,000-year-old campsite on the edge of an ancient river valley, but there is a humanistic component to its representation of a small family finding a good meat supply one fall week in a country known for its bitter winters. For many people, such a site also has a spiritual component in its manifestation of the anima of the past. All components are essential elements of archaeological resources, and the humanistic (or sometimes spiritual) values are frequently more important to the lay public.

When archaeological resources are identified, their management is usually assigned to the owner of the lands in or on which the resources have been found; thus, they are quickly tied to a property concept. The ascription of property rights to archaeological resources is a complicated legal, as well as social, issue (cf. Knudson 1986, 1991; see also Fowler, this volume). The identification of human remains as archaeological resources, much less some kind of property, usually has been culturally relative — human skeletal materials have generally been identified as archaeological resources, when they are not associated with known kin of the politically dominant subculture and thus assumed not to be subject to historically culturally biased state or local human burial laws and regulations. Inclusion of human remains within those archaeological materials designated as "property" may relate to distant common-law concepts, but is more likely a condition that prevails primarily in the absence of public question. In the basic Judeo-Christian value system, human remains have a special character and are not appropriately treated as property, whether the remains be of American Indians or Norwegian Americans, but they have archaeological as well as other cultural values.

This article uses the term "archaeological resources" to include *all* materials from the human past; some of which are appropriate for scientific study; some of which are valued because of their spiritual significance and may not be appropriate for nonbeliever involvement; and some of which have significant spiritual, humanistic, and scientific qualities that all merit attention.

# THE ARCHAEOLOGICAL PUBLIC TRUST

The assertion that initiated this article is based on the assumption that every human being has an inalienable right to intellectually understand, and be spiritually secure in, her or his place in the physical and social world, within that individual's natural capabilities. We have a right to our own values about ourselves and our world, and we must be socially responsible in acting out those values.

To be comfortable, each individual must have confident expectations of other people's behavior; that is, there must be trust. A "public trust" is a society's collective fulfillment of individual responsibilities to respect individuals' rights, as expressed either informally through group behavior or more formally through institutionalized processes.

Individuals' inalienable rights to knowledge and belief have a diachronic dimension — they involve our past as well as our present and/or future. In complement, each of these dimensions has value only in the context of the rest of time and space. Archaeological resources are corporeal entities (material remains, things) that embody incorporeal intellectual and spiritual values of the past (and present and future; cf. Lipe 1974,1984). Following the basic tenet that initiated this article, access to these resources so that they can be used to fulfill knowledge and belief needs is desirable for all people. How to use them without "using them up" is always the dilemma of managing irreplaceable things.

It is noted that most cultures, in some manner, restrict the use of some past (and present) things and places that have spiritual value, by circumscribing access to them. As stated elsewhere in this article, managing these past remnants in the real multicultural context involves finding a common ground if at all possible. In conflicts between "system" vs. "lifeworld" cultural patterns (Habermas 1989), finding this commonality may be extremely difficult. In lieu of that, it generally involves a process of intracultural triage (Stoffle and Evans 1990) (i.e., making choices among values held within a single cultural system).

The complex temporal aspect of archaeological resources is significant in their "nonrenewable" label. Each of them is a somewhat unique reflection of past human and natural environments and behaviors, with information relevant to contemporary entertainment, religious comfort, or sociotechnical problem solving (e.g., how to manage wastes, how to live with environmental change). At the same time, these presently useful and past-reflecting resources are a "bank" of unique values for future recreationists, believers, and scientists.

Given all this, each individual within society has an ethical responsibility to deal with past cultural remains in their contemporary (and projected future) collective sociocultural context — this is an *archaeological public trust*. The basic principles underlying this public trust concept, and its derivation from the public trust doctrine of Euroamerican water resource law, are described elsewhere (Knudson 1991).

Fulfillment of this trust responsibility begins when archaeological resources are first identified, whether they are arrowheads in a plowed field, human skeletal remains in a waterline trench, or shipwreck timbers in a dredge line. It includes the protection of the identified material in place, insofar as is possible and feasible, until all of the remains' archaeological values can be initially evaluated and publicly responsible decisions made about their treatment. To dig, and if so, how? To analyze, and if so, how and how much? How to treat in the long run (discard, curate, inhumate)? These decisions must be made in consideration of the common ground among potentially conflicting scientific, humanistic, and spiritual values, and in the context of contemporary socioeconomics and politics.

Following the basic ethical value asserted at the start of this article, protecting archaeological resources — the secrets of the past — is then basically a public trust to protect human values within diverse cultural contexts, to protect the things so that human access to the use of the items is sustained to the maximum extent possible in a diverse and dynamic world context.

## CONTEXT OF PROTECTION

Archaeological aficionados, be they professional scientists, devoted avocationals, or more casual museum visitors, are familiar with the use of "context" in reference to the relative position of artifacts, samples, and features within a prehistoric or historic site. Protection or management decisions must be made in consideration of several other archaeological contexts (cf. Costa et al. 1988).

The management responsibility for *in situ* archaeological resources is initially very place oriented in the context of resource location — where it is found in or on the ground, or under water. Variations in national property and/or heritage laws and/or regulations differentially assign this to private landholders or public trustees (Cleere 1989; Knudson 1986, 1991). In the U.S., "The Federal Government shall provide leadership in preserving, restoring, and maintaining the historic and cultural environment of the Nation" (Executive Order 11593 Sec. 1 [1971]). Land managers, acting as archaeological resource management decision makers, must consider the rights of the users of the land or river- or lakebed in or on which the archaeological materials are found. The stormwater sewer needed by a metropolitan community, the money-making housing development desired by the entrepreneur, or the grazing lease held by the rancher with children in college may each have to be considered when deciding whether or how to protect an archaeological site and its included values.

Private landholders also bear responsibilities for archaeological resource management. While the U.S. Constitution Fifth Amendment (the "taking clause;" Bosselman, Callies, and Banta 1973) requires compensation for the public use of private property, in the past two decades there has been much broader application of the Public Trust Doctrine in U.S. land law (Knudson 1991). The doctrine relies on common property concepts, asserting the rights of society over individual rights when both are involved in the management of community resources. Issues of the social responsibility of private individuals and corporations have been frequent topics of discussion lately (e.g., Preston and Post 1975). These various perspectives mean that there is a need to find a common ground in managing publicly valued archaeological resources when they are in or on private lands. Traditionally, landowners have the first responsibility for actions that affect their property. They are participants in the public archaeological trust.

The physical context of an undisturbed archaeological resource is a primary constraint on resource protection decisions. Given that an undisturbed site can or must be moved, decisions about the manner of removal and subsequent disposition must be made within multiple social, cultural, and political contexts. The individuals whose inalienable heritage rights are being protected live and function within those multiple contexts.

First, all individuals must be recognized as members of a worldwide human community with multiple and frequently conflicting values and needs. Within that world view, individuals are members of different cultures and culturally relative value systems, and decisions about archaeological resources must consider both the cultural relativity and world community trust responsibilities. Cross-cutting the cultural variations are the sociopolitical rules and regulations that variably assign land ownership/management responsibilities as well as responsibilities for preserving, protecting, and managing included archaeological resources.

All the required ethical considerations for managing archaeological sites must also be addressed in managing the site-derived archaeological artifacts, ecofacts, and documentary evidence.

## CONCLUSION

Each individual and each governmental unit (or individual/organization operating under a governmentally provided authority) has a responsibility to protect the human community's past. This includes education of the general public (both adults and children), the individuals responsible for managing direct adverse impacts to archaeological materials (e.g., development planners, engineers, farmers, miners, foresters), and the individuals with archaeological management responsibilities (both of the sites and of the derived materials) (cf. Archaeological Assistance Division 1990). It includes enforcement of stewardship laws, regulations, guidelines, and policies, where they are relevant.

At its most basic level, there is a public trust to recognize and fulfill a commitment to respecting the worldwide value of heritage resources to help each of us fit within our present world.

## ACKNOWLEDGMENTS

Bennie Keel, Frank McManamon, Velouta Canouts, and Muriel Crespi made useful comments on an early draft of this paper, and Alan Downer and Mark Leone inadvertently led me to ideas useful in developing the final version.

## REFERENCES CITED

Archaeological Assistance Division (1990) The many publics for archaeological public education, *Fed. Archeol. Rep.*, 3(2),1–5.

**Bosselman, F., Callies, D., and Banta, J.** (1973) *The Taking Issue. An Analysis of the Constitutional Limits of Land Use Control,* Council on Environmental Quality, Washington, D.C.

**Cleere, H. F., Ed.** (1989) *Archaeological Heritage Management in the Modern World,* Unwin Hyman, London.

**Costa, F. A., Neves, W. A., and Caldarelli, S. B.** (1988) Rescue archaeology in Brazilian Amazon: retrospect and perspectives. In *Archaeology and Society: Large Scale Rescue Operations—Their Possibilities and Problems,* ICOMOS ICAHM Stockholm-88, ICAHM Report No. 1, Trotzig, G. and Vahlne, G., Eds., The Nordic Secretariate of ICAHM, Stockholm 277–285.

**Deal, T. E. and Kennedy, A. A.** (1982) *Corporate Cultures,* Addison-Wesley, Reading, MA.

Executive Order 11593 Sec. 1 (1971).

**Frazer, J. G.** (1890) *The Golden Bough: A Study in Magic and Religion,* 2 vols., MacMillan, London.

**Green, E. L., Ed.** (1983) *Ethics and Values in Archaeology,* Free Press, New York.

**Habermas, J.** (1989) *The Theory of Communicative Action,* Vol. 2: *System and Lifeworld,* Becon Press, Boston.

**Kelley, K. and Francis, H.** (1990) Documenting Navajo traditional history. In *The Plenary Case Study, "Beyond Historic Properties: Cultural Resource Management in the 1990s,"* Present. First Natl. Conf., Cultural Conservation: Reconfiguring the Cultural Mission, American Folklife Center, the Library of Congress, Washington, D.C.

**Knudson, R.** (1983) Ethical decision making and participation in the politics of archaeology. In *Ethics and Values in Archaeology,* Green, E. L., Ed., Free Press, New York, 243–263.

**Knudson, R.** (1986) Contemporary cultural resource management. In *American Archaeology Past and Future,* Meltzer, D. J., Fowler, D. D., and Sabloff, J. A., Eds., Smithsonian Institution Press, Washington, D.C., 395–413.

**Knudson, R.** (1991) The public trust and archaeological stewardship. In *The Public Trust and the First Americans,* Proc. First World Summit Conf. on the Peopling of the Americas, Vol. 5., Knudson, R. and Keel, B. C., Eds., Center for the Study of the First Americans, Corvallis, OR, in press.

**Lipe, W. D.** (1974) A conservation model for American archaeology, *Kiva* 39,213–245. (A slightly shortened and revised version of this paper was published in *Conservation Archaeology,* Schiffer,    M. B. and Gummerman, G. J., Eds. (1977), Academic Press, New York, 19–42.)

**Lipe, W. D.** (1984) Value and meaning in cultural resources. In *Approaches to the Archaeological Heritage*, Cleere, H., Ed., Cambridge University Press, Cambridge, 1–11.

**Malinowski, B.** (1955) *Magic, Science and Religion*, Doubleday, New York.

**McGimsey, C. R., III.** (1983) The value of archaeology. In *Ethics and Values in Archaeology*, Green,     E. L., Ed., Free Press, New York, 171–183.

**Nelken, D.** (1984) *Science as Intellectual Property. Who Controls Intellectual Scientific Research?* Series on issues in science and technology, American Association for the Advancement of Science, Washington, D.C.

**Neufeldt, V. and Guralnik, D. G., Eds.** (1988) *Webster's New World Dictionary of American English* (3rd College Edition), Webster's New World, Cleveland.

**Preston, L. E. and Post, J. E.** (1975) *Private Management and Public Policy. The Principle of Public Responsibility*, Prentice-Hall, Englewood Cliffs, NJ.

**Shanks, M. and Tilley, C.** (1987) *Re-Constructing Archaeology: Theory and Practice*, Cambridge University Press, Cambridge.

**Stoffle, R. W. and Evans, M. J.** (1990) Holistic conservation and cultural triage: American Indian perspectives on cultural resources, *Human Org.*, 49(2),91–99.

**Wildesen, L. E.** (1983) The search for an ethic in archaeology: an historical perspective. In *Ethics and Values in Archaeology*, Green, E. L., Ed., Free Press, New York 3–12.

# PUBLIC ATTITUDES TOWARDS ARCHAEOLOGICAL RESOURCES AND THEIR MANAGEMENT

David L. Pokotylo and Andrew R. Mason

## INTRODUCTION

Few archaeologists would disagree that a large segment of the public is fascinated by the ancient past. We often cite public interest in archaeology as the basis of heritage conservation legislation and research programs in both Canada and the U.S. (see Lipe 1977; King 1981). The public's interest in archaeology also has a negative aspect. Despite the gains made in passing heritage conservation legislation, site looting and vandalism remain major threats to the archaeological resource base. More stringent laws alone will not resolve this problem. Rather, an effective solution requires a major change in public opinion to increase awareness and understanding of our archaeological heritage.

As effective heritage resource conservation comes to depend more and more on public understanding and support of archaeology, the profession must take responsibility to foster an archaeologically well-informed public. Archaeologists, however, still remain at odds about how to best respond to the public interest in archaeology (Fagan 1984). Lipe (1977) recognized this problem in his classic paper on conservation archaeology and recommended that the discipline find out just what the public finds appealing about archaeology and then use the results to promote the case for conservation, research, and education activities. Epp and Spurling (1984) also note the critical need for such information, given the more active and influential role that public hearings, opinion polls, and lobby groups now play in the heritage resource decision-making process.

Although information on public interests in archaeology can contribute to the future success of resource conservation programs, little research on this topic has been attempted by either the academic or management communities. Davis (1978) identifies five principal forms that the public's interest in archaeology can take: (1) romanticism, (2) aesthetics, (3) nature of the human community, (4) social roots, and (5) technical avocation. However, we do not have systematic data on how widely held these interests are. We are acutely aware that our discipline attracts a pseudoscience fringe that enjoys a high public profile (see Cazeau and Scott 1979; Cole 1980; Wauchope 1962). Over the past decade, the entertainment media have also fueled public interest, producing more and more movies, television programs, books, and newspaper articles on archaeology, which range dramatically in their depictions of the profession and its activities. Archaeologists deal with a public that often has romantic and simplistic notions of what the discipline studies, and views archaeology as remote from the main concerns (and fiscal priorities) of modern society (Fagan 1984).

A number of studies have conducted survey research to more accurately monitor public interest levels. Feder (1984) surveyed Central Connecticut State College students to assess their acceptance of pseudoscientific claims in archaeology and related fields presented in the popular media. Based on his analysis of responses to questions on archaeological and paleontological topics, Feder noted that large percentages of the student sample simply did not know whether pseudoscientific claims were true or not. Students also considered television and teachers to be equally reliable sources of information. Feder (1984:536) concluded that "students are largely ignorant of archaeology and related topics" and "are a ripe audience for pseudoscientists and charlatans who parade as archaeologists and would have the public accept all sorts of unacceptable nonsense about the past and its study."

In Canada, two opinion polls have indirectly addressed public awareness of archaeological topics. In a province-wide survey, the Alberta Environmental Commission Authority (1972) found that 96% of the residents sampled were concerned about preservation of the province archaeological and historic heritage. Opinions on ownership of heritage objects favored the finder slightly more than the government (53 vs. 47%). Sixty-seven percent of the sample believed that public education was the most practical way of preventing the continued destruction of Alberta heritage sites, and 85% agreed that heritage education should commence as early as the first grade in school. A poll by the Ontario Heritage Foundation shows that archaeology in Ontario has a low level of public support (White 1982). Only 31% of the sample was aware that the foundation awarded grants for archaeological research, while 43% thought grants for archaeology were important. However, respondents were much more supportive of architectural conservation, suggesting that the public is more enthusiastic about heritage when the resources are familiar and tangible (White 1982).

The above results are intriguing, but we need further attitudinal data dealing specifically with current archaeological issues, to better utilize our available resources to improve public understanding and support for archaeology. In this article we present some preliminary results of a continuing survey of Vancouver, BC, area residents' opinions on prehistoric archaeology and heritage conservation legislation, compare the results to previous surveys, and assess potential ways to promote positive perceptions of the profession, the resource, and its conservation.

## SURVEY METHODS

University of British Columbia students enrolled in an applied archaeology course taught by the senior author conducted public opinion surveys in February and March of 1985 and 1989. The survey involved the distribution of questionnaire forms to 550 households equally distributed among 11 select neighborhoods in greater Vancouver. The 1985 survey sampled 300 households. Two hundred and fifty households were sampled in 1989. The neighborhoods were selected by the students' location of residence. This admittedly judgmental sampling method, nevertheless, provided a good cross-section of socioeconomic areas in Vancouver. The survey questionnaires were hand delivered directly to the occupants, and the surveyor returned 2 to 3 days later to pick up completed forms. Occupants returning completed forms were given a free admission to the UBC Museum of Anthropology. The return rate average of both surveys was 73% (64% in 1985 and 84% in 1989).

Questions were designed to elicit from the respondents their understanding of prehistoric archaeology and archaeological resource conservation and the sources of this information. The questionnaire presented bounded answers in a multiple-choice format that ensured standardized responses for statistical analysis. Although the specific content of the questionnaire form varied each year, 29 questions common to both surveys are reported here. The questions are grouped into four categories:

1. Demographic data on the respondent's age, education, and length of residence in the province
2. Knowledge of prehistoric archaeology in general and British Columbia archaeology in particular
3. Opinions about the value and significance of prehistoric archaeology in modern society
4. Awareness of heritage conservation legislation

# SURVEY DATA AND RESULTS

## Nature of the Survey Sample

In terms of age, 98% of the sample was over 18 years of age. The majority (56%) ranged in age from 18 to 35 years; 33% were 36 to 55 years old, and 9% were over 55 years. The sample mode was 18 to 25 years (32%).

Twenty percent of the sample listed a high school degree as the highest education level completed, and 8% did not graduate from high school. Seventy-three percent had some form of postsecondary education. In this latter group, 10% had a technical-vocational diploma, 18% had an undergraduate university degree, and another 11% held a postgraduate degree. The sample proportion with postsecondary education was higher than the 51.3% value recorded in the 1986 Vancouver census. The major discipline of postsecondary study was arts (38%), followed by science (19%), and applied science (14%). Ten percent listed commerce as the main discipline, 8% were in education, and the remaining 11% were in other fields ranging from physical education to law.

The median duration of residence in British Columbia was 21 years, and ranges from less than 1 year to 99 years. Upper and lower quartiles of the distribution were 14 and 32 years, respectively.

In summary, the sample tended to be relatively young and well educated in the arts and sciences. Most lived in the province for an appreciable period of time to have some familiarity with its environmental and cultural setting.

## Knowledge of Prehistoric Archaeology

Residents were asked about their visits to heritage sites, museums, and archaeological site excavations, to monitor general levels of heritage awareness and interest. Ninety-three percent of the sample had visited a museum that exhibited archaeological artifacts, and 61% had visited a heritage site. These figures suggest that heritage interests are popular recreational activities. However, few people (5%) had visited an archaeological site excavation. This low value more likely reflects the limited opportunity for on-site visits in the province, rather than lack of interest, given the higher numbers for developed heritage sites.

The high general-interest level in heritage is countered by considerable misunderstanding of the scope and practice of prehistoric archaeology. Most respondents selected "remains of past cultures" when asked to identify what prehistoric archaeologists study (see Table 1). However, over half of the sample chose "fossils, such as dinosaurs," and 52% selected *both* responses. No significant association exists between the two opinions — people selecting the "remains of past cultures" were not more likely to reject the "fossils" response. Although the results reveal misconceptions about the scope of prehistoric archaeology, few respondents admitted that they were uncertain about the subject. Ten percent of the sample did not respond when asked to specify what archaeologists do, which suggests a higher level of uncertainty on this topic. The majority of those responding identified the appropriate response — "studying lifeways of past cultures" (see Table 2) — and were more likely to reject the notion that archaeologists excavate burials for valuable art objects and that archaeologists purchase artifacts for their collections (chi square significanct at $p < 0.01$). Nevertheless, 19% of the sample selected both the "lifeways" and "burial excavation for valuable art objects" responses.

## TABLE 1
## PUBLIC OPINIONS ON THE SCOPE OF ARCHAEOLOGY

| Response | N | % of respondents (N = 401) |
|---|---|---|
| Study fossils, such as dinosaurs | 227 | 56.6 |
| Study the remains of past cultures | 377 | 94.0 |
| Study living cultures | 65 | 16.2 |
| Uncertain | 11 | 2.7 |

## TABLE 2
## PUBLIC OPINIONS ON ARCHAEOLOGICAL PRACTICE

| Response | N | % of respondents (N = 360) |
|---|---|---|
| Excavation of valuable art objects | 155 | 43.1 |
| Purchase artifacts for museum collections | 105 | 29.2 |
| Develop museum collections and exhibits | 41 | 10.2 |
| Study lifeways of past cultures | 232 | 64.4 |
| Other | 55 | 15.3 |

A question on the antiquity of human occupation in British Columbia monitored substantive knowledge on regional archaeology. Respondents were asked, "In your opinion, how long have people lived in the region now known as British Columbia?" and could select one of nine time intervals (Figure 1). Thirteen percent of the sample did not answer the question. Of those responding, only 19% chose the time interval supported by present research (5,000 to 10,000 years). Over 21% selected time ranges less than 1000 years B.P., while 22% indicated ages greater than 20,000 years B.P.

The above results question the effectiveness of present means of transmitting information about archaeology as a discipline and substantive research results to the public. What information sources do the public use to obtain their archaeological knowledge? Respondents were asked, "Where have you learned about prehistoric archaeology?" and could select any number of sources listed. Table 3 shows the distribution of responses. Television programs are the predominant information source, followed by magazines and books. Approximately equal numbers of people learned about archaeology from courses vs. newspapers. Movies were the least-selected information source and were the only source in just one case. This should partially alleviate the profession's concern about the fallout from Hollywood's "Indiana Jones" archaeological stereotype.

## Relevance of Prehistoric Archaeology

When asked, "Is archaeology relevant in contemporary society?" 84% of the sample chose "relevant," and 4% checked "not relevant." The remaining 12% were uncertain.

The profession assumes that education is the foundation of a better-informed public, but would the public support prehistoric archaeology taught in the education system curriculum, and at what level? Responses to this question are tabulated in Table 4. The majority of the sample

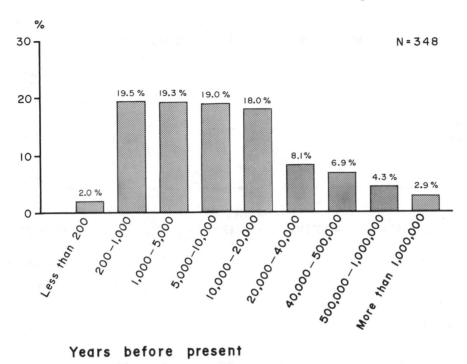

FIGURE 1. Public opinion levels on antiquity of human occupation in British Columbia.

thought that archaeology should be taught as early as the elementary school level. The value is considerably less than the proportion of the Alberta survey sample agreeing that heritage education should start in grade one (56 vs. 85%). A minimal number considered archaeology to have no place in the education system.

Looking beyond the education system, 67% of the sample indicated that they would like more information on prehistoric archaeology made available to the general public. Respondents desiring more information were asked to select preferred sources. The results are tabulated in Table 5. Television programming is the most-preferred information source. A high proportion of respondents expressed an interest in visiting on-site excavations, ranking only slightly behind museum exhibits. This high level of interest in site excavation is important when compared to the proportions of the sample that are uninformed about archaeological scope and methods, and the small number who have visited excavations in progress.

Respondents were also queried about the political role of archaeological research in current native land-claim issues in British Columbia. Forty-six percent of the sample maintained archaeological research should be used to support land-claim cases, 18% did not think such data should be used, and 36% were uncertain about the issue.

## Understanding of Heritage Conservation Legislation

Figure 2 shows opinion levels on three heritage conservation issues: the need for legislation, awareness of current legislation, and legal penalties for archaeological site destruction. A great majority of the respondents thought there should be legislation to protect archaeological sites. This was slightly less than the 96% level of concern about heritage preservation expressed in the Alberta survey. Only one third of the sample were aware that provincial heritage conservation

TABLE   3

## SOURCE OF INFORMATION ABOUT ARCHAEOLOGY

| Information source | N | % of respondents (N = 368) |
|---|---|---|
| Television | 297 | 80.7 |
| Newspapers | 174 | 47.3 |
| Courses | 172 | 46.7 |
| Movies | 110 | 29.9 |
| Magazines | 241 | 65.5 |
| Books | 216 | 58.7 |

TABLE   4

## LEVEL THAT ARCHAEOLOGY SHOULD BE INTRODUCED IN THE SCHOOL

| Level | N | % of respondents |
|---|---|---|
| Elementary school | 220 | 55.7 |
| Secondary school | 123 | 31.1 |
| University | 30 | 7.6 |
| Should not be taught | 8 | 2.0 |
| Uncertain | 14 | 3.6 |
| Total | 395 | 100.0 |

TABLE   5

## PREFERRED SOURCES OF MORE INFORMATION ON ARCHAEOLOGY

| Information source | N | % of respondents (N = 268) |
|---|---|---|
| Television | 205 | 76.5 |
| Newspaper | 108 | 40.3 |
| Education system | 155 | 57.9 |
| Archaeological dig visit | 177 | 66.1 |
| Museum exhibits | 182 | 67.9 |
| Magazines | 124 | 46.3 |
| Books | 106 | 39.6 |

legislation presently exists, and over half were uncertain whether laws existed or not. Ninety percent of the sample believed that an individual or corporation should be penalized for knowingly destroying a site.

When queried about the nature of a penalty for site destruction, 21% selected a jail term, 72% chose a fine, and 31% favored both. In the 1989 survey, respondents who identified a fine or jail penalty were also asked to suggest appropriate amounts. Fines ranged from $50 to $5,000,000, with a median of $10,000. The median suggested jail sentence was 5 years, and the range was from 1 to 20 years. Twenty-seven percent of the sample felt that developers should be required to pay all salvage excavation costs when land development projects threaten archaeological sites, 36% thought that developer should pay some of the costs, and 37% stated none.

The relationship between the antiquities market and the looting and destruction of archaeological sites is well documented (Vitelli 1984). In British Columbia, legislation to assign ownership of archaeological artifacts to the province in trust is currently being drafted (British

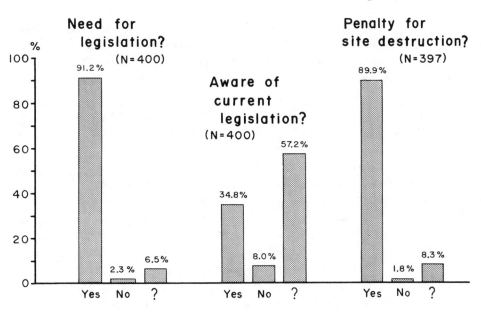

FIGURE 2. Public opinion levels on heritage conservation legislation.

**TABLE 6**
**PUBLIC OPINION ON OWNERSHIP OF ARCHAEOLOGICAL ARTIFACTS**

| Legal ownership | N | % of respondents (N = 327) |
|---|---|---|
| Finder of artifact | 48 | 14.7 |
| Landowner of site | 50 | 15.3 |
| Nearest Indian band | 51 | 15.6 |

Columbia Ministry of Municipal Affairs, Recreation and Culture 1990; Project Pride Task Force 1987). However, a lasting solution to the problem also requires heightened public awareness of the problem. Table 6 presents responses to the question of who should have legal rights to prehistoric archaeological artifacts. Respondents could select any number of choices. The province was the preferred legal owner, ranking well above all other choices and the 47% level in the Alberta survey. Approximately equal numbers selected the Indian band nearest to the site of origin, and the owner of the land on which the artifacts were found.

## Comparative Analysis

To better understand the basis of the above opinions, we treated education and knowledge of archaeological scope and practice as control variables. These were revised, cross-tabulated with other opinion questions, and tested by chi square analyses for statistical significance at the 0.05 probability level.

Responses to the scope and practice of archaeology questions were initially grouped into "informed" and "uninformed" opinions. People informed about the scope of archaeology identified only "the study of remains of past cultures;" those informed on practice selected either "the development of museum collections and exhibits," or "study of past lifeways" responses.

Any other response to either question was classified as uninformed. Respondents informed about the scope of archaeology were more likely to make informed selections about archaeological practice (87%), but only half of those informed on practice chose correctly for scope. We also defined a "well-informed" group that was informed on both questions, for comparison with other opinion variables. Only 29% of the respondents met this criterion.

The sample was classified into groups with and without postsecondary education. Approximately equal proportions of each education level group had informed opinions about the scope (high school, 40%; postsecondary, 43%) and practice (high school, 71%; postsecondary, 73%) of archaeology. Antiquity estimates showed the largest difference between education groups: 20% of the postsecondary sample selected the acknowledged time range vs. 14% for the high school group. None of these relationships are significant.

Respondents lacking postsecondary education were more likely to be uncertain, or to consider archaeology not relevant, than those with postsecondary schooling (23 vs. 13%). However, the proportion of well-informed respondents with this opinion was similar to the rest of the sample (15 vs. 17%). No significant associations exist between the respondents' education or information level, and opinion about whether archaeology should be taught in the education system. Education level has a significant association with opinion on land claims: the sample with postsecondary education was less likely to be uncertain, and more likely to support the use of archaeology in land claims, than those with no postsecondary schooling.

No significant relationships exist between opinions on need for legislation, knowledge of present laws, penalty for destroying sites, developers' financial responsibility, and education level or knowledge of archaeology. Education level is significantly associated with opinions on provincial ownership of artifacts and the finder's legal rights to artifacts. Respondents with high school as the highest education level were more likely to support the finder's legal rights to artifacts than the postsecondary sample (22 vs. 12%), but were less likely to support government ownership (60 vs. 76%). There were no significant relationships between individuals well informed about archaeology and any of the ownership variables.

## CONCLUSION

The survey data show that the public has a high level of interest in archaeology and is concerned about heritage resource conservation. The results also indicate considerable support for legislation to protect cultural resources, public ownership of archaeological resources, and continuing archaeological education and research.

The study also reveals that present means of transmitting information about archaeology and archaeological conservation to the public are inefficient. Although the sample had a higher than average education level, it lacked both a clear understanding of what archaeology is and a basic knowledge of regional prehistory and was unaware of existing legislation. In most cases, the respondent's education level and current archaeological knowledge made little difference to the extent of erroneous opinions. We obviously need to improve the general level of public knowledge about archaeology; but how can this be best accomplished? The survey results suggest some general means by which this knowledge can be effectively increased.

Television programming should be considered an ideal vehicle for delivering information to the public: most respondents had viewed television programs on archaeology, and this medium is the most preferred source of further information. The museum system is another viable means of increasing public awareness. Almost all respondents had visited museums, and over half preferred museum exhibits as a source of further information. We should also recognize the very high interest level in on-site visits to see archaeological research in progress, and make efforts to incorporate a public programming component in research projects whenever possible. Articles in magazines and newspapers, and books with topics related to archaeology have exposed many sample respondents to archaeology. Well-written, accurate, informative, and (most importantly) entertaining reports could receive a higher profile if they were regularly published in media that have wide public distribution. We should also not discount the positive role that archaeological fiction can play in exposing the public to the prehistoric past. Jean Auel's *Earth's Children* series (1980, 1982, 1985) has enjoyed massive success, with over 2 million hardcover copies and 12 million paperback editions sold (Fagan 1987:132). More archaeologists may want to follow Kurten's (1986a, 1986b) and Thomas' (1987) example of scientists writing archaeological fiction (see Fagan 1987) to bring current research to a much wider audience.

The subject of public interest in archaeology is timely, and this study represents an initial step to achieve a better understanding of the topic. The results of the present survey are intriguing and certainly warrant further work. We hope that the results will encourage similar studies in other regions to see if larger scale patterns are evident.

## ACKNOWLEDGMENTS

UBC students enrolled in Anthropology 424, *Applied Archaeology,* assisted in the questionnaire design and conducted the surveys. Heather Koulas, Brad Smart, Jim Spafford, Philip Walker, and Dick Woo participated in the 1985 survey. The 1989 survey involved Catherine Bartl, Vicki Feddema, Deborah Hayles, Lee McFarlane, and Andrew Mason. The Department of Anthropology and Sociology, UBC, covered costs for duplicating the questionnaire forms. Computing funds were provided by the UBC Faculty of Arts. Michael Ames, Director of the UBC Museum of Anthropology, generously donated the museum passes that contributed to the high response rate. Kathryn Bernick prepared the graphics. An earlier version of this paper was presented at the 43rd Northwest Anthropological Conference, Eugene, OR, March 1990.

## REFERENCES CITED

Alberta Environment Commission Authority (1972) The conservation of historical and archaeological resources in Alberta: report and recommendations, Edmonton, Alberta.

**Auel, J. M.** (1980) *The Clan of the Cave Bear,* Crown Publishers, New York.

**Auel, J. M.** (1982) *The Valley of the Horses,* Crown Publishers, New York.

**Auel, J. M.** (1985) *The Mammoth Hunters,* Crown Publishers, New York.

British Columbia Ministry of Municipal Affairs, Recreation, and Culture (1990) Toward heritage legislation: a proposal for public review, Victoria, B.C.

**Cazeau, C. and Scott, S.** (1979) *Exploring the Unknown: Great Mysteries Re-examined,* Plenum Press, New York.

**Cole, J. R.** (1980) Cult archaeology and unscientific method and theory. In *Advances in Archaeological Method and Theory,* Vol. 3, Schiffer, M. B., Ed., Academic Press, New York, 4–33.

**Davis, E. M.** (1978) Archaeology, a matter of public interest. In *Papers in Applied Archaeology,* Gunn, J., Ed., Center for Archaeological Research, University of Texas at San Antonio, 15–18.

**Epp, H. T. and Spurling, B. E.** (1984) The other face of Janus: research in the service of archaeological resource management. *Can. J. Archaeol.,* 8, 95–113.

**Fagan, B. M.** (1984) Archaeology and the wider audience. In *Ethics and Values in Archaeology,* Green, E. L., Ed., Free Press, New York, 175–183.

**Fagan, B. M.** (1987) Life with Ayla and her friends: Jean Auel and the new phenomenon of Ice Age fiction. *Sci. Am.* 256(6), 132–135.

**Feder, K. L.** (1984) Irrationality and Popular Archaeology, *Am. Antiquity,* 49, 525–541.

**King, T. F.** (1981) The NART: a plan to direct archaeology toward more relevant goals in modern life, *Early Man,* 3(4), 35–38.

**Kurten, B.** (1986a) *How to Deep-Freeze a Mammoth,* Columbia University Press, New York.

**Kurten, B.** (1986b) *Singletusk: A Novel of the Ice Age,* Pantheon Books, New York.

**Lipe, W. D.** (1977) A conservation model for American archaeology, *Kiva* 39, 213–245.

Project Pride Task Force (1987) Stewardship and opportunity: report of the Ministerial Task Force on Heritage Conservation, British Columbia Ministry of Tourism, Recreation and Culture, Victoria, B.C.

**Thomas, E. M.** (1987) *Reindeer Moon,* Houghton Mifflin, Boston.

**Vitelli, K. D.** (1984) The international traffic in antiquities: archaeological ethics and the archaeologist's responsibility. In *Ethics and Values in Archaeology*, Green, E. L., Ed., Free Press, New York, 143–155.

**Wauchope, R.** (1962) *Lost Tribes and Sunken Continents,* University of Chicago Press, Chicago.

**White, J.** (1982) The 1982 annual meeting banquet address by Mr. John White, Chairman of the Ontario Heritage Foundation, *Can. Archaeol. Assoc. Newsl.,* 2(1), 12.

# Chapter 2

## ARCHAEOLOGY AND THE LAW

"I got my rights and this is a free county. I pay taxes and I can dig there if I want to — I've been doing it for years and nobody cares. I ain't bothering nobody. I got my rights! If I can't dig here I might as well go to Russia." (Excerpt from an interview with a looter, Big Cypress National Preserve, 1981)

# THE LEGAL STRUCTURE FOR THE PROTECTION OF ARCHAEOLOGICAL RESOURCES

## John M. Fowler

## INTRODUCTION

Laws for the protection of archaeological resources have existed in the U.S. for over a century. Early enactments to protect specific Anasazi sites in the Southwest led to the Federal Government's first historic preservation statute in 1906, the Antiquities Act. Since then archaeological protection laws have evolved within the broader context of the program to protect all aspects of the historic and prehistoric patrimony (see Friedman, Cheek, Neumann, and Rogers, this volume, for further discussion of historic preservation law). As a result, the legal framework today reflects a variety of forces and considerations, only a few of which are strictly related to the inherent nature of archaeological resources.

The structure of preservation law in the U.S. is determined largely by the principles of federalism and the traditional allocation of legal authority and political power to the various levels of government. As a result, while a cohesive program of administrative structures and legal protections exists at the national government level, the most stringent protections are provided for historic properties at the local level, the traditional repository of land-use control authority. Indeed, it is important to note that no provision of federal law exists to prohibit the destruction of a historic resource unless it is in federal ownership.

Within this general constraint, the body of archaeological protection law has evolved in much the same way other aspects of the national historic preservation program have. A threat is perceived to resources that a constituency holds dear, and legislative enactment of protective strictures follows. While the most far-reaching legal activity has occurred at the federal level, recent years have witnessed an upsurge of state and local laws designed to combat growing threats to archaeological resources beyond the reach of federal protections. The result is an increasingly comprehensive tapestry of legal protections.

All levels of government have a role to play in protecting archaeological resources. Essentially, the Federal Government sits at the top of the pyramid of the legal structure, focusing its powers on those resources in which there is some national interest, either through ownership, significance, or involvement with federal activities. The states participate in many of the federal protective systems and add their own layer of state law to the tools available for archaeological resource protection. Finally, local government, with its ability to directly regulate the use of private property, offers legal tools to protect the widest range of resources.

## FEDERAL PROGRAMS AND PROTECTIONS

At the outset, a distinction must be drawn between federal laws that apply to federal and nonfederal lands. Not surprisingly, the most stringent protections for archaeological and historic properties apply only to those properties in government ownership. It is also important to note that the broader provisions of laws concerning all kinds of historic properties are augmented by several federal laws that are designed specifically for the protection of archaeological resources.

The keystone of federal preservation law is the National Historic Preservation Act (NHPA) of 1966 (16 U.S.C. 470). It establishes the basic elements of the national historic preservation program and strongly influences the shape of state and even local preservation laws. The NHPA creates a comprehensive system for the identification, evaluation, protection, and enhancement of historic resources. It also provides an administrative structure to carry out these authorities.

At the center of the program is the National Register of Historic Places. This embraces the buildings, sites, districts, structures, and objects that are significant in American history, archaeology, architecture, culture, and engineering at the national, state, and local level. Listing on the Register, or meeting the criteria of eligibility for it, is a basic prerequisite for a property to benefit from NHPA protection and assistance. The National Register is administered by the Secretary of the Interior, acting through the National Park Service.

The Register caps a nationwide inventory process for identifying significant historic properties. Conducted primarily at the state level through individual state historic preservation officers (SHPO) in accordance with federal standards and criteria, surveys are ongoing to develop a nationwide data base for planning and resource allocation decisions affecting historic properties.

Properties meeting the Register criteria are afforded protection through Section 106 of the NHPA. This requires that a federal agency "take into account" the effects on such properties of activities that it carries out, funds, or otherwise assists or approves. When a historic property is affected, the agency must obtain the comments of a cabinet-level historic preservation body, the Advisory Council on Historic Preservation (Council).

The Section 106 process, set forth in regulations as 36 CFR Part 800, is the basic protection in federal law for historic properties. It applies to all properties on, or eligible for, the National Register, regardless of ownership, as long as there is some federal involvement in the action affecting them. In practice, it is a conflict resolution process, bringing together the project sponsor, preservation experts (the council and the SHPO), and interested members of the public. Agreement is sought on measures that will preserve significant features of the historic resource, but also allow the project to go forward.

While agreement is reached in the vast majority of cases, failure to agree results in the council issuing formal comments to the head of the federal agency proposing the project. The agency is obligated to consider the comments in reaching a decision, but is not required to follow them. It is important to recognize that this system provides no final authority to veto a federal action that might destroy a historic property, regardless of the importance of the resource.

A related program provides for the recovery of historic and archaeological data that is threatened with loss as a result of a project with federal involvement. Under the Archaeological and Historic Preservation Act of 1974 (16 U.S.C. 460), an agency must notify the secretary of the Interior when significant data will be lost. The agency or the secretary is authorized to undertake recovery of the data in accordance with specified standards, and project funds are allowed to be used for this purpose. This program is administered by the National Park Service.

For archaeological resources located on federal lands, substantially greater protections exist. The Archaeological Resources Protection Act of 1979 (16 U.S.C. 470aa-ll) prohibits the unauthorized excavation of archaeological sites and artifacts on federally owned lands and establishes civil and criminal penalties for violations. A permit system regulates the conduct of legitimate scientific investigations.

A final provision of general application to federal agencies is Section 110 of the NHPA. This obligates federal agencies to manage historic resources under their control in accordance with professional preservation standards and policies. In 1988 the National Park Service issued "Guidelines for Federal Agency Responsibilities under Section 110 of the National Historic Preservation Act" (Federal Register 1988a). These complement the "Secretary's Standards and

Guidelines for Archeology and Historic Preservation" (Federal Register 1988b), which generally apply to governmental activities affecting historic properties.

As previously noted, there are particular provisions of federal law and regulations that deal
with the interests of Native Americans in historic resources. The regulations implementing
Section 106 make special provision for the involvement of Indian tribes and Native Americans
in the project-review process. Likewise, the Advisory Council has adopted specific policies
regarding the treatment of human remains and grave goods in Section 106 cases.

The American Indian Religious Freedom Act (16 U.S.C 1996) declares it to be the policy of
the U.S. to protect the free exercise of traditional religions by American Indians and provide
access to sacred sites and the use of sacred objects. A second provision required federal agencies
to evaluate their programs to accommodate this policy. While this has not provided specific legal
protection to traditional sites and objects, it has influenced the implementation of other federal
preservation laws, such as the NHPA, and is occasionally referred to in regulations and
guidelines relating to archaeological and historic preservation.

In summary, the federal program provides for the identification of archaeologically and
historically significant resources and ensures their careful consideration in the planning of
federal and federally supported projects. Likewise, federally owned archaeological resources
are given stringent protection against vandalism and looting. However, the reach of federal law
to privately held resources is limited, and its strictures only apply to the actions of federal
agencies that may harm such properties.

## STATE HISTORIC PRESERVATION LAWS

The role of the state government is essentially threefold: a partner with the Federal
Government in carrying out the provisions of federal law; an implementor of state preservation
laws; and an authorizer for the conduct of preservation regulation at the local government level.
The first role is embodied in the state historic preservation program through which the SHPO
participates in the survey and inventorying activities related to the expansion of the National
Register and plays an active role in the conflict resolution process of Section 106.

The second role varies greatly from state to state. A number of states have project review
processes similar to Section 106 of the NHPA, covering activities where there are state agencies
involved. These are often tied to state inventories of historic properties, similar to the National
Register, but usually embracing a larger number of properties than the state has nominated to
the federal list. Only a few states, however, extend these protections to private actions that have
no governmental involvement.

Closely related are state environmental policy acts requiring consideration of the impacts of
state and local government-sponsored projects on the cultural and natural environments. These
laws customarily mandate the preparation of environmental impact statements and often provide
a mechanism for rejecting projects that have unacceptable impacts. They are often used to
protect historic and archaeological resources.

Most states have enacted special laws for the protection of archaeological sites. Most
common are laws that parallel the protections for federally owned lands. They establish a permit
system for excavation on state-owned lands and often place the administration of the system
under a designated state archaeologist. A few states have extended protection to private lands,
requiring the consent of the owner before anyone disturbs an archaeological site.

A related area of state activity to protect archaeological resources extends to those resources
located underwater. With authority from the Federal Abandoned Shipwreck Act of 1987 (43

U.S.C. 2101), states now have title to historic shipwrecks within their jurisdiction and can issue permits to regulate salvage. The 1987 law clarified state authority and is expected to generate a number of new or revised state laws.

Another somewhat arcane area of law is also used for archaeological protection: this is legislation enacted to protect cemeteries. While not always specifically directed at historic cemeteries and burials, their stringent prohibitions on the disturbance of grave sites offer a  legal tool that can be quite effective. Cemetery laws are also found at the local level.

Finally, under the U.S. Constitution, those powers not given to the Federal Government are reserved to the states. As a result, the exercise of such authorities as the police power by local governments, which are creatures of the state, must be based on delegations of authority from the state government. Accordingly, the basis for local government regulation must be found in state constitutions or legislative enactments. Thus, the state plays an important role in shaping the protection of historic resources at the local level.

## LOCAL REGULATION OF HISTORIC PROPERTIES

It is at the local level of government that direct regulation of private activity affecting historic resources occurs. Consistent with state enabling legislation, general zoning authority, or constitutional provision, a local government may enact a system that requires approval from a governmental body before a private action is allowed to modify or destroy a historic property. This has been done in hundreds of communities throughout the nation (see Kearns and Kirkorian, this volume, for a discussion of site protection at the local level).

Essentially, the protective process requires formal designation of a property as a local landmark and then establishes a governmental commission to review and approve proposed alterations or demolition. While this process can be used for individually listed properties, it is most often found applied to historic districts. The extent of control may vary from simply delaying the proposed action for a period of time to allow negotiation, to outright prohibition.

While these techniques have been primarily used to protect historic structures and neighborhoods, they have also been employed in some jurisdictions to protect archaeological resources. When so used, a similar kind of public agency review of proposed private action that may disturb a recognized archaeological site occurs, leading to approval or disapproval.

## A PRIVATE LAW APPROACH TO PRESERVATION

The foregoing discussion has focused on public regulation to protect historic properties. One of the most effective tools for long-term preservation of historic and archaeological resources comes from consensual arrangements among private parties and government agencies. Through the use of easements or preservation restrictions, private properties are voluntarily removed from the threat of development.

An easement essentially is the surrender of certain development rights by the owner of a property, usually in exchange for money or some tax benefit. A holding organization, either a governmental body or a nonprofit organization, is given the legal right to review proposed changes to a historic property or alterations are prohibited altogether.

These restrictions "run with the land;" that is, bind successive purchasers in accordance with the terms of the easement. As they are not imposed on an unwilling owner by a governmental body, they tend to be more successful in achieving their preservation objective. Easements are widely used to protect open space and archaeologically significant properties.

# CONCLUSION

Protecting historic resources in the U.S. relies upon the interplay of three levels of government. While the standards for deciding what is significant are largely derived from the Federal Government, their application and the most effective imposition of controls occurs at the state and local levels. Only at the local level does the authority exist to absolutely prohibit the destruction of a privately owned historic property. However, the integration of historic preservation concerns into the planning of public projects is highly developed and achieves substantial success in accommodating development and preservation goals.

This segmented system does not necessarily result in a lesser level of protection for historic properties, but indeed dictates the political dynamics of establishing and administering protective programs. Recognition of where the effective legislative and administrative decision making occurs is essential to the effective creation and use of legal tools to protect historic resources. That is the real challenge confronting those who advocate a more effective system of archaeological resource protection.

# REFERENCES CITED

16 U.S.C. 470 (1966) National Historic Preservation Act of 1966.

16 U.S.C. 460 (1974) Archaeological and Historic Preservation Act of 1974.

16 U.S.C. 470aa-ll (1979) Archaeological Resources Protection Act of 1979.

Federal Register (1988a) Guidelines for federal agency responsibilities under Section 110 of the National Historic Preservation Act, 53 Fed. Reg. 4727.

Federal Register (1988b) Secretary's standards and guidelines for archaeology and historic preservation, 48 Fed. Reg. 44716.

16 U.S.C. 1996, American Indian Religious Freedom Act.

43 U.S.C. 2101 (1987) Federal Abandoned Shipwreck Act of 1987.

# ANTECEDENTS TO CULTURAL RESOURCE MANAGEMENT

## Edward Friedman

## INTRODUCTION

The federal historic preservation program, as it exists today, has a long developmental history. The early preservation movement was made up of two groups: antiquarians/archaeologists and those involved with endeavors to preserve historic properties. Oftentimes the two groups were working together on archaeological and historic properties projects. In addition, these two groups often joined together to participate in legislative efforts to advance the preservation movement (King et al. 1977).

According to Hosmer (1965), "The American preservation movement appears to have been a truly grass-roots effort. It sprang up spontaneously all through the nation as an amateur activity, and therefore it did not possess a national organization or leadership of the kind usually encountered in comparable movements." King et al. (1977) see an unraveling of this long-standing movement during the Great Depression, with each of the two groups, archaeologists and those oriented to historic properties preservation, going its separate way. King et al. point out that "A major problem for modern historic preservationists is to bring archaeology and preservation together again . . ." (1977:22).

This article presents a chronological summary of the development of the historic preservation program through 1974. Post-1974 development is discussed in Fowler, Cheek, Neumann, and Rogers, this volume. Detailed research on the historic preservation movement is abundant. It has been interpreted by authors of various disciplines. The historian's perspective is provided by Hosmer (1965, 1981, 1987) and Lee (1970); an archaeological viewpoint is provided by Willey and Sabloff (1973) and Fowler (1985); an anthropological position is presented by King et al. (1977); and a legal outlook is contained in Rogers (1984).

## PRESERVATION IN THE 1700s

Don Fowler (1985:138) notes that one of the earliest efforts at preservation of an archaeological site was recorded in 1788 in Marietta, Ohio. While preparing the townsite for construction, the Ohio Land Company "reserved . . . the two truncated pyramids and the great mound, with a few acres attached to each, as a public square."

Thomas Jefferson, in 1793, prior to becoming president of the U.S., undertook systematic archaeological excavations on his Virginia property in an attempt to determine the origin of the mound sites. For this effort he has been referred to as the "father of American archaeology," but it should be noted that "Jefferson's influence as an archaeologist apparently was not important for either his contemporaries or even the next generation" (King et al. 1977:12; Willey and Sabloff 1973:38). He established a model for archaeology in terms of (1) stratigraphic approach, (2) testing explicit hypotheses, and (3) immediate publication of results. From today's perspective, Jefferson's only fault was in not issuing a call to conserve archaeological sites for future study or appreciation (Fowler 1985:138).

## PRESERVATION IN THE 1800s

The effort to save Independence Hall from demolition was the century's first preservation

27

undertaking. Efforts to preserve the structure began in 1813; the final victory was achieved in 1816. This project was to set the tone for most preservation activities for more than 100 years; it was based on private funding for the preservation of properties important to the history of the Revolution (King et al. 1977:13).

The federal government, in 1846, entered into preservation with the establishment of the Smithsonian Institution. This same year saw the first governmental sponsorship of archaeological research, as the Smithsonian provided support for Squire and Davis's investigations of the mound-builder sites (Fowler 1985:136; King et al. 1977:12).

Up to this point preservation proponents had been very successful in advancing their position. The first setback also came in 1846. In Deerfield, Massachusetts, there was a community drive to save "Old Indian House," the last remaining Indian structure from the site of a 1704 massacre. Though the action was unsuccessful, the effort set a tone for community involvement in historic preservation that continues up to this day (King et al. 1977:13).

A major impetus to the preservation movement was the reverence the people had for their great men — Washington in particular. As the Washington Monument was under construction in 1850, another effort to memorialize Washington was being undertaken by the state of New York. The state acquired the Hasbrouck House, Washington's headquarters during the last 2 years of the Revolutionary War. This action is noteworthy because prior to the 1870s, preservation was almost exclusively a private affair (King et al. 1977:13). In 1853 the Mount Vernon Ladies Association was formed and began a national campaign to raise funds to purchase and preserve Washington's home. By 1858 the association had raised enough money for the purchase and initial restoration projects (Hosmer 1987:5).

While the loss of the "Old Indian House" in 1846 was a setback, 1863 witnessed a major defeat. After a 4-year battle, John Hancock's home was lost to the wreckers. Hosmer (1965:13) points out that "In dying, the Hancock house contributed more to the preservation movement than it ever could have by remaining intact. Throughout the next five or six decades many preservationists used the Hancock Mansion as their rallying cry."

The Centennial Celebration in 1876 saw a significant change in the fabric of the preservation movement, with federal and state governments providing funding. One facet that did not change was the focus on sites associated with the Revolutionary War (Hosmer 1987:6; King et al. 1977:17).

The year 1879 was a pivotal one for American archaeology. Lee (1970) identifies five significant developments within the preservation movement that later led to the adoption of the Antiquities Act (1906) as the first national historic preservation policy of the U.S. The first of these events was the organization of the Anthropological Society of Washington (in 1902 it joined with other organizations to form the American Anthropological Association), which started publication of the *American Anthropologist* in 1888. The second development was the founding of the Archaeological Institute of America, with the express goal of promoting and directing archaeological research. On the governmental side of the equation was the establishment of the Bureau of American Ethnology within the Smithsonian Institution. The publication of the "Report Upon United States Geographical Surveys West of the One Hundredth Meridian," edited by Frederick Putnam, is considered the fourth event of the year. The book deals with the pueblos of Arizona and New Mexico and heightened public awareness of the spectacular nature of the sites of the Southwest. The final event of 1879 was the election of Lewis Henry Morgan, an anthropologist, as president of the American Association for the Advancement of Science.

The decade of the 1880s began with an expedition to the Southwest. In the account "Report on the Ruins of the Pueblo of Pecos" (Norris 1881), Bandelier testifies to the extensive looting of sites. The report aroused wide interest and deep concern on the part of Archaeological Institute of America members, who were moved to submit a petition to Congress to protect the sites. The petition, introduced by Senator Hoar of Massachusetts, suggested reserving selected lands from public sale and protecting antiquities from ruthless destruction. The petitioners were unable to gather enough support, so the effort failed to pass out of the Committee on Public Lands in 1882. (King et al. 1977:15; Lee 1970:9; Meltzer et al. 1985:140; Rogers 1984:3).

President Ulysses Grant, in 1872, signed legislation establishing Yellowstone as the first national park. In 1881 Yellowstone's superintendent, P.W. Norris, issued a staff directive that established policy for future parks and their personnel:

> . . . Comrades: Organized as we are for the protection and improvement of the Park, every member is expected to faithfully obey all the recently published rules and regulations for its management . . . . As all civilized nations are now actively pushing explorations and researches for evidences of prehistoric peoples, careful scrutiny is required for all material handled in [maintenance] excavations; and all arrow, spear, or lance heads, stone axes and knives, or other weapons, utensils or ornaments; in short, all such objects of interest are to be regularly retained and turned over daily to the officer in charge of each party for transmittal to the National Museum in Washington.

In 1886, Frank Cushing, of the Smithsonian's Bureau of American Ethnology, headed the privately funded Hemenway Southwestern Archaeological Expedition, which travelled to Casa Grande. In his reports Cushing noted serious damage to the ruins at the hands of looters. These reports served as the basis for preservationists to again petition Congress to protect sites (Lee 1970:18).

In 1889, as in 1882, a petition was submitted by Senator Hoar to Congress to enact legislation to protect Casa Grande. On this occasion, the drafters of the document, having learned from their previous setback, lined up several prominent citizens to sign the petition, which this time was successful. As a result of the petition, an executive order signed by President Harrison in 1892 established Casa Grande as the first national archaeological reservation in U.S. history (Lee 1970:19; Rogers 1984:3). The executive order designated that lands around the ruins were to be withdrawn from sale and settlement, and federal funds were to be set aside to protect and repair the site. The task of managing the reservation was given to the Department of the Interior (King et al. 1977:15; Lee 1970:20; Rogers 1984:3).

As the 1800s drew to a close, there were indications of greater public awareness, interest, and appreciation for archaeology and historic preservation. This period also had its negative side; the Chaco Canyon site of Pueblo Bonito was looted and the materials sent to the Swedish Museum as well as the American Museum of Natural History (King et al. 1977:18; Rogers 1984:5–6). According to Lee (1970:29), the display of these materials created a ". . . rising public interest in the history and art of the southwest Indians [which] was accompanied by a swelling demand for authentic prehistoric objects."

## PRESERVATION IN THE 1900s

After the activities of Chaco Canyon came to light, the preservationists determined that a method to protect the site was needed, and according to Rogers (1984:6), the only means open to them was to have the lands withdrawn. After years of bureaucratic maneuvering, the whole area of Chaco Canyon was withdrawn in 1905, pending its possible designation as a national park.

The Antiquities Act was passed in 1906. To pass, this legislation required a massive effort spanning 6 years, three sessions of Congress, and seven versions of the bill. H.R. 13349 was introduced in early January 1906 and was passed in March. The Senate version was introduced in February and was approved in May. On June 6, 1906, President Roosevelt signed the bill into law (Lee 1970:47–77). In 1907 uniform regulations were developed by the Departments of Agriculture, Interior, and War (King et al. 1977:19).

During the second decade of the 1900s, the Federal Government became deeply involved in preservation activities. The centralization of responsibility for the management of federally owned historic properties in the Department of the Interior occurred in 1916 and was furthered by the establishment of a unified National Park Service (King et al. 1977:19).

A new development in archaeology had its beginnings in the 1920s. The construction of federal hydroelectric plants and flood control projects that threatened a large number of archaeological sites in river valleys ushered in the era of salvage archaeology (Meltzer et al. 1985:145).

The 1930s and the Great Depression was a time of unparalleled growth in the federal preservation program. To staff the Civilian Conservation Corps, Works Progress Administration, and Tennessee Valley Authority, the Federal Government hired architects, archaeologists, historians, landscape architects, and engineers. Also during this period, the National Park Service assumed responsibility for the management of Revolutionary and Civil War battlefields from the War Department. To handle this new responsibility, the National Park Service absorbed the initial programs of the New Deal in order to locate Civilian Conservation Corps personnel in many of the historic areas (Hosmer 1987:7).

In 1933 there was a major reorganization of federal land management responsibilities. The reorganization delegated the responsibility for the administration of all federal parks, monuments, battlefields, and historic sites to the National Park Service (King et al. 1977:19). In 1934 the National Park Service was the recipient of a new program, the Historic American Building Survey (HABS). The HABS program was another Depression make-work program that was to employ thousands and last for 6 months.

On the archaeological front, the Society for American Archaeology was chartered in 1934. One objective of the organization was, and still is, the conservation of archaeological sites.

In 1935 President Roosevelt signed into law the Historic Sites Act. According to King et al. (1977:23), ". . . for the first time asserted a broad federal concern for the nation's historic properties and authorized the National Park Service to conduct a tremendous variety of programs to locate, record, acquire, preserve, mark, and commemorate properties of national significance."

On the eve of World War II, major gains had been made by the preservation movement, most of these a result of the make-work programs of the Great Depression. The U.S. entry into the war placed all preservation activities on hold. It was not until 1949, with the congressional charter of the National Trust for Historic Preservation, that the national preservation movement was set in motion again.

Between 1949 and the passage of the National Historic Preservation Act of 1966, only one major piece of legislation was created. In 1960 the Reservoir Salvage Act, with its antecedents in the Missouri Basin Survey, was signed by President Kennedy ". . . to provide for the protection of historical and archaeological data which might otherwise be lost as the result of the construction of a dam" (Scovill 1974:2).

In 1974 Congress amended the Reservoir Salvage Act of 1960 as the Archaeological and Historic Preservation Act. This act extended the provisions of the 1960 act to all federal construction activities and all federally licensed or assisted activities that would cause loss of scientific, prehistoric, or archaeological data. It requires the Secretary of the Interior to coordinate this effort and to report annually to Congress on the program. It permits agencies either to undertake necessary protection activities on their own or to transfer to the Secretary up to 1% of the total amount authorized for expenditure on a federal or federally assisted or licensed project, to enable the secretary to undertake the necessary protection activities.

To address the increased amount of archaeological looting and vandalism that was taking place in the 1970s, the professional archaeological community, federal agencies, and Congress set about the task of developing protective legislation that would provide additional protection for archaeological sites located on federal and Indian lands. This effort resulted in the passage of the Archaeological Resources Protection Act (ARPA) in 1979. Development and implementation of ARPA is discussed in Cheek, Neumann, and Rogers in this volume.

## CONCLUSION

Protecting the past has been a special concern in this country for over 200 years. The role of the Federal Government in this effort has been, and continues to be, very important. The preservation of archaeological resources on lands managed by the Federal Government, roughly one third of the nation, acts to conserve archaeological resources for future generations. Our country has a long and rich past that belongs to and is part of all Americans. A substantial part of that past is represented only by archaeological remains. At the request of a concerned public, the Federal Government has developed laws, regulations, and guidelines to protect those archaeological resources. Although the laws have been modified over the years to respond to changing ideas and needs, they have collectively provided the basis upon which current archaeological resource protection rests. Without them, little of the past would be left. We all have benefited from those who protected the past for us. It is now our turn to protect the past for the future.

## REFERENCES CITED

Fowler, D. D. (1985) Conserving American archaeological resources. In *American Archaeology Past and Future: A Celebration of the Society for American Archaeology 1935 –1985,* Meltzer, D., Fowler, D. D., and Sabloff, J. A., Eds., Smithsonian Institution Press, Washington, D.C.

Hosmer, C. B., Jr. (1965) *Presence of the Past: A History of the Preservation Movement in the United States Before Williamsburg,* G. P. Putnam's Sons, New York.

Hosmer, C. B., Jr. (1981) *Preservation Comes of Age: From Williamsburg to the National Trust, 1926–1949,* University of Virginia Press, Charlottesville.

Hosmer, C. B., Jr. (1987) Preservation — a historical perspective In *Cultural Resources Management,* Johnson, R. W. and Schene, M. G., Eds., Robert E. Krieger Publishing, Malabar, FL.

King, T. F., Parker Hickman, P., and Berg, G. (1977) *Anthropology in Historic Preservation: Caring for Culture's Clutter,* Academic Press, New York.

Lee, R. F. (1970) *The Antiquities Act of 1906,* Office of History and Historic Architecture, Eastern Center, Washington, D.C.

Norris, P. W. (1881) Fifth Annual Report of the Superintendent of the Yellowstone National Park, Washington, D.C.

Rogers, K. O. (1984) Visigoths revisited — The prosecution of archaeological resource thieves, traffickers and vandals, *J. Environ. Law Lit.,* 2, 217.

Scovill, D. H. (1974) History of archaeological conservation policy and the Moss-Bennett Bill. In *Proc. 1974 Cultural Resource Management Conf.,* Lipe, W. D. and Lindsay, A. J., Eds., Museum of Northern Arizona Technical Series No. 14, Flagstaff, Arizona.

Willey, G. R. and Sabloff, J. A. (1973) *A History of American Archaeology,* W.H. Freeman, New York.

# PROTECTION OF ARCHAEOLOGICAL RESOURCES ON PUBLIC LANDS: HISTORY OF THE ARCHAEOLOGICAL RESOURCES PROTECTION ACT

Annetta L. Cheek

## INTRODUCTION

Throughout the 19th century, the inquisitiveness of the American spirit fostered an interest in the prehistoric ruins and objects the pioneers discovered as they moved westward. Late in the century, public interest in the art, history, and prehistory of North America reached a fevered peak, stimulated by the discovery of the major ruins of the Southwest. As the century drew to a close, it seemed that our very enthusiasm was going to destroy the objects of our interest, as more and more ruins were stripped and their contents hauled east to grace the walls of museums and private collectors.

A growing concern over this phenomenon at the turn of the century resulted in pressure being brought on Congress to pass legislation protecting antiquities on public and private land. As a result, Congress passed the Antiquities Act of 1906 (16 U.S.C. 431-433). Not only did this act protect "any historic or prehistoric ruin or monument, or object of antiquity" located on public lands, it also provided authority for the President to withdraw lands from the public domain and set them aside as national monuments and to accept land relinquished for such purposes by private landowners.

This act remained the keystone of our efforts to protect archaeological resources on public lands until 1974. As far as we know, the first legal challenge to the act was the case of *United States vs. Diaz,* decided in the Ninth Circuit Court of Appeals, which covers many of the western states. In that case, Diaz had been convicted for a violation of the act, for stealing a number of recent religious objects from a cave in the San Carlos Indian Reservation. In 1974 the Appeals Court overturned the lower court's conviction stating that the terms "object of antiquity," "ruins," and "monuments" were vague, and on that basis found the act to be unconstitutional.

While several convictions were obtained under the act over the next few years (Collins and Green 1978), the *Diaz* case rendered the act useless in the Ninth Circuit. In 1977 a case in New Mexico resulted in a U.S. Magistrate's decision that the act was unconstitutional. Furthermore, it was becoming apparent that with the escalating prices for prehistoric artifacts, particularly from the Southwest, the minimal penalty provisions of the Antiquities Act were no longer sufficient deterrents to looting and vandalism. In addition, the $500 fine associated with the Antiquities Act, although close to the average yearly salary for Americans in 1906, is not the deterrent it was in the early 20th century.

## THE ARCHAEOLOGICAL RESOURCES PROTECTION ACT OF 1979

Several individual archaeologists decided to work for new legislation to supplement or replace the Antiquities Act (Collins and Michel 1985). The support of the Society for American Archaeology was solicited. Congressman Morris Udall of Arizona, chairman of the House Interior Committee, which had jurisdiction over any such legislation, was contacted; he promised support for a strong bill. In 1977 initial contact with the Department of the Interior revealed that Interior was developing draft legislation. After a frustrating wait of many months,

33

however, Interior's bill was revealed to contain little more than minor revisions to the Antiquities Act, which would resolve the definitional problems revealed by *Diaz,* but would do little else.

As a result, a small group of archaeologists resolved to draft their own bill. They intended the bill to be a comprehensive reform of the provisions for protecting publicly owned archaeological resources. They wanted to prohibit looting as well as selling, purchasing, bartering, trafficking in, transporting, or receiving looted artifacts from federal lands. Trafficking in interstate commerce was also banned if the violation of a state or local law was involved. Greater criminal penalties were included, and a system of civil penalties was included to cover damages and repair of the damage done to sites.

Initially, the archaeological community intended to continue to work through Interior, and a draft bill was provided to the department and to Congressman Udall in April 1978. At about the same time, U.S. District Judge William Copple of Phoenix ruled that the government could not prosecute three men who had been caught looting a prehistoric site on a national forest in Arizona. The government, knowing that the Antiquities Act had been declared unconstitutional in that jurisdiction, sought to prosecute the men for theft of government property. The judge ruled that the theft of government property charge was inappropriate and that the men should be prosecuted under the Antiquities Act. But since that act was unconstitutional, they could not be prosecuted at all. The judge himself suggested that Congress should correct the situation with legislation.

This decision made the situation even more desperate. After waiting throughout the summer for Interior to produce a viable bill, the archaeologists decided to try to get their own bill introduced. The Society for American Archaeology, for the first time in its history, agreed to commit funds for a professional lobbying effort in Congress. A bill was introduced on February 1, 1979.

Over the next 9 months, considerable effort was expended working with Congress (the role of Congress is discussed further in Domenici and Neumann, this volume) and with various special interest groups to hammer out a bill that could be passed. A number of controversial issues developed. The issue of "arrowheads" was one of the most difficult, due to concern about making surface collecting by casual collectors illegal (Beaty 1985:93–94). Eventually, compromises on the remaining issues were worked out. The Archaeological Resources Protection Act of 1979 (16 U.S.C. 470 aa-ll) (ARPA) was signed into law by President Carter on October 31, 1979. The act was considered a great victory for archaeology and was to be a major tool in antilooting and vandalism efforts.

ARPA contained a number of important new provisions. In addition to imposing new and severe penalties for the excavation or destruction of archaeological resources, it imposed the same penalties for the unauthorized "removal" of such resources and their sale or purchase. It even imposed penalties on interstate commerce in such artifacts when removed in violation of ARPA or in violation of *any* state or local ordinance. This last provision essentially makes it an ARPA violation to transport across state lines any artifacts stolen from a state park or even private land. ARPA also provides for the forfeiture of any vehicles or other equipment involved in a violation — a provision that has proven to be an important tool in the hands of federal prosecutors. The act refined and extended the permitting provisions of the Antiquities Act. It also set up a system of civil penalties for minor violations. Clearly, Congress intended these penalties to be an easy-to-use tool to deter minor violators of the act (Senate Committee on Energy and Natural Resources 1979). However, federal agencies do not seem to be using these tools to the extent Congress intended.

## Uniform Regulations

As soon as ARPA was passed, federal agency personnel began using it in the battle against vandalism and looting. It quickly became apparent that without the uniform regulations called for in the act, implementation would be difficult if not impossible. Many problems during the development of the statute were "solved" by deferring to the regulations. Many critical definitions and processes were not specified in the act.

The job facing the rule writers was a mammoth one. The act called for "Uniform Regulations"; this meant that all four of the Executive Branch units named in the Act—the Departments of Interior, Agriculture, and Defense, and the Tennessee Valley Authority (TVA)—had to agree on the text of the regulations. The individual agencies involved (including the National Park Service, the Bureau of Land Management, the Fish and Wildlife Service, the Army Corps of Engineers, the TVA, and the Forest Service) represented a great diversity of interests in, and commitments to, archaeological resources.

Even though the agencies began meeting to develop regulations before the act was passed, it was $4^1/_2$ years after the act became law that the regulations were adopted (compare this to the regulations implementing the Antiquities Act of 1906, which were promulgated 6 months after passage). How did this delay happen?

For anyone who has not worked within the environment of the Federal Government on a project as complex as uniform regulations, it is hard to imagine what transpires. In the case of these regulations, an overly large and ever-changing group of subject-area specialists from agencies with different and often competing interests met to try and accomplish the task. Membership shifted, old issues had to be revisited, and critical members of the overall federal resource protection team — law enforcement specialists — were not represented (Friedman 1985). After an initial flurry of activity, staff from the Department of the Interior, which had the lead, consistently failed to meet designated deadlines.

Early in 1980 it was announced that public hearings would be held to solicit the views of concerned citizens on the direction the regulations should take and what issues needed to be considered. This public participation process, which is now a required component of regulatory development, provided valuable insight into the views of private citizens, but at the same time raised issues that required extensive and time-consuming work to resolve.

A number of major issues were highlighted by the public hearing process. Most significantly, the definition of archaeological resources presented a thorny problem. This section of the regulations drew the most public comment, and regulators had to balance the apparent intent of Congress, that a "laundry list" of such resources be developed, with the need to ensure that currently unnamed resources would be protected. Ultimately, a broad definition that includes specific, but noninclusive, examples was developed (Friedman 1985:97). Other issues also were raised that bogged down the regulatory effort.

In March 1982 the director of the Bureau of Land Management recommended to the Secretary of the Interior that the regulatory task force be disbanded because of the lack of progress. Instead, the department changed the personnel involved and placed the Departmental Consulting Archaeologist in control of the group (Keel and Cheek 1985:101).

With the change in personnel, final drafting of the regulations began. By June the document was completed, and a host of other requirements were met over the next several months. By March 1983 all other agencies in the Department of the Interior completed their review, and the rules were sent to the other two departments and the TVA. By May Defense, Agriculture, and TVA gave their approval. The last stop was the Office of Management and Budget, which had

10 days to review the rule and 60 days to review the permit application. Then, after one final departmental review, the rules went to the Federal Register for final publication on September 26, 1983.

Those of us who were working on the rules at the time breathed a great sigh of relief when we delivered the rules to the Federal Register. Bennie Keel and I had not been involved in the early development of the rules and had missed the opportunity to discuss the major technical and administrative issues that had to be resolved. However, Keel and I had the "pleasure" of shepherding the rules through their last 18 months of bureaucratic review, changing "therefore" to "therefor" and making other such significant changes. We were personally delighted to see the last of the document.

The next day disaster struck. The Federal Register called and said the rules were in the wrong format. We had used a regulation number in the National Park Service regulation system. The Federal Register had recently decided that uniform regulations issued by several agencies had to be promulgated separately by each agency and had to have a regulation number specific to each agency. So back we went to reformat the whole thing, break it out into four separate but identical packages, call the other departments and explain the situation, and get new numbers assigned. Of course, the final package had to go through the bureaucratic "surname process" in each department all over again and ultimately be signed by the head of the department. All in all, this process took an additional 3 months. The new final package went back to the Federal Register and was published on January 6, 1984. Because of legal procedural requirements, they could not go into effect for 30 days, until February 6, 1984 — $4\frac{1}{2}$ years after ARPA was passed. At last, federal managers had the regulatory tools they needed to enforce ARPA.

## ARPA Amendments

In 1988 two amendments to ARPA were enacted (see Domenici and Neumann, this volume, for additional discussion of the ARPA amendments). Although it is too early to determine the extent to which these amendments will impact federal programs, the provisions corrected weaknesses in ARPA that were identified by the Congress, the Executive Branch, the law enforcement community, and the profession, as needing resolution.

The first amendment, enacted October 28, 1988, requires the four agencies who were named as having principal responsibilities under ARPA — the Departments of Interior, Agriculture, and Defense and the TVA — to develop plans for surveying lands under their control. The surveys are to determine the nature and extent of archaeological resources on those lands. This requirement reflects the concern that the major federal landowners are not being successful in protecting archaeological resources on their lands, in large part because the exact nature, extent, and location of those resources are not know. The amendment further requires those agencies to develop documents for the reporting of suspected violations of ARPA and to establish when and how those documents are to be completed.

The second amendment, enacted November 3, 1988, lowers the threshold of site damage that can result in a felony conviction, large fine, and imprisonment of 2 years. As a result, damage of only $500 can result in severe penalties. This provision reflected the concern of archaeologists and law enforcement staffs that too much effort was being spent establishing that the threshold previously listed in ARPA for such penalties (damage greater than $5000 was exceeded in specific cases).

The same amendment requires that all federal land managers establish a public awareness program on the significance of archaeological resources and the need to protect them. This requirement responds to the growing awareness among federal managers and resource protection staffs that the looting and vandalism problem cannot be solved without the active assistance of a concerned public.

As a result of these amendments, the four principal agencies published proposed uniform rules on January 29, 1990. These would amend the uniform regulations to include in the description of prohibited acts to include the *attempt* to remove, deface, etc. archaeological resources.

Additionally, the Department of the Interior has developed preliminary proposed rules that would amend the uniform rules to lower the threshold of felony violations and to establish public awareness programs and schedules and plans for archaeological surveys. The draft also provides for the Secretary of the Interior to report to Congress on public awareness programs and on agency programs to document violations (Michele Aubry, personal communication April 1990).

## The Situation Today

Clearly, federal agencies have made significant efforts to improve the protection of archaeological resources on lands they own and manage. The most recent reasonably accurate and complete data available (National Park Service 1989) shows, in fiscal years 1985 and 1986, that federal agencies spent at least $74 million on archaeological work, surveyed over 13 million acres, and determined approximately 5600 sites eligible for inclusion in the National Register of Historic Places. Through about the same time period, the Bureau of Land Management surveyed about 7.5 million acres and recorded over 100,000 sites. The Forest Service surveyed 18.4 million acres and also recorded over 100,000 sites (Schalk 1988).

A number of agencies have specifically recognized the importance of public awareness efforts in their resource protection programs through the initiation of interpretive and educational programs and public lectures. Training programs for employees and contractors are included as a routine part of cultural resource management programs, by several agencies. Other agencies encourage the participation of volunteers in their programs. Archaeological contractors are sometimes required to prepare articles and slide or video presentations for use in interpretive programs. Site steward programs have been established in some areas to enlist private citizens in the task of guarding individual resources from vandalism and looting (see Hoffman, this volume, for a discussion of site stewardship programs).

In addition to numerous area and site-specific efforts by federal agencies, the national spotlight continues to be focused on the issue of protecting archaeological resources. Both the Senate and the House as well as the General Accounting Office (GAO) have examined the problem in recent years (Senate Committee on Energy and Natural Resources 1986; House Committee on Interior and Insular Affairs 1988; General Accounting Office 1987).

Despite this attention and the efforts of federal agencies, the loss of publicly owned archaeological resources continues at an alarming pace. Of the approximately 0.8 billion acres of public land, less than 10% has been surveyed, and it is unlikely that a significant portion of the remainder will be surveyed in the foreseeable future. Looting and vandalism is clearly continuing almost unabated. In fiscal years 1985 and 1986 (National Park Service 1989:32) there were over 1000 documented cases — and this is likely the tip of the iceberg. Furthermore, there was a sharp increase from 1985 to 1986. On the other hand, there were just 33 arrests and 82 citations for ARPA violations, and only 43 convictions; the majority of these occurred in 1985. A recent General Accounting Office report that focused on the Four Corners area reported that commercial looting has not been deterred and scientific information continues to be destroyed (General Accounting Office 1987:21). The three major federal land managers in that area, the National Park Service, the Bureau of Land Management, and the Forest Service, had a total of three people in fiscal year 1985 whose primary responsibility was the protection of archaeological resources on over 104 million acres of public lands. The three agencies had surveyed only about 7% of their lands in that area and had recorded about 136,000 sites. They estimated a total of almost 2,000,000 sites, of which approximately one third have been looted or vandalized. Often the sites that are looted or vandalized are those with varied, stratified deposits that hold both the greatest amount of scientific information as well as the most commercially valuable artifacts.

## CONCLUSION

When ARPA was passed, archaeologists expected that the rate of looting and destruction of our country's archaeological heritage would subside. Unfortunately, this has not proven to be the case. While casual looting may be on the decline, clearly, commercial looting is not, and archaeological resources on public lands continue to be seriously endangered.

An article of this scope cannot discuss the possible solutions to this problem in even a remotely thorough manner. Instead, I'll examine a few individual ideas about what might be done to make some impact on the problem.

First, it is obvious that passing a law is just the beginning. Agencies need to be convinced that it is important to enforce the law, that of the many responsibilities they have, this one should be near the top of the list. Furthermore, even if they are convinced, they must have resources to implement those responsibilities. This is something that both the archaeological profession and the interested public can help with through lobbying efforts in the Congress. We also need to keep in close contact with top executive agency management who need to be educated about the problems and who need to be convinced that enough of the public cares so that *they* need to care. However, as LeBlanc points out, this must be a joint effort between professional archaeologists, grass roots interest groups, and professional lobbyists and not just an effort by archaeologists alone (LeBlanc 1985:16).

Second, a major component of fixing this problem is public education in the largest sense (see Chapter 4, this volume, for discussions of archaeology and education). This has been the main thrust of the Society for American Archaeology "Save the Past for the Future" project, jointly sponsored by the society and a number of cooperating federal agencies (see Reinburg, this volume, for a discussion of the "Save the Past" project). By education I do not mean simply presenting school children with the facts and figures of archaeology. I include educating federal land managers, federal law enforcement personnel, and everyone involved in our judicial system. A major problem with obtaining prosecutions under ARPA has been the reluctance of the judicial bureaucracy to take on cases of this nature. It is up to the archaeological community to change that. We need to educate our local, state, and national legislators about the problem and the need for resources to be *focused* on the problem in an effective way.

Finally, we all need to do whatever we can do locally to help protect the archaeological resources in our own backyards. Participate in site steward programs; get friends and relatives to do the same. Report any violations you know about, even if they seem minor.

The passage of ARPA did not achieve all the results we expected. However, it was, and remains, a major victory. Public awareness of, and concern about, the looting problem has increased, but the job of protecting these resources has barely begun. Federal agencies simply do not have the fiscal and personnel resources to do the job, and they never will. We all have to do our part.

## REFERENCES CITED

**Aubry, M.** (1990) Personal communication, April 1990.

**Beaty, L.** (1985) ARPA enacted: the legislative process, *Am. Archaeol.,* 5(2), 90–94.

**Collins, R. B. and Green, D. F.** (1978) A proposal to modernize the American Antiquities Act, *Science,* 202, 1055–1059.

**Collins, R. B. and Michel, M. P.** (1985) Preserving the past: origins of the Archaeological Resources Protection Act of 1979, *Am. Archeol.,* 5(2), 84–89.

**Friedman, J.** (1985) The regulations: the early years. *Am. Archeol.,* 5(2), 94–101.

General Accounting Office (1987) Problems protecting and preserving federal archaeology resources, GAO/RCED-88-3, General Accounting Office, Washington, D.C.

House Committee on Interior and Insular Affairs (1988) The destruction of America's archaeological heritage: looting and vandalism of Indian archaeological sites in the Four Corners States of the Southwest, Committee Print No. 6, U.S. Government Printing Office, Washington, D.C.

**Keel, B. C. and Cheek, A. L.** (1985) The regulations: the late years, *Am. Archeol.,* 5(2), 101–103.

**LeBlanc, S.** (1985) ARPA: some lessons, *Am. Archeol.,* 5(2), 115–117.

National Park Service (1989) *Federal Archeology: The Current Program,* National Park Service, Washington, D.C.

**Schalk, L.** (1988) Looters of the past: an enforcement problem in the Pacific Northwest, *CRM Bull.: Archeology and the Federal Government,* Vol 11, National Park Service, Washington, D.C., 32–34.

Senate Committee on Energy and Natural Resources (1979) Hearing before the Subcommittee on Parks, Recreation and Renewable Resources of the Committee on Energy and Natural Resources. Senate Hearing 96-26.

Senate Committee on Energy and National Resources (1986) Management of archaeological and paleontological resources on federal land. Senate Hearing 99-463.

16 U.S.C. 431-433 (1906) Antiquities Act of 1906.

16 U.S.C. 470aa-ll (1979) Archaeological Resources Protection Act of 1979.

# THE POLITICS OF ARCHAEOLOGY AND HISTORIC PRESERVATION: HOW OUR LAWS REALLY ARE MADE

Loretta Neumann

## INTRODUCTION

The U.S. Congress publishes for its constituents a booklet, "How Our Laws Are Made" (Willett 1986). It is an informative treatise on the rules and procedures for the legislative process; however, it provides only part of the story. Lost between the lines are the tales of specific bills and real-life people who make our nation's laws. Yet these stories are important, not just as entertaining vignettes for the historical record, but as a way to understand how laws are really made. They are especially useful to archaeologists and preservationists more familiar with scientific disciplines and scholarly pursuits. No scientific method is involved in making laws. The legislative process is often unpredictable and sometimes uncontrollable. It is also fascinating and — especially for archaeological and historical resources that depend so heavily on federal law for their protection and enhancement — indispensable.

This article will provide an archaeological perspective on how our laws are made. It will describe the legislative process, including information about people who helped make the laws possible. It will conclude with some insights about the political future of preservation as our nation looks forward to a new century (discussion of the history of preservation legislation can be found in Fowler, Friedman, and Cheek, this volume).

## THE WORKINGS OF CONGRESS

To understand how laws are made, a few basic facts are helpful. The U.S. Congress, composed of the House of Representatives and the Senate, meets in 2-year terms starting in January of odd-numbered years. Congressional elections are held in even-numbered years. All members of the House are elected for 2-year terms. Senators are elected for 6-year terms; every 2 years only one third of the Senate is up for election. The political party with more than half of the members in the House or the Senate is called the "majority;" the party with less than half is the "minority." The majority party holds the leadership posts, including the positions chairing committees (the minority party counterparts are called the "ranking members"). Since the early 1950s, the Democratic party has been the predominate majority party in both the House and Senate. The only exception was from 1981 through 1986, when the Senate majority was Republican.

### Introduction of Legislation

Legislation may be prompted for several reasons : to remedy problems in a previous law or to establish new programs in response to emerging needs. A bill may be recommended in several ways : by the executive branch, by lobbyists, or by members of Congress and their staffs. Regardless of the reason or the source, only a member of Congress may actually introduce a bill. The following are some examples of why and how some recent preservation acts were initially introduced. (the term "bill" is used until legislation passes the House or Senate; after that, the term "act" is used).

1.    ARPA was based on suggestions in the late 1970s by the Society for American Archaeology (SAA), through the efforts of Drs. Raymond Thompson, Charles McGimsey, Don Fowler, and other archaeologists concerned about the growing problem of the looting and vandalism of archaeological sites. The proposal was in response to a federal court decision in 1974 *(United States vs. Diaz)*, which held that the penalties section of the 1906 Antiquities Act was unconstitutionally broad and, therefore, largely ineffective. The SAA approached Representative Morris K. Udall (D-Arizona), chairman of the House Committee on Interior and Insular Affairs, and Senator Pete Domenici (R-New Mexico). The members' staffs worked with the SAA, with other committee staffs, and with professionals in the Interior Department to develop the legislation that Representative Udall and Senator Domenici later introduced.

2.    The 1980 NHPA Amendments began with legislation initially introduced in 1977 by Representative John F. Seiberling (D-Ohio). Meanwhile, President Carter's administration proposed legislation to create a national heritage program combining historic preservation and natural resources conservation programs. In 1979, at the administration's request, Representative Philip Burton (D-California) introduced legislation for such a new program. At about the same time, Seiberling introduced a new version of his bill which addressed solely historic preservation issues. It was Seiberling's bill that later resulted in the NHPA Amendments of 1980.

3.    The Abandoned Shipwreck Act was first introduced in the late 1970s by Representative Charles Bennett (D-Florida), who had a personal concern about the protection of historic shipwrecks. (He is the "Bennett" of the Moss-Bennett Act of 1974 and a long-time champion of archaeology and historic preservation.) He reintroduced versions of the legislation in succeeding Congresses. In 1984 Bennett introduced the bill again. A version of it was also introduced by Representative Walter Jones (D-North Carolina), chairman of the House Merchant Marine and Fisheries Committee; the Jones bill passed the House, but died in the Senate. Bennett reintroduced legislation in the next Congress, as did Senator Lowell Weicker (R-Connecticut), but again the bill was not enacted. In 1987 Bennett reintroduced the bill, and Senator Bill Bradley (D-New Jersey) introduced a similar one in the Senate. These bills, as amended, resulted in the final legislation enacted in 1988.

What all of this shows, of course, is that once an issue gets popular, other members want to get involved. They can do so by "cosponsoring a bill," which means that their name is added to the bill, with the original sponsor listed first. In the case of the 1980 NHPA amendments, 80 members of the House joined Representative Seiberling in cosponsoring the bill. Members can also introduce identical bills or completely different ones addressing the same issue. For example, the two 1988 ARPA amendments amend the same statute, although in quite different ways, and were introduced separately by Senator Domenici and Representative Sam Gejdenson (D-Connecticut).

## Committee/Subcommittee Consideration

Once a bill is introduced, it is referred to one or more committees. Legislation to authorize archaeological and historic preservation programs and regulations (such as the NHPA and ARPA) are handled by the Committee on Interior and Insular Affairs in the House of Representatives, and the Committee on Energy and Natural Resources in the Senate. Since 1977 the chairman of the Interior Committee has been Representative Udall, the only member now serving who was on the committee in 1966 when the NHPA was passed. In the Senate, the chairman of the Energy Committee is Senator Bennett Johnston (D-Louisiana); his Democratic predecessor was Senator Henry ("Scoop") Jackson, who died in 1983. At his death, Jackson was the last member of the committee who had served in 1966 when the NHPA was passed. The chairman of the Energy Committee from 1981 through 1986 was Senator James McClure (R-Idaho).

Legislation sometimes gets referred to more than one committee. For example, while both ARPA and the NHPA were referred in the House only to the Interior Committee, the Abandoned Shipwreck Act was referred both to the Interior Committee (because of its jurisdiction over historic preservation law) and to the Merchant Marine and Fisheries Committee (because of its jurisdiction over maritime and admiralty law). Both committees held hearings and took action on the bill before it went to the House floor. In the Senate the bill was referred only to the Energy Committee.

Subcommittees are usually the first forum for consideration of legislation. In the House, the Interior Committee's Subcommittee on National Parks and Public Lands has jurisdiction over archaeology and historic preservation. The subcommittee has been chaired by Representative Bruce Vento (D-Minnesota) since 1987, when his predecessor, Representative Seiberling, retired. Seiberling's subcommittee had jurisdiction over such legislation from 1981 through 1986. Seiberling's predecessor was Representative Philip Burton (D-California), who switched his chairmanship to another committee in 1981. Burton, who died in 1983, was a close friend of Seiberling's — so much so that he allowed Seiberling to chair the hearings and handle the details of the NHPA of 1980 (including writing the committee report) while Burton was still chairman of the subcommittee.

In the Senate, the Energy Committee's Subcommittee on Public Lands, National Parks and Forests has jurisdiction over preservation legislation. The chairman, since 1987, has been Senator Dale Bumpers (D-Arkansas). From 1981 through 1986, the subcommittee was chaired by Senator Malcom Wallop (R-Wyoming).

Bills normally receive their most thorough consideration by subcommittees. Usually at that level, hearings are held to give witnesses a chance to express their views. In the House, but less often in the Senate, a subcommittee holds a "mark up" on the bill, where subcommittee members review a bill, line by line, and offer amendments to it. If a majority of the subcommittee approves, the bill is then referred favorably to the full committee. In full committee, the bill must again be marked up and approved by majority vote before it goes to the floor. In the Senate, usually mark up occurs only in the full committee, after a subcommittee hearing.

Many things can happen to a bill during a mark up. The original ARPA bill was changed to exempt arrowheads taken from the surface of the ground; this was the result of an amendment in the full House Interior Committee by then-Representative James Santini (D-Nevada). During consideration of the NHPA Amendments of 1980, the so-called "owner consent" provision was added in full committee at the urging of former Representative Richard Cheney (R-Wyoming). The intent was to require the consent of an owner before a property could be listed on the National Register. In subsequent negotiations the provision was modified simply to provide an owner with notification and an opportunity to object to such a listing. If the owner objected, the Secretary of Interior would still be required to determine whether the property was "eligible" for the Register and, if so, it would still receive the same protections of federal law, although it would not be formally listed.

After mark up, the full committee must approve the bill by majority vote before it goes to the floor. This is called "ordering the bill reported." The committee's action is then officially brought to the attention of the House by the filing of a committee report, a separate document usually written by the subcommittee chairman and representing the official position of the committee. Among other things, a committee report states the purpose and effect of the bill and includes background information, a section-by-section analysis, cost estimates, views of the administration, legislative history, and proposed changes in existing laws, if any. Individual members of the committee may also include additional statements, under their own names, in support of, or opposition to, the legislation. An example is the committee report to the NHPA amendments of 1980, which provides an overview of federal preservation laws as well as a description of the bill itself.

## Floor Action

A House bill goes to the floor in one of three ways:

1.  "Unanimous consent" is a way to bring up noncontroversial bills that do not authorize over $1 million. As the name of the procedure suggests, a single objection by any member can block the bill. The NHPA amendments of 1980 were brought to the floor in this manner. In that case, the bill was more controversial than most largely because it contained several new provisions, such as the "owner objection" provision, described earlier. As part of the negotiations over this provision, Representative Cheney promised that if it were included in the legislation when it went to the floor, he would support the entire bill and urge other members not to object to it. The bill then passed without a dissenting vote.
2.  "Suspension of the rules" is a legislative shortcut for considering relatively noncontroversial bills, usually with less than $100 million authorization. A two-thirds vote of members present and voting is needed to suspend House procedures and pass a bill. Debate on the bill is limited to 20 minutes for each party, and no floor amendments may be offered. Most relatively noncontroversial Interior Committee bills are brought to the floor in this manner, including the two amendments to ARPA passed in 1988.
3.  A "rule" is a simple resolution prepared by the Rules Committee, which stipulates the length of floor debate time and whether or not amendments may be offered. The rule must be approved by a majority of those voting, the same as regular bills. Once the rule is approved, the bill itself can then be considered, amended, and voted upon. Again, only a majority of those voting is required. Sometimes bills that were defeated initially under suspension of the rules (because of the two-thirds vote requirement) later succeed under a rule with a simple majority vote. An example of this was the Abandoned Shipwreck Act, which fell a few votes short of the needed two thirds under suspension, but later passed under a rule by a vote of 340 to 64.

The Senate procedures for floor consideration are quite different from those of the House. As a practical matter, the Senate operates on the basis of "unanimous consent agreements," whereby bills that are subject to any controversy are considered on the floor only after a unanimous consent agreement is achieved that limits debate. At that point they usually pass quickly by voice vote. A "hold" may be placed on a bill by one or more senators, which means they are not ready to consent to such an agreement. This can prevent its consideration by the Senate until the hold is removed.

In the case of the Abandoned Shipwreck Act, for example, several "holds" were put on the bill; when proponents of the bill were able to get one hold released, another senator would ask for a new hold. Fortunately, Senator Bradley finally prevailed, with much personal persistence and intensive lobbying from the supporters of the legislation. The bill was brought to the Senate floor and passed unamended. The bill then went to the House for action, where several unsuccessful amendments were offered on the floor. To be sent to the President, legislation must pass both the House and the Senate in identical form. Had the Abandoned Shipwreck bill been amended by the House, it would have either been returned to the Senate, where further action may have been difficult to achieve, or it would have been sent to a conference committee to iron out the differences, in which case both the House and Senate would have been required to pass the bill again.

### Presidential Action

After final passage by both the House and Senate, a bill then is sent to the President for action. Once it reaches the White House, the President has 10 days (Sundays excluded) to act on the bill. If the President does not act on the bill in this time limit, it will automatically become law unless Congress has adjourned.

The President may choose to sign the bill into law or veto it. If he sends it back unsigned to the originating chamber and notes his objections, the bill has been vetoed. For it now to become law, both the House and Senate, by roll-call votes of two thirds, must agree to override the veto. If the Congress has ended the session and adjourned *sine die,* the President may also "pocket veto" the bill by not acting on it for 10 days after receiving it. In this case the bill dies without a formal veto and without an opportunity for the Congress to vote to override it. No legislation solely directed to protection of archaeology and historic preservation has ever been vetoed.

## ROLE OF CONSTITUENCIES

None of this legislation would have been accomplished without the support of national organizations that are concerned about the protection and enhancement of our nation's archaeological and historical resources. Among the most active on archaeological issues, in particular, are the Society for American Archaeology (SAA) and the National Conference of State Historic Preservation Officers (NCSHPO). Both were active on the 1980 amendments to the NHPA and to the ARPA of 1979 and its amendments in 1988. In addition, a major force behind the Abandoned Shipwreck Act was the Society for Historical Archaeology, helped by SAA, NCSHPO, and other organizations such as Preservation Action and the National Trust.

As Representative Seiberling often noted, good legislation does not necessarily pass because it is good, and bad legislation does not necessarily get defeated just because it is bad. People who care about archaeological resources need to inform members of Congress about the importance of legislation that will benefit these resources, either through programs that enhance them, such as the historic preservation fund in the NHPA, or through regulatory programs that protect sites from deliberate or inadvertent harm, such as the permitting and penalty provisions in ARPA Section 106 reviews under the NHPA, or Section 4[f] in the Highway Act. At the same time, it is necessary for archaeology and historic preservation groups to be ever vigilant to prevent the passage of legislation that would weaken or eliminate these provisions. An informal alliance — the National Preservation Coordinating Council — has been formed among the leaders of a dozen national organizations who meet regularly to discuss pending and proposed legislation.

But national groups cannot do it alone. As former Speaker of the House Tip O'Neill used to say, "All politics is local." In a democracy, members of Congress respond best to those who elect them. Only an enlightened and active public can assure that good legislation is passed and bad legislation is prevented. We do so by electing members of Congress who are responsive to our concerns and then by keeping them informed about the way that legislation can affect those concerns. This is no less true for cultural resources than for any other endeavor.

## CONCLUSION

Indeed, much work remains to be done. New legislative tools may be needed to meet the challenges that lie ahead. Of the 435 members of the House and 100 members of the Senate, only 32 representatives and 6 senators were members when the NHPA was passed in 1966. Nearly half of the Senate and well over half of the House has been elected since ARPA was enacted in 1979. As we move through the last decade of this century, we must reinforce our efforts to educate members of Congress to the needs of archaeology and historic preservation. Archaeological sites are still far too vulnerable to looting and vandalism; historic buildings are still too often lost to the wrecking ball. Making or amending a law is not easy, but when it is necessary, we must be there. We can do no less for ourselves and for future generations.

## REFERENCES CITED

House of Representatives (1980) National Historic Preservation Act Amendments of 1980, Report No. 96-1457. House of Representatives, Washington, D.C.
*United States vs. Diaz,* 499 F.2d 113 (9th Cir. 1974).
**Willett, E. F., Jr., Ed.** (1986) How our laws are made, Document No. 99-158, House of Representatives, Washington, D.C.

# MODEL STATE/TRIBAL LEGISLATION AND JURY EDUCATION: CO-VENTURING TO COMBAT CULTURAL RESOURCE CRIME

Kristine Olson Rogers and Elizabeth Grant

## INTRODUCTION

In many respects, 1988 and 1989 were banner years for archaeological resource protection and "archaeophiles," admirers of the ancients. National media focused attention on the Slack Mounds burial desecration case in Kentucky (Harden 1989), the Thai temple lintel demonstrations at the Chicago Art Institute, (Wilkerson 1988), the Italian government's efforts to recover an ancient Sicilian statue at the Getty Museum (Anonymous 1988a; Stille 1988), and a U.S. District Court judge in Indianapolis who ordered the return of stolen Byzantine mosaics to a Cyprus church (*Autocephalous Greek-Orthodox Church of Cyprus vs. Goldberg and Feldman Fine Arts, Inc.,* 1989). Federal shipwreck legislation finally made it through the rocky shoals of Congress (P.L. 100-298, 102 Stat. 432 [1988]).

The House Committee on Interior and Insular Affairs held field hearings in the Four Corners area, which resulted in the passage of two more significant pieces of legislation in Congress' 100th session (Act of Oct. 28, 1988, P.L. 100-555, 102 Stat. 2778; Act of Nov. 3, 1988, P.L. 100-588, 102 Stat. 2983). Doonesbury lampooned presidential candidate Bush's association with the secret Skull & Bones Society at Yale, holding its members up to ridicule as grave robbers of Martin Van Buren's tomb (G. Trudeau, Dec. 27, 1988). The Hopis were successful (aided by a National Park Service archaeologist) in blocking potential depredations by LucasFilm in its plans to shoot its latest "Raiders" episode at Mesa Verde National Park (Anonymous 1988b).

The tide has turned against archaeological looters, and it is time for archaeophiles to take advantage of it. Unfortunately, when this tide turns and the artifact supply dries up, the antiquities market also heats up, as evidenced by the record Sotheby auction prices from the Indian Art Sale held in November 1988 in New York City (Reif 1988; Grimes 1989). Hence archaeophiles need to move on several fronts, and move *fast*.

This analysis will begin with a summary of the recent federal legislation amending the Archaeological Resources Protection Act (16 U.S.C. §§ 470aa-470ll) of 1979 (ARPA), followed by a discussion of how states and tribal governments can follow suit and how federal agencies can be instrumental in building an intergovernmental protection partnership. Finally, readers will be directed to ways of enhancing preservation partnerships to join three essential entities: (1) tribal governments, (2) museums, and (3) private property owners.

## CONGRESSIONAL BACKDROP — PUBLIC LAWS 100-555 AND 100-588

Senate Bill (S.B.) 1985 — Senator Domenici's Bill (P.L. 100-555, signed by former President Reagan on October 28, 1988) — had its impetus in the findings of the 1987 GAO report about archaeological looting on federal lands (see Cheek, Neumann, this volume, for further discussion of ARPA and the 1988 amendments). In introducing the legislation, Senator Domenici remarked:

> Most of the archaeological surveys performed in recent years have been conducted to obtain clearances for development projects (or timber sales) and therefore are not necessarily directed at those areas

having the greatest archaeological resource potential. S.B. 1985 would strengthen the provisions of ARPA by directing BLM, the Park Service, the Forest Service, and other federal agencies to develop plans to survey the lands under their control to determine the nature and extent of archaeological resources on those lands (Domenici 1988).

P.L. 100-555 also directs federal land managers to develop processes for reporting suspected incidents of looting. Domenici said, "Improved documentation of looting activity would provide the land management agencies with better data to use in deciding the amount of funds and staff to request for ... the protection of sites and for the apprehension and prosecution of looters" (Domenici 1988).

The principal author worked with Representative Sam Gejdenson (D-Connecticut) on the House of Representatives amendments to ARPA. There was some trepidation about tinkering with ARPA, for fear that it would bring out the pothunting lobby in droves or that the political process would result in a weakened version. The first fear really didn't materialize, but the second did, in part.

After conducting a tour and field hearings in Cortez, CO, Representative Gejdenson drafted amendments to ARPA with three objectives:

1.  To clarify the definition of archaeological resource by eliminating the "laundry list" and eliminating the phrase "of archaeological interest"
2.  To reduce the age limit of protected archaeological resources from 100-years to 50-years old (Representative Craig from Idaho was adamantly opposed to this change)
3.  To eliminate the $5000 felony threshold; to provide instead the Arizona model of misdemeanor penalties for surface collection and felonies for digging (Comm. Print 1988)

The final legislation was House Bill (H.B.) 4068 (P.L. 100-588), signed November 3, 1988 by the President. As a result of committee compromise, ARPA has now been amended by:

1.  Adding an attempt provision (to reach those defendants who are caught before they do any damage at a site, but have tools, etc. with them). Unfortunately, Congress didn't define what constitutes an attempt
2.  Substituting $500 for the $5000 felony cut-off, which *may* make felonies easier to prove, but which doesn't eliminate the problems with jurors disparaging archaeological damage figures and with battles of the experts over definitions and professional fees (Rogers 1985:110)
3.  Requiring each federal land manager to "establish a program to increase public awareness of the significance of the archaeological resources located on public lands and Indian lands and the need to protect such resources," summarized in periodic reports to Congress. This last addition is a step, but doesn't go far enough.

The primary legal attacks on ARPA have concerned the definition of "archaeological resource" (Rogers 1987:70). A convicted pothunter in Oregon recently appealed to the Ninth Circuit on vagueness grounds, but the court upheld the guilty verdict. The issue is now pending on a petition for *certiorari* before the U.S. Supreme Court (*United States vs. Austin,* No. 88-3300 [9th Cir. 1990]). Unfortunately, P.L. 100-588, as amended, does nothing to address ARPA's definitional problems (which will continue to be raised across the nation, regardless of the circuit court ruling in the *Austin* appeal).

As a matter of fact, as this article was being revised, the principal author received an inquiry about a pothunting case in Grand Junction, CO (in the Tenth Circuit). In March 1990, a U.S. Magistrate there acquitted a defendant (caught with screen and shovel, digging in an archaeological site), citing concerns over ARPA definitions. The U.S. Attorney's office sought *de novo* review in the U.S. District Court.

## CONGRESSIONAL FALLBACK

Federal/state/tribal partnerships need to be built to develop model state statutes and tribal ordinances that supplement federal laws, and to consider joint investigative efforts that could be prosecuted through the state and tribal courts if the federal courts are unavailable (either because federal prosecutors decline ARPA cases or because of unfavorable federal court rulings on ARPA). This is exactly what the Bureau of Land Management (BLM) did in the 1970s in Utah's Grand Gulch Primitive Area (when the legality of the criminal provisions of the 1906 Antiquities Act was in doubt), and it resulted in 11 convictions of pothunters within a 5-year period, under the Utah State statute (Fike 1980).

Reliance on the state courts where there are inadequacies in federal legislation is also what former Oregon State Supreme Court Justice Hans Linde has advocated in speeches and opinions, echoing similar suggestions by former U.S. Supreme Court Justice Brennan. When federal constitutional protections were being eroded by a conservative U.S. Supreme Court, Justice Brennan remarked, "The diminution of federal scrutiny and protection ... mandates the assumption of a more responsible state court role" (Brennan 1986:548).

Author Olson Rogers teaches an Archaeological Resources Protection Law seminar at Lewis and Clark's Northwestern School of Law and assigns law students to draft model regional legislation. Fifty such models have been prepared for various states, U.S. territories, Canadian provinces, counties, and tribal lands (on file at the law school). Many states have undertaken similar revisions to outdated antiquities legislation, sometimes prompted by these students' inquiries.

## MODEL STATE/TRIBAL LEGISLATION: CULTURAL PROPERTY PROTECTION ACT

Thirteen prescribed provisions of this law reform effort follow in an annotated outline:

### Section I: Introduction

The preface to any legislation should set the tone by emphasizing that the purpose of the act is for protection and preservation (not excavation and display). The introduction should be modeled after Arkansas (Ark. Stat. Ann. 13-7-301 [1987]), Pennsylvania (Pa. Stat. Ann. tit. 71, §§ 1047.1b[3], [6] [Purdon Supp. 1988]), and the Warm Springs Tribal Ordinance (Code Chapter 490). It should also cite duties of state officials to report and investigate violations (Domenici Bill) (Act of Oct. 28, 1988, P.L. No. 100-555, 102 Stat. 2778) and to prosecute (N.M. Stat. Ann. § 18-6-9[D]); and, on the part of private citizens, to report discoveries.

The state of Utah has one of the broadest provisions with respect to reporting discoveries:

> Any person who discovers any site or specimen on lands owned by the state shall promptly report such discovery to the Division of State History. It is the intention of the Legislature that discovery on privately owned lands of sites or specimens should be immediately reported to the Division of State History and that field investigation should be discouraged except in accordance with this act (Utah Code Ann. § 63-18-27 [1986]).

Arkansas Statute Ann. 13-6-3-3(b) (1987) and North Carolina General Statute 70-1 (1985) contain similar language.


## Section II: Definition

A model definition of cultural property would be based on information and sacred values, not on artifacts and would be geared to *regional* resources (hence the crucial role of *state* and *tribal* authorities). ARPA was originally drafted by Southwestern states advocates (Collins and Michel 1985:84), so its definition is slanted toward Southwest ruins and pottery (16 U.S.C. § 470bb[1]). "Resource" should be broadly defined as it was in the original Gejdenson Bill (Gejdenson 1988): "sacred object" per the Oregon statute (Oregon Rev. Statute §§ 358.905[6][a]-[b] [1987]); "contextual information" per the Columbia River Gorge National Scenic Area interim guidelines (U.S. Department of Agriculture 1987); age limit set at 50 years to conform to most agency and tribal regulations (36 C.F.R. §§ 1.4[a] and 261.2 [1988]) and to include most Western historical sites. Tribal ordinances should be incorporated by reference into other jurisdictions' laws to include cultural vegetation and other items of tribal identification. Human remains should *not* be included in the definition of "resource", but treated separately (Section IV, VII, X).


## Section III: Permitting

A permitting program should make clear that the state or tribe possesses the exclusive right to explore and excavate archaeological resources located within the state or tribal lands (Alabama Code § 41-3-1 [1982]). A system must be established for research following Dr. William Lipe's "conservation ethic." Permits should be issued only in keeping with conservation and preservation goals. The goal of the conservation model is "to see that archaeological resources everywhere are identified, protected, and managed for maximum longevity" (Lipe 1977:21), which in the case of some, should be indefinitely.

A board should be established to determine what research is absolutely necessary. The Veterans' Administration Human Subjects Research Review (45 C.F.R. §§ 46.101-24 [1988]) provides an analogous forum. Indian representatives are essential (one for each affected tribal government). Permitting fees would fund patrols, surveys, and public education at the state, county, and tribal levels.

Clear title to any objects found should be vested in the state or tribal government (no percentage to finder!). Unfortunately, a number of states with underwater archaeological sites treat the resources as salvage items and allow salvors to retain a portion of what they recover (see, e.g., La. Rev. Stat. Ann. §§ 41.1605-.1606 [West Supp. 1989] [percentage of cash value of objects found]; N.C. Gen. Stat. § 121-25 [1986] [portion of all relics may be sold or retained by the licensee]). Oregon (O.R.S. §§ 273.718 *et seq.)* allows people to obtain permits to explore state lands for "goods, money, or treasure trove." If the state chooses to place the property in a museum, it must compensate the finder for the value of the goods up to $5000 and 50% of any value above that amount. These types of statutes encourage the exploitation of resources and are contrary to the goal of conservation archaeology.

Finally, an ongoing supervision requirement is critical to the success of this system, to allow the tribal or SHPO agent access to the site throughout the project (Washington, Ch. 44, Laws of 1989; Utah Code Ann. 63-18-25 [1986]). With respect to *private land,* recording and removal conditions should be specified, providing for condemnation in the case of noncompliance. Programs for funding private preservation efforts should be initiated, and financed through fines and permitting fees (Mo. Rev. Stat. §§ 253.400-407 [Supp. 1989] [Historic Preservation Revolving Fund Act]; N.Y. Parks & Rec. Law §§ 17.01-.11 [McKinney 1984] [Outdoor Recreation Development Bond Act]; Pa. Stat. Ann. tit. 32, § 5001 [Purdon Supp. 1988] [Open Space Lands Act]).

## Section IV: Criminal Conduct

Prohibited behavior should include "*Entering* archaeological area with intent ..." (Utah Code Ann. § 63-18-25 [1989]); *possession* of illegal artifacts (Northey 1982:81); *trafficking* without certification of origin (Oregon Rev. Stat. §§ 358.920[3]-[4] [1987]); and *removal* of cultural property from the state. The state of Alabama has declared ownership of all objects found on aboriginal mounds, earthworks, ancient or historical forts, and burial sites, situated within the state and forbids the sale or disposal of those objects outside of the state unless they are exchanged for other objects from other states museums, libraries, or individuals (Alabama Code § 41-3-5 [1975]).

All "garden variety" applicable criminal statutes (e.g., theft, trespass, vandalism, etc.) should be incorporated in this provision (Rogers 1987:81–86). *Human remains* should be addressed in a separate section with increased penalties. For instance, Washington law provides that the knowing removal, mutilation, or destruction of historic graves is a felony, and in the event of inadvertent disturbance, the remains must be reinterred. In addition to criminal prosecution, Indian tribes or members are given a civil action for equitable relief or damages against those who have disturbed grave sites. A successful plaintiff may recover attorney fees and punitive damages under this provision (Washington, Ch. 44, Laws of 1989).

## Section V: Penalties

A misdemeanor should be penalized by a maximum one year imprisonment or a $100,000 fine, or both, for *surface* collection if the value of the stolen object is less than $100; *felony,* by five years, $250,000 fine, or both, for surface collection of artifacts worth more than $100 and *for all excavation* (Ariz. Rev. Stat. Ann. § 13-3702.01 [Supp. 1988]).

## Section VI: Forfeiture

State drafters should follow the ARPA model allowing forfeiture in conjunction with, or apart from, any criminal or civil cases (16 U.S.C. § 470gg[b][3]), plus *mandate* forfeiture of illegal artifacts in the defendants' possession (Northey 1982:88) (Idaho Code § 67-4122 [1980]; Kan. Stat. Ann. § 74-5408 [1985]; Or. Rev. Stat. § 273.711 [1987]). Forfeiture should also be allowed for items purchased with *proceeds* of illegal trafficking activities: similar to many criminal narcotics trafficking statutes.

## Section VII: Civil Penalties

ARPA regulations are generally adequate, as long as they are enhanced by provisions for *treble damages* (Idaho Code § 67-4118 [1980]). With respect to burial violations, a separate right of action should be provided for tribes or enrolled members, allowing tribal court jurisdiction (Washington, Ch. 44, Laws of 1989, § 3).

## Section VIII: Private Right of Action

Civil enforcement should not be reliant on the state Attorney General's Office to pursue. Individuals, tribal governments, or public interest organizations should have available: damages (actual, punitive, plus emotional distress), declaratory and injunctive relief, and provisions for successful plaintiffs to recover attorneys' fees (Or. Rev. Stat. § 358.955; Washington, Ch. 44, Laws of 1989).

## Section IX: Rewards

ARPA's system is an acceptable model, except the maximum reward should be increased to $5000. ARPA allows a reward to any person who furnishes information that leads to the finding of a civil violation or to the conviction of a criminal violation and for which a fine was paid. If several persons provide information, the money is divided among them. A government employee acting in the scope of employment is not entitled to claim a reward.

The maximum reward under ARPA is $500. Originally, ARPA called for a $1000 reward, but "several members of Congress feared the higher figure might encourage vigilante-type activity or, more likely, frivolous allegations" (Collins 1980:7–8). These fears have proven to be unfounded. In the first 8 years of ARPA's operation, only two cases of penalty awards to private citizens were reported (Mott 1987).

## Section X: Tribal Rights

A model statute *must* require notification to tribal authorities regarding recovered sacred objects (Oregon Rev. Stat. § 358.945 [1987]), mandate forfeiture of items to identifiable tribes or descendants (16 U.S.C. § 170gg[c] [1982]), ensure tribal access to sites (42 U.S.C. § 1996 [1982]), contain a conflict resolution process such as that called for in Charles Wilkinson's exemplary "Ethic of Place" (Wilkinson 1988:401), specify disposition of remains (immediately returned to identifiable tribe or descendant except when temporarily needed for prosecution or for critical scientific investigation, as determined by the representative permitting board).

In 1976 Iowa passed a law providing for reburial of disinterred Native American remains. As one commentator noted, the law was the product of a cooperative effort between archaeologists and Indians to resolve the conflict between them and to face the problems created by their common enemies' construction projects and looting (Anderson 1985: 48). The cooperation between the archaeologists and Indians of Iowa has continued through a series of conferences and other educational programs. Anderson suggests that archaeologists work on a regional or with the appropriate tribal officials to develop procedures that are tailored to the problems that exist in the area (Anderson 1985:51).

## Section XI: Incentives to Private Landowners

There are numerous tax incentive schemes to draw upon for protection of cultural resources on private land (Alaska Stat. § 29.45.050[b][2][B] [1988] [municipality may by ordinance classify and exempt from taxation historic sites, buildings, and monuments]; N.M. Stat. Ann. § 7-2-18.2 [1988] [tax credit for onehalf of the cost of restoration, rehabilitation, or preservation of a cultural property, up to a maximum of $25,000]). A land exchange program, such as that provided by Washington statute, should be expanded to specifically include archaeological resource sites (Wash. Rev. Code § 79.08.109 [Supp. 1989]). Protective measures can also be required as parts of state land-use plans, such as the Oregon Land Conservation and Development Commission's Goal Five (Oregon Land Conservation and Development Commission [1985] [programs shall be provided that will protect scenic and historic areas and natural resources for future generations]; N.J. Stat. Ann. § 40:55D-28[b][6] [West Supp. 1988] [master plan, where appropriate, should include information on historic sites and their relation to surrounding areas, in keeping with site-specific secrecy requirements outlined in next Section].

Eminent domain is a more drastic possibility (Alaska Stat. § 41.35.060[b] [1988]). New Mexico provides for an emergency classification of private land, whereby a site can be temporarily placed on a register, pending further investigation (N.M. Stat. Ann. § 18-6-12 [1978]). An owner may receive a fair rental value for land to the extent the classification affects the normal use of the property. Historical district designation must be facilitated (Hawaii Rev. Stat. § 6E-2 [1984]). Mining activities must be curtailed. Mississippi Code Ann. § 53-7-51 (Supp. 1988) gives anyone the right to petition the state to declare an area unsuitable for mining that might damage the area's archaeological value. The Supreme Court of Indiana has recently held that the state's designation of an archaeological site on privately owned land as unsuitable for surface coal mining did not amount to an unconstitutional taking (*Dept. of Natural Resources vs. Indiana Coal Council, Inc.*, 542 N.E.2d 1000 [Ind. 1989]).

In addition, political pressure can be a form of powerful persuasion and can lead to negotiated deals between governments and private landowners to prevent the destruction of valuable sites. For example, Hawaii's Governor Waihee was able to convince a land developer to cancel plans to develop a hotel on an ancient burial site and to rebury the remains in return for the state's promise to purchase the land (Anonymous 1989c).

## Section XII: Exemption from State Freedom of Information Acts

No site-specific information should be available to the public. Sales of public land with known sites should be prohibited (Arkansas Stat. Ann. § 13-6-305 [1988] [the Commissioner of State Lands, upon written notice given by the Arkansas Archaeological Society, shall reserve from sale any state lands on which sites or artifacts are located or may be found]; Vermont Stat. Ann., Tit. 22, § 765 [1988] [when transferring real property that contains archaeological resources, the state, upon recommendation of the state archaeologist, may condition the transfer in such a way as will protect the resources]). A right of first refusal could also be granted to the SHPO, a tribe, or an archaeological conservancy.

## Section XIII: Public Education

Overall objectives for any state cultural resource program include appropriating 50% of "state ARPA" fines to fund designated public education programs; devoting one fifth of SHPO's job description (i.e., one day a week) to public education activities (Rogers 1986:13; also see Chapter 4, this volume, for additional discussion of archaeology and education); and requiring paraprofessional components in all state-funded research projects.

# PUBLIC EDUCATION PLATFORM — 13 PLANKS

All archaeophiles conducting public education programs should begin with the Airlie House Report (see McGimsey, this volume). In 1974, with the help of the National Park Service, Dr. McGimsey organized several Airlie House seminars. One, in particular, focused on public education. In the Airlie House Report, Chapter 4 is entitled "The Crisis in Communication" and deals with getting the archaeophiles' message out to the general public (McGimsey 1977:78). Its recommendations are

1.   To teach public relations methods to archaeology graduate students
2.   To give professional recognition to public relations as a worthwhile endeavor (not just to "scholarly journals"). Give credit for pieces in popular magazines
3.   To *talk* to pothunters

> "[t]here will always be certain individuals, generally labeled 'pothunters' who are either uncon- cerned or simply unaware of the damage they are doing to the resource base. It is important to the profession that communication is maintained with these individuals. In individual instances, it may be impossible to convince them to adhere, to whatever degree, to proper scientific methodology. It certainly is impossible if you do not talk to them at all. Even those individuals that show no prospect of being converted can be helpful in giving information on what they find, which again would be a total impossibility if they had been alienated because of the attitude of the professional. Destruction of sites or materials by pothunters should not be supported or condoned in any way, but it should be possible to remain in communication with such individuals without doing either. At least the attempt should be made" (McGimsey 1977:84).

4.   To adopt a logo for public recognition
5.   In dealing with the media and laypersons, to *always* ask yourself the following seven questions:

" 'Am I sufficiently stressing the need for preservation of archaeological resources?' (Avoid creating the impression that archaeological sites are there to be exploited by archaeologists or anyone else)" (McGimsey 1977:85), Since Dr. Lipe's seminal article in 1974, archaeologists have generally internalized his plea to save study subjects for future scientists, rather than rummage through them all in a fit of professional fervor.

" 'Am I fully recognizing the humanistic appeal of archaeology?' (Avoid portrayal of archaeology as a dry-as-dust activity)" (McGimsey 1977:86). In the successful *Cortiana* prosecution in Arizona, the expert witness, Dr. Adovasio, personalized the main exhibit (a mummified Anasazi infant) by referring to her as "this little girl," clearly conveying to the jury that this was someone's *child,* not a collectible curio (Adovasio 1988).

" 'Am I fully presenting the *scientific* nature of archaeology?' (Avoid looking like a treasure hunter — forget objects, talk *information.*)" Professional topics for lay audiences should communicate *concepts,* not frame artifacts as "objets d'arts."

" 'Am I pointing out the pertinence of my work to the modern world?' (Present the social-scientific basis for your research.)" In *U.S. vs. Jaques,* an Oregon pothunting prosecution, Dr. C. Melvin Aikens, the government's expert witness, described for the jury how soil and pollen research from the vandalized site could provide data useful to local farmers and agricultural researchers, with respect to grazing patterns and crop rotation (*United States vs. Jaques,* No. 83-129FR [D. Or. 1983], *aff'd,* 753 F.2d 1084 [9th Cir. 1984], *cert. denied,* 470 U.S. 1087 [1985]).

" 'Am I representing archaeological considerations in a manner compatible with the law and with good cultural resource management concepts?' (Consider that next year you or some other archaeologist may want the local legal authority to pass a law protecting sites. Lay the groundwork for that understanding and support.)" Probably the finest example of this kind of foresight can be found in McGimsey's own pioneering work in Arkansas (McGimsey 1972).

"Am I presenting the *interconnected* nature of archaeology with other disciplines?" Most local newspapers have a science section that seeks contributions from community residents. Rob Freed, former archaeologist with the U.S. Army Corps of Engineers (Portland District), has been a regular correspondent with *The Oregonian,* concerning such subjects as dovetailing geological and archaeological research theories in the Columbia River Gorge (Freed 1988).

" 'Am I making clear the limitations on archaeology and archaeologists?' (Don't create unreasonable expectations. Avoid letting people think that if they find a site and report it, somebody will appear from the big university in the sky, pat them on the head, and excavate everything for free.)" In *U.S. vs. Barnes,* another early Oregon prosecution, an unfortunate example of apparent failure to heed this warning may be found. A defense witness testified as follows:

Q. Did you ever send any of your [artifacts] ... to Oregon State University, to Dr. Cole?

A. Yes, I did.

Q. And did you ever show Dr. Cole the site?

A. Yes, I did. I took him to the site. It was the first time that the university had knowledge of the site.

Q. Well, did he express an interest in excavating the site?

A. ... I urged him to do so, and he *definitely* said that if they were funded ..."
(Trans. p.585) (*United States vs. Bender,* No. 81-119BE (D. Or. 1981)).

[Later testifying about a prehistoric rabbit snare from the site which the same witness had sent up to the university for examination.]

Q. [Mr. Cole] kept the basket and its contents for approximately 2 years, and refused to acknowledge my letters requesting him to share what knowledge he had learned from the study of the material. I stopped at the university while I was in Corvallis and asked him if he had written a pamphlet on the basket as he had promised. He said no, he had written nothing and didn't even know where the basket was. He eventually found it buried under a heavy stack of old newspapers, somewhat crushed and deteriorated in comparison to its condition when he borrowed it. I was disappointed with both the treatment to myself and the loaned material ...

Is that statement true?

A. That statement is true.
(Trans. pp.602-03) (*United States vs. Bender,* No. 81-119 BE (D. Or. 1981)).

Given those seven questions as a constant backdrop, 13 strategies for public education have emerged. To be most effective, all should be offered simultaneously as part of an integrated program.

## 1. Native American Political Participation

Nothing brings the protection message home in a more heartfelt way to the public than tribal outrage over desecration of sacred sites. Nez Perce leaders concerned with the *Kelly* prosecution in Idaho rented buses to attend proceedings and maintained a "victims' court watch" (Loftus 1986). Allen Slickpoo, a Nez Perce elder, made the point vehemently by saying, "These are *my* relatives whose skulls you're selling" (see Anyon, this volume, for further discussion of Native American concerns).

Hopis were able to make their presence felt at Mesa Verde in raising objections over the disturbance of sacred lands. As reported in the Rocky Mountain News in August 1988, "Lucas Films... bowing to the concerns of the Hopi ... canceled plans to film part of an Indiana Jones adventure movie at Mesa Verde National Park"(Anonymous 1988).

An executive producer was quoted as saying, "We discovered that this was holy ground to the Hopi Indians.... We feel we have to respect their heritage ...." The Hopi elders' objections were raised by actor Jon Voigt and by Jack Smith, National Park Service archaeologist. The producer noted, "The thing that put us over the top on this was to discover how upset the Indians would be, and certainly we didn't want to cause any kind of disrespect or problem there ...."

The Hopi Cultural Preservation Officer was writing a letter of objection to the Park Service when LucasFilm withdrew. He expressed relief, saying, "... these [ruins] have become a complex shrine system for us. Mesa Verde was the home of the Flute Clan."

Another avenue for Native American activists to explore is the use of hex mythology. Virtually every culture has its version: the Egyptian mummy curse (Larson 1986); the AKU AKU warning on Easter Island (Heyerdahl 1958); misfortune spells surrounding the Viking rune stones (Dixon 1963); the chilling coincidences (?) that befell pocketers of potshards at Chaco Canyon, as noted on the NPS tourist information center bulletin board. The point is that many pothunters are superstitious and therefore a receptive audience to the rumor that contact with illegal artifacts is not good for one's health.

There is nothing to prevent Native Americans from taking advantage of publicizing these cultural taboos. And there is every reason to cultivate Hollywood stars willing to assist in this endeavor. Exploitation of cult heroes is fair in this campaign.

## 2. Elementary and Secondary School Programs

The "Young Igors" of the world have to be set straight. Oregon archaeologists salt sandbox stratigraphy with representative artifacts to give grade school amateurs an opportunity to participate in a professionally supervised "dig" (Wilson 1985). The Head Start Program on the Warm Springs Indian Reservation in Oregon has an elder-devised curriculum promoting cultural pride in preschoolers. Provincial leadership in Alberta, Canada, provides an antipothunting unit for fourth graders (Knudson 1989:106). (For additional information on school programs see Lerner, Rogge, Smartz, McNutt, and Hawkins, this volume.)

### 3. Private Landowners Outreach

There are many vehicles for converting citizens who are happenstance custodians of cultural resources. The most direct approach is taken by organizations such as the Archaeological Conservancy and the Trust for Public Lands, which negotiate for preservation easements or outright purchase (Ford 1983:221; also see Michel, this volume). Conversion is also accomplished through proselytizing in popular magazines such as *Archaeology* (Herscher 1989:67). Praise and other positive reinforcement for enlightened private action to preserve sites also win support. A model program in Kentucky, the Kentucky Archaeology Registry (KAR), has adopted this approach with great success. Its executive summary contains this description:

> KAR provides cost-effective site protection to significant archaeological sites by educating landowners about their site's significance, involving them in site stewardship, and providing management assistance and advice on stronger protection options. Recognition of the landowners' commitment takes the form of personalized awards.
>
> Landowner contact/site registration can be useful site protection strategy in and of itself, or it can be used as the first step in a multifaceted site protection program. That includes the use of recorded land-use agreements, public education, grass roots support, enforcement of existing antiquities laws and active site management (Henderson 1988).

### 4. Museum Exhibits, Presentations, etc.

There *are* some museums that are not wholly preoccupied with scoring "coups" in the illegal marketplace. To cite some positive examples of museum contributions to the cultural resource protection message: (1) the National Geographic Society's "Stolen Treasures" exhibit interpreting the confiscation of Peruvian burial goods from a convicted New York art dealer (Lewis 1982); (2) the Washington Archaeological Resource Center's traveling show with an integrated team of local, tribal, and professional consultants assembling the information packet that accompanies the display; and (3) the Oregon Art Institute's Northwest Native American Art Council which sponsored a panel on pothunting, featuring an archaeologist, an attorney, and a representative of the tribal governments in the state. This is the direction in which museum management of the 1990s should be headed (see Brose, this volume).

Superb examples of this form of public education may be found in the tribal cultural centers on Western reservations. The Makah Cultural Center in Neah Bay tells the story of the excavation of the Ozette site on the Washington coast. The Gila River Indian Cultural Center just south of Phoenix abuts and interprets the site of the great Hohokam excavation at Salt River. None of these "objectify" artifacts by showcasing aesthetic values.

### 5. Site Stewardship and Signage

The Arizona State Historic Preservation Officer, Dr. Shereen Lerner, has instituted an aggressive site steward program that has received national attention (Destruction of Archaeological Heritage 1988:53; also see Hoffman, this volume). Sites with citizen watchdogs have advocates when they are violated. It is far more impressive to have hiking enthusiasts as witnesses (who had the presence of mind to photograph pothunters in trenches), than to parade a string of government law enforcement agents in court (Clayton 1982).

Creative signage can also impact captive audiences (see Jameson and Kodack, this volume). A roadside sign in Alaska takes advantage of a prime whale-watching spot to tell the story of missing pieces in an archaeological puzzle. A river-rafting launch-site posting heightens recreationists' sensitivity to archaeological areas downstream. The use of signs like these, physically *removed* from attractive resources, can educate without inviting invasion.

### 6. Participatory Archaeology

Fortunately, there are now many fine examples of programs that entail supervising amateurs involved in archaeological fieldwork (see Davis, this volume). Peter Pilles, archaeologist on the Coconino National Forest in Arizona, has received national recognition for his summer work with volunteers of all ages in the Flagstaff area (Dagget 1989:12). Dr. William Lipe spends his summers with amateurs at Crow Canyon. Earthwatch provides international opportunities.

Paraprofessional training can backfire. Care must be taken to provide an acceptable (and exhausting!) outlet to those with pothunting tendencies, reinforced by unremitting propaganda about the information potential of legitimate fieldwork. Archaeophiles cannot afford to provide training and "inside" information to those who will use it to promote their own treasure hunts. State and tribal governments might begin with a paraprofessional training and certification program, such as that provided by New Hampshire law (N.H. Rev. Stat. Ann. § 227-C:10 [Supp. 1988]).

### 7. State Commission

As with so many public relations offensives for archaeology, Arizona has taken the lead in using its state's *political* resources to cultivate a constituency for its *cultural* resources. When Bruce Babbitt was governor, the first state archaeological protection commission was formed and the first Archaeology Awareness Week proclaimed (Proclamation, Arizona Archaeology Week, Office of the Governor, State of Arizona, signed by Gov. Babbit on Jan. 18, 1983). (See Lerner, this volume, for additional information on Arizona Archaeology Week.) Oregon has followed with a proclamation under Governor Goldschmidt and with conferences and legislation sponsored by the State Commission on Indian Services. Washington has adopted Arizona's "Thieves of Time" poster theme for its own campaign, substituting a Northwest carving for the Southwest pottery in the original design.

It is most appropriate, as states undertake revisions of their cultural resource laws, that official commissions be established in conjunction with such efforts. It is these commissions that can coordinate all the public education planks advocated in this article.

### 8. Amateur Archaeological Groups

Almost every state has a club of would-be archaeologists. In the last few decades, these organizations have struggled to make the difficult transition from a loose-knit hobbyists' and collectors' "kaffeklatch" to a serious supplement to professional archaeological groups (see Davis, this volume). Two that have largely succeeded in this evolution are the Mid-Columbia

Archaeological Society (MCAS), under the leadership of the late Nick Paglieri, and the Oregon Archaeological Society (OAS).

The MCAS regularly exhorts its members to get involved in protection efforts and has been very industrious in "watchdogging" federal and state agencies (see, e.g., Anonymous 1989b), advising readers to write to Congress to protest a U.S. Army Corps of Engineers decision to reduce cultural resource staff in the Portland, OR District. The OAS, through its newsletter *Screenings,* has recently reminded its membership that:

> We also believe that by protecting sites from indiscriminate digging, we can conserve many of these vanishing pages of history for future generations, whose scientific technique may be vastly superior to ours.... The artifact in itself should not be the primary objective, but rather the knowledge attained with its recovery....Indiscriminate digging and vandalism by the few negate the efforts of the many....All violators will be dropped from membership rolls and, if the incident warrants, will be reported to the proper authorities....Remember, once a site has been destroyed, it can NEVER be repaired (OAS 1987).

As news of this enlightenment spreads, professionals are gradually becoming more attuned to working with amateurs (rather than scornfully keeping them at bay). One positive example, again in Oregon, involved the close working relationship between the local discoverer of a Clovis-like point in eastern Oregon and an archaeologist (and lithics expert) from the Corps of Engineers (Dreyfuss 1986:5). The professionals who excavated the site ended up naming it after the amateur who had called it to their attention. For an opposite point of view on the success of this endeavor and an indication of the attitudes (on both sides) that will need to be overcome, readers should skim the June 1989 issue of *Indian Artifact Magazine* (Anonymous 1989a).

### 9. Professional Archaeological Societies

The Society for American Archaeology has been traditionally open to public membership and regularly sponsors public conferences. It also holds workshops training professionals in public education programming. The society has recently initiated a special project, "Saving the Past for the Future" to assemble interdisciplinary "think tanks" that will concentrate on developing new approaches to promote public efforts for resource protection (Neumann 1989; also see Reinburg, Judge, this volume).

### 10. PSAs, TV Documentaries, etc.

Media communication that has the greatest impact comes in dramatic 30-second "spots" produced free for "public service announcements." Various states and tribal governments have been experimenting with a version of the environmental message borne by the profile of an Indian on horseback by a polluted stream, showing a tear rolling down his cheek. The archaeophiles' edition portrays an Indian father and son entering a Protestant pioneer cemetery, carrying a pick and shovel, excitedly discussing what "treasures" they can find buried among the graves.

Other longer television productions include successful documentaries, such as Arizona's "Thieves of Time" and Oregon Public Broadcasting station's "Time Bandits." Hollywood actors and national political figures can also be drafted for cameo appearances and radio spots.

Another successful video is "Assault on Time," produced by the Federal Law Enforcement Training Center in cooperation with several federal agencies. For this approach to reach its potential, it must be cast and directed as an aggressive public relations campaign.

### 11. Law Enforcement Press Releases

Closely related — indeed, another component of the public relations offensive — is the issuance of press releases reporting law enforcement activities. One of the objectives of a criminal prosecution is deterrence; yet federal land managers are often reluctant to trumpet indictments and convictions of their "customers." Not only must this reticence be overcome, but managers should go one step farther and also publicize "preventive" law enforcement measures, such as monitoring and electronic surveillance of sites (see, e.g., United States Corps of Engineers 1989 [describing how increased surveillance of sites along the Columbia River resulted in the arrests of two men for illegal digging]). (See Des Jean, this volume, for discussion of a monitoring program at a National Park in Tennessee/Kentucky.)

A note of caution, however — it is imperative that public information officers work *with* law enforcement officers in coauthoring press releases of this nature. Ongoing investigations can be seriously compromised, or undercover operatives endangered, by unguarded communications with media representatives.

### 12. Fact-Finding/Propaganda Trips for Policy Makers

Some public education needs to be *targeted* at public officials. Greater levels of awareness can be almost instantly achieved by such attention-getting ventures as hosting a member of the court at an archaeological field station on a wildlife refuge; taking prosecutors on river trips to vandalized areas; organizing "field trips" for FBI agents, in conjunction with training sessions; urging land managers to accompany elders to looted burial sites and to attend a reinterrment ceremony; busing advisory councils to the scenes of archaeological crimes to observe, first-hand, bulldozer blade gouges in ancient kiva walls and skeletal material eroding from the shoulders of newly constructed logging access roads. Media representatives may be invited along on any or all of these excursions.

### 13. Operation SAVE Prototype

The Bureau of Land Management (BLM) recognized that the best way to protect archaeological research was through a multifaceted approach and instituted Operation SAVE (Save Archaeological Values for Everyone) in 1987 (see Schalk, this volume). The program's three areas of emphasis are public education, interagency employee training, and law enforcement. The BLM efforts to increase awareness of the importance of cultural resources include distribution of posters printed with a toll-free number for citizens to call to report archaeological crimes. Stickers featuring the same Wishram Indian rock art design as the posters are distributed to school children. The toll-free number has prompted numerous calls.

In its first year of operation, SAVE sponsored training programs for over 400 governmental employees, including both managerial and field staff. Through Operation SAVE, the BLM assists federal and state agencies in investigating violations and increasing enforcement of laws protecting archaeological sites. The BLM also conducted an aerial surveillance program that led to the detection of 14 archaeological violations and recovery of 70 artifacts in one weekend. Future goals of Operation SAVE include strengthening ties to local communities, increasing patrols on public lands, and developing a monitoring program for vulnerable sites (BLM 1989; for a detailed description of SAVE, see Schalk, this volume). The Operation SAVE logo "Tsagaglalal" has been adopted by the Society for American Archaeology "Save the Past for the Future" project.

## COVENTURING

At the Third Annual Northwest Tribal Cultural Resource Protection Conference in Silverdale, WA, the executive director of the National Advisory Council on Historic Preservation, together with the primary author of this article, found themselves cast in a "bit part" mediating role, much like the cook in Moliere's "The Miser" (Moliere 1956:205–207). However, a reconciliation between Indians and archaeologists proved to be a much tougher challenge than that involving an estranged father and son competing for the same woman! That shouldn't be the case.

Cultural resources are mute. Not that they don't have much to convey to those who take the time to listen, to observe, and to learn, or to those whose ancestors or heritage they contain. But when their integrity is violated, they cannot testify for themselves.

The 1980s has witnessed the effectiveness of the victims' rights movement, as "reform" legislation swept 47 states and the Federal Government. The combined political clout of victims and their friends and relatives has resulted in increasing resources for investigation, more arrests of offenders, greater acceptance of evidence at trials about the impacts of crimes, and enhanced penalties at sentencing. When cultural resources are victims of pothunters, private developers, or governmental project depredations, they likewise need voices to protest their plight.

Frequently in the courtroom, cultural resources are disembodied, objectified. To speak of cultural resource "victims" as dehydrated remains, as items of scientific curiosity, serves to further degrade them. To allow them to go advocateless is to permit their continuing victimization.

That is why Adovasio's description of the mummified infant in the *Cortiana* case as "this little Anasazi girl" was so compelling. The jury at this trial was less able to disregard the invasion of this human being, because she became more than a "site" or abstract artifact in the jurors' minds. That's also why the *Kelly* case resulted in the serious penalties imposed (including costs of reburial) — because Nez Perce elders rented a bus and appeared at court hearings, held press conferences, and carried picket signs saying, "We don't dig Kelly!" and bore witness in the back of the courtroom whenever the case appeared on the docket.

Instead of bogging down in internal squabbles over past slights, why can't the preservation forces *join* forces? Why has there been no coalition of archaeologists and tribal leaders to go on the public relations offensive in these cases? It is time for the "thieves of time" message to be proclaimed by a chorus of *blended* voices at every opportunity: in the press, in the courtroom, in the legislature, and in the public arena, wherever cultural resources are threatened. It is time to expand the partnership. Tribal governments are essential to this enterprise. They have never been allocated adequate funding to be meaningful players in the protection of their own heritage.

For instance, when the Columbia River Gorge National Scenic Area Act was passed, Oregon county governments received monies from the state legislature for planning purposes. The four affected tribal governments named in the legislation received nothing until the Gorge Commission applied to Congress for a small appropriation under the tribal government Self-Determination Act (25 U.S.C. § 450[h]) (Hansell 1988). This underfunding is unfair and shortsighted, because gorge protection cannot be achieved without tribal participation.

The National Historic Preservation Act contains a heretofore unused provision that is of particular interest in this regard. Title 16 U.S.C. § 470-1(d)(3)(B) empowers the secretary of the Interior (in consultation with the SHPO) to "make grants or loans ... to Indian tribes ... for the preservation of their cultural heritage." It would be a productive step to begin this partnership if representatives of the Department of the Interior would urge SHPOs to work with tribes to apply for such grants.

The second prong of this partnership has got to be museums. Museums have, unfortunately, often taken an adversarial role vis-a-vis preservationists and Indian tribes: for instance, by lobbying against the UNESCO cultural property convention, or by proposing legislation to have museums exempted from the National Stolen Property Act (Meyer 1973:284; Wald 1977; Moore 1988:466). But new curators and directors, like Ellen Herscher, are starting to push for cooperation with tribes on repatriation issues and for tighter acquisition policies (Herscher 1989:70). Governmental agencies could play a major role in supporting this "new wave" of museum management and in offering joint ventures in assembling traveling exhibits or interpretive programs.

The third partnership category is another obvious one — private property owners. It will be impossible to achieve consistent cultural resource management if it only applies on public lands. The Kentucky model mentioned earlier is one worth emulating. Working through SHPOs, federal agencies could enter into agreements with their private citizen neighbors to preserve sites jointly held. Contributing its expertise, the federal agency could foster private site steward programs, offer "Take Pride in America" awards to citizens who do the most for cultural resources, etc.

There are *lots* of opportunities to nurture this relationship if private outreach becomes a priority. After all, the Kentucky program is funded, in part, by the National Park Service. That agency is a natural to take the lead in forming these kinds of partnerships, and the mandate from Congress is in Representative Sam Gejdenson's legislation.

According to Ruthann Knudson: "We need to develop an overall archaeological research [and preservation] plan for the whole continent. To do it will take scientific and political skills as well as courage and chutzpah" (Knudson 1989:73). Moreover, the proposed partners must envision sinking or swimming *together*. Otherwise the archaeophiles' audience will lack confidence in the ability of these coventurers to go the distance.

## REFERENCES CITED

**Adovasio, J. M.** (1988) Potholder found guilty in jury trial, *Am. Anthropol. Assoc. Newsl.*, 29(1), 28.
**Anderson, D.** (1985) Reburial: is it reasonable? *Archaeology*, September/October 1985, 49.
Anon. (1988) The Getty Statue: beyond legality. *Connoisseur*, October 1988, 202.
Anon. (1989a) *Indian Artifact Magazine*, June 1989, 17.
Anon. (1989b) Cultural heritage threatened. *Mid-Columbia Archaeol. Soc. Bull.*, 2.
Anon. (1980) Government rangers pursue robbers of ancient Indian graves in Southwest, *New York Times*, June 23, 1980.
Anon. (1988b) Indiana Jones won't raid Mesa Verde, *Rocky Mountain News*, p. A1, April 24, 1988.
Anon. (1989c) Hawaii, *USA Today*, p. 6A, April 20, 1989.
**Brennan, W.** (1986) The Bill of Rights and the states: the revival of state constitutions as guardians of individual rights, *N.Y.U. Law Rev.*, 61, 535, 548.

Bureau of Land Management (1989) Operation S.A.V.E.: Annual Status Report, Oregon State Office, Fiscal Year, U.S. Department of the Interior.

Clayton, R. (1982) 3 fined for Indian burial ground violation, U.S. Forest Service Pacific Northwest/Southwest Log.

Collins, R. and Michel (1985) Preserving the past: origins of the Archaeological Resources Protection Act of 1979, *Am. Archaeol.,* 5, 84.

Collins, R. (1980) The meaning behind ARPA: how the act is meant to work. U.S. Department of Agriculture, Forest Service, S.W. Region, 7–8.

Dagget, D. (1989) Rocks of ages. *Arizona Highways,* April 1989, 12.

Dixon, F. (1963) *The Hardy Boys: The Viking Symbol Mystery.*

Domenici, P. (1988) 134 Congressional Record.

Dreyfuss, C. (1986) Legacy of a vanished people, *The Oregonian, Northwest Magazine,* p. 5, June 1, 1986.

Fike, R. (1980) Antiquities violations in Utah: justice does prevail. In Cultural resources law enforcement: an emerging science, 49 U.S. Department of Agriculture, Forest Service, Region 3.

Ford, R. (1983) The Archaeological Conservancy, Inc.: the goal is preservation. *Am. Archaeol.,* 3, 221–224.

Freed, R. (1988) Major landslide 900 years ago shaped life in Columbia Gorge. *The Oregonian,* D3, February 25, 1988.

General Accounting Office (1987) Cultural resources — Problems Protecting and Preserving Cultural Resources. GAO/RCED-88-3, General Accounting Office, U.S. Congress, Washington, D.C.

Geranios R. (1988) Indian sites, relics intact at Hanford,. *The Oregonian,* p. C7, August 26, 1988.

Gejdenson (1988) 134 Congressional Record E. 486 (daily ed.), March 2, 1988.

Grimes, W. (1989) Antiquites boom — who pays the price? *New York Times Magazine,* 6:3, July 16, 1989.

Hansell, S. (1988) Letter from the chairman of the Columbia River Gorge Commission to Representative Sidney Yates, February 22, 1988.

Harden, H. (1989) Who owns our past? *Natl. Geogr.,* March 1989, 376.

Henderson, L. (1988) The Kentucky Archaeological Registry: citizen-based preservation for Kentucky's archaeological sites, Kentucky Nature Preserves Commission.

Herscher, E. (1989) A future in ruins, *Archaeology,* January/February 1989, 67.

Heyerdahl, T. (1958) *Aku-Aku,* Rand McNally, Chicago.

Knudson, R. (1989) North America's threatened heritage, *Archaeology,* January/February 1989, 71, 106.

Larson, G. (1986) The Far Side, *The Oregonian,* p. 13, March 17, 1986.

Lewis, C. (1982) Peru's lost worlds, *Washington Post,* p. D1, August 5, 1982.

Lipe, W. (1977) A conservation model for American archaeology. In *Conservation Archaeology,* Schiffer and Gumerman, Eds., 21.

Loftus, B. (1986) Grave robbers sentencing delay angers Nez Perces, *Lewiston Tribune,* p. A7, April 8, 1986.

McGimsey, C. (1972) *Public Archaeology,* Seminar Press.

McGimsey, C. (1977) *The Management of Archaeological Resources: The Airlie House Report,* Society for American Archaeology.

Meyer, K. (1973) *The Plundered Past,* Atheneum Press, 284.

Moliere, A. (1956) *The Miser in Six Prose Comedies of Moliere* (G. Gravely transl.), 205–207.

Moore, J. (1988) Enforcing foreign ownership claims in the antiquities market, *Yale Law J.,* 96, 466.

Mott, W. P., Jr. (1987) Letter from the director of the National Park Service to Senator Pete Domenici, March 13, 1987.

Neumann, L. (1989) Saving the past for the future, SAA embarks on project to prevent looting, *Bull. Soc. Am. Archaeol.,* January 1989, 1.

Northey, L. (1982) The Archaeological Resources Protection Act of 1979: protecting prehistory for the future, *Harvard Environ. Law Rev.,* 6, 61, 81.

OAS (Oregon Archaeological Society) (1987) President's Comments, *Screenings,* October 1, 1987, 1.

Rogers, K. O. (1985) Viable forensic archaeology through interdisciplinary deference and dialogue: a prosecutor's prescription, *Am. Archaeol.,* 5, 110.

Rogers, K. O. (1986) Practical problems in ARPA prosecutions, SAA Annual Meeting, New Orleans.

Rogers, K. O. (1987) Visigoths revisited: the prosecution of archaeological resource thieves, traffickers and vandals, *J. Environ. Law Lit.,* 2, 217.

Reif, R. (1988) A season that has seen records toppled daily, *New York Times,* December 11, 1988.

Reif, R. (1988) Was this statue stolen? *Natl. Law J.,* November 1988, 1.

Reif, R. (1988) The Getty's Aphrodite: fruit of an illegal dig? *Natl. Law J.,* November 1988, 33.

U.S. Corps of Engineers (1989) U.S. Corps of Engineers News Release No. PA 88–90, June 13, 1989.

USDA (U.S. Department of Agriculture) (1987) Columbia River Gorge National Scenic Area Interim Guidelines (Pacific Northwest Region 1987), at 9.

Ward, P. (1977) Letter from the Assistant Attorney General to Honorable Charles A. Vanik, Subcommittee on Trade, Committee on Ways and means, July 26, 1977.

Wilkerson, C. (1988) Temple Lintel pits Thais against art museum, *New York Times,* p. 8, July 17, 1988.

Wilkinson, C. (1988) Law and the American West: the search for an ethic of place, *Univ. Colorado Law Rev.,* 59, 401.

**Wilson, L.** (1985) Students dig into history, *The Oregonian,* p. B1, September 13, 1985.

*Autocephalous Greek-Orthodox Church of Cypress vs. Goldberg and Feldman Fine Arts, Inc.,* 717 F. Supp. 1374 (S.D. Ind. 1989).

Public Law (P.L.) 100-298, 102 Stat. 432 (1988).

Act of October 28, 1988, P.L. 100-555, 102 Stat. 2778; "Domenici Bill".

Act of November 3, 1988, P.L. 100-588, 102 Stat. 2983; House Bill (H.B.) 4068.

16 U.S.C. §§ 470aa–470ll (1979) Archaeological Resources Protection Act.

*United States vs. Austin,* No. 88-3300 (9th Cir. 1990).

Arkansas Stat. Ann. 13-7-301 (1987).

Pennsylvania Stat. Ann. tit. 71, §§ 1047.1b(3), (6) (Purdon Supp. 1988).

Warm Springs Tribal Ordinance (Code Chapter 490).

New Mexico Stat. Ann. § 18-6-9(D).

Utah Code Ann. § 63-18-27 (1986).

Arkansas Stat. Ann. 13-6-3-3(b) (1987).

North Carolina Gen. Stat. 70-1 (1985).

Oregon Rev. Stat. §§ 358.905(6)(a)-(b) (1987).

36 C.F.R. §§ 1.4(a) and 261.2 (1988).

Alabama Code § 41-3-1 (1982).

45 C.F.R. §§ 46.101-24 (1988).

Louisiana Rev. Stat. Ann. §§ 41.1605–.1606 (West Supp. 1989).

North Carolina Gen. Stat. § 121–125 (1986).

Oregon Rev. Stat. (O.R.S.) §§ 273.718 et seq.

Washington, Ch. 44, Laws of 1987.

Missouri Rev. Stat. §§ 253.400–407 (Supp. 1989), Historic Preservation Revolving Fund Act.

New York Parks & Rec. Law §§ 17.01–.11 (McKinney 1984) (Outdoor Recreation Development Bond Act).

Pennsylvania Stat. Ann. tit. 32, § 5001 (Purdon Supp. 1988), (Open Space Lands Act).

Utah Code Ann. § 63-18-25 (1989).

Oregon Rev. Stat. §§ 358.920(3)-(4) (1987).

Alabama Code § 41-3-5 (1975).

Washington, Ch. 44, Laws of 1989.

Arizona Rev. Stat. Ann. § 13-3702.01 (Supp. 1988).

16 U.S.C. § 470gg(b)(3) (1979).

Idaho Code § 67-4122 (1980).

Kansas Stat. Ann. § 74-5408 (1985).

Oregon Rev. Stat. § 273.711 (1987).

Idaho Code § 67-4118 (1980).

Oregon Rev. Stat. § 358.955 (1987).

Oregon Rev. Stat. § 358.945 (1987).

16 U.S.C. § 170gg(c) (1982).

42 U.S.C. § 1996 (1982).

Alaska Stat. § 29.45.050(b)(2)(B) (1988).

New Mexico Stat. Ann. § 7-2-18.2 (1988).

Washington Rev. Code § 79.08.109 (Supp. 1989).

Oregon Land Conservation and Development Commission, Department of Land Conservation, Oregon's Statewide Planning Goals 5 (1985).

New Jersey Stat. Ann. § 40:55D-28(b)(6) (West Supp. 1988).

Alaska Stat. § 41.35.060(b) (1988).

New Mexico Stat. Ann. § 18-6-12 (1978).

Hawaii Rev. Stat. § 6E-2 (1984).

Miss. Code Ann. § 53-7-51 (Supp. 1988).

*Dept. of Natural Resources vs. Indiana Coal Council, Inc.,* 542 N.E.2d 1000 (Ind. 1989).

Arkansas Stat. Ann. § 13-6-305 (1988).

Vermont Stat. Ann., Tit. 22, § 765 (1988).

*United States vs. Jaques,* No. 83-129FR (D. Or. 1983), *aff'd,* 753 F.2d 1084 (9th Cir. 1984), *cert. denied,* 470 U.S. 1087 (1985).

*United States vs. Bender,* No. 81-119BE (D. Or. 1981) (Trans. pp. 585, 602–603).

New Hampshire Rev. Stat. Ann. § 227-C:10 (Supp. 1988).

25 U.S.C. § 450(h).

16 U.S.C. § 470-1(d)(3)(B).

# THE TEAM APPROACH TO ARCHAEOLOGICAL RESOURCES PROTECTION

Sherry Hutt

## INTRODUCTION

While the court house presents a new domain for the archaeologist, in the context of a typical function of site protection, those who find the turf familiar, such as lawyers and law enforcement agents, may be equally unaccustomed to including archaeologists as an integral component. Yet it is essential that the players brought together by the Archaeological Resources Protection Act of 1979 (ARPA) become comfortable working as a team in site protection efforts.

## BASIS OF THE TEAM APPROACH

The team approach to ARPA enforcement is not merely an option, but a necessity. The added options and responsibilities within the law make teamwork practical if the goal of effective use of the court process is to be achieved. The statutory provisions of ARPA (Public Law 96-95 found in Title 16 of the U.S. Code, section 470 aa, *et seq)* set forth the requirements to pursue a criminal case in court. Every crime is composed of easily identifiable elements that a law enforcement agent will satisfy with accumulated evidence before presenting the matter to an Assistant U.S. Attorney, who will prosecute the case. ARPA cases are unique in that not all elements may be obtained through traditional criminal investigation. Proof that the site or item affected is an archaeological resource is an element that requires input from an expert. Thus, the law has created the need for a forensic archaeologist.

"Archaeological resource" is defined (Title 16 U.S. Code section 470 bb) as "any material remains of past human life or activities which are of archaeological interest," and are "at least 100 years of age." Therefore, by statutory mandate, the archaeologist is thrust into the litigation arena to provide essential expert information. No ARPA case may proceed without an analysis of age, interest, and human involvement, which must be made by a qualified scientist.

The Archaeological Resources Protection Act made available a number of new tools to utilize in site protection and strengthened the grasp of law enforcement, all of which created a heightened interest in site protection beyond the archaeological community. As a potential felony, ARPA added another substantial crime to the agenda of law enforcement agents. The spectrum of stiff penalties made the transgressors worth pursuing. The prospect of asset forfeiture made ARPA cases truly attractive.

Another facet of ARPA, however, was the new responsibilities placed on land managing and enforcement agencies to involve Indian tribes in site access decisions and protection. There are requirements for intergovernmental coordination and cooperation with private individuals throughout the act.

Of course, the cost of all this attention must be satisfied through the expenditure of resources, and a law that becomes too costly, given its relative priority, is a law that is soon abandoned. It is axiomatic that no agency has sufficient resources to give quality attention to all of its charges. Therefore, if ARPA is to be a viable tool, it must find life within existing resources. As a matter of practicality, a team approach provides a salient option.

If one assumes that the quintessential ARPA case will be brought to court with little preparation, which is an unrealistic assumption in any criminal case, and that an archaeologist working alone may submit credible testimony to satisfy the appropriate legal elements, the case may still falter in the legal process before it is resolved. It would be appropriate to assume that the purpose of an investment in ARPA prosecution is to realize success in court and to achieve, through successful resolution, the deterrence of site destruction, or, at the least, retribution. Preparation is key to the successful litigation of any case. Therefore, if the goal of effective court presentation is to be achieved, there must be communication between those involved on the team, which will enhance the performance of each team member.

## ROLE OF EACH TEAM MEMBER

There are three members of the ARPA prosecution team; the attorney, the archaeologist, and the law enforcement agent. Each player must be knowledgeable not only in the unique skill they bring to the team, but also in the role they play within the team. Court cases can be jeopardized and a team may become dysfunctional when the members are unclear as to how their piece operates in the overall scheme.

Each member may have an ongoing role in site protection, but the focus here is on the part each team member assumes in the preparation of an ARPA case for trial. The respective functions begin with the reporting of a violation and continue through the investigation, preparation for court, and trial.

### Archaeologist

Archaeologists, prime moving forces in the creation of ARPA legislation, have often had firsthand experience with looted sites. Therefore, they most likely will be involved in the reporting of violations, when involved in field work. It is their obligation to know of the law enforcement agency having responsibility for a site regardless of whether a disturbance has occurred. Hopefully, over time, a personal contact will emerge, and the foundation of a team will begin.

Once a disturbance is observed and reported, the role of the archaeologist remains centered on the site. Site stabilization or curation of artifacts, and later a damage assessment, all fall within the scope of the archaeologist's domain. Confrontation with suspected ARPA violators should be referred to law enforcement personnel.

An archaeologist should not become involved in the "who did it" aspect of the investigation except under circumstances where they personally observed an offense during the commission and are later needed to identify a perpetrator. At all other times, the archaeologist serves the team by focusing on "what occurred."

As a case is readied for trial, the reason for the rigid separation of function becomes apparent. An archaeologist who has been asked to prepare a site damage assessment for trial will find their credibility sullied to the point of rendering their testimony useless if they are perceived to have become zealously involved in nabbing the defendant. Jury perception, properly based on common sense, will grant little weight to the best scientific rendering if they feel the witness has lost the appropriate perspective.

At trial, those people who observed the acts in progress may testify as "fact" witnesses. Facts are to be related without speculation or embellishment. Such testimony might not go beyond statements as originally given to investigating agents. It is not until the archaeologist testifies in the capacity of an "expert" witness that one can venture opinions. Experts are allowed to give opinions to be considered as evidence in a trial, based on their specialized training and expertise. It is the obligation of the scientist to project their sense of professionalism, in work product as well as demeanor. One may be passionate about the occurrence at a site and the loss of information, or the mutilation of human remains, but they must stop short of visiting vengeance upon the defendant.

In the federal system, the archaeologist will always gain access to the prosecuting attorney through the law enforcement agent. Again, the personal contacts that are created may cement the team and allow a more open flow of communication. Though the lawyer may be a skilled litigator, their background on the site or the protected item may be limited. One potentially fulfilling aspect of team involvement for the archaeologist may arise from the educational interaction with the lawyer.

The archaeologist will add two vital aspects to the mounting of a trial, beyond the fact or expert testimony previously discussed. First, they may prepare the lawyer with recent treatises on site protection and assist the lawyer in evaluating the background of government and defense experts. Second, in the course of providing background on the site to satisfy the archaeological interest element that is mandated in an ARPA case, they can give the lawyer much nontechnical information that will make the case meaningful and even enjoyable for a jury. The lawyer is then able to build on the experiences of their team member to create a captivating open statement at trial.

## Law Enforcement Agent

It is the law enforcement agent, designated by their agency in each individual case to be the lead agent, who has the responsibility to determine what may occur at a site once a violation has occurred. It is the nature of such "reactive" law enforcement that causes the agent to be primarily concerned with "who" committed the act. Therefore, having an archaeologist, with whom a working relationship is established, to respond immediately to a site to augment investigative efforts maximizes evidence accumulation. Where mutual respect between agents and archaeologists is established, they can develop "proactive" protection strategies by identifying sites most vulnerable to attack in the future.

The agent is the team member with direct access to the prosecutor. In a reactive situation, a report will be submitted to the Assistant U.S. Attorney for action. Here again, with the development of a working relationship, the agent may seek legal guidance for proactive investigations.

At the time of trial, the agent will remain in the courtroom with the lawyer, to assist in technical details. Also, the agent is responsible for the handling of all evidence from the scene until the items are admitted into evidence at trial. After a trial, all three team members should have input as to the disposition of former items of evidence, with deference to the agency policies of each as well as the tribal considerations required by ARPA.

## Attorney

The decision of whether to prosecute, for what and under what statutes, civil or criminal, is the unique responsibility of the attorney. A number of considerations and policies will enter into the decision, some of which go beyond the realm of ARPA and are more the result of competing demands on the attorney's time. Over time, prosecution policy with regard to ARPA will become more defined, although the policies will vary between districts. The law allows for such flexibility.

Ideally, in the furtherance of site protection, the well-informed attorney, supported by the team, will be able to offer knowledgeable and workable prototypes for policy that will gauge how the various violations are to be addressed within their district. A case of first impression requires an inordinate amount of attorney time because a pervasive perspective is lacking. The attorney's resources will be better spent preparing for trial or giving ongoing legal advice once the team is fully functional.

# JOINT ACCOUNTABILITY

In addition to the separate functions of each team member, there are areas of joint accountability that must be acknowledged and coordinated. These areas include, at a minimum, a concern for the disposition of the site, the care to be given to artifacts or human remains, the need to serve the public, and a recognition of appropriate interaction with the media.

## To The Site

During the pendency of an investigation, the archaeologist may determine that a looted excavated site should be back filled to preserve the remainder from erosion. However, the attorney may need to allow time for the defense to examine a site prior to restoration. Each circumstance has attendant variables that will affect anyone's judgment of what is appropriate. It is possible that the needs of information preservation and evidence collection will be in conflict. While there are no absolute correct procedures, a rational basis for the action taken is almost always defensible in court. On this point, it is essential that team members promptly communicate their respective positions and needs.

The ARPA uniform regulations (36 CFR 296.1, Agriculture; 32 CFR 229.1, Defense; 43 CFR 7.1, Interior; and 18 CFR 1312.1, Tennessee Valley Authority) specify who may have custody of excavated items. Very simply, items taken from Indian lands become the property of the tribe having rights of ownership over the land, and items taken from public land belong to the U.S. The law and regulations do not address the sensitive cultural and religious factors involved, regardless of ownership. This void is left to the team to resolve so that the need for information, for educational tools, and for respect for ancient peoples, may be addressed. It should be recognized by the team that just as evidence collection is necessary for prosecution of a case, the eventual disposition of evidence may impact future defence efforts.

## To The Public

All three team members are public servants. The statutes and regulations make repeated reference to working with private individuals. If the short-term focus of convicting a violator is allowed to obliterate the impact on the greater public, the intended beneficiaries of the knowledge and cultural preservation to be wrought from site protection will be ungrateful. Jurors, as reflections of the public, may express their displeasure by rendering unfavorable verdicts. Unpopular laws are not well enforced.

The team members must temper their expectations with the reality that the public as a whole does not always share their fervor for preservation. Not every violation is a felony or deserving of criminal resolution. Not every case should be treated to the full barrage of possibilities under ARPA. While the attorney makes prosecutorial determinations, each member of the team must remember their actions create an opportunity for heightened public awareness or for public reproach.

Every encounter with the public, whether at a site or in front of a jury, may be utilized by each team member as a positive educational experience. Each team member has an obligation to step beyond their basic job function to educate the public.

### To The Media

The team cannot control the media, but they can interact with the media to maximize positive results. Press releases may educate the public in ARPA and utilize convictions for further deterrence. However, ill-timed releases may compromise investigations. Also, comments to the press by a government agent during the course of a case, which discuss the case, are prohibited by court rule in most districts. Archaeologists are included as agents in this regard. Failure to adhere to the rule may be seen as an attempt to try the case in the media and may result in its dismissal. It is imperative that the team act in consort when dealing with the media.

## CONCLUSION

The experienced team will enjoy a more efficient, predictable, and successful venture in using the law and the legal system for site protection than will any potential member acting alone. If the goal underlying all legislative, judicial, and agency efforts is the protection of archaeological sites from destruction, then cooperation is the critical tool to achieve those ends. The team approach is, quite simply, a practical device.

## REFERENCES CITED

Public Law 96-95 sec. 6, Oct 31, 1979, 93 Stat. 724
Title 16 U.S. Code sec. 470 aa-470 mm.
36 CFR 296.1 et seq. (Deptartment of Agriculture)
32 CFR 229.1 et seq. (Department of Defense)
43 CFR 7.1 et seq. (Department of Interior)
18 CFR 1312.1 et seq. (Tennessee Valley Authority)

# *Chapter 3*

## *ARCHAEOLOGICAL SITE DESTRUCTION*

"It takes only a period of about a dozen years to implant a basic culture in the mind of man — the period between the age of two and the age of fourteen. In a psychobiological sense, history, tradition, and custom are only about 12 years old." (Beardsley Rumi, World Trade and Peace Address, 1945)

# THE DESTRUCTION OF ARCHAEOLOGICAL SITES AND DATA

## Paul R. Nickens

## INTRODUCTION

Archaeological sites are widely recognized as being limited in number and nonrenewable, much like several other natural resources. What distinguishes archaeological sites from many of the other resource concerns is their fragility, informational context, and necessary role in the theoretical, methodological, and technical approaches for archaeological investigations of the past. Archaeologists and the interested public are acutely aware of the intrinsic nature of this resource base and of the need to protect it, both for wise use for research and for preservation of significant resource elements for future generations.

Unfortunately, the characteristics of the archaeological record that make it so valuable also render it highly vulnerable to destructive forces generated from both natural and human origins. Cultural materials that make up the archaeological context range from being highly perishable, capable of being preserved only under the most unusual conditions, to nearly indestructible items such as stone and ceramic artifacts. However, for the archaeologist the spatial and temporal relationships are as important to reconstruction and interpretation of the past as the cultural debris itself.

This article provides a brief overview of the destructive processes that lead to alteration or loss of archaeological sites and data. We need to understand the stresses in today's environment, and we need to be able to predict the severity and rate of loss associated with the various threats. This forum only allows for a superficial examination of the overall situation, but the discussion will provide a background for other articles in this volume, which outline various approaches for protecting archaeological sites.

## ARCHAEOLOGICAL SITES AS RESOURCES

Before the various forces contributing to loss of archaeological sites and data are examined, a brief review of why archaeological sites deserve protection is beneficial. Historically, archaeological sites have been of great interest and value to the professionals and concerned avocational archaeologists who study the remains and lifeways of past human communities. Many of the larger important sites have also generated interest among the public in their appreciation for things of the past. Over the past few decades, our society has come to realize that archaeological sites are finite in number, and there has been an awareness that vestiges of our cultural heritage are being methodically destroyed, often at an alarming rate. The increasing demands upon our natural resources and the ever-growing use of land surface throughout the country have prompted increased concern for the archaeological sites that remain in place.

While the archaeological site is often the center of the concern, we should remember that our concerns are better targeted at a larger picture that may be designated as the cultural resource base. Lipe (1984) has defined the cultural resource base as "the material things produced by past human activity — the artifacts, manufacturing debris, middens, structures, monuments, and the like, that have survived from some time in the past into the present." Lipe also notes that the landscapes of past cultures may also qualify as cultural resources.

Professional interest in the preservation of such resources lies in the fact that archaeological remains are a limited, fragile, nonrenewable part of the environment, and any disturbance creates irreversible and cumulative impacts. The following quote from an article by Scovill, Gordon, and Anderson (1977:44) succinctly expresses the important characteristics of archaeological resources for the professional community:

> The investigation of the archaeological record of the American continent is the serious and scientific study of humankind over a span of time numbered in the tens of thousands of years. The study seeks knowledge — knowledge to describe, to explain, and to understand the behavior of past peoples and their interactions as integral parts of changing cultural and natural systems. Cultural history, cultural physiography, cultural ecology, and cultural processes are the current emphasis in the anthropological study of the past through the archaeological record.
>
> Archaeological resources predominantly consist of the physical evidences, or cultural debris, left on the landscape by past societies.... Of high significance to the investigation, analysis, and interpretation of the cultural debris are the local and regional geomorphological sequences, soil composition, and modern biological and botanical baseline indicators. Critically essential to the methodologies, techniques, and processes of studying archaeological resources is the preservation of the undisturbed stratigraphic context of the cultural debris. Directly stated, the cultural debris of this nation's archaeological resources have no value for studying the past once they have been rearranged on the landscape by a bulldozer or a dragline.

These two paragraphs by Scovill and his co-authors clearly convey the feeling of the professionals regarding archaeological sites as significant resources and point to the reasons why protection of these resources is important for those charged with the management of the nation's public lands. In addition to protection and wise use of the resource base today, we also need to be concerned with proper stewardship and preservation of resource elements for the future. As noted some years ago in an article by William Lipe (1974), it is highly desirable to save archaeological sites in place whenever possible, as opposed to excavating them without consideration of preservation and thereby promoting removal of yet another piece of the rapidly disappearing resource. Lipe's arguments for a conservation ethic within the profession still have considerable relevance today.

## AN OVERVIEW OF ARCHAEOLOGICAL SITE DESTRUCTION

A number of agents can be identified that, in most cases, result in either damage, alteration, or complete loss of archaeological sites and data when the agent and the resource come into conflict. An outline of these destructive agents is shown in Figure 1. To be sure, additional sources of disturbance could readily be identified and added to the list; however, those categories indicated cover the major threats to the resource base.

Before these categories are examined, some general comments can be offered concerning the various agents of destruction as they relate to site and data loss. The first and perhaps most obvious fact is that a large degree of interrelationship exists between the agents and modes of resource destruction noted in Figure 1 in that much association, with respect to cause and effect circumstances, is clearly evident among the various categories. For example, in some cases recreation on public lands and hobby collecting (or even malicious vandalism) may be considered interrelated activities. In other instances, the two may be quite differentiated. Likewise, a combination of erosion impacts and land reclamation undertakings may create an environmental battlefield, with archaeological sites being among those resources caught in the middle.

The agents of destruction under discussion are not in every case completely harmful to archaeological sites and data. For example, many important archaeological sites would go

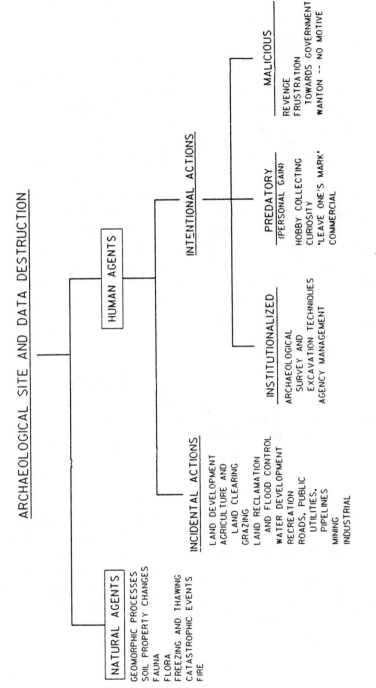

FIGURE 1.  Agents and modes of resource destruction.

unrecognized if not for natural erosion or human-caused land alteration or even as a result of the efforts of interested hobbyists. Some of these agents, particularly the human incidental categories, lead to critical funding for data recovery programs when such activities take place on federal or state lands. However, far more archaeological sites are lost to these agents than are preserved, on public and private lands alike. It is well recognized that with the present legal, funding, and management situations, every worthy site cannot be investigated or even saved. On the positive side, though, the impacts generated by certain forms of destructive activities can be mitigated through increased effectiveness of educational and protective programs. Moreover, interest in reducing the effects of vandalism and finding ways to physically protect endangered resources is on the increase, and meaningful results should be evident in the near future.

We also need to keep in mind that the archaeological record, by its very definition, is one that has lost important elements of critical information due to various destructive processes. As Schiffer has noted in his various writings (e.g., 1976, 1983, 1987) on the formation processes affecting the archaeological record, cultural materials suffer varying degrees of informational loss as they are transformed from a systemic or ongoing behavioral system to the archaeological context. The rate of loss is especially calamitous for perishable items. Schiffer goes on to point out that the archaeological record may undergo changes that transform cultural materials from one state to another within the archaeological context (e.g., natural erosion or human intervention such as plowing or land leveling) and that the archaeological context may even return to a systemic one when the archaeologist (or vandal) retrieves the cultural materials. Our concern in this discussion is limited to the destructive processes that take place within the archaeological context and, more importantly, the conflicts that arise as the materials come face to face with the systemic contexts of today.

# AGENTS OF DESTRUCTION

Sources of potential destructive forces for archaeological sites and data come from almost every conceivable source in the environmental setting. The two major categories include those of a natural origin and those associated with human activities on the landscape. The human agents can be further subdivided into incidental and intentional actions.

## Natural Agents

Natural processes and events that affect archaeological sites are legion, ranging from the effects of earthworm and crayfish soil mixing to the devastating consequences of volcanic and earthquake events. In between these extremes, we find that the activities of various plants and animals and erosive actions of wind, water, and temperature take a great toll on cultural materials, in the archaeological context, leading to a loss of items and abundant variation in the record. For the interested, excellent descriptions and discussions of these processes as they relate to archaeological sites can be found in Mathewson (1989), Schiffer (1987), Wildesen (1982), and Wood and Johnson (1978).

## Human Agents

Human-caused actions that have harmful effects on archaeological sites and data are also multitudinous and continue to increase in number and magnitude as lands are developed and exploited and the pressures of population expansion increase. By and large, legislative actions at both the federal (see McManamon, this volume) and state levels have been enacted to lessen or mitigate the effects of associated impacts to archaeological sites on public lands; however, the problems associated with many types of activities have in no way been totally eliminated. As they pertain to archaeological sites, destructive actions can be divided into two subcategories: incidental and intentional. As noted previously, the various actions that may be listed under either one of these headings are not totally independent of each other. The advent or growth of a land development activity, for example, will surely create a host of interrelated potential impacts, both in the short- and the long-term, including, in all probability, a rise in the incidence of vandalism or depreciative behavior.

### Incidental Actions

These activities may be defined as those destructive actions associated with the many forms of land development and resource exploitation that take place on the landscape. In other words, the destruction of archaeological sites and data is not the primary motive behind such actions, but the end result is that another part of the archaeological record disappears from the landscape. These activities may be generally categorized as (1) land development; (2) agriculture and land clearing; (3) grazing; (4) land reclamation and flood control; (5) water development projects; (6) recreational pursuits; (7) construction of roads, public utility features, and pipelines; (8) mining and quarrying; and (9) industry.

In many cases, the precise effects of these types of land alteration activities have not been quantified; however, it is not difficult to imagine that each undertaking creates special and ultimately harmful results for the archaeological record, if allowed to continue unchecked. These impacts lead to either partial or total destruction or, at best, mixing and displacement of the resources.

Fortunately, the recent emphasis on proper resource management on public lands has brought about a better understanding of the range and seriousness of impacts resulting from such activities. This emphasis has also led to regulated identification and evaluation of archaeological resources in the impact zones and, when needed, effective mitigation of the adverse effects resulting from those impacts.

The body of literature examining the interplay between human occupation and use of the landscape and the protection and preservation of archaeological sites and data has grown over the past 20 years as archaeologists have become more aware of the need to better understand the overall effects of such undertakings. Thus, we can find references providing data on such potentially destructive and diverse activities as military training (Carlson and Briuer 1986), livestock grazing (Osborn et al. 1987), forest chaining (DeBloois et al. 1974; Haase 1983), river navigation (Gramann 1981), agricultural practices (Ford and Rollingson 1972; Medford 1972; Roper 1976; Knoerl and Versaggi 1984), reservoir inundation (Lenihan et al. 1981), stream channelization (Schiffer and House 1977), traffic vibrations on prehistoric structures (King and Algermissen 1985), fire (Kelly and Mayberry 1980; Noxon and Marcus 1983; Switzer 1974), and tourism (Gale and Jacobs 1987). In spite of these and other studies, many gaps still exist in our knowledge pertaining to the nature of specific impacts on archaeological resources from the various land-disturbing activities listed above.

### Intentional Actions

Intentional actions that lead to a loss of archaeological sites and data are critical in that they are inherently harmful to the resource base, but, in most cases, are guided by motives that are difficult to prevent or control. The worst of these actions, those related to vandalism, are particularly damaging, since they lead to destruction without any return of scientific informa-tion. Intentional actions causing resource destruction can be subdivided into three categories: institutionalized destruction, predatory vandalism, and malicious vandalism.

### Institutionalized Destruction

Some forms of archaeological site and data destruction have been either tolerated or accepted over the years. In this category we refer to the loss of cultural materials and information that occurs during professional investigation or associated with the management of archaeological resources.

At first it may appear that to designate the activities of the archaeologist, whose goal it is to retrieve data from the archaeological context and make sense of it, as being destructive is somewhat contradictory. Realistically, however, it must be said that each and every archaeologi-cal endeavor leads to the loss of varying amounts of information. This situation will never be completely alleviated, since far too many factors are involved (e.g., professional competence, data recovery techniques, and time and funding constraints). Further, we must recognize that a tremendous amount of archaeological data was lost during the early phases of discovery and investigation in this country when zeal often took predominance over scientific discretion. It is, however, difficult to excessively castigate many of those early efforts, from our present-day vantage point. Undoubtedly, our successors will, at some point in the future, decry the "primitive" data recovery and analytical techniques used by archaeologists in the 1980s and 1990s and complain of the data loss that took place.

More to the point at hand, certain archaeological practices, which unfortunately continue to exist, do result in intentional and harmful effects to the resource base. These actions range from survey techniques in which, for example, artifacts are collected without corresponding mapping of artifact loci, to much more serious problems involving the use of limited research designs to guide excavation of archaeological sites. Even more damaging is the act of conducting investigative work and not pursuing the necessary analysis and reporting of the results. It is probably fair to state that in the past, and even today, some archaeological fieldwork was/is undertaken without any intention on the part of the investigator to adequately analyze the resultant data and make them available. Hopefully, the time is near when well-meaning but overworked investigators are no longer allowed to conduct field work beyond their capacity, professional or financial, to effectively complete the research process. As has been noted by others, this practice is little more than a form of archaeological vandalism.

Similar losses of archaeological sites and data can result from management practices on the part of agencies charged with this responsibility (see Spoerl 1988). Actions leading to resource destruction can include ineffective management orientations, a lack of rigorous evaluation methodologies for evaluating the significance of sites, or failure to fully realize the impacts that an agency's activities or operations may have on archaeological resources. Examples of the latter activities might include the side effects from timbering actions, or shoreline and downstream impacts to archaeological sites from the operation of a reservoir.

### Predatory Vandalism

This form of intentional activity is the most widespread and leads to the most serious consequences for archaeological resources (Nickens et al. 1981; General Accounting Office 1987). It is characterized by a motive dictated by personal gain, either of a noncommercial or commercial nature. In the first case, the effort may involve actions such as adding items to one's collection of relics, satisfying a curiosity about antiquities, or perhaps egocentric autographing of resource sites. Commercial ventures are guided by a motive of retrieving artifacts for sale and profit. In either case, the impact to archaeological resources is much the same: loss of cultural elements and contextual information.

To understand the problem, it will be useful to examine its extent, as indicated by one study completed a few years ago. In that investigation, Williams (1978) surveyed the management problem of cultural resource vandalism in federal and state agency recreation areas throughout the Rocky Mountain West. In compiling the results provided by resource managers throughout several states, Williams listed the following vandalism practices that impact cultural resource sites (arranged in decreasing order by reported absolute frequency):

- Excavation (digging, pothunting, use of heavy machinery)
- Carving, scratching, chipping, general defacement
- Surface collection of artifacts (especially lithic artifacts)
- Removing, shooting at, painting, chalking, making casts and tracings of rock art
- Theft of artifacts from structures
- Stripping weathered boards or other timbers
- Removing part or all of a structure or causing structural damage
- Dismantling; general destruction of structure (but apparently no removal)
- Arson
- Climbing or walking on resources
- Building new roads over, and using modern vehicles on, historic roads; offroad recreational vehicle use
- Rearrangement of or relocating of resources
- Breaking artifacts, objects, windows
- Breaking and entering
- Knocking structures over
- Use as firewood
- Throwing rocks into excavated ruin
- Handling, touching

### Malicious Vandalism

The final category of intentional vandalism includes acts that may be classified as those brought about by revenge or frustration with government policies, or those that result from no discernible motive at all (Chokhani 1979:10). Basically, this category of vandalism includes those inexplicable, unprovoked actions for which there are no avowed motives. Such behavior can be the result of wanton activities or even the end product of psychotic or inebriate conduct. Fortunately, this type of aggressive vandalism, quite often highly destructive in nature, occurs less frequently in comparison to other forms of vandalistic behavior. An example of such senseless vandalism occurred in 1979 at Arches National Park near Moab, Utah, where a highly significant rock-art panel was obliterated by brushing a chemical solvent across the panel face (Noxon and Marcus 1980).

## CONCLUSION

The aim of the foregoing discussion has been to review the various agents that interact to extirpate elements of our nation's archaeological heritage. The importance of maintaining archaeological sites in pristine conditions cannot be understated, nor can the need to provide protection and preservation for the vestiges of this resource. The actions of natural processes upon archaeological sites and the ever-expanding demands by our population on the landscape are agents of destruction that will continue to adversely affect archaeological resources. It is simply not possible to completely halt all the detrimental stresses resulting from environmental processes. The effects of such impacts can, in many cases, be mitigated by using physical protection technologies, given appropriate need and funding. It should be noted that the natural agents of destruction tend to occur more slowly than human-caused actions and therefore may be considered to have a lower overall priority in cultural resource management than those detrimental effects tied to human activities. However, given the amount of past destruction of archaeological sites and data, and that continuing today, we cannot afford hesitation on any front of the conservation battle.

While some problems still exist, incidental impacts to archaeological resources as byproducts of land alteration and resource exploitation are, by and large, mitigated by legislative enactments, at least on federal and state lands. Control of vandalism, however, continues to be a formidable challenge. Severe problems continue to be associated with destructive actions on private lands, with the result being that valuable archaeological remains are disappearing at an alarming rate. This fact makes it even more important that such resources on public lands be adequately protected.

## REFERENCES CITED

**Carlson, D. L. and Briuer, F. L.** (1986) Analysis of military training impacts on protected archaeological sites at West Fort Hood, Texas, U.S. Army Fort Hood, Archaeological Resource Management Series, Research Report No. 9, Fort Hood, TX.

**Chokhani, P.** (1979) Destruction on the public lands: a closer look at vandalism. *Our Public Lands,* 29, 9–11.

**DeBloois, E., Green, D., and Wylie, H.** (1974) A test of the impact of Pinyon Juniper chaining on archaeological sites, U.S.D.A. Forest Service, Intermountain Region, Ogden, UT.

**Ford, J. L. and Rolingson, M.** (1972) Site destruction due to agricultural practices in southeast Arkansas, Arkansas Archaeological Survey Research Series, 3, 1–40.

**Gale, F. and Jacobs, J. M.** (1987) Tourists and the national estate: procedures to protect Australia's heritage. Publication Series No. 6, Canberra, Australian Heritage Commission.

**Gramann, J. H.** (1981) Navigation-related impacts on cultural resources of the upper Mississippi River system, *Contr. Abstr. CRM Archeol.,* 2(3), 11–16.

**Haase, W. R.** (1983) Mitigation of chaining impacts to archaeological sites. *J. Range Manage.,* 36, 158-160.

**Kelly, R. E. and Mayberry, J.** (1980) Trial by fire: effects of NPS burn programs upon archaeological resources. In Proc. Second Conf. on Scientific Research in the National Parks, Vol. 1, U.S. Government Printing Office, Washington, D.C., 603–610.

**King, K. W. and Algermissen, S. T.** (1985) Seismic and vibration hazard investigation of Chaco Canyon National Park, U.S. Geological Survey Open File Report 85-529, Denver.

**Knoerl, J. J. and Versaggi, N.** (1984) Plow zone sites: research strategies and management policy, *Am. Archaeol.,* 4, 76–80.

**Lenihan, D. J., Carrell, T. L., Fosberg, S., Murphy, L., Rayl, S. L., and Ware, J. A.** (1981) *The final report of the National Reservoir Inundation Study,* 2 Vols., National Park Service, Southwest Cultural Resources Center, Santa Fe, NM.

**Lipe, W. D.** (1974) A conservation model for American archaeology, *Kiva,* 39, 213–243.

**Lipe, W. D.** (1984) Value and meaning in cultural resources. In *Approaches to the Archaeological Heritage,* Cleere, H., Ed., Cambridge University Press, Cambridge, 1–11.

**Mathewson, C. C., Ed.** (1989) Interdisciplinary workshop on the physical-chemical-biological processes affecting archaeological sites, U.S. Army Engineer Waterways Experiment Station, Contract Report EL-89-1, Vicksburg, VA.

**Medford, L. D.** (1972) Agricultural destruction of archaeological sites in northeast Arkansas, Arkansas Archaeological Survey Research Series, 3, 41–82.

**Nickens, P. R., Larralde, S. L., and Tucker, G. C.** (1981) A survey of vandalism to archaeological resources in southwestern Colorado, Bureau of Land Management - Colorado, Cultural Resources Series No. 11, Denver.

**Noxon, J. S. and Marcus, D. A.** (1980) The Moab panel site of southeastern Utah: its defacement and significance in Southwestern prehistory, *Am. Rock Writing Res. Newsl.,* 1(5-80), 1–3.

**Noxon, J. S. and Marcus, D. A.** (1983) Wildfire-induced cliff face exfoliation and potential effects on cultural resources in the Needles District of Canyonlands National Park, Utah, *Southwestern Lore,* 49(2), 1–8.

**Osborn, A., Vetter, S., Hartley, R., Walsh, L., and Brown, J.** (1987) Impacts on domestic livestock grazing on the archaeological resources of Capitol Reef National Park, Utah, National Park Service, Midwest Archaeological Center, Occasional Studies in Anthropology No. 20, Lincoln, NE.

**Roper, D. C.** (1976) Lateral displacement of artifacts due to plowing, *Am. Antiquity,* 41, 372–375.

**Schiffer, M. B.** (1976) *Behavioral Archeology,* Academic Press, New York.

**Schiffer, M. B.** (1983) Toward the identification of formation processes, *Am. Antiquity,* 48, 675–706.

**Schiffer, M. B.** (1987) *Formation Processes of the Archaeological Record,* University of New Mexico Press, Albuquerque.

**Schiffer, M. B. and House, J. H.** (1977) Assessing impacts: examples from the Cache Project. In *Conservation Archaeology: A Guide for Cultural Resource Management Studies,* Schiffer, M. B. and Gumerman, G. J., Eds., Academic Press, New York, 309–320.

**Scovill, D. H., Gordon, G. J., and Anderson, K. M.** (1977) Guidelines for the preparation of statements of environmental impact on archaeological resources. In *Conservation Archaeology: A Guide for Cultural Resource Management Studies,* Schiffer, M. B. and Gumerman, G. J., Eds., Academic Press, New York, 43–62.

**Spoerl, P. M.** (1988) Management impacts on cultural resources: an assessment of Forest Service research needs. In Tools to manage the past: research priorities for cultural resources management in the Southwest, Tainter, J. A. and Hamre, R. H., Eds., U.S.D.A. Forest Service, Rocky Mountain Forest and Range Experiment Station, General Technical Report RM-164, Fort Collins, CO, 17–25.

**Switzer, R. R.** (1974) The effects of forest fire on archaeological sites in Mesa Verde National Park, Colorado, *Artifact,* 12,1–8.

General Accounting Office (1987) Cultural resources: problems protecting and preserving federal archaeological resources, GAO/RCED-88-3, U.S. Government Printing Office, Washington, D.C.

**Wildesen, L. E.** (1982) The study of impacts on archaeological sites. In *Advances in Archaeological Method and Theory,* Vol. 5, Schiffer, M. B., Ed., Academic Press, New York, 51–96.

**Williams, L. R.** (1978) Vandalism to cultural resources of the Rocky Mountain West, U.S.D.A. Forest Service, Southwestern Region, Cultural Resources Report No. 21, Albuquerque, NM.

**Wood, W. R. and Johnson, D. L.** (1978) A survey of disturbance processes in archaeological site formation. In *Advances in Archaeological Method and Theory,* Vol. 1, Schiffer, M. B., Ed., Academic Press, New York, 315–381.

# SOME DIMENSIONS OF THE POTHUNTING PROBLEM

Thomas F. King

## INTRODUCTION

My purpose in this article is to explore the magnitude and other dimensions of the looting and vandalism problem, that following standard American practice, I'll refer to as the pothunting problem, for short. This is not as simple a task as it might seem.

When one refers to "magnitude" and "dimensions," one naturally tends to think about numbers — in this case, how many archaeological sites have been potted, how much information has been lost, how many violators have been prosecuted. We have some information on numbers, some of which will be presented below, but the reliability of our figures is often, if not usually, questionable. It is even more questionable whether it would be worth expending the time and effort needed to make our numbers more accurate. Numbers of sites damaged and quantity of information lost are important, but they measure only a few of the problem's dimensions and provide only a dry and dusty reflection of its magnitude.

Measuring the scope of the problem also requires some shared understanding of what the problem is. Each of us tends to worry about pothunting within our own frame of reference and, therefore, to define it somewhat differently. The federal land manager tends to think about it as a land management problem — violation of the Archaeological Resources Protection Act and misuse of public property. The state archaeologist tends to think about it in the context of his or her own state — its laws and administrative traditions, its particular kinds of archaeological resources, and the psychology of its citizens. The nongovernmental archaeologist tends to think about its impacts on his or her own research interests. Archaeologists who work in the U.S. and those who work elsewhere, though they have very similar concerns about the problem, tend to view it with reference to the geography and politics of their research areas.

In this article "pothunting" means all kinds of damage done to archaeological sites in the interests of artifact collecting, commercial trafficking in artifacts, and plain hell raising. It does not include damage done as a result of such activities as land development. I take the term to include such damage wherever it occurs, not just in the U.S. and not just on public lands. Finally, I take the term to include such damage regardless of whether it is illegal. With this definition in mind, let us look at some aspects of the problem that reflect its magnitude and, I hope, may provide a basis for evaluating different approaches to its solution.

## THE GEOGRAPHIC SCOPE OF THE PROBLEM

Pothunting is a phenomenon that expresses itself on public and private lands in all nations. Lately, pothunting in the southwestern U.S. has received considerable publicity. Studies have been conducted by the General Accounting Office (1987) and by a subcommittee of the Committee on Interior and Insular Affairs in the House of Representatives (Subcommittee... 1988) as well as by federal agencies. These studies document a problem that has reached crisis proportions.

Although at present the best documentation of the problem comes from the Southwest, it would be a serious error to view it as a southwestern problem. Although numbers tend to be lacking, anecdotal examples of large-scale pothunting abound from areas outside the Southwest.

The U.S. Army Corps of Engineers and South Dakota State Historic Preservation Officer (SHPO), for example, are fighting pothunters at the Anton Rygh site, a prehistoric site on the east side of the Missouri River in South Dakota; pothunters have been observed operating there who have come from South Dakota, North Dakota, and Wyoming, according to their auto license plates (Allison Brooks, personal communication 1989). On the Hanford Reach of the Columbia River in Washington State, I recently photographed a massive prehistoric site complex that has been potted so heavily for so many years that its sandy deposits have been largely blown away. Artifacts and fragments of human skeletons were scattered on the deflated surface, but fresh potholes indicated that digging there continues.

Much attention has been focused on the pothunting problem on federal lands, and rightly so; such pothunting not only violates the Archaeological Resources Protection Act (ARPA) and the Antiquities Act, but can be defined as theft of government property. But again, to view the matter as simply a problem of protecting the federal estate is to miss its larger dimensions and, hence, to fail to address them. The fact that a site is on private land makes its destruction no less a loss for science and humanity; it simply, in most cases, makes it legal.

Pothunting on private land, with or without the permission of landowners, is extensive in the U.S. and elsewhere. As usual, our evidence of the problem tends to be anecdotal. The now-famous Slack Farm Site in Kentucky, for example, was mined for artifacts until public outrage forced the work to be closed (cf. Arden 1989). In 1988, with the Advisory Council on Historic Preservation, I visited Navajo Springs, a large Chacoan Anasazi site that had been the scene of weekend pothunting parties sponsored by its owner until the Navajo Nation was able to purchase and protect it; the site was a moonscape of potholes and sprinkled with torn-apart architecture and broken artifacts.

Pothunting is also not simply a domestic problem. The depredations of pothunters in overseas venues are well known, reported regularly both in the professional literature and in popular publications. The October 1988 issue of *National Geographic,* for example, reported (rather incidentally to the main point of the article) the massive pothunting of Sipan, a complex of Moche sites in Peru (Alva 1988), and the *Wall Street Journal,* on September 8, 1988, ran an article entitled "How grave looter at a Mexican site drools over relics" (Kandell 1988). Public distaste for the practice notwithstanding, such depredations continue unchecked.

## SOME NUMBERS

Understanding how limited they are as true indicators of the problem's magnitude, let us turn to such figures as we have about pothunting. Figure 1, developed by the National Park Service, represents three things: the number of incidents of pothunting on public land in the U.S. reported to the Park Service by federal agencies; the number of arrests under ARPA and other federal statutes; and the number of convictions (National Park Service 1989).

As Figure 1 shows, we are experiencing an increase in reported incidents of pothunting on federal lands. Whether this reflects an increase in pothunting is open to question; the high level of attention recently focused on the problem by federal agencies and the Congress is undoubtedly causing incidents to be reported that in the past would have gone unremarked. The impression of those who prepared the reports, however, according to the House subcommittee and the GAO, is that commercial pothunting, at least, is on the rise (General Accounting Office 1987:21; Subcommittee... 1988:5). "Casual pothunting" — that is, pothunting for recreation — is reported by some to be stabilizing, or even declining, on federal lands (General Accounting Office 1987:21). Of course, reported incidents are only the tip of the iceberg. The National Park

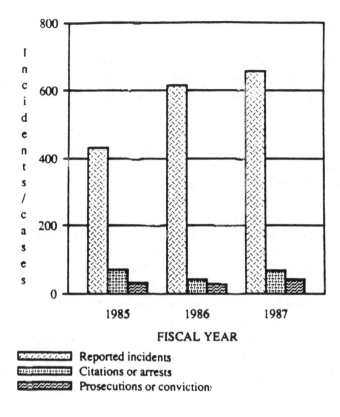

FIGURE 1. Pothunting statistics for federal lands in the U.S., fiscal years 1985
to 1987. (Source: Archaeological Assistance Division, National Park Service.)

Service has estimated, in testimony to the U.S. Senate, that reported incidents represent only about one quarter of the total of actual incidents in any given year (National Park Service 1989).

What is most clear from this graph, however, is the relationship among the level of potting, the level of investigations and arrests, and the level of prosecutions. Clearly — especially when you consider that the actual incident level is four-times larger than the reported level — the vast majority of pothunters on the public lands are getting away with it.

The GAO estimates that there are some 2 million archaeological sites on federal lands in the Southwest (1987:16). It indicates that at least one third of the *known* sites there have been potted to some extent; the House subcommittee report puts the percentage at between 50 and 90% (General Accounting Office 1987:22–23; Subcommittee...1988:6–8). If we extrapolate the lowest of these estimates to the total estimated universe of sites, this would mean that some 660,000 sites have been potted on federal lands in the Southwest alone. The House subcommittee also reports that as of 1987, there had been a total of 233 criminal investigations of pothunting incidents and 44 convictions under ARPA and other statutes. If 660,000 sites have been potted, this suggests that the potting of approximately one site in 2833 is being investigated, and the potters of one site in some 15,000 are being convicted.

Of course, these estimates are painfully inexact, and extrapolating from them not only compounds whatever errors are present, but results in the mixing of a good many apples and oranges. The numbers are all we have to work with, however, and they comport well with the anecdotal evidence and the observations of workers in the field. The pothunting problem, especially the problem of commercial pothunting, is a big one on the public lands, and it is getting bigger.

If the pothunting problem is large and growing larger on public lands, what is happening elsewhere? The short answer is that we really do not know, but we must assume that pothunting is going on at least as frequently on nonfederal lands as on the federal estate, and possibly more frequently.

The Bureau of Indian Affairs, in testimony to the House subcommittee, has estimated that between 1980 and 1987, pothunting increased by 1000% on the Navajo reservation; presumably, similar numbers would apply on many other Indian reservations. The subcommittee speculated that this increase may have reflected a shift in potting patterns away from federal lands, in response to increased ARPA enforcement (Subcommittee...1988:10). This, then, is another important dimension of the problem: enforcement of ARPA and other protective laws on the federal lands, paltry as this enforcement has been, may be *increasing* the level of potting on nonfederal lands. No one has collected usable figures regarding pothunting on private land, but if the problem is increasing on the federal lands, where ARPA applies and prosecutions occasionally occur, and on Indian lands, where ARPA applies, though prosecutions rarely occur, it has to be assumed that it is increasing even more on private and other nonfederal lands.

We lack useful figures for pothunting overseas, but we have a sufficiency of anecdotes. Archaeologists and antiquities agents have been gunned down or threatened in the bush by well-armed pothunters, often allied with drug dealers. Mayan stelae have been cut apart with chain saws preparatory to their transportation out of the country. At Rio Azul in Guatemala between 1979 and 1981, an estimated 80 pothunters were employed in the well-organized mining of an important Mayan site, digging some 150 trenches to destroy 32 tombs and constructing an airfield to fly out the plunder (Adams 1986:447). In El Salvador, the rich postclassic Cara Sucia site has been pocked with some 5000 potholes, and every known site in the area has been plundered to some extent, producing an estimated 30,000 artifacts that have gone into the international marketplace (Herscher 1989:68). Similar anecdotes can be recounted from virtually every country. The magnitude of the potting problem is huge. Its dimensions, however, go beyond the merely quantitative.

## ECONOMIC DIMENSIONS

There are two kinds of economic dimensions to the problem. First, although the bulk of potted artifacts that are trafficked in the marketplace go for a few dollars, or their equivalent, the international market in potted artifacts is a big business. An article in a recent *National Law Journal* estimates that over a billion dollars goes into the purchase of smuggled art and artifacts each year (Stille 1988:2). One group of investors is reported to have readily invested $80,000 on speculation for artifacts looted from Sipan in Peru (Decker 1989:144). Mimbres bowls from New Mexico go for anywhere from $2000 to over $6000, according to the GAO, while Mogollon pots have brought up to $20,000, and a Hohokam basket is reported to have been sold for $180,000 (1987:28–29). The Euphonios krater, the subject of intense controversy between the government of Italy and the Metropolitan Museum of Art in New York, is valued at a million dollars (Nagin 1986:22).

Second, there is a clear link between potting and the general economy of the area where potting takes place. In some areas potting is literally vital to the livelihood of local citizens. On St. Lawrence Island in Alaska, for example, residents are potting the middens of their ancestors for ivory, whalebone, and other artifacts, which are shipped out for sale in the art market. They have little other source of livelihood; their subsistence economy is no longer sufficient to sustain them, and they have few ways to participate in the modern cash economy except those offered by dealers in ivory and artifacts. So they have turned to what their ancestors have left them, to the obvious detriment of their heritage and the archaeological record. Alaska is by no means unique; the same economic pressures that drive the St. Lawrence Islanders to dig up their ancestors' artifacts motivate the pothunters of many third world nations. In the Southwest, too, increases in pothunting have been attributed, in part, to rising local unemployment (Bureau of Land Management 1985:433–413).

## THE LEGAL DIMENSION

Another important dimension is that of criminal justice: how readily one can catch and prosecute pothunters. I have touched on this dimension above; it is obvious from Figure 1 that on the whole, pothunters are not being caught and prosecuted in great numbers. There are good reasons for this. The GAO (1987:57; Table 4.1) reports that in the Four Corners area of the Southwest, there are all of 271 people on the federal payroll charged with enforcement of ARPA. Some 606 people have responsibilities that include surveillance of archaeological sites that might be subject to potting on the federal lands (General Accounting Office 1987:49, Table 3.3). There are about 100 million acres of federal land in the Four Corners area (General Accounting Office 1987:49, Table 3.3), so each surveillance person is responsible for looking out for about 167,000 acres, and each enforcement person is responsible for enforcing ARPA on about 370,000 acres: an imposing task, to say the least, particularly since ARPA surveillance and enforcement are by no means the only things these people are supposed to be doing.

Apprehending a pothunter is only the beginning of the battle, of course; one then has to prosecute — a long and tedious process with no sure guarantee of success. The seriousness of this aspect of the problem is illustrated by the fact that a jury handed down a felony ARPA conviction for the first time in 1987, 8 years after ARPA's passage. To get himself convicted, the pothunter in this case had to dig up a mummified baby girl and try to sell her for $35,000 (Trahant 1987).

It must also be remembered that one can prosecute only if there is a law under which to prosecute. ARPA applies only to federal and Indian lands; on most private lands, pothunting is perfectly legal unless done in violation of a state or local law or ordinance.

Many other nations regard all antiquities as the property of the state; in theory, pothunting is universally prohibited in such countries. Assuming the will to enforce protective laws, however, the governments of these nations are faced with the same problems that confront the U.S. government on federal lands — nowhere near enough enforcement personnel to cover the ground. And the will to enforce is not always very strong, particularly where pothunting is conducted by the same well-financed, well-armed, and often well-connected people who run the local illicit drug business, or where pothunting is an important component of the local economy.

Ostensibly, international traffic in antiquities is subject to control under the UNESCO Convention on the Means of Prohibiting and Preventing the Illicit Import, Export, and Transfer of Ownership of Cultural Property (cf. Herscher 1989:69; USIA 1988). Implementing the convention, however, is even more cumbersome than pronouncing its name; suffice it to say that the U.S. imposed import restrictions on a class of antiquities under the terms of the convention for the first time in 1987, 4 years after it enacted legislation to implement it (U.S. Information Agency 1988). In 1988 the *Los Angeles Times* reported customs seizure of four groups of artifacts and characterized this as a "clamp-down" (Spano 1988).

# THE PSYCHOLOGICAL DIMENSION

Finally, and perhaps most importantly, there is the psychological dimension of the problem. On the whole, as the GAO succinctly comments, "much of the public...condones the looting of archaeological sites..., both as a means of supplementing personal income and as a personal hobby" (1987:61). Simply put, to most people, pothunting is OK. Amassing and maintaining collections of beautiful and exotic artifacts, to most people, is more than OK; it's something that cultured, educated, upper class people do and gain status and prestige by doing.

Recognition of this fact, and of the infeasibility of stopping pothunting through law enforcement, has led many archaeologists to emphasize education as the best means of addressing the problem. Organizations like the Society for American Archaeology (see Reinburg and Judge, this volume), federal agencies (see McManamon, this volume) like the National Park Service and the Forest Service, and others, are hard at work on educational campaigns, and the reported decrease in "recreational" pothunting on federal lands in the Southwest may suggest that these campaigns are having salutary effects. Looking hopefully into the future, Ellen Herscher in a recent issue of *Archaeology* magazine suggested that the day will come when "private collecting itself may no longer be a socially acceptable endeavor, with the image of collectors as greedy fat cats replacing the 19th-century ideal of collectors as cultured gentlemen" (Herscher 1989:69).

# EDUCATION AND SITE PROTECTION

Education is attractive as an "answer" to the pothunter problem because it seems altogether positive and nonthreatening — a motherhood and apple pie kind of solution. The fact that a solution is attractive, though, does not necessarily mean that it is going to work; it may mean only that it is an easy one to think about, because it presents us, or seems to present us, with no hard choices. I suggest, however, that education does present us with some hard choices, choices so difficult that they make it improbable that education will have more than a marginal impact on the overall pothunting problem. Without intending to offend any individual or institution, I will conclude this article by discussing an aspect of the pothunter problem that I believe requires us to question our current strategies for addressing it and contemplate new ones.

One pleasant spring day recently, I strolled through a well-appointed complex of underground rooms in Washington, D.C. There I admired a handsome clay drinking vessel used in Persia, produced sometime between the third and seventh centuries A.D., probably in what is now Iran, and another of silver. I viewed pottery vessels from the Warring States period of Chinese history between the third and fifth centuries B.C., and scores of other ancient artifacts.

The rooms are those of the Arthur M. Sackler Gallery, a museum of Asian art at the Smithsonian Institution. There is little or no question that the artifacts they contain were exhumed from archaeological sites through nonscientific excavation; in other words, they are the fruits of pothunting. They were acquired and made available to the Smithsonian by an imminent collector of ancient Near Eastern and Oriental art, the late Dr. Arthur M. Sackler.

Dr. Sackler seems to have been an altogether admirable individual. An imminent psychiatrist and medical researcher, he was the author of some 140 scholarly papers (Spens 1987:10), more than most of us can claim. Linus Pauling has described him as a pioneer in studies of the molecular basis of schizophrenia (Pauling 1987:21). He was a vigorous campaigner for professional responsibility in his discipline, and against smoking, alcoholism, and drug abuse (Lasagna 1987:20). He established the Foundation for Nutritional Advancement and backed establishment of the Sackler School of Graduate Biomedical Sciences at Tufts University. Beginning his career as a collector after putting his two brothers through medical school and helping his parents through the Depression, he was, in time, responsible for endowing not only the museum that bears his name at the Smithsonian, but a museum at Harvard, a wing of the Metropolitan Museum in New York, and a museum of art and archaeology at Beijing University. Also, in China he founded the Sackler Foundation for China, which supports projects in health, art, and archaeology (Spens 1987; Wen Zhong 1987).

When Sackler died, the prestigious art journal *Studio International* published a commemorative issue in his honor. In it Frank Press, president of the National Academy of Sciences, characterized Sackler's death as "an incalculable loss" (Press 1987:34). Jean Mayer, president of Tufts University, described him as coming "close to the definition of a universal mind" (Mayer 1987:31). Joshua Lederberg, president of Rockefeller University, described him as "decades ahead of his time" (Lederberg 1987:34).

Recalling Ellen Herscher's prognostication, do we really think that education is going to turn people like Dr. Sackler, in the public eye, from the "cultured gentleman" that he obviously was, into a "greedy fat cat"? More to the point, should it?

If it should, we certainly have not made much of a start toward promoting such a change in perception. The Sackler Gallery was opened in 1987 with considerable and quite deserved fanfare and praise by the secretary of the Smithsonian, the imminent archaeologist Robert McCormick Adams; I presume Dr. Adams is proud of the gallery, and he should be; it is a wonderful addition to the Smithsonian's treasures. But you could search a long time, and in vain, to find anything in the gallery to indicate that people shouldn't emulate Dr. Sackler's example; there is no archaeologist general's warning that collecting may be harmful to the health of the world's archaeological heritage. It is of course hard to imagine inscribing such a warning on the walls of the gallery along with the names of those whose donations made the place possible; such a warning would seem churlish, at best. But if we are not ready to inscribe such warnings on the walls of the world's art galleries, then our educational message is discordant. We are saying that it is OK, in fact admirable, for rich people to collect pothunted artifacts and donate them to museums, but it is not OK for destitute Costa Ricans or St. Lawrence Islanders to pothunt them or for middle-class artifact dealers in Ohio to trade in them.

## THE "ESTABLISHED COLLECTIONS" DEFENSE

I know the classic response. Dr. Sackler bought and sold artifacts from "established collections;" presumably the drinking vessels and pots I admired in the gallery were dug up years, even centuries ago, and have been moving around from collection to collection ever since. Therefore, they are thought to be in a different category from the artifacts that are being dug up today. Presumably it is this theory that allowed *Archaeology,* in the same issue that included Ellen Herscher's article (1989), to run an advertisement for a sale of "folk, ethnic, and tribal arts" that included precolumbian artifacts discretely identified as "pre-1940."

The "established collections" defense reminds me of the response I got from a teenager recently when I suggested that as an animal lover, she ought not show the enthusiasm she does for fur coats. She saw no conflict in her values because, of course, the animals from which the furs came were already dead.

Even if all museums were honest and consistent in their application of the "established collections" policy — and, of course, one can hardly assume that they are (cf. Nagin 1986) — it seems to me as inevitable as the law of supply and demand that as the established collections move into the museums, those wanting to establish new ones will have to look elsewhere. That they do look elsewhere is manifest in the worldwide increase in pothunting. I am not necessarily saying that the "established collections" policy causes pothunting, but I do think that it does little or nothing to discourage it.

## WHAT CAN BE DONE?

Senator Pete Domenici, in his opening statement at a U.S. Senate hearing on pothunting in September 1988, expressed the belief that "...there is no cure for the problem" (see Domenici, this volume, for a discussion of his efforts to protect archaeological sites). I do not want to be that pessimistic; I think there are cures, or at least effective treatments.

I think we need to recognize, first, that there are at least two kinds of pothunters abroad in the world. One of these is the individual who digs and collects for his or her own enjoyment, deriving from the practice many of the same pleasures that archaeologists derive: the joy of discovery, the challenge of figuring out what happened in the past, the aesthetic pleasure of experiencing a beautiful object long lost to sight, the plain enjoyment of hard work in the outdoors. The other is the person who is in the work for the money either because he or she has little or no choice (like the St. Lawrence Islanders) or because it is easier or more fun or more remunerative than other available lines of work.

The two kinds of pothunters need to be dealt with in distinct ways. The first kind is a good target for education, but our educational campaigns should be "soft sells" designed to win people over to the cause of archaeology, not to excoriate them about the evils of pothunting. More importantly, such campaigns must be accompanied by the development of responsible ways for people to exercise their archaeological interests, through avocational organizations, participation in professional projects, and so on. Every federal agency that sponsors archaeological work in order to meet its responsibilities under the environmental and historic preservation laws should establish systems to ensure maximum public participation in such work. Federal land management agencies, whose relations with local communities are intimate and ongoing, should provide ongoing support to avocational archaeological organizations and other outlets for popular enthusiasm about archaeology.

There is nothing especially radical about the suggestions offered above; indeed, avocational programs are blossoming in many parts of the country (see Davis, this volume), as are public participatory programs sponsored by museums, research centers, and nonprofit organizations. More and more federal and state agencies are beginning to support such programs, albeit often only quietly and informally, uncertain about how such support relates to agency missions and about how to undertake them within the context of their legal responsibilities and procurement practices. These uncertainties can be addressed; the problem of the "casual" pothunter can be handled.

Treating the problem of the commercial pothunter, on the other hand, requires more drastic measures. With apologies to Michail Gorbachev, it requires *perestroika* — radical restructuring of our approaches to the matter.

In a nutshell, neither police action nor education is going to affect the commercial pothunter much. There will never be enough police or attorneys to address the problem, and in any event, much commercial pothunting is perfectly legal as long as it is carried out on nonfederal, non-Indian lands in the U.S., or in nations without comprehensive antilooting statutes. Education is not going to work because major collectors classify themselves, and are widely perceived to be, in a class with Dr. Sackler; the sales houses, like Sotheby's, that cater to them are similarly perceived, and the diggers who supply the sales houses don't give a damn.

To get at the commercial pothunter, it is necessary to coopt the market. To coopt the market, we have to participate in it, and to do this, we must get over the idea that it is wrong for a private individual to own and hold artifacts.

## CONCLUSION

I propose that the archaeological community and its allies in the executive and legislative branches of the U.S. Government initiate a dialogue with the communities of art and artifact collectors and suppliers, aimed at reaching agreement on what kinds of artifacts should and should not be held by private parties. Generally speaking, I propose that we should seek agreement that it is appropriate for private parties to own artifacts that have been excavated or otherwise acquired using appropriate archaeological methods, from public or private lands, in the U.S. and elsewhere, particularly if the sites from which such artifacts are recovered are threatened with destruction. Conversely, we should regard it as inappropriate for private parties to own artifacts that have been recovered in any other way, with provision for "grandfathering" old collections. We should then modify statutes like ARPA and the U.S. Tax Code to accommodate this agreement, and set about supplying the legitimate artifact market with artifacts from existing and newly acquired collections.

Would this work? Probably not entirely, but I think it could go a long way toward solving the problem. If dealers in antiquities, when deciding whether to acquire an artifact, asked "where is the documentation showing that this piece is the product of a proper archaeological project?" rather than "now, this wasn't acquired from federal land or in contravention of the UNESCO convention, was it?" I believe that the tilt of the field on which the pothunter/archaeologist game is played would be altered considerably. Can we do it? We can't know if we don't try. Is it too radical for the archaeological community to accept? I don't know; are we so set in our ways, so rigid in our ideological orthodoxy that we are less able to accept *perestroika* than are the communist parties of Eastern Europe and the Soviet Union? I certainly hope not.

## REFERENCES CITED

**Adams, R.** (1986) Rio Azul, *Natl. Geogr.,* 169(4), 420–450.

**Alva, W.** (1988) Discovering the New World's richest unlooted tomb, *Natl. Geogr.,* 174(4), 510–550.

**Arden, H.** (1989) Who owns the past? *Natl. Geogr.,* 175(3), 376-393.

Bureau of Land Management (1985) San Juan Resource Management Plan: management situation analysis. San Juan Resource Area, Moab District, Moab, Utah.

**Brooks, A.** (1989) Personal communication. South Dakota State Historical Preservation Center, Vermillion, SD.

**Decker, A.** (1989) Digging for dollars, *Art Auction,* March 1989, 142–147.

**Domenici, P.** (1988) Statement of the Honorable Pete V. Domenici, U.S. Senator from New Mexico. In Hearing Before the subcommittee on Public Lands, National Parks and Forests of the Committee on Energy and Natural Resources, United States Senate. Senate Hearing 100-943:23, U.S. Government Printing Office, Washington, D.C.

General Accounting Office (1987) Cultural resources: problems protecting and preserving federal archaeological resources, GAO/RCED-88-3, General Accounting Office, Washington, D.C.

**Herscher, E.** (1989) A future in ruins, *Archaeology,* January/February 1989, 67–70.

**Kandell, J.** (1988) How grave looter at a mexican site drools over relics, *Wall Street Journal, (New York),* pp. 1, 25, September 8, 1988.

**Lasagna, L.** (1987) Untitled tribute to Dr. Arthur Sackler, *Studio,* 200 (Suppl. 1), 20.

**Lederberg, J.** (1987) Eulogy to Dr. Arthur Sackler, delivered in the Sackler Wing of the Metropolitan Museum of Art, New York, June 17, 1987, *Studio,* 200 (Suppl. 1), 35.

**Mayer, J.** (1987) Eulogy to Dr. Arthur Sackler, delivered in the Sackler Wing of the Metropolitan Museum of Art, New York, June 17, 1987, *Studio,* 200 (Suppl. 1), 31.

**Nagin, C.** (1986) Patrons of plunder, *Boston Rev.,* August, 1986, 5–25.

National Park Service (1989) Fiscal year 1990 budget briefing statement, Ms, National Park Service, Washington, D.C.

**Pauling, L.** (1987) Untitled tribute to Dr. Arthur Sackler, *Studio,* 200 (Suppl. 1), 21.

**Press, F.** (1987) Eulogy to Dr. Arthur Sackler, delivered in the Sackler Wing of the Metropolitan Museum of Art, New York, June 17, 1987, *Studio,* 200 (Suppl. 1), 34–35.

**Spano, J.** (1988) U.S. works to stem flow of contraband artifacts, *Los Angeles Times,* pp. 3, 43, October 23, 1988.

**Spens, M.** (1987) Introduction: Dr. Arthur M Sackler special issue, *Studio,* 200 (Suppl. 1), 10–13.

**Stille, A.** (1988) Was this statue stolen? *Natl. Law J.,* 11(10), 1-3.

Subcommittee on General Oversight and Investigations (1988) The destruction of America's archaeological heritage: looting and vandalism of Indian archaeological sites in the Four Corners States of the Southwest, unpublished investigative report, Subcommittee on General Oversight and Investigations, Committee on Interior and Insular Affairs, U.S. House of Representatives, 100th Congress, Second Session, February 1988.

**Trahant, M. M.** (1987) Ancient mummy is more than evidence, Indians say. *Arizona Republic,* pp. B1–2, November 19, 1987.

United States Information Agency (1988) Facts on U.S. implementation of UNESCO Convention on the Means of Prohibiting and Preventing the Illicit Import, Export and Transfer of Ownership of Cultural Property. Fact sheet provided by Cultural Property Staff (E/B), USIA, Washington, D.C.

**Wen Z.** (1987) In memory of Dr. Arthur M. Sackler, *Studio,* 200, 83.

# LOOTING AND VANDALISM OF ARCHAEOLOGICAL RESOURCES ON FEDERAL AND INDIAN LANDS IN THE UNITED STATES

## Martin E. McAllister

## INTRODUCTION

The prehistoric and historic archaeological resources on federal and Indian lands throughout the U.S. comprise a large portion of this country's publicly owned national heritage. Tragically, they are being looted and vandalized at an alarming rate with each passing year. If this pattern of destruction is not substantially reduced in the near future, whole categories of the more impressive archaeological resource sites formerly present on federal and Indian lands soon will cease to exist, and many others will survive only as heavily damaged remnants of what they originally were. A large portion of the artifacts and other materials of interest the sites once contained also will be lost, and their potential to yield information about past human behavior will be greatly diminished (see Nickens, this volume, for further discussion of the destructive processes that lead to the loss of archeological data).

This article will deal with four aspects of the archaeological looting and vandalism problem on federal and Indian lands. Through reference to recent National Park Service (1989a, 1989b) and General Accounting Office (1987) findings, the magnitude of the current situation will be reviewed briefly, as will federal and tribal enforcement efforts. The remainder of the article is devoted to the situational context of looting and vandalism on federal and Indian lands and the behavior associated with these activities: topics that are currently addressed in only a few other studies (e.g., Nickens et al. 1981; Gramann and Vander Stoep 1986, 1987; Vander Stoep and Gramann 1987; McAllister 1988).

## THE CURRENT MAGNITUDE OF THE PROBLEM

Statistics assembled annually by the Archeological Assistance Division of the National Park Service, for fiscal years 1985 through 1987, show that the number of incidents of archaeological looting and vandalism reported by federal land managing agencies nationwide, including the Bureau of Indian Affairs, was 1720, and it is estimated that this figure may represent as little as 25% or less of the actual total (1989a:1–2; 1989b:chap. 5:3). These statistics also reveal a 51% rise in documented incidents over the 3-year period. Some of this increase is due to improved reporting, but unfortunately, it is obvious that rather than decreasing, the overall frequency of looting and vandalism on federal and Indian lands continues to grow. In addition, in the recent regional study of this problem conducted for Congress by the General Accounting Office, it was found that an estimated 32% of the known sites on National Park Service, Bureau of Land Management, and Forest Service lands in the Southwest are already damaged by looting and vandalism, and another 33% are in an unknown condition and potentially also affected (1987:22). These figures should force all those concerned with protecting the nation's archaeological resources to analyze the nature of the looting and vandalism problem (see King, this volume, for additional discussion of the magnitude of the looting problem).

# RECENT ENFORCEMENT EFFORTS

Recent federal and tribal law enforcement efforts to combat archaeological looting and vandalism have been only partially successful (see McManamon, this volume, for a discussion of federal efforts, and Anyon, this volume, for a discussion of tribal efforts. Also see Rogers, this volume, for a discussion of model tribal laws). The National Park Service statistics for fiscal years 1985 through 1987 show that only 183, or approximately 11%, of the 1720 incidents reported by federal land managing agencies resulted in arrests or citations (1989a:10–16; 1989b:chap. 5:3). Some would consider this to be a low enforcement rate, especially since the documented incidents probably represent only a fraction of those actually occurring. These statistics also show that there were at least 94 convictions under the Archaeological Resources Protection Act (ARPA) and other laws and regulations during this period, so the record for prosecuting the looters and vandals apprehended is good (approximately 51%).

It is interesting to note that between 1985 and 1987, there were more prosecutions of looters and vandals under other laws and regulations than under ARPA (National Park Service 1989a:10–16; 1989b:chap. 5:3). Also surprising was the fact that there was not a felony conviction by a jury in an ARPA case until November of 1987 *(U.S. vs. Cortiana)*. This situation probably was due to a continuing lack of familiarity with ARPA vs. other commonly used means of prosecution and also to weaknesses in the law, which now apparently have been rectified by the 1988 amendments (see Cheek, Neumann, and Rogers, this volume, for discussions of the 1988 ARPA amendments).

The statistics presented here can be interpreted either positively or negatively in assessing the effectiveness of recent federal and tribal law enforcement efforts to combat archaeological looting and vandalism. They certainly represent a significant advance over the meager record of success achieved with the Antiquities Act in the years between 1906 and 1979. (According to currently available information, there were fewer than 20 cases in which charges against looters and vandals were filed under the Antiquities Act during this 73-year period). Regardless of how these statistics are viewed, there is obviously a need for increased levels of enforcement until the number of violations occurring now can be substantially reduced through both enforcement and other deterrents. Truly effective deterrence of archaeological looting and vandalism will require a greater understanding of why and how these acts occur.

# THE SITUATIONAL CONTEXT OF ARCHAEOLOGICAL LOOTING AND VANDALISM

Four unfortunate situations contribute significantly to creating the archaeological looting and vandalism problem that exists in this country. Together they make effective solutions much more difficult than would otherwise be the case. Sadly, it is unlikely that any of these situations will change to any great degree in the future.

Of major importance is the proprietary status of archeological resources on private land in the U.S. Unlike most other countries in the world, where archaeological resources are public property wherever they are found, our cultural heritage belongs to the land owner, when located on private property. Consequently, the removal or destruction of archaeological resources on private property by the owner, or with their permission, is not generally illegal except when specific items, such as human graves, are protected by federal, state, or local law. Of course, looters and vandals may be aware of this fact, and many rationalize their actions by the logic that what is legal on private property also should be legal on federal and Indian lands. Moreover, if apprehended on these lands, they may claim they thought it was private property.

Because archaeological resources may be privately owned, possession of prehistoric and historic materials also is not prohibited, providing that they were legally obtained. The only exception to this rule is the National Park Service regulation that makes possession of any such items illegal within the boundaries of National Parks. Elsewhere on federal or Indian lands, looters and dealers found with archaeological materials may state that they came from private property regardless of their actual origin.

A related problem is the difficulty of determining where archaeological materials came from once they are removed from that location. These materials generally have no inherent characteristics that can be used to definitely identify where they were originally discovered. Obviously then, when looters are found with items in their possession that are suspected to be from federal or Indian lands, it is difficult to prove this fact unless they were observed removing them or admit to having done so. This makes the prosecution of looters and dealers difficult or impossible in many cases.

Finally, it is also unfortunate that there is no law in the U.S. prohibiting the sale of archaeological materials or at least those not proven to be obtained legally from private land. ARPA makes it illegal to traffic in artifacts and other protected items removed without authorization from federal or Indian lands, but as has been noted, establishing that they came from such lands may be difficult or impossible. It is unlikely that most dealers ask looters if they operate legally, and when they do, the answer received often may not be true. A law prohibiting the sale of all archaeological materials, or those without proper documentation, would be countered with an active black market trade, but would make enforcement easier.

## LOOTING AND VANDALISM BEHAVIOR

The most reliable information currently available on looting and vandalism behavior on federal and Indian lands is statistical data on violations, which can be generated from sources such as the LOOT Clearinghouse, a computerized archival data base maintained by the Archeological Assistance Division of the National Park Service (see Knoll, this volume, for a discussion of the LOOT Clearinghouse). As valuable as these data are, they can be used primarily only to identify basic patterns in the occurrence of looting and vandalism, such as what types of sites are most commonly targeted. They are less useful in analyzing why such behavior exists.

Except for a few regional studies (e.g., Nickens et al. 1981:81–127, 165–168), true behavioral research dealing specifically with archaeological looting and vandalism has been almost totally neglected until very recently. Fortunately, sociologists with expertise on vandalism affecting other types of resources are now beginning to analyze the archaeological problem, but widely applicable findings on the participants and their roles in this behavior are still in the future. Some observations, based on long experience with archaeological looting and vandalism, are presented here, but should be regarded as very basic and subject to extensive refinement as the necessary behavioral research begins to be accomplished.

Probably the most perplexing aspect of the problem for those entrusted with the protection of archaeological resources is wanton vandalism carried out for the intrinsic purpose of destroying these remains. This senseless destruction occurs in a wide variety of forms, but there are several common types. Rock art and other types of resources are regularly attacked by graffiti, shooting, and other forms of defacement. Structural remains at prehistoric and historic sites, such as walls and roofs, are frequently torn down or otherwise intentionally damaged. Four-wheel-drive vehicles, motorcycles, and other all-terrain vehicles are often deliberately driven over and through archaeological sites, permanently scarring or destroying them.

Unlike vandalism, the basic motivations for looting and collecting archaeological materials are more obvious. This behavior is caused by the widespread fascination with the past and the resulting desire to possess objects from earlier time periods, which many people experience. Clearly, there would be no looting and collecting of archaeological materials if no one were interested in them. It is ironic that the fascination with the past, which motivates all positive public behavior toward archaeological resources, also causes so much damage and destruction.

Deriving from the desire to possess physical remains of the past are the monetary values that have come to be associated with certain types of archaeological materials. Even relatively common artifacts, such as prehistoric projectile points and Civil War minie balls, are sought after and have value, though they usually sell for only a few dollars apiece. On the other hand, rare or exotic types of archaeological materials are often offered for sale for astronomical prices, and some collectors appraise the worth of their collections in the millions of dollars. These dollar values obviously induce some looters to attack archaeological sites, searching for the types of items that bring high prices.

The most numerous participants in looting behavior are those identified as "hobbyist" looters, who remove artifacts and other materials from archaeological sites primarily because of personal interest in the past and the desire to start or enhance their own collections. This group encompasses a wide variety of individuals, from one-time looters to avid devotees, many of whom have some particular type of interest, such as surface arrowhead collecting or metal detecting at Civil War battlefields. The more active participants view their behavior as a legitimate hobby and participate openly in well-organized clubs or associations, many of which publish newsletters and journals.

The other major group engaging in looting behavior are individuals referred to as "commercial" looters, who systematically remove artifacts and other materials from archaeological resource sites specifically for the purpose of profiting from their sale in the market that exists for these items. Some percentage started their careers as hobbyist looters, but monetary gain has replaced interest as the primary motivating factor. There are, in fact, individuals in the U.S. today who are full-time commercial looters and many others who substantially supplement their regular sources of income by this activity. The profit potential of commercial looting is indicated not only by the monetary values of collectible items, but also by the types of expensive equipment in use, including earth-moving machinery, all-terrain vehicles, helicopters, fixed wing aircraft, large ocean-going dive boats, and sophisticated terrestrial and underwater metal detectors.

Relative to the hobbyists, the commercially motivated individuals are a small, clandestine group who, by their own admissions, acknowledge that they intentionally and illegally loot archaeological sites on federal and Indian lands. Their knowledge that they are breaking the law is demonstrated by the fact that they often employ antidetection and alarm strategies, such as camouflage clothing, concealment of vehicles away from site locations, night time and other off-hour activities, and the use of radio scanners and lookouts. In addition, many are considered to be dangerous because they are likely be armed, and some have openly threatened to resist arrest.

Hobbyist looters commonly attempt to rationalize their activities by claiming that they do much less harm than commercial looters. It is true that in many parts of the country, commercially motivated individuals have heavily impacted the types of sites known to contain valuable items, and should continue to be seen as a major threat to archaeological resources. Certainly, a commercial looter systematically ravaging a site with a bulldozer or a back hoe will do more damage than someone surface collecting or digging with a garden trowel or a shovel. Quantitatively, however, their numbers are far lower than those in the ranks of the hobbyist looters, and always have been. Only a few people have the time, equipment, and personal inclination it takes to make all or a large part of their income looting archaeological sites for profit, while many collect artifacts as a hobby. In addition, sites containing desirable archaeological materials are frequently targeted repeatedly by large numbers of hobbyists, and they often seriously damage or completely destroy them by digging with tools or simply by surface collecting, especially when only surface remains are present. Both the sheer force of their numbers and the intensity of their activities cause the cumulative effect of hobbyist looting to be one of the most destructive factors affecting archaeological resources in the U.S. today. Also, as they become more actively involved in this pastime, some hobbyists begin to alter their status by participating in the buying and selling of collectible items, and some eventually become true commercial looters.

Another important role in the commercial aspect of looting and collecting behavior is occupied by a wide range of dealers who act as middlemen, buying and selling marketable items for a profit. The most sophisticated dealers operate large, very lucrative businesses with galleries or showrooms in major cities, resorts, and art centers, and often are involved in both the domestic and international trade in archeological materials. It has been reported that some higher level dealers actually employ commercial looters to obtain sought-after items. At the other end of the spectrum are part-time dealers in small towns or rural areas who buy and sell out of their homes or vehicles and also may be looting sites themselves.

There is also a cadre of what can be called support specialists, who provide technical assistance to looters, dealers, and collectors. Some individuals with backgrounds in art history and related fields have become experts in determining the commercial worth of prehistoric and historic items and are employed by dealers and collectors as consultants. Others are paid for their expertise in restoring damaged artifacts. Unfortunately, a few individuals with formal archaeological training, sometimes referred to as "rogue" archaeologists, have been known to work for looters and dealers. They help locate, remove, and sell collectible items, and serve as defense expert witnesses when the need arises. In some western states, at least, certain attorneys are recognized authorities in the area of defending accused violators of archaeological protection statutes. Also, there are a number of publishers who specialize in producing and distributing newsletters, magazines, and books that provide information on looting and collecting archaeological material. Others who intentionally or unintentionally fall into this category are those who supply equipment or services that aid looters, such as metal detector manufactures and dealers, charter dive-boat owners and operators, and outfitter guides. Of course, there may be other as yet unidentified specialists who are also involved.

Collectors of various types make up the final major group in this behavioral complex and are certainly one of the most important factors, since they create the demand for artifacts and other archaeological materials in the first place. One obvious and significant group of collectors is comprised of hobbyist looters whose basic motivation for removing items from sites is to add them to their personal collections. Another category consists of the commercial faction, the looters, dealers, and their support specialists, who are primarily interested in archaeological materials from a profit standpoint, but also often have personal collections of highly prized pieces that they do not wish to sell. A third important group can be referred to as the "pure" collectors, who find prehistoric and historic objects appealing and possess them out of interest, but will only add to their collections by purchasing from dealers or looters because they have no inclination to become directly involved in site looting. Also, there are individuals who are not particularly attracted to archaeological materials for aesthetic reasons, but buy and hold them mainly for investment purposes due to their strong potential to increase in value over time.

| | | | |
|---|---|---|---|
| DEMAND | —> | COLLECTORS | —> | HOBBYIST LOOTERS<br>COMMERCIAL LOOTERS<br>DEALERS<br>SUPPORT SPECIALISTS<br>"PURE" COLLECTORS<br>INVESTORS<br>EXHIBIT OWNERS |
| MIDDLEMEN<br>AND<br>SUPPORT | —> | DEALERS<br>AND<br>SPECIALISTS | —> | LOW TO HIGH LEVEL<br> DEALERS<br>APPRAISERS<br>RESTORATION EXPERTS<br>"ROGUE" ARCHAEOLO-<br> GISTS<br>DEFENSE ATTORNEYS<br>PUBLISHERS<br>EQUIPMENT/SERVICE<br> SUPPLIERS |
| SUPPLY | —> | PROCURERS | —> | COMMERCIAL LOOTERS<br>AND<br>HOBBYIST LOOTERS |

FIGURE 1.    Roles in the archaeological looting and collecting network.

Similarly, owners of so-called private museums, where large collections of looted materials may be exhibited to the public for an admission fee, often seek to obtain additional items in order to enhance their business.

The fact that hobbyist looters as well as many members of the commercial interest faction are also collectors demonstrates that any one individual may play more than one role in this behavior. As is shown in the diagram of the network in Figure 1, some are, for example, simultaneously hobbyists, commercial looters, dealers, and collectors. In reality, the badly needed behavioral research on this problem undoubtedly will show that the roles and patterns of interaction in archaeological looting and collecting are much more complex than we currently know.

## CONCLUSION

Until we understand more about the why and how of archaeological looting and vandalism, efforts to deal with the current problem on federal and Indian lands will remain less effective than they can be. Therefore, research on this behavior should have the highest possible priority. This is especially true, since it seems very unlikely that we will ever totally eliminate looting and vandalism behavior by substantially changing the basic situational context in which it exists. We may eventually develop new techniques that will allow us to determine more precisely where stolen archaeological materials were originally found, but it is highly improbable that we would succeed in attempts to pass laws establishing public ownership of all archaeological resources in the U.S. and prohibiting possession, buying, and selling of archeological materials.

Improved understanding of the problem will produce a more successful law enforcement response to active looters and vandals, which in turn will have a greater deterrent effect on would-be violators. Also, it will allow us to develop new and better approaches to archaeological public education and involvement programs that have the potential to prevent looting and vandalism before these acts occur. The future survival of many important archaeological resources on federal and Indian lands is dependent on significant progress in these areas in the near future.

## REFERENCES CITED

**Gramann, J.H. and G.A. Vander Stoep** (1986) *Reducing Depreciative Behavior at Shiloh National Military Park.* Technical Report No. 2. National Park Service Cooperative Park Studies Unit, Texas A&M University, College Station, Texas.

**Gramann, J.H. and G.A. Vander Stoep** (1987) Prosocial Behavior Theory and Natural Resource Protection: A Conceptual Synthesis. *Journal of Environmental Management* 24:247.

**McAllister, M.E.** (1988) Areas and Issues in Future Research on Archaeological Resource Protection. In *Tools to Manage the Past: Research Priorities for Cultural Resources Management in the Southwest.* Eds. J.A. Tainter and R.H. Hamre, U.S. Department of Agriculture, Forest Service, Rocky Mountain Forest and Range Experiment Station, Ft. Collins, Colorado.

National Park Service (1989a) *Briefing statement.* Department of the Interior, National Park Service, Archeological Assistance Division, Washington, D.C.

National Park Service (1989b) *Federal Archeology: The Current Program, Annual Report to Congress on the Federal Archeology Program, FY 1985 and FY 1986.* Department of the Interior, National Park Service, Archeological Assistance Division, Washington, D.C.

**Nickens, P.R., Larralde, S.L., and Tucker, G.C. Jr.** (1981) *A Survey of Vandalism to Archaeological Resources in Southwestern Colorado.* Cultural Resources Series No. 11. Bureau of Land Management, Colorado State Office, Denver, Colorado.

United States General Accounting Office (1987) *Report to Congressional Requesters, Cultural Resources: Problems Protecting and Preserving Federal Archeological Resources.* RCED-88-3. General Accounting Office, Washington, D.C.

**Vander Stoep, G.A. and Gramann, J.H.** (1987) The Effect of Verbal Appeals and Incentives on Depreciative Behavior Among Youthful Park Visitors. *Journal of Leisure Research* 19:69.

# Chapter 4

## PROTECTING ARCHAEOLOGICAL SITES THROUGH EDUCATION

"There is an undefined expectation in American society that once a problem is defined, no matter how, and understood by a significant number of people who have some relation to the problem, there is no problem any more." (Vine Deloria, Jr. 1969)

# SAVING SITES: PRESERVATION AND EDUCATION

Shereen Lerner

# INTRODUCTION

The term "archaeology" connotes different images and meanings to different people. Some people think archaeologists study rocks; others conjure up images of King Tut, Indiana Jones, and the romanticism of archaeology as a glorified science with a "thrill of discovery." Somehow a middle ground between these two images must be found to explain that archaeology includes everything from the study of rocks (lithics and groundstone, for example) to the discovery and excavation of ancient cities, temples, and shrines. One of the most rewarding exercises an archaeologist, as educator, can undertake is to introduce a novice to the archaeological experience for the first time. Be it through a lecture or actual fieldwork, the reaction is often the same: one of interest and excitement in discovery. It is said that archaeology can be equated to assembling a puzzle where some of the pieces may always be missing, thus requiring conjecture on the part of the scientist. It is piecing together the puzzle of past lives that is exciting, and bringing that excitement to the public is part of our mission in preservation and education.

Preservation of the past is accomplished not only by saving the physical remnants of previous cultures, but also through education of the value of learning about the past. People have an inherent curiosity about the past; in 1980 a National Park Service study on tourism found that visiting historic sites was the third most-cited reason people travel, following only visits to family and friends. In Arizona, archaeological parks such as Walnut Canyon, Wupatki, and Canyon de Chelly achieve high rates of visitation year after year. In Europe, tourism is focused on historic towns, churches, and other noteworthy sites; such places are considered primary reasons people choose to travel to European countries.

Reaching people and educating them about archaeology, preservation, and the past means trying to address some of these ideas about the past. Programs should be designed to foster a preservation ethic and inform the public of the value of archaeology as a science. We, as educators, must try to reinforce the preservation ethic in a positive way. First, we must determine the message(s) we are trying to convey. At a recent workshop ("Save the Past for the Future") on preventing vandalism of archaeological sites, the participants considered what we are trying to convey to the public through education, volunteer, and public outreach programs. The messages that we are trying to convey to the public are

1. Cultural resources are a nonrenewable and irreplaceable part of the heritage of all Americans.
2. Cultural resources can provide us with a unique sense of who we are as human beings and how we have come to be what we are today.
3. The study of cultural resources can be an adventure in discovery, providing educational opportunities and enhancing participants' quality of life.
4. The proper study of cultural resources can show us how we have affected, and have been affected by, our environment. Such lessons from the past may help us solve contemporary environmental problems.
5. Archaeologists can unlock the stories behind the artifacts for all of us to enjoy, and help us learn about other people, places, and times.

(See Reinburg, Judge, this volume, for discussion of the SAA's "Save the Past for the Future" project and the Taos Conference.)

## EDUCATION AS AN OPPORTUNITY

Education programs are currently used to teach an awareness of, and respect for, the past and to explain the importance of archaeological research and what archaeology and cultural resources can give to the public. These programs may be broken into a formal classroom style approach and one that targets particular groups. In this regard, there are a number of different types of educational programs that can be made available to both the young and old.

With regard to formal education, it appears that most educational programs in the school systems mandate history units between grades 4 and 8, thus providing a "window of opportunity" to address preservation issues. Programs such as summer field schools that teach field techniques and laboratory work and address theoretical issues are an excellent opportunity for hands-on application by the student. Incorporating archaeology directly into the school curriculum, whether as a separate unit or as part of an already existing topic (e.g., art history, history, social studies) is an approach taken by many. Curriculum guides have been developed that provide teachers with educational materials appropriate for the classroom, lesson plans, slide programs, and activities that can be used in the classroom. Workshops to train teachers are currently being conducted throughout the country by archaeologists and educators, to provide teachers with this newly developed information (Rogge and Bell 1989; also see McNutt, Hawkins, and Rogge, this volume, for further discussion of school curriculum). The Toronto public school system has hired archaeologists to work within the system, developing curricula and hands-on opportunities (see Smartz, this volume, for a discussion of the Toronto program). Coordinating with groups with related interests, such as environmental education, is also important. "Camp Cooper, Arizona; Archaeology is More than a Dig" (Shurban 1989) provides in-service teacher training, classroom materials, field camps, and participatory archaeology, integrated into an environmental curriculum. In Arizona recent legislation to fund an environmental education program came about as the result of the efforts of groups involved in both natural and cultural environmental issues.

While there are a number of excellent programs being used to disseminate archaeological information through public school systems, they have evolved with little coordination and direction. Currently, there is no nationally recognized mechanism for the exchange of information and ideas, and no guidance in the development of minimum standards for education programs. At present, there is little or no data available on the effectiveness of these programs, and process and outcome measures are significantly lacking. It is important that we establish a national clearinghouse for the exchange of information on program and curriculum development (see Knoll, this volume, for a discussion of a national clearinghouse for archaeology education: LEAP). Such a center would also enhance communication among educators. Finally, programs should be evaluated for their effectiveness, and results compared to those of other environmental programs. Such an evaluation will require consensus on desired outcomes and agreement on program goals and objectives.

Public education programs can be effectively used to take archaeology beyond the classroom by targeting special interest groups with activities and programs tailored to fit their needs, interests, and schedules. For example, senior citizens are often an excellent source for volunteers and can be reached via lecture series and special programs; service groups can both participate in preservation activities and may also be a source of project funds, when educated about preservation. Owners of archaeological sites may be enlisted to protect and preserve sites, while art museums can educate the public on the value of the artifact as both art object and source of information, and recreation groups can protect the cultural resources while they enjoy the natural areas and outdoor experience. Finally, legislators can play a major role through development of the legal framework to increase awareness and enhance preservation, and by committing funds directly and indirectly for both preservation and education (see Neumann, this volume, for a discussion of legislative involvement in archaeological site protection). There are numerous other special interest groups who can be reached through various educational programs, and efforts should be made to develop creative approaches to bringing the message of preservation to them.

## VOLUNTEERISM IN ARCHAEOLOGY

Volunteer programs are often used to provide a means for the public to enjoy archaeology, learn about the past, increase public awareness of cultural resource values, and change attitudes toward preservation as a goal. Volunteers are highly divergent in their interests and levels of experience; therefore, volunteerism messages and opportunities that are offered vary, depending on the group or organization being targeted. Through a variety of public programs, it is possible to build support in the general population to foster the preservation ethic. There are several excellent and creative programs now in existence that could be enhanced to increase membership and interest in archaeology.

The site steward program (Pilles 1989; also see Hoffman, this volume) consists of statewide networks of citizen volunteers who monitor archaeological sites on lands of all participating jurisdictions. In essence, these volunteers are used to safeguard and help preserve significant cultural resources. Presently, only six programs have been identified worldwide: in Saskatchewan, Ontario, Australia, British Columbia, Texas, and Arizona. In Arizona, the largest of these programs, volunteers are certified as stewards upon completion of an orientation program and function under volunteer agreements signed with each agency upon whose lands they work. The program includes a statewide coordinator, 22 regional coordinators, and more than 300 stewards, all of whom are volunteers. For the most part, stewards are not professional archaeologists, but citizens who have an appreciation and respect for heritage values. As a result of the efforts by the stewards, more than 250 archaeological sites are inspected on a regular basis. The program recently received the 1990 Governor's Award for Historic Preservation and has been highlighted on both the national and state level as an example of volunteerism in action.

Avocational archaeological societies are organizations that provide interested citizens the opportunity to learn about and participate in archaeology at their own pace and in accordance with their own schedules. These societies range in size and scope from loosely organized local clubs to state societies. Many enforce a code of ethics, and some have well-organized certification programs to train members in archaeological techniques and procedures. Certification programs exist in more than a dozen states, and all are designed to improve the competence of their members and volunteers. Such organizations may conduct their own excavations of sites or provide a pool of trained volunteers to assist in surveys, excavations, or rock art recording, in cooperative arrangements with professional archaeologists and land management agencies (see Davis, this volume, for further discussion of avocational archaeological societies).

Museum docent programs offer public tours of museum exhibits and outreach programs in local schools. Docent programs, such as that of the University of New Mexico's Maxwell Museum, serve the dual purpose of instilling preservation values in volunteers who train to be docents and spreading awareness to the general public by providing a forum for docents to teach others. By emphasizing the importance of archaeological context and the concept of artifacts as carriers of information rather than objects of art, volunteer docents can make a significant contribution to preservation awareness.

There are other worthy programs that involve volunteers in participatory archaeology, notably Crow Canyon and Earthwatch (Hays 1989), where volunteers pay their own expenses (and sometimes an additional amount to cover salaries of professional supervisory personnel) to participate in an archaeological project such as excavation or rock art recording. Federal and state agencies also have encouraged public participation in archaeology, for many years. Volunteers have been used to perform a variety of cultural resource management activities, including field inventorying, site patrolling, site fencing, archival researching, working with oral history projects, developing interpretive materials, excavating, and stabilizing. The U.S. Forest Service "Passport in Time" program includes all aspects of heritage management and protection, while increasing awareness of, and providing opportunities for, the public to enjoy archaeology.

As with public education, there is currently no formal mechanism for evaluating the effectiveness of volunteer programs in increasing preservation values. However, judging from the strong participation enjoyed by most of these programs, it can be assumed that they are successful in stimulating interest in archaeology. As an alternative to classroom instruction, volunteer programs are an excellent means of demonstrating the difference between archaeology and collecting while providing an experience that is both enjoyable and educational.

## PUBLIC PROGRAMS

A third means to reach the public is through public archaeology programs that do not necessarily require any long-term commitment from the public. In essence, the public participates by responding to the events placed before them. Structuring these events to bring across the message of understanding and respecting heritage resource values, and to develop a sense of public responsibility to preserve archaeological resources, is key to success. Specific objectives of these programs include sharing the archaeological experience with the public and teaching an understanding and respect for other cultures, values, and diversity; for archaeological resources, values and techniques; and for the laws that protect these resources.

There are numerous examples of public programs that are currently used to bring archaeology into the public eye. "Archaeology Week" (Hoffman and Lerner 1988, 1989) now occurs in more than half a dozen states and is designed individually by each state to promote and publicize the positive side of archaeology. These celebrations usually include, in a concentrated time period, many of the activities discussed in this chapter. Such activities also occur year round at individual events and locations and are not exclusive to archaeology week celebrations. Living history and demonstrations on prehistoric technology and life are extremely popular with adults and children who enjoy "reliving the past." Tours of archaeological sites, which range from 30 minutes to several hours, as well as those that are commercially organized and may last for several weeks and visit numerous sites, certainly bring the resource closer to the public. In this regard, open houses by museums and laboratories are valuable in bringing the public "behind the scenes" to view archaeologists in action, opening previously restricted collections for viewing, and providing opportunities to learn about the preservation of the artifact as part of a culture. Hands-on workshops, including such activities as stringing corn and seed necklaces or making canteens and pouches from gourds, give people the opportunity to recreate the past for themselves. Traveling exhibits are another means to bring archaeology to the public. Exhibits are specifically designed to illustrate some aspect of archaeology, ranging from artifacts to cultural history. They range from suitcase-size exhibits designed for classroom use to multimedia, gallery-size displays, such as the Tutankhamen exhibit.

A wide diversity of media-related activities have been used to communicate archaeology to the public. A recent incident in Arizona, where citizens banded together to halt construction on an archaeological site and burial ground, received sufficient media attention that it successfully increased public awareness of the lack of protection such sites currently have and resulted in public demand for legislative action to protect all sites and burial areas. Articles in periodicals that cater to special interest groups can be extremely beneficial in bringing the preservation ethic to the public. The incident at Slack Farm (Kentucky) that received national recognition as a result of the cover story in *National Geographic* increased public awareness of the problem of looting and vandalism of archaeological sites.

As with the other programs, there is, as yet, no mechanism in place to evaluate the effectiveness of public programs and media campaigns. It appears, however, that existing efforts have focused on educating the public about the past, rather than on messages of protecting the past, sharing the archaeological experience, or developing an understanding and respect for cultural values.

## CONCLUSION

Archaeology has traditionally viewed "informing the public about the past" as important, but not its primary goal. As a result, the objectives of developing understanding and respect for cultural resources and communicating archaeological values have not been effectively articulated nor brought to the public in a clear and accessible manner. Those currently being reached are people who are already sensitized to archaeology and who share its values; it is a self-selecting audience. There is a need to more effectively communicate these values to the majority of the American public.

In this regard, media-related activities have been more effective in communicating the preservation ethic than have most other public programs. The media can influence public attitudes, provide information on who people can contact if they wish to take an active interest, and provide an opportunity to recruit children and instill proper values before their attitudes become fixed. However, the media has not been used effectively, and the proper messages need to be brought to the public with regard to the preservation of archaeological sites, and the value that heritage resources bring to the general population (see Milanich, Bense, this volume, for further discussion concerning archaeology and the media).

By examining and evaluating the status of existing programs designed to bring archaeology to the public in an effort to foster the preservation ethic, it is apparent that virtually all efforts to communicate with the public have been done by individual archaeologists and at local or state levels. There is a need to create a single, coordinated effort to evaluate the success of these programs and to identify national strategies and objectives (see Harriman, this volume, for a discussion of a national strategy for archaeological programs in the Federal Government). The education process is a continuing one that can be molded for the audience, yet still provide an exciting and interesting experience for participants. Different experiences will foster differing images of archaeology and what it means to the public. The ethics of preservation cannot be easily taught, for there is no simple answer as to why it is important to prevent the further destruction of our nation's heritage resources. A positive approach in explaining the value of these resources, the information they provide, and the involvement of citizens in their preservation can instill this ethic. The more people gain from a positive experience of archaeology, the more likely they will be to ultimately embrace and support the goals of preservation.

## ACKNOWLEDGMENTS

I wish to thank the members of the "Preventing the Problem" workshop held during the "Save the Past for the Future" Conference. Many of the ideas presented in this article came as a result of discussions held during the workshop. Full responsibility for the contents of this article, however, rests with the author.

## REFERENCES CITED

Hays, K. (1989) Men, women and dirt: Earthwatch volunteers and the Homol'ovi research program. In *Fighting Indiana Jones in Arizona: Proc. 1988 American Soc. Conservation Archaeology*, Rogge, A. E., Ed., Portales, NM, 9–13.

Hoffman, T. L. and Lerner, S. (1988) Arizona Archaeology Week: promoting the past to the public. *Natl Park Ser. Tech. Bull. 2.*

Hoffman, T. L. and Lerner, S. (1989) Arizona Archaeology Week: promoting the past to the public. In *Fighting Indiana Jones in Arizona: Proc. 1988 American Soc. Conservation Archaeology*, Rogge, A. E., Ed., Portales, NM, 31–37.

Pilles, P. J., Jr. (1989) The Arizona Archaeology Advisory Commission and the Site Stewards Program. In *Fighting Indiana Jones in Arizona: Proc. 1988 American Soc. Conservation Archaeology*, Rogge, A. E., Ed., Portales, NM, 39–45.

Rogge, A. E. and Bell, P. (1989) Teaching teachers to teach *with* archaeology. In *Fighting Indiana Jones in Arizona: Proc. 1988 American Soc. Conservation Archaeology*, Rogge, A. E., Ed., Portales, NM, 69–74.

Shurban (1989) Archaeology is more than a dig. In *Fighting Indiana Jones in Arizona: Proc. 1988 American Soc. Conservation Archaeology*, Rogge, A. E., Ed., Portales, NM, 75–79.

# ARCHAEOLOGY IN THE SUNSHINE: GRASS ROOTS EDUCATION THROUGH THE MEDIA AND PUBLIC INVOLVEMENT

Jerald T. Milanich

*Who is she that looketh forth as the dawn,*
*Fair as the moon,*
*Clear as the sun,*
*Terrible as an army with banners?*
*(Song of Songs, 6:10)*

## INTRODUCTION: AN ARMY WITH BANNERS

It was Tuesday, May 19, 1987, and there was the headline on the front page of the *New York Times* science section: "De Soto's Trail: Courage and Cruelty Come Alive." Pulitzer Prize-winning journalist John Noble Wilford's article had as a subheading: "What may be the most important site found so far is under study in Florida." The half-page lead article, including a montage of graphics, was continued on page 3.

All in all, Wilford's story covered nearly a full page of the *New York Times*. It was distributed in regional editions across the U.S., where it was seen by more than a million people, including the governor and cabinet of the state of Florida, who were meeting that same morning to consider an emergency plan to initiate the purchase and preservation of a portion of the Governor Martin site (the native Apalachee Indian village of Anhaica where the de Soto expedition wintered in 1539–1540; the privately-owned site, discovered by B. Calvin Jones of the Florida Division of Historical Resources, was threated by imminent development; the Division's excavations at the site were featured in the *Times* story). On that Tuesday morning, I estimate that the number of people who read and learned about the Hernando de Soto expedition and the importance of archaeology in understanding our past was greater than all the people who will read everything I and my colleagues will ever write, teach, or say about the archaeology of Hernando de Soto.

## EDUCATION AND THE MEDIA

If archaeology is ever going to have the impact of "an army with banners," we must utilize the media and the public's interest in our research activities as an integral part of public education efforts. If the archaeological community is going to be successful in efforts to preserve archaeological sites, establish and maintain adequate levels of funding for resource management, and make known the archaeological viewpoints on creationism and the necessity for curation of systematic collections, we must take advantage of the public's interest in our discipline. Guidelines and statements issued by professional organizations, lapel buttons, and conferences with archaeologists talking to one another are not going to do the job, nor is publically emphasizing archaeological resource management and site protection as our primary goals.

Instead, we need to go to the public and tell them about our research. We need to bring our discipline and the information we are excavating out into the sunshine. The best ways to do this are through the media and in conjunction with activities that involve the public. As we learned from the de Soto *New York Times* article and other similar articles, a single story about archaeology on local television or in a local newspaper or magazine will reach tens of thousands of people; a story that goes national will reach millions.

Yes, we need to continue to publish our data and interpretations in our journals, and yes, we need to continue to lobby for archaeological resource management and to devise and refine our theories and methods of site management. But to be successful in these endeavors, we must attract and hold the public's attention, interest, and support. We need to take advantage of people's fascination with the past: something media professionals learned a long time ago. Archaeological stories sell newspapers and boost ratings. Archaeological stories can also sell archaeology, including resource management. However, before people can see the worth of protecting the past, the utility of archaeology for illuminating that past must be accepted. The American public must be aware of, and identify with, the non-Anglo history of human societies in the U.S.

How can an archaeologist who never took a course in public relations work with the media and the public to highlight archaeology? In this article I offer some methods and ideas that I and my colleagues in Florida have learned. Our skills in public relations are certainly not up to the standards of American politicians or corporations, but we are learning.

Most importantly, our efforts are paying dividends; archaeological research is booming in Florida, as is state-legislated funding. Working through the Florida Division of Historical Resources and with other state agencies, the archaeological community has been successful in pushing archaeological resource issues into the mainstream via laws and regulations. A number of significant sites have been purchased and are in public ownership. Some schools now have archaeological curricula, and at least some state officials see the utility of archaeology for helping build tourism in the state.

It is no accident that these efforts correlate with a half-decade-long media blitz. Over the last 5 years, newspapers have had a very large number of archaeology stories that related to specific Florida sites and topics (Windover, Fort Mose, San Luis, and other Spanish missions; Hernando de Soto contact sites; archaeology and developers; Warm Mineral Springs; Cutler Ridge; and various sites in southwest Florida, Pensacola, and St. Augustine, to name some that have been featured; see Bense, this volume, for a discussion of archaeology and the media in Pensacola, FL). Legislators and state officials have supported archaeology in Florida because they, too, read the papers.

## FAIR AS THE MOON

Many archaeologists, perhaps most, are loathe to allow members of the public to visit sites during excavations. They also often work to avoid publicity. Reporters, both newspaper and television people, might reveal a site's location, leading to vandalism, or they might report facts in a manner not to the archaeologist's liking. What the media sees as important — something often said to be "the oldest," "the first," or "the most important" ever found — is not necessarily what an archaeologist thinks is important (e.g., "our laboratory analysis is showing that 91% of the meat caloric intake is fish, not large mammal as previously surmised"). We can control graduate students and employees; we cannot control the media. Therefore, it is better to wait until the research is done, write our own press release or distribute a copy of our written report, and take no chances that we might appear silly on the nightly news.

This approach, one to which I used to adhere, probably accomplishes exactly the opposite of what is intended. Secrecy usually is interpreted by the public as meaning you are hiding something (gold, usually), leading to nocturnal visits and incidents of vandalism. And rumors about what might be going on at a site draw the interest of reporters who, as a result of brief, unstructured telephone calls with an archaeologist or land owner, are forced to write uniformed stories.

My approach changed 5 years ago while working near a small town in west-central Florida on a de Soto-related site. Two then graduate students, Brent Weisman and Jeffrey Mitchem, opened my eyes to archaeology in the sunshine, to incorporating the media and the public into field projects. I decided then that the long-term goal of archaeology was not simply to gather and interpret data about the past, but to produce and disseminate that information to people.

## CLEAR AS THE SUN

Here, then, are several ideas drawn from the collective experiences of archaeologists in Florida. Archaeology in the sunshine may not work for everyone, but it certainly has been beneficial in our state.

### Sunshine Tip 1: Make contact with the media

Media people (journalists, writers, and television reporters) are professionals as varied in personalities and abilities as are archaeologists. All of them get paid for preparing news stories, but there is a real hierarchy that ranges from student reporters, who often are interning with local papers and are learning the ropes, to national figures like a John Wilford Noble of the *New York Times,* who is willing to read the literature on a science subject, synthesize it, and prepare a story. Most reporters do not have that latitude; they are told by a news editor (their boss) to write or film a story about a topic, and they do it. As one gets more established in the field, one can suggest stories to be pursued.

Larger papers are specialized; some have science, outdoor, and environmental writers along with sports reporters and people who cover the social scene. Smaller papers do not have a wide variety of specialists.

Television stations also have news editors; sometimes they are the anchor people you see on the local six o'clock news; sometimes they are not. Television stations also have field reporters who cover stories; they are the people who travel in vans with a camera person who carries a mini-cam. Their video tapes are returned to the studios where they are edited for airing on news programs. Unfortunately, the people who tape the stories and do the on-site interviews are not always the ones doing the editing.

How does one make contact with the media and enter a realm so foreign to archaeology? If you work for a college or university or a large private firm, chances are your organization has a public relations department that already has the contacts and can guide you. If not, the simplest way is to call the appropriate news desk or news room and ask whoever answers if he or she would like to do a story on your project. Archaeology is viewed as "good" news; it is generally not about crime and corruption. Media people actually like archaeology stories, and they like to visit sites and see excavations in progress. It is much more interesting than covering a new jail dedication. Generally, with your cooperation, they will write a good story.

Stories appear at the local level, but they can also be sent out on a regional or national network. For instance, a written newspaper account might be sent out on the UPI or AP wire service and read by a UPI or AP reporter. The wire service reporters rewrite the stories and send them on the wire to newspapers all over the country. We have had stories written by local Florida reporters redone by UPI and appear the next day in the *San Francisco Chronicle* and a few days later in the English-language *Herald Tribune* distributed in Europe.

Reporters *like* to see their stories make the big time. They want to do well in their profession, just as we do. And do not forget to get the names and telephone numbers of your new media contacts. You will need one another again.

## Sunshine Tip 2: Cooperate with the media

What do you want from the media? You want them to prepare a news story that educates their viewers or readers about archaeology and what we can learn about the past. Your implicit message is "protecting archaeological sites is important because it is from such sites that we can learn new knowledge such as that being produced from this site (or survey)." What is the best way to try and head them in that direction? First, tell the media that is one of your goals. Education is a noble cause and the media knows it. Second, I have found that preparing a short overview — several pages — on your project that can serve as sort of a press-release/information packet for the media is a good practice.

Make it popular and nontechnical so real people can understand it. Anticipate what about the project the public might find most interesting. What do you want them to know? If something is controversial, say so. Include your name as author and a telephone number where you can be contacted for additional information. The newspaper reporters will take your literature away and may or may not use information from it. Most often they do. If the story goes out on the wire, the wire service writers can get your name and number from the local reporter if they want more information. Your overview will also serve as a quick introduction to television reporters and help to guide their questions and their on-the-air comments. The overview also serves as a good source of quotes that can be attributed to you.

I have found that the press overview is a great handout for students, field participants, relatives, sponsoring agencies, etc. If you update it regularly, when you finish the project you often have the basis of a good popular magazine article.

## Sunshine Tip 3: Media Day

Trying to utilize the media is work, and it is time consuming. If you do not budget your time, you can be swamped. One way to use your time efficiently and highlight the educational aspects of your project is to integrate "Media Day" with "Dignitary Day" and "Public Visitation Day." It sounds like a zoo, and it often turns out that way, but the results can be worth it. First, invite the press for a specific time: say 9 A.M. to noon. Have your handout information ready to give them and have artifacts and other "photo opportunities" (e.g., the field crew excavating features) available.

This also is a good time to invite appropriate dignitaries to visit the site. Start with your boss and your firm's president or your department's dean. Also, are there local politicians or officials that were involved in setting up the project? How about the landowner and officials from sanctioning state or federal agencies? Give all of them your handout, too. Local politicians love to have the chance to say a few informed words before cameras, and you will be giving them the opportunity to do that *and* to support archaeology. Often you will find that the media, administrators, politicians, and officials all know one another and do not find it at all strange that they are at what appears to be a contrived archaeology love-in. They probably all were at the new jail dedication last week. The media and people interested in establishing an image with the public have a symbiotic relationship.

Since Media Day takes up the morning (or afternoon) anyway, I like to use the occasion to invite the public to visit the site (this requires advance notification to the media). Schedule 30-min tours every hour and assign some of the field crew to handle parking, put up ropes to mark the tour route, and even lead tours. You or someone else will also want to give a short presentation to each tour group. The tours provide an excellent photo opportunity for the media ("archaeologist educates public"); and in reality you *are* educating them. Your boss and the local politicians will also smile on your foray into public education.

Media/Dignitary/Public Visitation Day is itself a newsworthy event and always draws attention and builds grassroots support. I have also found that opening things up to the public answers their questions about what is going on, generates information on other local sites and privately held artifact collections you might otherwise know nothing about, and instills in the local community protective feelings toward the site. And meeting local people can lead to all sorts of things, from cocktail invitations to barbecues to marriage.

## Sunshine Tip 4: Build local support by emphasizing local archaeology

In Florida we are fortunate to have the Florida Anthropological Society, which is largely made up of avocational archaeologists and which is affiliated with a number of regional chapters around the state. Whenever it is geographically appropriate, I make contact with the local chapter if I am doing a project in their locale. But in much of Florida, no chapters exist. When that occurs, I go instead to the local historical society. They are everywhere, it seems, and often are affiliated with small local museums.

The members of such organizations can be invaluable. They already have contacts with local organizations, schools, and the media. And they are a source of information on local archaeology. Invite the officers to Dignitary Day and the members to Public Visitation Day. Offer to give an evening slide presentation to their group (another photo/education opportunity for the media). Where appropriate, help them with an archaeology display in the local museum, which focuses on your project and the importance of *their* local archaeological resources.

My experience is that cooperation with local groups can pay extraordinary dividends (not the least of which was an individual that provided more than $70,000 for one project). Because archaeological societies are much rarer than historical groups, many members of the latter turn out to be persons who are actually more interested in your project than studying genealogy. Your presence in a community will give such people a chance to learn more about their local archaeology, and it will draw new members to the local historical society. Everyone benefits.

How far you want to go with your new friends depends on your resources and the time you or your field people can commit. For instance, on our west-central Florida project, Brent Weisman and Jeff Mitchem worked through the local historical group to help found a subgroup interested in archaeology. That group attracted new members to the society and ultimately grew to more than 200 people. We gave lectures at monthly meetings and utilized volunteers on a regular basis in our excavations and in survey work. Most importantly, we built a great deal of support and a sense of public stewardship for the local archaeological sites and the prehistory and history of the region. That support, coupled with related local museum activities, attracted the notice of legislators who in turn have been educated about archaeology.

Approximately this same approach is being applied at other locations in Florida and is paying huge dividends in terms of support and education. Teaching local people about local archaeology is the best way I know of to assure long-term support for archaeological research and archaeological resources.

## Sunshine Tip 5: Teach teachers so they can teach the kids

If you actually ever apply Sunshine Tips 1–4 to one of your archaeology projects, it is guaranteed that you cannot escape number 5. Everything said about school teachers is true: they are interested in education and they will take advantage of you and your project to bring new information to their students. But again, their goal is the same as yours: education.

Teachers, like top-notch reporters, are also willing to put in the time it takes to learn about a subject. When they contact me, I like to send them my handout and anything else that I can lay my hands on. A bibliography that includes overviews or popular articles is also a good idea. Teachers will take those materials and create curricula for their students.

Part of any curriculum is probably going to be a tour of your site with a talk from the archaeologist, or at least a slide show at school. And do not forget to send the students to see the museum exhibit you helped with (Tip 4). I have done several Saturday workshops for school teachers, arranged by local school boards. The teachers learned a lot, and they received school board-approved credits, which they liked. I was very proud when one teacher in a small west Florida county sent me a copy of the teaching materials she had prepared on Hernando de Soto and the Florida native peoples. I now refer other teachers to her for information.

## Sunshine Tip 6: Archaeologists are your friends; support them

If you have read this far, you probably do not need this advice. But unfortunately, you will find that not all of your colleagues will believe that public education and media coverage of archaeology are worthwhile. Snide remarks may be made about sunshine archaeology. Such naysayers are wrong and should stay hidden in their ivory towers.

It is much more constructive and better for the discipline if archaeologists support one another, especially when it comes to public- and media-related activities. Once you are on a reporter's contact list, you will again hear from them when news is slow. One will call and ask if you are doing anything newsworthy. If you are not, refer them to another archaeologist that you know has an ongoing project. Reporters are not used to having scientists support one another. A recommendation from you that "so-and-so's Spanish mission project is terrific" will leave them thinking just that. And do not forget the surveys and other contracted research projects your colleagues are doing.

United, archaeologists are a potent force, especially when they include everyone from the State Historic Preservation Officer's staff to the consultant archaeologist just graduated with an M.A. degree and a Society for Professional Archaeology license. If you have not done so already, organize yourselves in some fashion and plot strategy. And that leads to the next bit of advice.

## Sunshine Tip 7: Think big and do not be shy

Public interest, involvement, and support mean government support. Government support means money for research, education, and site protection. Organized archaeologists are an effective way to afford government the opportunity to exercise that support in meaningful ways. Examples are local and state archaeological resource management legislation, county and state archaeology curriculum in schools, support for historic preservation, and support for research and museum activities.

One the most recent examples in Florida is the "Year of the Indian" program that William H. Marquardt and the Florida Museum of Natural History have undertaken in conjunction with two local museums in the Ft. Myers area (the Nature Center of Lee County and the Fort Myers Historical Museum) and the Florida Division of Historical Resources. Funded by the Florida legislature, the project involves research in southwest Florida, media and museum/school education, and participation by the public. It is not going to be long until every school kid and adult in Lee County knows about the Calusa Indians and their prehistoric ancestors and the difference between a nonagricultural and agricultural chiefdom. And they "will come to better understand the need to protect and preserve the cultural riches of southwest Florida for themselves and for future generations" (from *Calusa News* 1989).

## CONCLUSION: WHO IS SHE THAT LOOKETH FORTH AS THE DAWN?

Hopefully, it is archaeology in the sunshine. Sharing our discipline with the public can only lead to increased public support. Utilizing the media is one of the best ways to reach that public. Giving the public the opportunity to learn firsthand about archaeology is another. Once people understand the contributions that archaeology can make to understanding their past, they will also be protectors of that past.

## REFERENCES CITED

Calusa News (1989) Newsletter of the Southwest Florida Project, Institute of Archaeology and Paleonenvironmental Studies, Florida Museum of Natural Resources, No. 4.

# ARCHAEOLOGY AT HOME: A PARTNERSHIP IN PENSACOLA, FLORIDA

Judith A. Bense

## INTRODUCTION

There is something very special about an archaeological site. Perhaps it is the silence surrounding the artifacts that once were a part of life. Perhaps it is the recognition of our own mortality and the inevitable loss of the context of things that are important to us and that identify us as individuals and a society. Most people generally understand that an archaeologist is trained to decipher the material from sites to reconstruct past ways of life. Despite this general perception, several misunderstandings are also prevalent: (1) the most important archaeological sites are somewhere else (Egypt, Mexico, Europe, China) and not in the U.S., (2) there is no important archaeology in their hometown, and (3) archaeologists think the spectacular artifacts are the most important ones. These misconceptions have been aggravated by the general avoidance of the public by many American archaeologists and has fostered an ever-increasing destruction rate of archaeological sites in the U.S.

Things are finally beginning to change as more and more archaeologists realize that, just like some natural resources, archaeological sites can be virtually eliminated during our generation. So, on the coat tails of the successful environmental movement, some alarmed archaeologists have become active as our nonrenewable resources are pushed up by bulldozer blades, without any protection. This article presents a case study about how a small group of alarmed people, using the organized tactics of the friends of the environment, have changed the perception and attitudes toward archaeological sites in a community. The key to this shift in attitude was organization, persistence, and working within the system to develop and implement local legislation and pressures that protect and conserve archaeological sites in the Pensacola, FL area. As a result, a mutual partnership has developed within the community. This partnership consists of professional archaeologists, a strong citizen advocacy group, the city of Pensacola, the media, and the historic preservation organization. This article explains how this partnership developed, how it works, and the kind of interrelationships that sustain it. It is hoped that the realistic approach to archaeology in Pensacola can be repeated in other communities in the U.S.

## PARTNERSHIP IN PENSACOLA

The answer to why there is a community archaeology program in Pensacola is simple: the existing well-intended but archaeologically uninformed leadership in Pensacola was essentially destroying the heart of one of the most significant archaeological areas in the state and was going to continue doing it because they perceived that they were doing nothing wrong. No one had raised a voice in protest, and unless something was done, it would have continued at an ever-increasing pace. Therefore, Pensacola picked us, rather than the reverse. This is our home, and what happens here to the archaeological resources on "our watch" is our responsibility. However trite this sounds, it is the driving force of the Pensacola archaeology program: either we find a way to protect archaeological sites at the local level or they will be destroyed, and we will be at fault. By looking the other way, professional and avocational archaeologists as well as the general public were allowing it to happen. That was a poor legacy to leave for the next generation. It was unacceptable.

Pensacola is an old town. It was a colonial military settlement permanently established by the Spanish in 1698, and it has been occupied ever since. The present urban core is in the same location as it has been for over 250 years, while the remainder of the city has sprawled into the interior and along the bays. Pensacola has a metropolitan population of approximately 250,000 and is the regional center for west Florida. It is located on the northern Gulf coast of Florida, out of the high-growth, more tropical areas to the south. Approximately 50% of the payroll in Pensacola is military and government related (especially Navy), with the remainder made up of heavy industry, tourism, and retirement. The higher education institutions include Pensacola Junior College and the University of West Florida (UWF).

In the late 1970s, large-scale urban renewal began in Pensacola, and demolition of block after block of deteriorated buildings as well as excavations were common place in the older areas of the city. Associated with these activities, unfortunately, was an increasing, unintended, yet devastating destruction of significant archaeological deposits from the Indian, Colonial, and Early American occupations of Pensacola. One of the largest building programs was "Direction 85," which included a 12-million-dollar civic center, an 8-million-dollar city hall, and a new police station, all in the downtown area. By this time, an archaeology program was being established at the University of West Florida, and university archaeologists and students saw first hand the unintended destruction. Despite being untrained in historic archaeology materials and literature and having no sources of funds, a core group of alarmed professional archaeologists, historians, and concerned friends of archaeology felt forced to do something to bring this destruction under control.

## THE FIRST PARTNERSHIP

The first partnership in the Pensacola archaeology movement was between concerned professional and avocational archaeologists. This small group had the simple but immediate goal of finding a way to prevent this almost constant destruction of archaeological sites in downtown Pensacola. These first partners developed a key ingredient of the ensuing larger and successful archaeology movement in Pensacola. They recognized that a confrontational approach would not be productive and that a positive, pragmatic, yet assertive approach would be the most effective means of reaching a solution. No longer did they sit on the sidelines and wring their hands, complaining about lack of funding, training, and the like. These partners were advocates who used public pressure, negotiation, whistle blowing, and persistence to protect and conserve archaeological resources in Pensacola.

This first partnership successfully developed and pushed through city legislation in 1985 to protect archaeological sites on city-owned property, in rights-of-way, and on city-sponsored projects. While not comprehensive, this accomplished the goal of protecting sites that were being destroyed indiscriminately in the urban renewal process that was sponsored primarily by the city. It should be noted that the archaeological review resolution is not tailored to Pensacola; it is a carbon copy of federal-level Section 106 compliance procedures found in the National Historic Preservation Act of 1966. (For further information and background about the Pensacola archaeological review resolution, see Bense 1987.)

In addition, the group approached private companies and developers planning construction projects for which no compliance was required, with unsolicited proposals to at least survey the parcel to determine if significant archaeological deposits were going to be damaged. If this was the case, negotiations were held with the developer until sponsored archaeological investigations were agreed to. The approach remained the same: positive, pragmatic, and persistent. One of these unsolicited, noncompliance projects sponsored by the local electric utility, Gulf Power Company, won the first Department of Interior National Public Service Award for archaeology awarded to a public utility.

## THE SECOND PARTNERSHIP

With the passage of the archaeological review resolution, the city became the third partner in Pensacola archaeology. Compliance archaeology projects generated by the archaeology resolution began to be regularly performed. These projects included street improvements, affordable housing developments, and utility improvements.

In addition, the three partners designed and implemented an archaeological survey of the city of Pensacola using their own resources as well as grants from private foundations. Each of the partners contributed their share, and this project exemplifies the partnership approach to Pensacola archaeology. The university contributed the professional archaeologist's salary for teaching archaeology students, facilities, and equipment. The archaeological society provided volunteer labor and obtained a large grant from a private foundation to pay for two trained supervisors (experienced students), supplies, and report production costs. The city paid for the costs of supervisors and supplies for a survey of city-owned property. This survey resulted in a professional quality technical product (Bense 1989) that can be used by city staff as well as professional archaeologists in planning and making management decisions that can effect significant archaeological deposits.

A fourth partner was also brought into the Pensacola archaeology movement during the city survey: the media (see Milanich, this volume, for information on using the media to educate the public about archaeology). It was realized early on that one of the major obstacles to archaeological site conservation was an uninformed public. While a small group of people (less than 50 at the time) knew that Pensacola had large areas of archaeological deposits that were generally in excellent condition, no one else did. Therefore, a high profile public education campaign was initiated to teach the who, what, when, where, and why of Pensacola archaeology. However, the vast majority of people do not read books or journals and do not regularly attend classes or meetings on archaeology. That meant that they were not going to come to us. Therefore, we had to go to them by placing archaeology information in the things they did read, watch, and listen to: i.e., newspapers, television, and radio.

Subsequently, much attention and time were devoted to the media. Events such as ground breakings, kickoffs, and press conferences became a regular part of most archaeology projects. The press corps was cultivated by quick leads on new discoveries and "finds." Articles began to appear with increasing frequency. Editorials summarized the articles and added credibility to archaeology, to the power structure, as well as to the general public. A weekly radio program on archaeology in Pensacola, broadcast on the local segment of the National Public Radio Station at the university, provided archaeological information to the public, many of whom were temporarily captive in their cars on their way home. This public education mechanism has become a mainstay of increasing archaeology awareness in Pensacola.

## THE FINAL PARTNERSHIP

The last, but far from the least, partner brought into active participation in Pensacola archaeology was the local historic preservation board. This had been a typical historic house-restoration and museum-oriented organization supported by state historic preservation funds. Its primary missions were to prevent demolition of historic structures and to establish historic architectural districts. This had been successful, and the historic district in downtown Pensacola continues to draw over 100,000 people annually, including public school children on field trips to the "Old City" of Pensacola to experience Pensacola history by viewing the restored buildings and visiting the museums. Only one thing was missing in this historic experience: the archaeology. Because of the combination of an existing audience and an excellent archaeological record containing the authentic, though buried, pieces of Pensacola's ancient and historic past, it was decided to expose and develop the archaeological deposits that lie just beneath the surface in the "Old City."

The first step was to simply move the base of operations from the university (located on the fringe of town) to the heart of the historic district to establish a presence for archaeology there. The Historic Pensacola Preservation Board (HPPB) was requested to (and has since) provide several field headquarters in the historic district, for all archaeology projects in the downtown area. This includes city compliance, university field schools, and youth archaeology programs.

The second step was to design a high-profile public archaeology project that focused on the Colonial period forts that were in downtown Pensacola. This concept resulted in a "Colonial Archaeological Trail" project that was the first archaeology project to receive a special big-ticket legislative grant from the state of Florida. The trail is now open, with three outdoor exhibits, a brochure, and an Archaeology Center in the heart of the historic district where visitors can see artifacts and maps from Colonial Pensacola on exhibit. Archaeology is becoming a part of historic preservation in Pensacola. It has provided a new and continuing source of public interest in the historic district and now presents the full spectrum of historical resources to the public.

## HOW THE PARTNERSHIP METHOD WORKS: THE FORT OF PENSACOLA EXAMPLE

In the seemingly constant stream of city construction projects in the historic "Old City" area, a large utility and street-scape improvement project was designed for several blocks, which completely crossed through the Colonial fort area of Pensacola. Plans called for massive new utilities, street surfaces, street lights, and sidewalks, and scores of large trees were to be planted. In addition, much of the existing buried utilities were to be removed, and new lines were to be placed in deep trenches. When the plans went out for bid, the city consulting archaeologist developed a compliance plan that began with a modest testing of several sidewalk areas and the identification of several areas of significant deposits that would be impacted.

On the second day of construction, as the asphalt was being removed in an area thought to be previously disturbed, a British cannon was discovered. The press was notified, and while the cannon was being hoisted from the street, with the cameras rolling, foundations from a Colonial building inside the 200-year-old fort were exposed in the street. With the press already there, a second story developed: the British Fort of Pensacola. This became the largest archaeological event in Pensacola, and as more and more of the fort was exposed in the street, public fascination grew. Finally, the stockade remnants and interior buildings in the main gate area were exposed. This gate happens to be the one that Andrew Jackson walked through to accept Florida from Spain in 1821, resulting in the first official American flag over the state. This construction project was in the heart of Pensacola, in the street, right next to a park, and at the foot of the largest museum in the historic district. Public accessibility was excellent. Hundreds of people came to watch the 200-year-old archaeological site being brought into the late 20th century. People wanted maps to see how the remnants of the old fort fit into today's environment. They were excited and were eager to sign petitions to save the site for the public. The partners then went to work.

More funding had to be secured from the city, as this was an unexpected discovery and an expensive one. The university lead the way with the president attending a crucial budget meeting of city staff, which resulted in additional funding for the project. Scores of volunteers from the archaeological society provided the labor and staffed an information table for the public. This meant that the only paid staff were three supervisors and a public tour guide. The media took to this story, and the uncovering of this piece of Colonial Pensacola grew into a national story, appearing on ABC's "Good Morning America" and twice on CNN, as well as receiving extensive local coverage. A "fort watch" was held by the local newspaper, and several editorials appeared throughout the duration of the project. The public and press immediately were concerned that the city would destroy the fort and its buildings by putting a large storm-water main through it. A petition circulated to close the street, excavate the fort, and turn it into an upscale outdoor archaeology exhibit to be incorporated into the Colonial Archaeological Trail. The Historic Pensacola Preservation Board immediately put the cannon on display and pressed hard for the street closing. Regular tours of the area incorporated the excavations, and the media used the historic preservation staff for stories and background.

The result was a typical negotiation between the partners. Each had a range of priorities within which a plan could be acceptable; however, the most powerful partner was now the public. The city knew that if the site was destroyed, the public would rise up and literally storm city hall. The public's interest in this case was represented by the city consulting archaeologist and, in the negotiations, held the highest position. The city felt pressure to keep the street in, but could avoid impacting the site by eliminating parking and moving the street to the far side of the right-of-way. The Preservation Board and its staff requested additional budget funds from the state for the excavation and interpretation of the site. The press kept the pressure on.

The compromise plan was a city-funded documentation and limited sampling of the Colonial features. The street design was changed to a serpentine pattern around the intact deposits, and the utility trench was placed on the other side of the street from the fort. The city provided sturdy filter cloth to cover the site, and two feet of fill to buffer it from impacts. The legislative delegation is now being lobbied to keep the funds in the preservation board budget so that the excavation and exhibit can continue. Even if it takes longer to secure the funding, everyone knows that this site was saved because the city had professional archaeologists on the job and on their payroll and because of the archaeological review resolution. The question of the worth of the resolution is now answered.

Everyone came out a winner (as well as a paying partner) in this project. The university archaeologists recovered priceless information and protected nationally significant deposits. The city wears the white hat because it had the leadership to have archaeologists on the job when the construction took place, and paid its way. The historic preservation board took the lead in initiating the large funding request, providing historical information, and exhibiting the main artifact: the cannon. The archaeological society provided the labor, telephones, and an information table. As a result they gained scores of new members. The media had a field day, and the reliable reporters had bylines and feature stories for several weeks. This is how it works in Pensacola, and we handle it one project at a time, giving each partner their respect, yet demanding that each shoulders their responsibility.

# CONCLUSION

Pensacola archaeology is now alive and well because concerned residents realized that it was up to them to find a way to stop the irreversible destruction of our archaeological deposits. This is not an especially rich, poor, big, or small city. The residents here consist of the full spectrum of American citizens. This partnership approach can be developed between the key players in any town. The essential ingredient is the acceptance of responsibility by the archaeological community, both professional and avocational, to do something to stop the destruction and neglect of nonrenewable archaeological resources. It is possible to mainstream archaeology. The long suit in all of this is that the public already has a natural interest in archaeology, and once educated and involved in it, they have the power to make changes (see Pokotylo, this volume, for additional discussion concerning public attitudes about archaeology). This is the key to the growing strength of Pensacola archaeology. Now almost all of the 250,000 people living here know that there is archaeology in Pensacola and it is a valuable community resource. It can be managed just like other public concerns, such as water, runoff, air quality, and the like. It is time to start the involvement now before more archaeological sites are gone and we leave a biased legacy for future generations.

# REFERENCES CITED

Bense, J. A. (1987) Development of a management system for archaeological resources in Pensacola, Florida. In Living in cities: current research in urban archaeology, Special Publication Series No. 5.

Bense, J. A. (1989) The Pensacola Archaeological Survey, Technical Report, Vols. I and II, Publication No. 1. Pensacola Archaeological Society, Pensacola, FL.

The National Historic Preservation Act of 1966 (Public Law 89-665; 80 Stat. 915; 16 U.S.C. 470) as amended by P.L. 91-243, P.L. 93-54, P.L. 94-422, P.L. 94-458, P.L. 96-199, P.L. 96-244, and P.L. 96-515.

# ROMANCING THE PUBLIC*

## Jean M. Auel©

In looking over the schedule, this meeting of the Society for American Archaeology promises to be informative, exciting, provocative, perhaps controversial, and stimulating.

All the elements, in fact, are here for a good work of fiction, except the stories that will be told here are true — or at least as close to truth as anyone can come when dealing with information derived from artifacts and sites of ancient times.

I am the writer of fiction here, though some of the newest information emerging from the study of prehistory truly verifies the old saying that "truth can be stranger than fiction." The current work being done by researchers working in the field and in laboratories is truly amazing! New revelations are following so closely on the heels of new discoveries that it's hard to keep up.

One of the important issues to be raised during this conference is the question of preserving the archaeological record. Talking to this group about the importance of preserving archaeological sites is indeed a case of preaching to the converted. Archaeologists know the fascinating and important knowledge to be gained from a site that is undisturbed. The question is, why aren't people interested in preserving archaeological sites and artifacts? How do you overcome public apathy toward learning about prehistory?

Part of the problem is that many people don't identify the sites or artifacts with anything important to themselves. In this country, some think it's just a bunch of old Indian stuff; who cares about Indian history? For others, the problem is just the opposite.

Many people like to collect fossils and artifacts, not only because of the lure of selling them for easy profits, but to put on their own shelves, if only to collect dust. After all, someone is buying the illegally sold artifacts. The interest is there; many people simply don't know the importance of undisturbed sites, or even of archaeology itself.

There is still a tendency for people to look upon hunting and gathering peoples, whether modern or prehistoric, as savages: a view expounded, often very colorfully and imaginatively, in earlier days by Victorian Antiquarians, though modern anthropologists have been trying to overcome it for many years. In a recent issue of *Current Anthropology,* in an article entitled "Hunter-Gatherers and Their Neighbors from Prehistory to the Present," Thomas Headland and Lawrence Reid point out that "ethnocentric and racist statements...still appear in print, and the prejudice they reflect continue to be widely held."

They maintain that while few anthropologists today would accept any part of the 19th century evolutionary theories, many lay people continue to believe in the fiction that human peoples evolved culturally from savagery to barbarism to civilized status. "Implausible as this viewpoint is, in the light of new archaeological, linguistic, archival, and ethnographic data, it continues to overshadow recent scientifically sound analyses...." But the authors also criticize some anthropologists for reinforcing the view by presenting them as "primitive," "the savage other," rather than as fully modern human beings, and for failing to recognize the extent of their associations and accomplishments.

---

\* *This article was presented at the 1990 Society for American Archaeology Conference in Las Vegas, Nevada as part of the Special Plenary Session on archaeological looting. It is presented in the style it was given at the conference.*

No one has more respect and admiration for scientists and researchers than I do. It is their dedication that enables all of us to know about our ancestors — and therefore ourselves. In fact, I'm sort of an "archaeology groupie." I enjoy talking to the professionals; but more than that, I have a vested interest in the archaeologist and archaeology.

You, as archaeologists, make your living by "mining" the sites for information, then adding your own skills, knowledge, insights, and interpretations. The result is increased information, knowledge, and insights about who we are, where we came from, and where we may be going; and on the practical side, you get to keep on doing what you are doing: earning a living at something you enjoy.

I earn my living by "mining" your results — your reports and papers and conversations — then adding my interpretations, insights, imagination, and skills. The result is increased knowledge and insights, and stories grounded in a solid core of scientific information that, among other things, helps people understand more about prehistory and the people we were and are, in a human and entertaining way. On the practical side, I get to keep on doing what I am doing, earning a living at something I enjoy.

I also must "dig" for my information, though not in the dirt. Let me give you an example of the kind of digging I do. I read a small item about musical instruments made out of mammoth bones found in Eastern Europe and dating to the Upper Paleolithic, but I could not find any in-depth information about them. Finally, I made a research trip to Europe, which included the Soviet Union (the Ukraine), and managed to find a copy of Bibikov's book describing his research that led to the discovery that the decorated mammoth bones were musical instruments. Unfortunately, the book was written in Russian.

I bought it, along with a record of a jam session by Russian musicians played on those old mammoth bones. When I returned, I paid for a complete translation of the book. It was a fascinating piece of archaeological detective work, and I included much of that information in the third book, *The Mammoth Hunters.*

*The Mammoth Hunters* was published 5 years ago, and I have been trying ever since to give that translation away to some university or academic press to publish so the information would be available to researchers here. It would require obtaining permissions, I believe, and copies of the many photographs, but I am still willing to donate the translation.)

In a recently released publication, *Save the Past for the Future: Actions for the '90s,* which is the final report from the Taos Working Conference on Preventing Archaeological Looting and Vandalism, published by the Society for American Archaeology (1990), in the "Summary of Major Findings," it was stated: "Americans need — indeed, deserve — to know about their heritage and the history and prehistory of the nation. Professional archaeologists in government, private practice, and academia must be more accessible and forthcoming to the public [see Lerner, Milanich, and Bense, this volume, for discussions of archaeology and public education]. Archaeologists must explain clearly and concisely (1) why archaeology is important, (2) what public benefit is derived from archaeological activities, and (3) how looting and vandalism damage that public benefit. These messages must be expressed with a unified voice and articulated in a compelling manner to all Americans."

It is a vested interest of the archeologist to have the cooperation of the public; your jobs may depend on it — and at least for as long as I choose to write fiction about prehistory, so does mine. Therefore, I'd like to tell you a little about some of the difficulties I had finding archaeological information — besides having to go to Russia...before glasnost! — to give you some insight into what it is like to come to this subject cold, without the usual university background.

Some archaeologist/scientific specialists make information very difficult for the ordinary intelligent person to understand. If the scientist wants the cooperation of the public, it is the responsibility of the scientist to communicate in ways that are understandable.

They must not only express their wishes and needs clearly to obtain funding, but to gain enthusiastic support they need to convey the fascination, the excitement, the pure fun of discovery. They need to involve adult members of the general public in putting together the pieces of the puzzle of who our ancestors were and how they lived, and they need to encourage children so they will grow up wanting to know more.

Archaeologists and anthropologists who work in this country need to make it clear that it is not just Indian history. It is all of humanity's history (see Knudson, this volume, for a discussion of archaeology and the public trust). People of European heritage, for example, tend to forget that their ancestors didn't spring full blown from agricultural or urban cultures, complete with writing and monumental architecture. Their ancestors also spent their first several million years as foragers, gatherers, and hunters. Studying about the lives of any ancient people gives insight into understanding ourselves better.

But that requires helping people to understand that ancient people who lived in what is today Russia, or France or Israel or Africa or Asia or America, were the same as we are. They had hopes and dreams; they loved and hated, knew compassion and jealousy, bravery and fear, ambition and loss of hope. They were brave and daring and very human.

I've tried to do it by telling stories, the way people have been doing since the beginning of time to remember and understand the legends, oral histories, and necessary lessons of survival. Though that isn't quite how I started. I began with an idea for a short story about a young woman living in prehistoric times, but when I tried to write it, I discovered I didn't know what I was writing about.

I thought I would do a little research and discovered an exciting world full of real people, which I hadn't known existed and which no one else seemed to know about either. It made me a little angry. Why didn't I know it? Why don't most people know it? It was all there in the nonfiction scientific material. Then I realized why. It was not written in a way that was accessible to people, and that was when I decided I was going to tell it in a way that was: in a story; but for all my enthusiasm, it was not easy to research.

I started with *Encyclopedia Britannica* and went from there to the library. What I found was scientific jargon: Pebble culture, Mousterian, Aurignacian, Clovis, microblade, burin, *in situ, Rangifer tarandus, Chenopodium album, Betula nana, Salix, Picea, Pinus,* Pleistocene, Paleolithic. I know what those terms mean now because I was determined to learn; but when I started, I didn't understand a word. I still don't know if I pronounce them correctly, because in many cases, I have not heard the words spoken; I have only read them. I had to expand my vocabulary a great deal, in effect, learn a whole new language, your language, before I could make sense out of the information in libraries and journals so I could write my stories.

Should that be necessary to find out something about prehistory? Probably yes, in my case, because I needed to know as much as possible in order to create an entire prehistoric world for my fictional characters to inhabit. But I don't think it should be true for most people if all they want is a little more understanding.

How many textbooks giving an overview of history begin by condensing "prehistory," — the 5 billion years from the "Big Bang" to the discovery of writing — into the first one or two chapters, with a page or two on the Ice Age, and the remainder of the book devoted to the 5 thousand years since then? No wonder the creationist's claims about 6 thousand years being the total length of time from the beginning, when God created everything, until now are believed by so many people. We have learned that fully modern humans have been around for at least a hundred thousand years, but the last 5 thousand are given the most attention.

Part of the problem is the result of the very dedication and years of study that are necessary to become a trained archaeologist. In that closed environment, speaking about archaeology only to teachers, colleagues, and students, it becomes easy to forget that not every one understands the specialized language that invariably becomes a part of any field of study. It is true that scientific words may be more precise, but only when talking with a peer: only if the meaning is clearly understood by both the one who is speaking and the ones being addressed.

In science there is a tendency for many to speak in long-winded specialized words when addressing the public. And in the written material, it is almost as though there is a competition to see who can write the longest sentences and use the longest words. I recall hearing a young man speaking about "mastication of deciduous dentition." It took me a few moments before I realized that what he meant was "chewing with baby teeth." I sometimes think scientists are required to take a class entitled "Obfuscating English."

Unfortunately, the media doesn't help the situation. Few reporters take the time to decipher the language of science, and many are scientifically illiterate. And with electronic media, they want "news bites" of exciting events. For example, they prefer to publicize something like the macho "first of the big-game hunters" theory to account for the extinction of Ice Age animals, because it sounds more exciting, more bloody and terrible, more newsy, and it's a simplistic definition. It conveys another message. It says, in effect, not only "we're so bad," but it implies, "we're so powerful." It's easier than explaining alternative theories that are more complex, but more logical.

The question is, how do you make the more interesting, complex information more clear? And how do you communicate the excitement of science and the scientific process? In addition, for some scientists the idea of communicating to the public carries with it a stigma. They are afraid of incurring the dreaded "carlsaganism", a disease to be avoided like the plague. Unfortunately, as long as that view prevails, scientists may well defeat themselves. Yes, he may have been a little overly dramatic on occasion, but he communicated and performed a worthwhile service.

In researching for my stories, I have been most excited and moved to learn about the humanity of ancient peoples and to understand that savagery and violence are not what define us or what make us human. A careful study of the archaeological record shows that humanity is defined by compassion and curiosity and by art and invention. It wasn't just being able to survive, because our early ancestors did more than that. They flourished. They obtained knowledge from their environment and had the intelligence to apply it.

Since my stories were set in the Ice Age, I had to ask what that environment was like. Was it harsh and miserable, forcing a bare hand-to-mouth, hard scrabble existence, as so many believe? But then why did people come north in the first place? Humans are tropical animals, not naturally adapted to living in a cold land; why didn't they stay south where it was warm? Were they driven out by competition of fellow human beings? Or were they intelligent and adaptive, curious explorers by nature? I think they were curious. Curiosity is a strong survival trait that makes intelligent humans want to learn about their environment and the world around them. We still are.

That leads me to the thought I'd like to leave with you: romance the public. Let them know that what you are doing is not only important, but fun, exciting, fascinating. Get them involved.

Show them how sharp a stone tool is — nothing turned my thinking around so dramatically as the first time I made a blade out of obsidian and cut a piece of leather with it.

Write at least some of your reports in clear, understandable language. It doesn't have to be fancy, but don't leave it to the media to misinterpret your findings. Get down to the level of a kid, which may be higher than some adults, and get them involved early. Imagine a Saturday morning cartoon with accurate information! Yes, it will take your time, but it's essential that people get their information from the best source. And you'll find its worth it.

# TEACHING *WITH* ARCHAEOLOGY: AN ARIZONA PROGRAM

A.E. (Gene) Rogge

## INTRODUCTION

As we enter the last decade of this century, archaeologists find themselves in a crisis. The archaeological sites we study are disappearing because of intentional looting and vandalism, myriad types of development, inadvertent damage, and benign neglect. Although the parameters of the crisis are not easy to specify, it is clear that we must enlist the aid of many nonprofessionals if we are to stem the loss of our primary data base. We need large, vocal archaeology advocacy groups, analogous to the many environmental groups that have organized over concern about threats to our natural environment. This means we need to educate more people about the values of archaeological research and the perspective it provides on our modern lives.

Coincidentally, the schools of our nation also find themselves in a crisis of performance, public confidence, and relevance to students (National Commission on Excellence in Education 1983). Public perception of the significance of the educational crisis far outweighs concerns over vanishing archaeological resources, which are not widely appreciated. When a third of the students in your state public school system are not graduating from high school and more than 50% of the teachers will burnout and leave the profession within 5 years, it is difficult to get much concern focused on the values of archaeology. But by casting our archaeological curriculum materials in a format that is relevant to the educational crisis, we clearly enhance our chances of introducing some archaeological concepts to a broader audience of precollege students who, in turn, can help us address our own archaeological crisis. If the current generation of school-age children grows up with a truer sense of what archaeology is all about and comes to appreciate the informational and heritage values embodied in archaeological resources, they are bound to be stronger advocates for preservation of archaeological sites in years to come.

Precollege teaching of archaeology, and more generally anthropology (its mother discipline in the U.S.), has been an area of research and development for at least three decades. Interest continues today (see, for example, Holms and Higgins 1985; Selig and Higgins 1986) and is the focus of a 4-year task force formed by the American Anthropological Association in 1988 (Erickson 1989). However, the major efforts of the 1960s left no lasting results when the federal funding for such programs disappeared in the 1970s. The valuable curriculum materials developed by those efforts have been characterized as "curious remains from another time" (Rice 1986:6).

Injecting some anthropology and archaeology into precollege classrooms faces numerous challenges. In this article I describe how one group of volunteers, the Archaeology for the Schools Committee of the Arizona Archaeological Council, has addressed this challenge. The council is a group of about 150 professional, student, and avocational archaeologists with active interests in public archaeology. The schools committee has been in existence about 5 years and has averaged about 10 active members (about 10 additional sympathetic corresponding members have promoted our goals in their individual corners of the state, but have not been able to participate actively in committee meetings and projects). Committee members include professional archaeologists working for universities, museums, federal and state agencies, and private consulting firms. More importantly, classroom teachers and museum educators have been recruited to serve on the committee. (For more specific information about the goals of the committee and the history of its activities, see Rogge and Bell 1988.)

Our experience reflects both what dedicated volunteers can and cannot accomplish. Our efforts are small scale and not at all comparable to the major curriculum development projects of the 1960s. Rather than promoting the teaching of full-blown courses in archaeology and anthropology, we characterize our more modest goal as encouraging teachers to teach *with* archaeology rather than teaching archaeology per se. We promote the introduction of some archaeological concepts through the use of supplemental materials that can be used to support, reinforce, and extend the required curriculum.

## THE CLASSROOM CONTEXT

The first requirement for promoting archaeology in precollege classrooms is the acknowledgment that this is a worthwhile goal. This may seem simple, but the fact that elementary and secondary schools have been largely ignored by archaeologists suggests otherwise. Undoubtedly, this stems in part from the lack of professional rewards for anyone teaching archaeology at the precollege level. There are also concerns on the part of both teachers and archaeologists that, somehow, archaeology is not quite appropriate at the precollege level. It is, after all, a rather marginal, arcane discipline and can be a source of conflict with the Eurocentric perspective on American history that is typically taught as part of the core curriculum in our schools (see Kehoe 1989). Some archaeologists also worry that a little information can be dangerous and could create a new generation of looters and vandals. So the decision to promote archaeology at the precollege level should be made in conscious recognition of the contextual challenges of the precollege classroom.

Once a decision has been made to become involved with school systems, there are basically two strategies for working toward that goal: a grass roots, bottom-up approach, or a top-down imposition of new requirements.

Our committee has explored both. One of our first activities was to prepare an eight-page packet for teachers. It included a number of short supplemental classroom activities and a summary of the state's prehistory. We raised funds for mailing a copy to almost every one of the almost 1000 schools in the state. The mailing was coordinated with the statewide celebration of "Archaeology Week" in 1986, and we expected a substantial return of the mail-back form we included for comments, suggestions, and requests for further information. To say the least, we were disappointed that our brightly colored packet generated only about a dozen inquiries.

Our analysis of the experience taught us that (1) teachers are typically overwhelmed with mandated curriculum requirements, (2) the best curriculum material in the world will not sell itself, and teachers receive lots of unsolicited supplemental educational materials; and (3) personal contact is an essential ingredient for successful outreach.

Our response was probably predictable and not particularly well thought out. We initiated contacts with the state Department of Education to explore the possibility of mandating the teaching of some archaeology, perhaps in conjunction with the course on state history that is required for all fourth graders. We received encouragement, help in identifying other groups with similar interests, and a polite refusal to impose any more top-down requirements. Clearly the department has more pressing priorities, such as basic literacy, drug prevention programs, and sex education. We concluded that archaeology would have to be adopted on its own merits.

Many of our committee members regularly make presentations to classrooms, but we were not satisfied with the scope of this strategy. It would never get our message through to more than a minuscule percentage of the more than half a million elementary and secondary students in the Arizona public school system. We decided that an alternative strategy worth pursuing was to enlist the assistance of classroom teachers who could multiply our efforts by each spreading the archaeological message to perhaps 25 to 30 or more students per year.

## WORKING WITH TEACHERS

With the advice and assistance of the teachers and educators on our committee, we developed a weekend workshop for teachers. The workshop includes a fast-paced 40-minute slide lecture that introduces archaeology as a scientific, anthropologically based study of the past and summarizes the culture history of the American Southwest (the presentation has subsequently been converted to videotape format to facilitate broader use in other contexts). Teachers are then divided into small work groups that spend 1/2- to 1-hour blocks of time participating in various types of hands-on activities that we developed or adapted from other curriculum materials we had identified. Lesson plans have been prepared in formats that teachers are used to, and the workshop participants are encouraged to adapt the activities for presentation in their own classrooms. The activities include

- Trowel It: a dig-in-a-box activity
- Garbage Can Archaeology: an activity for exploring the concept of stratigraphy, artifact interpretation, and hypothesis testing
- Culture History Mystery: an examination of how artifacts reflect changing adaptations and lifestyles
- Culture Universals: an exploration of the concept of culture and commonalities among all cultural groups
- Dating Methods: a review of relative and chronometric techniques for determining how old something is
- Simulating Prehistoric Pottery: an investigation of ceramic technology and the implications of ceramic variability

Our workshops typically close with a session focused on preservation legislation and discussion of some aspect of local ongoing research projects.

We have presented our workshop 5 times during the last 3 years, and it has also stimulated a couple of similar spin-off programs. Through these efforts approximately 200 teachers have been introduced to supplemental archaeology curriculum materials. This is on the order of only 1% of all the precollege teachers in the state. Although we have yet to meet the challenge of spreading our message very far and fast, we have learned several things through this experience.

Few teachers have ever been exposed to archaeology courses, and most will not be interested in, or feel qualified to teach, archaeology per se. Our challenge is to quickly educate them to some basic concepts so that they feel comfortable in presenting our materials as supplemental augmentations and extensions of aspects of the mandated curriculum.

Teachers must perceive the archaeology materials to be relevant. Archaeology is almost inherently intriguing and can often stimulate the interests of unmotivated students. Additionally, archaeology is very amenable to hands-on activities that encourage student participation and retention of information well beyond the 10% rate typical of textbook-driven presentations (see Bruner 1963; Clark 1986; Wonder and Donovan 1984). Archaeology is also ideally suited for integrating artificially compartmentalized subjects and encouraging cooperative learning — both of which are currently recognized as educational goals. A California high school teacher argues that some of the spin-off benefits of archaeological activities include realistic exposure to scientific methods, encouragement of personal involvement and social interaction, and maturation of reflective thinking (Onderdonk 1986). One Tucson teacher has told us that an archaeology unit involving gridding and plotting of artifacts has improved her students' scores on standard skills tests. These types of reactions from their peers and testimonials from other teachers who have experimented with archaeology (for example, Carroll 1987; Catalina 1983; Cotter 1979; Dyer 1983; Passe and Passe 1985; Watts 1985) influence teachers more than any pitch made by archaeologists.

Teachers operate within their own reward system and are unlikely to participate in our workshops unless they perceive some direct benefits. We work with local school districts to make arrangements for in-service credit because such credits are relevant rewards for teachers in maintaining and advancing their careers. Nevertheless, we are experiencing difficulty in filling our workshops and obviously have to become more effective at marketing them. Personal contacts with teachers seems to be essential to effective recruitment.

Through small workshop fees and proceeds from sales of books, they are paying for themselves as long as the volunteer efforts of the presenters continue. But the workshops take substantial effort, and clearly, a group of ten volunteers can never hope to present workshops to more than a small fraction of the teachers in our state. We must also realize that most archaeologists are only avocational educators, at best, and need the expertise and experience of trained curriculum developers and teachers. Institutional support in terms of full-time personnel and funding, such as the program developed by the Toronto School Board, is essential if any outreach effort to the schools is ever going to have a broad impact (Smardz and Hooge 1989; also see Smardz, this volume, for further discussion of the Toronto program).

## ARCHAEOLOGICAL LITERACY

The current educational crisis has been recognized as a challenge and opportunity by several special interest groups. "Literacy" has become a theme of the crisis since Eric Hirsch (1987) first challenged schools to produce culturally literate citizens. At first glance this seems like a goal remarkably compatible with archaeology and its mother discipline anthropology, but a reading of Hirsch's book quickly reveals that his goal is to simply enculturate students into our own culture. The American Association for the Advancement of Science (1989) has echoed Hirsch's theme by initiating a program to achieve a "scientifically literate" population by 2061, the year Halley's Comet will return. Recently, historians have launched a new program to produce "historically literate" students (Gagnon 1989). The challenge of producing "archaeologically literate" citizens thus faces stiff competition for teacher interest and time.

Historians have recently benefitted from Billy Joel's hit song "We Didn't Start the Fire," which promotes the relevance of their discipline. Scholastic, Inc. and CBS records are distributing 40,000 free copies of a tape of the song along with an interview with Joel and other materials for classroom use. Science education has also received considerable attention by the media, including a recent cover story for *Newsweek* (April 9, 1990). We archaeologists have the singularly popular Indiana Jones movies to promote interest in our discipline, but the image portrayed in those movies is off base.

We have come to realize that our committee's activities in Arizona are not an isolated case. Other groups in numerous states (such as Colorado, Florida, Georgia, Kentucky, Louisiana, Maine, Missouri, Ohio, South Dakota, South Carolina, Texas, Vermont, Virginia, and Utah) and in Canada have produced a variety of curriculum materials and are pursuing a variety of approaches (see Rogge and Bell 1989 for a listing of some of the materials prepared by these groups; also see McNutt, Hawkins, this volume, for further discussion of school curriculum materials). It seems clear that the level of interest in archaeological education outreach is growing across the country, and an archaeologically literate citizenry is an achievable goal.

## CONCLUSION

My basic conclusion is that we must recognize the perceived marginality of our discipline, hone our themes for archaeological literacy to the essential core implications of our research, and develop an effective delivery system that combines local personal contact with locally relevant material and national coordination. In our current enthusiasm, we could work to prepare top-quality curriculum materials, such as those prepared in the 1960s, but unless we implement an ongoing system to effectively promote and deliver these materials, they will soon be forgotten.

The best model we have identified for developing and delivering supplemental materials is that provided by environmental protection proponents, who are far ahead of archaeologists. The level of their activities is such that it has led to the creation of a *Journal of Environmental Education*. We are still at the newsletter stage (for example, *Anthro Notes* produced by the Smithsonian Institution, *Teaching Anthropology Newsletter* published by Saint Mary's University in Halifax, *Heritage Education Quarterly* from the Preservation and Library Resource Center in Madison, GA, *Archaeology and Education* that was recently launched by the Toronto Board of Education, and the new *Archaeology and Public Education* newsletter of the Society for American Archaeology, Committee on Public Education.

One of the best models for outreach that we have identified is "Project Wild," a program of supplemental elementary and secondary environmental curriculum that is disseminated through workshops in almost every state in the nation and parts of Canada and is being introduced into India (Western Regional Environmental Education Council 1988). The initial materials (a volume of activities for elementary use and another for secondary levels) were developed over a 3-year period in the early 1980s, with funding (on the order of a quarter million dollars) and cooperation of state game and fish agencies and departments of education throughout the western U.S. (Charles 1988). Today, a self-sustaining organization with a national director continues to guide a nationwide network of cooperating organizations and promote the program. The materials are made available to teachers through weekend workshops that are promoted by various local organizations in each state. Approximately 5% of all the teachers in the country have participated to date (Project Wild 1988). This is an enviable record archaeologist should work to emulate.

Our Archaeology for the Schools Committee demonstrates that volunteers can accomplish a great deal working at the state level, but I suggest the efforts in Arizona and other parts of the country need to be substantially increased. We need some existing or new organization to take on the challenge of national coordination. If other disciplines can do it, so can archaeologists. Nevertheless, I realize that a nationally coordinated program is not likely to happen very soon. In the meantime, I urge all archaeologists to pursue, or at least support, some form of local or regional public education outreach. Even individual archaeologists working with one teacher or one classroom should not be daunted by the challenge. Individual classroom presentations are still one of our most effective grassroots approaches to outreach.

# REFERENCES CITED

American Association for the Advancement of Science (1989) *Science for All Americans,* Washington, D.C., 1–217.

**Bruner, J.** (1963) *The Process of Education,* Vintage, New York.

**Carroll, R. F.** (1987) Schoolyard archaeology, *Social Studies,* 78, 69.

**Catalina, L. S.** (1983) Digging into hometown history, *Cobblestone Mag.,* 4(June), 10.

**Charles, C.** (1988) Summary of research findings on Project Wild, *North Am. Wildlife Nat. Resour. Conf. Trans.*

**Clark, B.** (1986) *Optimizing Learning: The Integrative Education Model in the Classroom,* Merrill, Columbus, OH.

**Cotter, J. L.** (1979) Archaeologists of the future: high schools discover archaeology, *Archaeology,* January/February 1979, 29.

**Dyer, J.** (1983) *Teaching Archaeology in Schools,* Shire, United Kingdom.

**Erickson, P. A.** (1989) AAA on the way to precollege anthropology, *Teaching Anthropol. Newsl.,* 15(fall), 4.

**Gagnon, P., Ed.** (1989) *Historical Literacy,* Macmillan, New York, 1–338.

**Hirsch, E.D., Jr.** (1987) *Cultural Literacy,* Houghton Mifflin, Boston, 1–251.

**Holms, K. A. and Higgins, P. J., Eds.** (1985) *Archeology and Education: A Successful Combination for PreCollegiate Students,* Anthropology Curriculum Project, University of Georgia, Athens.

**Kehoe, A. B.** (1989) In fourteen hundred and ninety-two, Columbus sailed . . .: the primacy of the national myth in American schools. In *The Excluded Past: Archaeology in Education,* Stone, P. and MacKenzie, R., Eds., Unwin Hyman, London.

National Commission on Excellence in Education (1983) A nation at risk: the imperative of educational reform, U.S. Department of Education, Washington, D.C.

**Onderdonk, R.** (1986) Piaget and archaeology, *Archaeology,* November/December 1986, 80.

**Passe, J. and Passe, M.** (1985) Archaeology: a unit to promote thinking skills, *Social Studies,* 76, 238.

Project Wild (1988) Repc ·t of program activities from a national perspective, summer, 1988, Boulder, CO.

**Rice, M. J.** (1986) Curriculum artifacts: the remains of three anthropology projects, *Pract. Anthropol.,* 8(3–4), 6.

**Rogge, A. E. and Bell, P.** (1988) Teaching teachers to teach with archaeology. In *Fighting Indiana Jones in Arizona, American Soc. Conservation Archaeology, 1988 Proc.,* Rogge, A. E. and Montgomery, J., Ed.S., Agency for Conservation Archaeology, Portales, NM.

**Rogge, A. E. and Bell, P.** (1989) Archaeology in the classroom: a case study from Arizona, *Archaeological Assistance Program Tech. Brief No. 4,* National Park Service, Washington, D.C.

**Selig, R. O. and Higgins, P. J., Eds.** (1986) Practicing anthropology in precollege education, *Pract. Anthropol.,* 8(3–4).

**Smardz, K. and Hooge, P.** (1989) Teaching people to touch the past: archaeology and education in Toronto and Ohio. Paper presented at third annual Presenting the Past Conference, Minneapolis, MN.

**Watts, L. E.** (1985) They dig archaeology. *Science Children,* 23(September), 5.

Western Regional Environmental Education Council (1988) *An Introduction to Project Wild,* Project Wild, Boulder, CO.

**Wonder, J. and Donovan, P.** (1984) *Whole Brain Thinking,* Morrow, New York.

# TEACHING PEOPLE TO TOUCH THE PAST: ARCHAEOLOGY IN THE TORONTO SCHOOL SYSTEM

Karolyn E. Smardz

## INTRODUCTION

When we speak of history, archaeology, and other heritage-oriented disciplines, what image appears in the mind of the average North American? Hollywood adventure films, museum displays, and dry tomes full of dates and "facts" are probably high on the list. Better-informed members of the public may have a clearer picture of what archaeologists do — research, excavation, analysis, and so on — but the key image even here is of activities that are mainly the province of the academic community. Heritage is something done by heritage professionals, and sometimes ordinary people get to look at the results of their labors, but usually through a glass case in a museum.

For children, exposure to heritage data may range from schoolroom lessons in "what Indians did before white men came" through more productive visits to living history sites where they actually get to card wool, bake bread, and perhaps dip candles. The impact of the latter is infinitely superior to "book learning" in interesting the young in the remnants of past cultures. They experience history rather than simply hearing and reading about it.

Yet even in experiential teaching situations, the young participants are well aware that the objects they are handling are usually reproductions, that the activities in which they engage are ones where they "can't do any harm," and that the entire exercise is established as a "learning experience," as opposed to an actual pursuit with defined goals. It isn't real.

With archaeology, educators have a unique opportunity to involve ordinary people and even school children in the actual process of scientific and cultural research. Students can not only see the various methods of discovery in operation, but they can reach out and touch artifacts, hearths, layers, and postmolds. Participants can experience their texture, their scent, color, and weight for themselves. They can be the first humans to handle an object since it was left behind in the earth a hundred or a thousand years ago. They can actually touch the past.

A few years ago in Toronto, a group of archaeologists and educators explored the possibilities of their respective disciplines and came up with a combined research and teaching package whereby children of public schools, as well as large numbers of city residents, could take part in archaeological research. The system which sprung from this most profitable partnership encompass both the various concerns inherent in cultural resource management and the "putting into practice" of modern educational theory.

## CULTURAL RESOURCE MANAGEMENT: THE ROLE OF EDUCATION

The very term "cultural resource management" subsumes a public and political role in preserving the past. It coordinates the efforts of a plethora of heritage and related professions, special interest groups, consultants, and both public and private sector institutions, in the pursuit of a common goal: the discovery and conservation of man-made heritage resources.

By definition, cultural resource management assumes the commitment of both tax dollars and private monies in the achievement of its objectives. Further, it requires official support from the immense variety of governmental organizations and establishments upon which its activities must impact. Planners, developers, commercial interests, and ordinary landowners, as well as the vocational and avocational cultural communities, are all thrown into the pot together to interrelate in ways that range from the direct, and sometimes violent, to the highly subtle. Yet cooperation between all such groups and individuals is necessary, for they have a crucial role to play in saving our nations' (and I use the plural advisedly) inheritance from the past.

Efforts in cultural resource management perforce compete with the compelling needs of modern societies and governments. Loss of heritage resources seems a small price to pay for progress, especially at a time when the public purse is strained to its limits from demands for housing, hospitals, medical care, and other indisputable priorities. Yet the cultural wealth that heritage resources represent is irreplaceable, and our generation is not its sole proprietors. It is also our legacy to the future.

In trying to ensure that some remnants of earlier human cultures will be preserved for later generations, those professions that have assumed responsibility for research and conservation of such resources must take a leading role. It is to ourselves that the public looks for guidance in respect to the very disciplines we have chosen as our own. In pursuit of our higher research goals, it is perhaps as well to remember to whom the sites, heritage buildings, and artifacts belong — the public — and who has been paying, directly or indirectly, for the research so far — the public.

Reflection upon the objectives of cultural research and their more tangible benefits predicates a demonstration by heritage professionals to the public of just what these benefits are. From a humanities viewpoint, the goals are clear. But when a municipal government must defend itself to a voting population clamoring for affordable housing, reasons for leaving large tracts with archaeological "potential" undeveloped are perhaps less than self-evident. After all, the sites relate to people long dead, and the concern of modern elected officials is with the living.

What role, then, do cultural resources serve in the modern world? "Quality of life" is the immediate and rather pat response we tend to make. Yes, but . . . how does the salvaging of historical buildings, the excavation of sites, the conservation of bits of ceramic and glass used centuries ago translate into a *direct* benefit to the modern community? The answer is, all too often, that it doesn't. Small wonder, then, that heritage conservation receives ever-diminishing support from public sources.

Clearly, what is needed are answers to queries regarding the importance of cultural resource management, now and for the future: queries made by the people whose heritage it is and who are being asked to pay for the work. The solutions lie in either demonstrating, or actually creating, a relevance beyond the usual institutional purview of "higher learning."

## THE ARCHAEOLOGICAL RESOURCE CENTRE: ARCHAEOLOGY IN EDUCATION

In Toronto an unusual experiment has taken place over the past several years. It was undertaken for a very specific purpose: to give the city's urban archaeology a direct bearing on the everyday lives of the townsfolk of every age and at every income level. In formulating the methodology for so doing, a group of archaeologists and educators turned the goals of "public" archaeology around; instead of doing education for the sake of publicizing the importance of archaeology, it is doing archaeology for the sake of education. Thus, archaeology becomes an important and permanent part of the city infrastructure because it does not serve only the needs of research and cultural resource preservation; it becomes a vehicle, in and of itself, for teaching the public to enjoy its past.

In 1985 the Toronto Board of Education was granted nearly a quarter-of-a-million dollars by the provincial government. The monies were earmarked for the design and implementation of a new type of educational facility — the Archaeological Resource Centre (ARC). Serving a tripartite mandate of education, heritage research, and conservation, the center is fully supported as a permanent part of the public school system. It is, to date, the only such facility in the world.

The philosophy of the ARC is that ordinary people, including school children, have a stake in the conservation of their area's heritage resources. By providing them with opportunities to · reach out and "touch the past," heritage professionals can encourage a sense of ownership of and ·' pride in their own city's cultural wealth. With this sense of ownership comes protectiveness for · a valued possession. The public therefore becomes the driving force behind efforts to conserve · its heritage.

On the other hand, students of our schools have long been taught information which is (or should be) archaeologically derived. This is especially true of the teaching of North American prehistory, but also is true of the history of early European immigration into our continent. Yet only rarely are students exposed to how this information is acquired. Involvement of school children in archaeological excavation, recording, and interpretation of data serves as a highly effective tool in the more general realm of public education. They learn scientific process rather than "facts," and develop skills that are applicable to a wide variety of other subject areas.

The ARC operates an annual calendar of excavation, curriculum development and implementation, and publicity aimed at involving as many people as possible in heritage programs. A major objective was, and is, to create entire generations of Torontonians for whom urban archaeological projects are a normal, familiar, comprehensible, and highly valuable part of their cityscape.

It should also be noted, however, that in developing a facility for the teaching of archaeology, we also created a system, with full public sector commitment, for doing urban archaeology on a permanent basis. This provides a superb opportunity to implement long-range research goals, develop a local artifact reference collection, and hone both methods and understanding to a fine edge. This ongoing work affords to both the archaeological community and the educational system an ever-growing corpus of information about Toronto's 19th and early 20th century heritage.

## EDUCATION IN ARCHAEOLOGY

Intrinsic to the ARC development was an assessment of archaeology's potential in light of modern educational theory and practice. Skills and abilities borrowed from such diverse areas as marketing, media relations, environmental assessment, and community service were mixed into the formula. The initial phases of creation seemed at times more like the conduct of a political or military campaign than the familiar and comfortably private research in which archaeologists expect to involve themselves. High-profile programs were initiated, efforts were made to create a market for archaeology in a highly diverse milieu, and the archaeological framework itself was examined to allow for modifications required by this new conceptual approach to the discipline.

The result was the creation of a comprehensive and cohesive system of education and archaeology whereby ordinary members of the public, and especially school-aged children, actually conduct some of the research. New approaches to field and laboratory methodology had to be devised to provide for the meeting of research goals and the proper execution of scientific analysis processes in such a situation. Basic criteria for the type of sites to be investigated, the goals of research to be conducted, and the kinds of programs that could be safely and effectively offered in both the outdoor, on-site context and in the schoolroom had to be established. In addition, the archaeologists had to learn a great deal about how teachers teach. They had to immerse themselves in the needs, methods, and mandate of the institution of which they were becoming a part — the Toronto Board of Education — but which had, as yet, no mechanisms for dealing with the requirements and practices of an archaeological unit.

Archaeology actually suits modern educational theory extremely well. It is by its very nature multidisciplinary and thus can serve as a focus for education in a great many subject areas. In addition, archaeology's process of preliminary formulation of research goals, subsequent implementation of research projects, analysis of acquired data, and final interpretation is directly relevant to today's pedagological concept of learner-centered education within a realistic learning environment. Problem solving is a major focus of current educational theory, and the application of acquired skills for implicit and specific purposes is common to both teaching and archaeological practice.

## TEACHING THE PAST: MEANS AND METHOD

Since the concept of teaching archaeology at the pre- or extrauniversity level is a relatively recent phenomenon, little in the way of printed documentation on the subject exists. Teaching methods, instructional media materials, and field excavation and recording systems for use in public projects are all in the process of development in various places around the world. In many cases, individual teachers and archaeologists are operating in isolation and thus "reinventing the wheel" when it comes to just how to go about educating people about archaeology. However, there are some bright lights on the horizon.

A great many groups are currently exploring the possibilities of education and archaeology as a means for increasing public support for cultural resource conservation (see McNutt, Hawkins, and Rogge, this volume). The various professional organizations on this continent — the Society for American Archaeology, the American Anthropological Association, the Society for Historical Archaeology, and the Canadian Archaeological Association to name only a few — have taken great strides forward in recent years in this regard. In Britain, English Heritage has long played a leading role in this endeavor. Where once the argument over whether public archaeology ought to be done at all dominated discussion, we now find entire sessions at conferences, and even whole symposia (for example, the University of Minnesota's "Presenting the Past to the Public" series of meetings), devoted to not the "whys," but the "hows" of teaching people about the need to conserve the past (see Wells, this volume, for a discussion of the "Presenting the Past" conference series).

Newsletters have sprung up *(Teaching Anthropology Newsletter* out of St. Mary's University in Halifax, the SAA's *Archaeology and Public Education,* and *Archaeology and Education* produced between individuals in Britain, America, and Canada) to provide an information exchange between teachers, archaeologists, museologists, and other heritage professionals engaged in meeting these common goals. At least one book has been published on the subject. The latter was produced as part of the "One World Archaeology Series" (published by Unwin Hyman in 1990, entitled *The Excluded Past: Archaeology in Education,* and edited by Peter Stone and Robert MacKenzie) as a result of the World Archaeology Congress efforts to provide an international perspective.

# TAKING ARCHAEOLOGY TO THE PUBLIC: THE "HOWS"

The concept of taking archaeology to the public is neither new nor unique to Toronto. But the means by which this is being conducted in that city is highly unusually and bears closer scrutiny.

The Archaeological Resource Centre has a staff of seven professional archaeologists, each with experience on a wide variety of sites and with expertise in a specific area of archaeological research. In addition, these individuals have a deep and abiding commitment to the importance of teaching people of all ages about the need for conserving their common heritage as human beings. In forming this team, nearly as much emphasis was placed on each person's educational and public service experience as on archaeology credentials.

Through this group's remarkable initiative, the role of archaeology in Toronto has taken on a completely new thrust. Archaeology is done in a formal context with fully-developed scientific research goals, but with an institutional commitment provided by public government for a purpose contiguous with, but different from, the traditional academic one. Here, annual urban projects are operated for the purposes of education, education on a broad and highly relevant scale — teaching school children and interested adults about their city's past through participating in the recovery of its heritage remains. Thus, archaeology takes on a new form and a new function. Rather than the public being a necessary and politically desirable adjunct to research programs conducted by professional archaeologists, professional archaeologists run digs that have as a main objective the meeting of curriculum goals set by professional educators.

The heritage professionals on the Archaeological Resource Centre staff have always been more than aware of the potential pitfalls inherent in doing archaeology where the majority of the finds are made by people under the age of 16. But the argument for teaching the public the reasons for cultural resource conservation through encouraging ordinary people to help do it was indisputable. The first task was the development of systems where research and education (hands-on education on real archaeological sites) could be carried out safely, profitably, and efficiently.

The success of both the educational programs and the seven excavations that have been conducted by the Centre to date bear out the effectiveness of the comprehensive system of teaching, excavation, recording, analysis, and reporting that has been created for use in Toronto schools. Anyone wondering whether "teachers will go for it" should note that all programs are booking 1 year in advance, and we have not advertised since 1986.

To provide for both educational and research needs, an operational structure was formulated for public education projects in archaeology. Paramount, from the professional point of view, was a research design whose goals were realistic and could be met within this new and rather overwhelming context. This research design was, of necessity, dictated by the types of sites that could safely be excavated with large groups of the uninitiated making up part of the crew. But it was also developed with a strong sense of the pedagological objectives of running archaeological projects with an educational bent. The purposes of the dig and the physical framework of the educational experience had to be both effective as a learning environment and archaeologically relevant.

Toronto has a strong multicultural population. As freshly styled educators, the archaeologists sought research goals that also would best serve the needs of the children who were to be the audience. Since many classes are made up of New Canadians, the archaeological research focused the exploration of Toronto's 19th century immigrant heritage. The choice was made to dig domestic and commercial sites once occupied by ordinary people, people just like the families of the children who were to take part in their excavation. Clearly defined stratigraphy, substantial subsurface structural remains, and a high artifact count ensure that there are sufficient familiar and understandable elements in each site to excite both the imagination and the intellect of even very young participants.

In most cases, students dig in areas where demolition debris ensures secondary deposition. When sensitive levels are reached, the professional staff and experienced volunteers take over, and student groups are moved to another area of the site. Approximately twice the area is opened that could reasonably be expected to be completed within a 6-month period. Students receive the same experience as if they were digging *in situ* remains; yet the site's research potential is protected.

An exploration of the urban milieu at the lower-to-middle income level has not to date been undertaken in Toronto, so the research design serves a real and appreciable purpose in increasing archaeological knowledge of the city's development. Furthermore, these sites usually would not be considered "delicate" from an archaeological standpoint, nor would they be the first choice of most researchers working in the area.

The next step in the Centre's development was the establishment of an annual calendar to allow the maximum number of students in both site and classroom programs while permitting sufficient man-hours for the execution of those aspects of archaeological research that must remain the purview of the professional staff.

A public archaeology project spans the period from May through November each year. This permits the operation of half-day class field trips in the spring and fall terms, as well as the administration of two 6-week credit courses — field schools in every sense of the term — for secondary students in the summer months. Further, it takes place at the time when most city residents seek recreational/educational activities in which to take part — the summer months. The projects of the Archaeological Resource Centre are as "public" as we can make them. Throughout the digging season, literally anyone can come to the site, book in for an introductory program in the method and theory of historical archaeology, and then volunteer on the dig as often as they wish. All programs are offered free of charge, and most are available in either English or French. A surprising number of Torontonians and tourists avail themselves of the opportunity.

Modification of modern excavation and recording methods has produced a highly detailed, yet comprehensible, system where even school children can make a significant contribution. Recording forms are written in simple English, but are just as detailed as the more technical ones ordinarily used on research projects. Sites are laid out so groups can be effectively supervised, while areas of higher sensitivity can be left for the professional and experienced volunteer to investigate.

All artifacts are mapped in place; this teaches both mathematical and archaeological skills while ensuring that slow, careful work is conducted by even the most junior (age 9) of participants. An unexpected byproduct of this highly structured hands-on system is the benefits it brings in teaching mathematical, cartographic, and dexterity skills to students in special education, learning disabled, and English-as-a-Second-Language classes. Small-group learning and problem solving are inherent in the normal functioning of an archaeological project, as are the development of integrated learning skills drawn from different disciplines. All in all, even a 3-hour program on a site can provide an excellent learning experience for school children.

Prior to taking part in the dig, an introduction to archaeological method and theory is offered in a nearby classroom. Students are cautioned to maintain proper methodology "because you have the privilege today of taking part in a real archaeological dig, and we are trusting you. If you make a mistake, we can't fix it, and that part of your history will be lost forever." The more skeptical readers may be surprised at how well this works. Of more than 50,000 participants to date, only a handful have been removed from the site for carelessness. We all respond well to being trusted to do something "very, very important," and small children are no exception to this rule.

At the end of each program, a site button and brochure is distributed to each student. This not only increases the educational impact, but broadens the lesson in heritage conservation to parents and siblings when the child returns home. Before they leave, students are thanked for their "help in saving Toronto's heritage" through their work on the site.

During the winter months, seven half-day programs per week are offered at the Centre's classrooms for children and adults. Subjects range from prehistoric art through the archaeology of early Toronto. All programs emphasize problem solving in a group-learning context, and the handling of real (if less than unique) heritage artifacts is a component. Coming to understand the use of primary source materials for documentary interpretation ensures that students gain an understanding of how archaeologists find and interpret urban sites.

In addition to class field trips, the Centre offers night school courses for adults, cooperative education programs (where individual secondary students help in data and artifact processing over an entire school year), seniors classes at community centers and facilities throughout the city, elementary school outreach programs (small people love bones), and volunteer workshops. During the winter, participation by volunteers and students in artifact processing greatly aids in achieving the annual reporting goals of the Centre. Reports are, of course, produced by the archaeologists on the staff. The carefully constructed calendar sets time aside for meeting research and analysis goals.

Yet even the site reports, normally extremely technical in content and of, ahem, limited appeal to the average reader, serve an educational purpose. Information contained in the report does not rest on a shelf, gathering dust. Every discovery, every interpretation, every new perspective on Toronto's urban heritage is fed back into the school system in some way. Booklets for use in schools are produced, new curricula for day programs are developed, and slide sets are loaned out to teachers to encourage the use of archaeologically derived information in schools throughout the system. Thus, the archaeological programs also provide a self-generating corpus of new teaching data each year.

Because there are few curricula and very little in the way of instructional media materials or even books designed for the teaching of archaeology at a preuniversity level, all teaching materials (quizzes, games, educational kits, and the like) must be produced in-house at the Archaeological Resource Centre. These are used throughout the school system by consultants, teachers, and students.

The Toronto Board of Education has taken archaeology to heart in a big way. The Board has more than 200,000 students and adults in its programs; at some point in their education, the majority of these will be impacted by archaeology at the ARC.

In addition, the Archaeological Resource Centre operates an intensive year-round public information program. Displays, special events, published articles, and public talks ensure that a far wider audience is reached than will ever visit a site or take part in an archaeological excavation. Media attention has been consistent and enthusiastic, making the efforts of the board in the realm of heritage conservation and education widely known. Apparently the concept of school children digging up their own city's past is one that has an extremely broad popular appeal.

# CONCLUSION: TEACHING PEOPLE TO TOUCH THE PAST

This brings us to what is perhaps the most important impact of the Archaeological Resource Centre on the preservation of Toronto's cultural resources. Because urban archaeology is being conducted by the Board of Education, more people know about and care about saving heritage sites and structures. These resources are thus valued not only as a significant part of the city's past, but as a focus for the future through their role in education.

By doing archaeology for the purposes of education, instead of education for the purposes of archaeology, the Archaeological Resource Centre in Toronto has, in a large metropolitan area, achieved a climate of popular and political support for heritage conservation that showing people what archaeologists do through lectures, slides, newspaper articles, or impassioned exhortations on the part of heritage professionals could not have achieved.

In developing the Archaeological Resource Centre, both educators and archaeologists have created an entirely new vehicle for transmitting and interpreting the urgency of cultural resource conservation to the general public. A whole generation of school children is learning how archaeology can help them take part in saving their own past, not for themselves alone, but for their children and their children's children. The Centre continues to develop new systems of education, new instructional media materials for use in the classroom and beyond, and more effective and comprehensive methods for conducting quality research projects within a completely public setting. The process is far from finished.

The people who take part in Toronto public archaeology projects know that they are not just learning something and having fun. They are helping to discover and preserve Toronto's heritage — their heritage — no matter how long they have been here or where their original homeland was. By taking part in digs, the people and the school children of the city of Toronto learn that they have an important stake in saving what is now their own past, as Torontonians, for the future.

# ARCHAEOLOGY FOR THE CLASSROOM —
# PROJECT ARCHEOLOGY: SAVING TRADITIONS

## Nan McNutt

## INTRODUCTION

Archaeology education is perceived differently by different people. Archaeologists view archaeology education from the stand point of archaeology. Educators look at the compatibility of archaeology to the existing curriculum. Native people focus on cultural awareness. Although these goals may not be in opposition, meeting the expectation of each interest group can be challenging. However, sometimes upon closer examination, the goals are found to be so compatible that they are one in the same.

Within archaeology education there are a number of goals to be considered; two will be discussed in this article. One goal is to establish good educational practices that are fun and exciting, allowing students to problem-solve real life issues in their communities. These practices should address students' learning skills through interdisciplinary themes, increasing the understanding of the relationship between science, technology, and society. Students need to challenge their higher level thinking, and above all, they need to succeed (Carnegie Council on Adolescent Development 1989; American Association for the Advancement of Science 1989).

Another goal within archaeology education is to stop the destruction of our national heritage and future data source. Archaeological sites, despite antilooting laws, continue to be destroyed at an alarming rate (see Domenici, Nickens, King, and McAllister, this volume, for further discussion of the level of site destruction). Attention must be paid to developing an ethic and civic responsibility that creates respect of others' property even when the ownership is unknown. It is an ethic that does not blossom on its own, but must be nurtured with intentional and sequential intervention. This type of care will produce an advocacy group. Archaeology needs an advocacy group that understands the importance of conservation archaeology and embraces this challenge with tenacity and enthusiasm.

## CHILDREN AS ADVOCATES FOR ARCHAEOLOGY

Children are the bottom line. They need to be part of something fun and exciting that engages them with real life situations that stress and stretch them to higher thinking skills. Children need recognition for what they can do when empowered (Carnegie Council on Adolescent Development 1989; American Association for the Advancement of Science 1989; also see Smardz, this volume). Children can be the advocacy group that falls in love with the adventure of archaeology and carries it through, taking civic pride in their involvement to protect our national heritage.

Many actions can be taken to develop an advocacy group, but none will be as important as insuring the instruction of archaeology education in the classroom and other centers of learning. To be effective, the instruction must meet the needs of both conservation archaeology and good educational practices.

## A NATIONAL MODEL FOR ADVOCACY

Clumps of students are scattered throughout the grounds of the Bush Home, an historic home

143

site in Seattle, WA. Laughter, shouts, and murmurs of discussions surround each group as a few students photograph the paintworn walls. Others draw specific details of the main house, and still others, with the use of compasses, metric tapes, and centimeter grid paper, begin the process of mapping this piece of heritage that is quietly rotting away.

These students have already completed an initial inventory, combed the early newspapers for references, and interviewed several old timers who remember the Bush family. During this final visit, they are to complete their "survey" and then send their record to the State Historic Preservation Office.

This process, which instills civic responsibility and an ethic of conserving our past, is part of the final unit in the interdisciplinary curriculum *Project Archeology: Saving Traditions (P.A.S.T.)* (McNutt 1988). *P.A.S.T.* is a unique middle school/junior high curriculum concerned with conservation archaeology and educating children. Students are actively involved with ten major principles in archaeology, which include absolute and relative time, stratigraphy, importance of provenience, rates of decomposition, and sites as nonrenewable resources.

Science, social studies, language art, and mathematics comprise the core studies that strengthen the students' basic skills while applying them in a real situation. Most of the classroom lessons are set up to help the students to become problem solvers. They understand the expectations of the situation, explore the variables, and explain their outcome. Finally, students expand new information into new experiences.

Questioning strategies for critical thinking, included in the teachers manual and the students' field notebooks, moves the students beyond asking questions for questions' sake. Students are encouraged to ask questions about things they want to know while involving the skills of analysis, synthesis, and evaluation. Students' questions then become relevant and thought provoking, stimulating their critical thinking process.

Although validated as a Washington State curriculum, *P.A.S.T.* applicability to any region sets it as a national model for teaching conservation archaeology. Designed within its scope are opportunities to apply regional materials when available, so that the curriculum encompasses both a global and regional view of archaeology (see Messenger and Enloe, this volume, for a discussion of archaeologists as global educators).

*Project Archeology: Saving Traditions* was specifically designed for students of the 6th through 8th grades; however, the concepts and some activities also apply to the lower and upper grades. In Petersburg, AK, students in the high school surveying course, with the guidance of a local archaeologist, took on the responsibility of mapping five prehistoric fish traps and surrounding areas. This activity has helped the students apply their surveying knowledge and has fostered an understanding of site conservation.

In Tucson, AZ, third graders constructed an example of an archaeological site by layering soil within clear-plastic shoe boxes. Studiously they measured and graphed the contours of each layer. This is just one example of how the presented skills are applicable to the lower grades. Upon completion of their graphs and discussions on how archaeological sites are formed, the teacher scooped up a large portion of soil from one of the student boxes and dumped it back into the newly made hole. Some students shrieked and others groaned, "You ruined it!" The teacher had just set the stage for these students to discuss archaeological site looting and vandalism and what they as a group can do about it.

This curriculum is not the only instructional material to embrace the challenge of archaeology education. There are a host of others, some singular activities, others regional materials, all developed to foster student appreciation for our national heritage and to address the problem of site destruction (Smith 1990; also see Hawkins, this volume).

## CRITERIA FOR INSTRUCTIONAL MATERIALS

Not since the controversial national banning of *Man A Course of Study (M.A.C.O.S.)*, a curriculum in anthropology developed in the early 1970s, has there been such a quantity of archaeological materials available to the schools. *M.A.C.O.S.*, which presented other cultures' values, so outraged many Americans that the curriculum was banned from schools (Rice 1986). Funding sources to develop other anthropological/archaeological materials disappeared immediately, and institutions of education found other social science studies to take the place of anthropology. In 1975 *Project Archeology: Saving Traditions* was funded for 5 years to develop and test an archaeology program that was interdisciplinary and scientifically based. By the mid 1980s, when archaeologists, themselves, began developing materials to counter the destruction of archaeological sites, a large quantity of instructional materials became available to the schools. A compilation of all these materials, published in *Pathways to the Past* (Smith 1990), identifies and briefly describes what is available. Since its printing, new materials have been developed. These materials range from instructions for a simulation dig, to the video story of looters among the Mayan ruins (Sunburst Communications 1989).

Some of these materials have been developed as isolated activities, allowing teachers to pick and choose which activities best fit their classroom studies. Some are units of study to be used as part of the social studies curriculum. Few have a scope and sequence that allows archaeology education to be part of an interdisciplinary study.

Archaeology is a science and uses the scientific method, along with other related disciplines, such as geology, biology, and chemistry. But at the elementary, middle school, and high school levels, archaeology is often taught in social studies textbooks by teachers with little training in the scientific process. Students graduate from high school thinking that archaeology is a mixture of glamorous adventure and stories portraying the ancient world. The vast majority go through life with this misconception, giving little heed to the worthiness of archaeology as a scientific study or to their own role in stopping the destruction of archaeological sites.

In 1988 a task force was established by the American Anthropological Association to explore efforts for teaching anthropology in North American schools (Selig 1989). Perhaps it is time archaeologists, along with educators nationwide, develop a set of criteria regarding what constitutes effective archaeology education. These criteria can be used to review developed materials and make recommendations concerning appropriate modifications.

## ARCHAEOLOGISTS BENEFITTING STUDENTS

In their publication "Archeology in the Classroom: A Case Study from Arizona," Rogge and Bell acknowledge the importance of developing a strong relationship between educators, the community, and archaeologists. In Arizona, these three groups have joined together to form the Arizona Archaeological Council (AAC). The challenge of archaeology being part of classroom instruction lies "in getting the ear" of the education system (Rogge and Bell 1989; also see Rogge, this volume).

In order that classroom instruction focuses on the concerns of archaeology, archaeologists must first address the concerns of educators. Becoming familiar with state, district, and school guidelines will inform archaeologists about the essential skills, knowledge, and attitudes addressed by educators. The following are examples taken from the state of Connecticut's "Common Core of Learning" (Connecticut State Board of Education 1987), which defines skills, attitudes, and applications crucial to learning.

Students will

1.  Recognize the necessity for moral and ethical conduct in a society. (Conservation archaeology places greatest importance on protecting the whole: sites, artifacts, and context. It is part of the existing ethical system that teaches, along with respect for yourself and for others, respect for property, cultures, and the environment.)
2.  Understand the roles played by various racial, ethnic, and religious groups in developing the nation's pluralistic society. (Through the study of past peoples, we can better understand the development of different cultures and how different groups of people relate to one another).
3.  Understand the implications of limited natural resources, the study of ecology, and the need for conservation. (Archaeological resources are finite resources, once destroyed they are gone forever).

A dialogue between educators and archaeologists will facilitate the understanding of these educational and archaeological needs. The vehicle for this dialogue, in most cases, is already established. Throughout the U.S., educators meet according to disciplines, i.e., social studies coordinators, science coordinators, etc. These groups include university and college professors, museum educators, and fellow educators from industries, who align themselves with similar educational interest.

Educators must hear that archaeology can be used to meet some of the essential skills, knowledge, and attitudes included in their educational guidelines and that archaeology can be used as a focus for a variety of subjects, i.e., science, mathematics, social studies, language arts, and art. Archaeology is an inquiring discipline and can be used to stimulate students to ask questions and to think critically.

Informing education professors, social studies and science coordinators, other administrators, and museum and industry educators as to how archaeology benefits education is paramount. These core groups understand the educational system and will be instrumental in gaining entry into the classroom. Archaeologists' reception by an education group depends largely on how instrumental archaeologists are in meeting the group's needs and, in turn, demonstrating the needs of archaeology.

Within this role, archaeologists can serve as advisors, providing information about regional archaeology and resources for classroom use. Archaeologists along with educators can identify instructional materials that meet archaeology education criteria. They can assist in teacher training/in-servicing and preteacher education. While the responsibility remains in the hands of the educator, archaeologists must be persistent in seeing that archaeology and archaeologists are included in this educational process.

As volunteers in the classroom, archaeologists should be considered a luxury. Their audience is limited; if they were to spend the same amount of energy assisting in preteacher/teacher education, their efforts would be multiplied. However, while volunteering in the classroom does not create a multiplier effect, it can be a most enjoyable and educational experience for both archaeologist and students.

To make this a quality experience, archaeologists involved with a classroom or a field trip should ask that participatory instruction take place prior to and following the visit. The previsit instruction serves to reduce the novelty of the occasion, thus preparing the student for the new information (Kubota 1985; Falk et al. 1978). In this manner, the archaeologist has not just heightened the students' interest in archaeology, but has prepared an instructional sequence of concepts and skills concerning archaeology.

Before visiting classes, archaeologists should review the information to be presented, identifying ways students can participate through activities or small group discussions. This type of learning has been demonstrated to produce retained learning: the least effective way people learn is through reading (10% retention), hearing (20% retention), looking at pictures (30% retention), while people tend to remember 90% of what they both say and do with real experiences (Edgar 1989). Activities involving individual or small group participation increase the students' retention. Examples include experimentation with raw materials, i.e., clay for pots (Ehrenhard and Ehrenhard 1988), or small group discussions of archaeological dilemmas, i.e., what to do after finding an old pioneer's cabin (Ellick 1990), or classification of fish hooks according to types (Oi and Tamura 1980). Following this type of involvement, the students are better able to extend their learning and use their higher level thinking skills to analyze, synthesize, and evaluate (Bloom 1985).

## TEACHER SUPPORT AND TRAINING

The development of instructional materials that meet prescribed criteria and the inclusion of archaeologists in the education community do not insure the success of an archaeology education program in the classroom. These are two important elements, but training of teachers and follow-up support by archaeologists empowers the teachers to create effective archaeology education for their students.

Project Archeology: Saving Traditions (P.A.S.T.) has incorporated a model of teacher training and follow-up support that introduces teachers to the global view of archaeology, with regional emphasis. An educational facilitator and an archaeologist team together, with the P.A.S.T. facilitator presenting the classroom materials, including various instructional strategies.

Modeling forms the basis of instruction, with the education facilitator presenting the activities just as they are to be taught in the classroom. Too often in workshops as well as college courses, teacher training becomes a lecture format, quickly passing over the practicum of "hands-on" experience. Teachers need to be taught in the way they will teach. At the same time, the P.A.S.T. facilitator instructs on an adult level, recognizing the teachers as experts in their field. This may seem counter to the idea of modeling, but in fact it is part of the modeling process. Students as well as adults need to know that their ideas and actions are valid.

The facilitator encourages the teachers to share their ideas and experiences and to modify the materials to their own situation. This act of ownership by the teachers is vital if the program is to succeed. Scheduling time for feedback from the teachers following each activity is one way to implement ownership. During this time teachers begin to perceive how they might use the materials within their own classrooms.

A regional archaeologist is selected to assist with the P.A.S.T. workshops, based on this person's command of regional archaeology and willingness to work with the teachers after the workshop is over. As the archaeologist attends the workshop, a familiarity with the instructional materials and each teacher is established. A mutual trust is important, enabling the teachers and the archaeologist to work together once the teachers have gone back to their classrooms and the P.A.S.T. facilitator has departed. This follow-up support has taken many forms. In some cases the teachers call the archaeologist to ask questions and share their students' work. In other instances, the teachers ask for periodic meetings as a group, and in some areas avocational and professional archaeological organizations have welcomed the teachers as new members.

Although this support of teachers by archaeologists appears as a "nicety," it is the element that makes or breaks a program. Repeatedly, good instructional materials have simply sat on the school shelves because teachers began to question the worthiness of their instruction and because they lacked the inspiration to continue. Some form of archaeological support is imperative for ongoing classroom success.

## CONCLUSION

The integrating of archaeology into society at large, and most specifically into the classroom, is essential if we are to preserve the sources of future archaeological data and our common heritage. In order to accomplish this, archaeology and education need to be integrated to meet the goals of archaeology education. The players are clear: students, educators, and archaeologists. We have the instructional materials, and we have, collectively, the knowledge to undertake the challenge. What we need is the will.

## REFERENCES CITED

American Association for the Advancement of Science (1989) *Project 2061, Science for All Americans,* American Association for the Advancement of Science, Washington, D.C., 7–8.

Bloom, B. S. (1985) *Taxonomy of Educational Objectives,* Longman, New York and London, 144–192.

Carnegie Council on Adolescent Development (1989) *Turning Points, Preparing American Youth for the 21st Century,* Washington, D.C., 55–106.

Connecticut State Board of Education (1987) Connecticut's Common Core of Learning, CT. State Board of Education, Hartford, 13–16.

Edgar, D. (1989) Experience and learning, *J. Coll. Sci. Teaching,* November 1989.

Ehrenhard, J. and Ehrenhard, E. (1988) Did Indians eat pizza? Clay pots, *Heritage Educ. Q.* 3, 2.

Ellick, C. (1990) *Archaeology Dilemma Cards,* Tucson, AZ, unpublished.

Falk, J. H., Martin, W. W., and Balling, J. D. (1978) The novel field trip phenomenon: adjustment to novel settings interferes with task learning, *J. Res. Sci. Teaching,* 15(2), 127–134.

Kubota, C. (1985) Effects of Novelty-Reducing Preparation on Exploratory Behavior and Cognitive Learning, unpublished dissertation.

McNutt, N. (1988) *Project Archeology: Saving Traditions,* Sopris West, Longmont, CO.

Oi, A. and Tamura E. (1980) Behold Hawai'i, 3.3 Department. of Education, HI.

Rice, M. J. (1986) Curriculum artifacts: the remains of three anthropology projects, *Pract. Anthropol.,* 8(3–4), 6, 19.

Rogge, A. E. and Bell, P. (1989) Archeology in the classroom: a case study from Arizona, Archaeological Assistance Program Technical Briefs, 4.

Selig, R. O. (1989) The AAA Task Force on Teaching Anthropology, *Anthro Notes,* 2.3.

Smith, K. C. (1990) *Pathways to the Past,* Museum of Florida History, Tallahassee, FL.

Sunburst Communication (1989) *The Second Voyage of the Mimi*, Pleasantville, N.Y.

# CLASSROOM ARCHAEOLOGY: INCLUDING ARCHAEOLOGY IN EXISTING CURRICULA; AN EXAMPLE FROM LOUISIANA

Nancy W. Hawkins

## INTRODUCTION

For more than 20 years, archaeologists and teachers have explored many ways to include archaeology in classroom teaching. Some of the most impressive strategies are (1) resident week-long teacher workshops with excavation and laboratory components (Holm 1985), (2) excavation projects for students (Cook 1985; Cotter 1979; Tirrell 1983), (3) programs at archaeological sites or museums for school groups (Harrison 1984; Tirrell 1983), and (4) lengthy units or courses with a substantial classroom component (Abell 1985; Anderson 1979; Chu 1982; Corbin 1985; Dyche 1985; Hartman 1985; McNutt 1988; Parren 1987; Thomas 1967; also see McNutt, this volume).

Educators support and endorse these kinds of activities because of their hands-on, interdisciplinary nature and their ability to develop skills in reasoning, problem solving, critical thinking, and social interaction (Abell 1985; Carroll 1987; Dyche 1985; Gettings 1970; Higgins and Holm 1985; McNutt 1988; Rogge and Bell 1989). They provide highly stimulating, enriching experiences that cannot be replicated in other settings.

All of these programs, however, require somewhat extraordinary conditions. For the first three types, the most obvious conditions required are proximity to an organization offering these programs and awareness of their availability. Even in regions in which these may be available and publicized, success depends on (1) teachers financially able and intellectually motivated to travel to a resident field workshop, (2) students financially and emotionally able to participate in an excavation, (3) students being taken to a museum or site with an outstanding educational program, or (4) an exceptional school that allows somewhat unusual electives or great flexibility within the existing curriculum.

In Louisiana, educational archaeology programs were first developed by the state archaeologist's office in the early 1980s. At that time, no resident workshops or field schools designed for teachers or precollege students were regularly offered in the state or in any of the bordering states. No archaeology courses for any students were offered in schools, and archaeology programs for school groups at museums and sites were limited. Furthermore, the specific content of school courses and length of time to be spent on each topic were outlined at the state level.

Severely limited funding for state archaeological projects forced consideration of how effectively to reach the widest school audience, with the least expenditure of staff time and money. Excavation projects were immediately eliminated from consideration because of their expense in both time and money and because of the limited number of persons who could participate annually.

Strategies that were explored and ultimately implemented in Louisiana were (1) booklets, (2) classroom materials to be used in existing courses, (3) presentations at social studies and science conventions, (4) displays at teachers' conventions, (5) in-service training sessions for teachers, and (6) working with the state Department of Education to amend the state guidelines for basic content of one or more required courses.

# PLANNING

The first concern was deciding what it is about archaeology that a majority of students should know. A course taught to a group of highly motivated teachers or students for 8 hours a day for 7 days or to academically advanced students for 50 min a day for a semester can include a broad introduction to archaeology. Difficult priorities have to be set for less intense interaction with less-motivated participants. This was accomplished in Louisiana in a loosely step-by-step process.

The first step was to articulate the purpose of endorsing the teaching of archaeology. Educators want an exciting way to help students gain basic knowledge and skills. Archaeologists should take advantage of this aspect of teaching archaeology, but in the planning stage must focus on the archaeological goals. What is it about archaeology that this educational experience should teach? Generally, the hope is that the content should enhance an appreciation for archaeology and for "the resource." Specifically, two basic interests directed all of the Louisiana public archaeology programs: the obligation to share with the public information discovered through archaeology, and the hope that better understanding of archaeology will result in better site preservation.

The next step was to clarify what about archaeology should be taught. In reaching the goal of sharing information about the past as revealed through archaeology, the appropriate content was relatively easy to identify:

- general and specific information archaeological research has discovered about the people of the state
- the relative length of prehistory compared to history
- general dates of human arrival in the Americas and how that compares with the time dinosaurs lived
- technologies used in the past
- what archaeologists have discovered about the historic era that written documents do not tell
- places to visit to learn more about people in the past

For the goal of improving site preservation, a major stumbling block was encountered and still exists. It is that archaeologists do not know what specific content will result in an interest in site preservation. Some options are

- the range of material remains archaeologists study and how they reflect the life of people who left them
- the importance of context in interpreting archaeological remains
- how sites are recorded
- the techniques and purpose of excavation
- special scientific and technical analyses in archaeology
- archaeological reasoning, hypothesis testing, conclusion drawing
- the importance of stratigraphy in establishing chronology
- the methods of determining relative and absolute dates
- the importance of publishing results of archaeological research
- the importance of conserving sites, threats to sites, and preservation options

The decision then had to be made about which medium or type of experience would best communicate these specific messages. Consultation with teachers and education supervisors indicated that teachers want materials to enhance the teaching of existing topics, that require little preparation and that do not require becoming an expert in another subarea.

For information about archaeological findings, it was decided in Louisiana to use booklets, slide/tape programs, and hands-on artifact kits and to attempt to include archaeological findings in a social studies course. To try to foster an understanding of the principles and processes of archaeology, an activities guide, called *Classroom Archaeology* (Hawkins 1987), was developed.

Another decision had to be made about which grade level to target. Although resourceful teachers of any grade can manage to slip archeology in sometime, it helps in the development of materials to select a specific grade and subject. After consultation with educators, the Louisiana Division of Archaeology decided to focus on eighth grade Louisiana Studies.

A difficult issue was determining a realistic expectation of the amount of class time that teachers will spend with archaeology and how many activities can be covered in that time. In the published Louisiana Studies guidelines, only one week is allocated to Louisiana Indians, past and present; so targeting the prehistoric time period would limit the time in the semester that archaeology could be used. Materials about findings of archaeology would be developed that could also be used in units about exploration, colonization, and the Civil War.

A major consideration of the educational program in Louisiana was how to publicize and distribute the materials. It was decided to establish several networks for getting materials to teachers. These include teacher's workshops, teacher's conventions, and through parish (county) social studies supervisors. Additionally, the products are publicized through an office newsletter and are included on a list of materials that is enclosed with any item requested from the office.

An essential step in developing the project was the commitment to developing ways to monitor use and, someday, to evaluate effectiveness. It was decided to include an evaluation card with all classroom exhibits and to develop a follow-up questionnaire for *Classroom Archaeology* users.

## PHASE ONE IMPLEMENTATION

While the planning of the educational programs in Louisiana followed this general sequence, implementation did not always flow steadily and logically. The enabling legislation of the state archaeological agency stated that the program would include "promulgation...of historic and prehistoric findings" (La. R.S. 41:1607). This directive guided early educational programs that were oriented toward creating and making available information about the results of excavations.

A booklet series was already underway before the formal educational effort began. Continuation of this seemed to be the most cost-effective single step that could be taken to provide information to both "the general public" and to teachers.

Before beginning any new projects, the outreach coordinator for the Louisiana Division of Archaeology consulted with the social studies supervisor for the Louisiana Department of Education and with teachers. They pointed out that teachers have more than enough to cover in one year and are barraged with worthwhile supplementary materials. The social studies supervisor also discussed learning techniques and social studies skills and said that any creative activities that develop these skills would be more important contributions than those that simply cover content in a traditional manner.

The Division of Archaeology's next step was to develop kits, which are referred to as classroom exhibits. These provide actual artifacts that students can handle, illustrations, maps, overhead transparencies, and an accompanying slide/tape show. Included in the kits are sheets for an inquiry learning activity with the artifacts and illustrations. This is a technique to engage students in active, rather than passive, learning (Beyer 1979). The self-contained kits require minimal teacher preparation and elicit enthusiastic comments from teachers. Approximately 5000 students use them annually.

Additionally, a slide/tape show about Louisiana archaeology was developed and placed on deposit with the state Department of Education's slide lending library. This agency duplicates slide programs and lends them to teachers around the state. The slide/tape show, the classroom exhibits, and the booklets were all oriented toward promulgating findings of prehistoric and historic archaeology.

Several shortcomings in these programs were identified. First, access to the audiovisual programs and exhibits was limited by the number of copies available, and required advanced planning. Second, the booklets and slide shows were clearly noninnovative in the method of instruction. Third, the activities were brief, so no additional programs were available to teachers who were interested in spending more time on archaeology. Finally, and most importantly, was the concern that the materials might not encourage site preservation because they emphasize the findings of archaeology rather than the process of archaeology.

## PHASE TWO IMPLEMENTATION

It was decided to develop a collection of self-contained, self-explanatory activities to be taught in nonexpository style. These activities include the messages identified as possibly being important in developing a greater appreciation for archaeology and archaeological sites.

The guide *Classroom Archaeology,* is divided into six sections. The first includes background material for teachers: vocabulary, an outline of Louisiana prehistory, recommended books for various ages, magazines and journals, other materials available from the Division of Archaeology, materials available from other sources, and places to visit.

The second part is composed of 17 short activities, each of which can be used alone and can be completed in one class period. The remaining sections require more than one class period. The third part is a series of card games students can play with cards they make showing culture traits of various prehistoric Indian groups. The fourth part is a class activity recording a site. The fifth provides printed information about archaeological findings at a historic contact site. The students interpret the site based on the artifacts, features, and historic maps.

The sixth activity is a simulated excavation in which either students (long version) or teachers (short version) create a site; then students excavate and interpret it. This activity was developed in response to a review of *DIG 2* (Lipetzky 1982), a commercially produced simulated excavation activity that is very well received by students and teachers. *DIG 2* does a good job of teaching social studies skills and excavation techniques, but it is weak in analysis and interpretation techniques. Its emphasis on the most exciting and exotic aspects of classical archaeology might foster an image of archaeology as being primarily concerned with digging up exotic and wonderful artifacts.

The *Classroom Archaeology* simulation was designed to encourage creation of a site more likely to reflect those found in Louisiana and to show that archaeology is not continuous fun, that context is important, and that analysis, interpretation, and reporting are also part of archaeology.

*Classroom Archaeology* was first published in July 1984 and was originally targeted for eighth grade Louisiana Studies classes. Interest from teachers of other subjects and grades showed that the activities were also useful for other classes. A second edition of the guide, printed in 1987, included coded symbols to suggest activities to be used in language arts, science, and art, as well as social studies.

More than 2600 copies were distributed between July 1984 and January 1990, with approximately 200 sent out of state. During the 5 years since the guide was printed, conversations with users of the guide and other educators raised several questions. Are the Louisiana state curriculum requirements too demanding to allow enough flexibility to use the guide? Are the guides going to people who actually use them, and is the distribution network adequate to ensure that potentially interested teachers are receiving them? The high cost of reproducing the 179-page guide led to consideration of its content. Are the activities useful? Should some be eliminated? The simulated excavation was considered to be too complex for teachers to conduct successfully. Teachers might simplify the project and develop a substitute that would fail to teach the processes involved in archaeology.

In an effort to evaluate the use of *Classroom Archaeology,* a questionnaire was sent to Louisiana residents who had requested the guide, in writing or by telephone, from July 1984 through October 1989. This excludes those who received the guide at workshops, conventions, or via a supervisor or curriculum specialist. Twenty-five percent returned the questionnaire. While this represents only a small percentage of respondents, the results are useful in showing activities that are used relatively more often than others.

The brief questionnaire had a series of six multiple choice questions followed by three open-ended questions. The questions in the first section were accessing who requested the guide, what happened to it, how many teachers used it, whether the respondent personally had used it with students, which activities were used, and how many activities the respondent used annually. The short answer section asked with what grade level and subject area the activities were used, which activity the respondent considers best and why, and which activity is considered least useful and why.

The results showed that approximately 80% were teachers, other education supervisors or specialists, education students, librarians, museum docents, scout leaders, and other persons likely to use the guide. Although 12% of the nonteachers used the activities with young people or in teaching demonstrations, the results relating to teacher use will be described here.

Of the respondents who knew how many teachers used the guides they received, 36% said one teacher used it, 32% said two teachers used it, 12% said three teachers used it, 4% said more than three used it, and 16% said none used it.

Teachers using the guide taught in kindergarten through college, with elementary teachers and middle school teachers using it equally, followed by high school, college, and kindergarten. The teachers had used the activities three times as often with social studies classes as with science classes. Approximately 20% of the teachers reported using the guide with gifted/talented students.

The questionnaire included a listing of the table of contents of the guide, and respondents were asked to check which activities they had personally used. Of the teachers who used any part of the guide, 100% reported using the "resources" section of background material, with a mean of four resources used. The most-used parts were the lists of recommended books, places to visit, and the outline of Louisiana prehistory. The least used were lists of suggested magazines, journals, and materials that may be purchased from other sources.

Of the teachers using the guide, 89% used one or more short activities, with a mean of four activities. The three most frequently used ones (used by more than 40%) were "Newspaper Archaeology" (students compile "for sale" ads that could have been placed by an imaginary family, exchange sets of ads, then analyze a family's "artifacts"), "Today's Artifacts" (students pretend to be archaeologists in the future who must describe and assign a function to 20th century artifacts), "Time Line" (from 10,000 B.C. until today), and "Archaeology Words" (a vocabulary activity).

Four were used by no more than 10%: "Pottery Reconstruction" (students reconstruct simulated ceramics), "Archaeology in the Library" (students read and report about an archaeology article), "Special Techniques" (students identify scientific techniques used in analysis of a shipwreck), and "Stratigraphy and Chronology" (students place in order, by age, letters representing strata at sites).

Twenty-one percent of the teachers using the guides used the games activity, 10% used the recording a site activity, 16% used the interpreting a site activity, and 16% used the excavating a site simulation.

Concern about the usefulness of the simulated excavation activity was heightened after (1) reading a questionnaire from a college student who said he used the simulated excavation instructions to conduct an actual excavation, (2) seeing a newspaper article about a teacher-led "dig," and (3) reading the following teacher's questionnaire statement: "We carried out three digs in DeSoto Parish during the month of May 1986. This guide was our 'Bible'...." The hope is that these sites were simulated, but the fear is that they were actual sites.

In the short answer section of the questionnaire, teachers expressed no consensus about the best or worst activities in the guide. The other added comments were complementary regarding both content and format of the guide.

The results of the questionnaire have led to several future plans. The guide, now out of print, will be reprinted. The simulated excavation activity will be omitted from future editions of the guide because of ethical concerns, and consideration will be given to omitting the four rarely used short activities. A smaller percentage of science teachers than expected are using the activities. Consultation with science educators will be undertaken to explore the possibility of adding short activities for science classes.

Teachers in a wider range of grades than expected are using the guide. Use might be increased further by keying all activities to the specific objectives and content of various courses as outlined by the state Department of Education. This would make it easy to identify places in the school year to use various activities. It is still expected that any one teacher will be able to use only a few activities each year, but it is more efficient to provide one guide to be used in a wide range of grades than to provide separate packets for various classes.

Distribution of *Classroom Archaeology* could be improved. When it is reprinted, effort will be made to get more copies to science teachers and to teachers of gifted and talented students. Science teachers are an important avenue to students because of the current emphasis in science education on conservation issues and because of the frequent use of discovery learning techniques in science classes. Teachers of gifted and talented students are expected to provide enrichment activities that supplement the basic content of their courses, and therefore, they have more flexibility than many teachers. While exceptional students are not targeted as the primary school group for whom *Classroom Archaeology* was designed, they are a part of the school population, and they certainly can be expected to be among the decision makers of the future.

Within the education program of the Division of Archaeology, several additional future activities have been identified. The outreach coordinator is working with the state Department of Education to include in the Louisiana Studies course outline, information gained through archaeology and to explore how information about archaeological techniques or site preservation could be included. This provides a way to get information about archaeology to every Louisiana Studies teacher in the state.

Additionally, the need has been identified to conduct more half-day or one-day in-service training sessions for teachers. The more familiar teachers are with a topic, the more accurately they can present it. While the goal is not to reach all teachers or to expect in-service training before use of the materials, it would provide a core of teachers who are more aware of materials and techniques that can be used to teach archaeology. A final, long-range goal is to provide an intensive one-week workshop for selected teachers within the state during the summer. Perhaps this could be modeled on the South Carolina program (Judge 1989) that offers this training to prepare teachers for using the guide *Can You Dig It* (Hawkins et al. 1989), a South Carolina adaptation of Louisiana's *Classroom Archaeology.*

## CONCLUSION AND RECOMMENDATIONS

Archaeologists have at least four motives for working with educators to include archaeology in schools: to communicate results of archaeological research, to increase appreciation for other cultures, to improve awareness of archaeological methods, and to increase site preservation. Educational programs, such as those in Louisiana, clearly accomplish the first three goals. The unanswered question is whether these lead to increased site preservation.

This is probably the most critical issue facing those involved in research in archaeology and education today. More than 25 collections of classroom activities have now been developed (Smith 1990). The need now is not for more activities to be developed but, instead, for existing activities to be evaluated for effectiveness in discouraging unscientific investigation of sites and in encouraging site preservation. One program, *Project Archeology: Saving Traditions* (McNutt 1988; also see McNutt, this volume), has been evaluated and has demonstrated through student testing that it is effective in teaching ten principles of archaeology, including "archaeological sites are a nonrenewable resource whose conservation is essential if we are to learn of the unwritten past" (McNutt 1988:4).

Not only must programs as a whole be evaluated, but the components of these programs must be studied. Archaeologists need to determine exactly which activities enhance the development of preservation interests, how many activities it takes to communicate the message, how much class time is needed to teach them, and whether they can be taught by teachers with no previous training in archaeology.

Archaeologists must recognize that most teachers will never have the opportunity to attend an in-depth workshop, will never be able to purchase a set of classroom materials, and cannot spend weeks teaching the subject. Excellent programs that require one of these elements are extremely rewarding to students fortunate enough to benefit from them, and are likely to promote site preservation. The unanswered question is whether inexpensive, self-contained activities requiring no previous teacher training can also be effective in promoting site preservation.

## REFERENCES CITED

**Abell, R. P.** (1985) Inference-making and testing in a high school archeology course. In *Archeology and Education: A Successful Combination for Precollegiate Students,* Holm, K. A. and Higgins, P. J., Eds., Anthropology Curriculum Project, University of Georgia, Athens.

**Anderson, D. C.** (1979) Iowa's P.A.S.T. (Programming Archaeology for School Teachers). Final Grant Report, The University of Iowa, Office of the State Archaeologist, Iowa City.

**Beyer, B. K.** (1979) *Teaching Thinking in Social Studies: Using Inquiry in the Classroom,* rev. ed., Charles E. Merrill, Columbus, OH.

**Carroll, R. F.** (1987) Schoolyard archaeology, *Social Studies,* 78, 69.

**Chu, J.** (1982) *Kidigger: Exercises in Critical and Creative Thinking Through Archaeology,* Hanson, Silver, and Associates, Moorestown, NJ.

**Cook, T. G.** (1985) Using students in research: the Lagoon site. In *Archeology and Education: A Successful Combination for Precollegiate Students,* Holm, K. A. and Higgins, P. J., Eds., Anthropology Curriculum Project, University of Georgia, Athens.

**Corbin, D.** (1985) Introduction to archeology: a unit for middle schools. In *Archeology and Education: A Successful Combination for Precollegiate Students,* Holm, K. A. and Higgins, P. J., Eds., Anthropology Curriculum Project, University of Georgia, Athens.

**Cotter, J. L.** (1979) Archaeologists of the future: high schools discover archaeology. *Archaeology,* 32, 29.

**Dyche, B.** (1985) Why Archeology when your curriculum is thinking skills? Developing a sequential archeological curriculum for grades 6 to 12. In *Archeology and Education: A Successful Combination for Precollegiate Students,* Holm, K. A. and Higgins, P. J., Eds., Anthropology Curriculum Project, University of Georgia, Athens.

**Gettings, D.** (1970) Unearthing an Indian culture: a total involvement program, *Sci.Teacher,* 37, 59.

**Harrison, M.** (1984) *Archaeology Walney,* Fairfax County Park Authority, Fairfax, VA.

**Hartman, D. W.** (1985) Understanding science through anthropological inquiry: two cases. In *Archeology and Education: A Successful Combination for Precollegiate Students,* Holm, K. A. and Higgins, P. J., Eds., Anthropology Curriculum Project, University of Georgia, Athens.

**Hawkins, N. W.** (1987) Classroom archaeology: an archaeology activity guide for teachers, 2nd ed, Division of Archaeology, Office of Cultural Development, Department of Culture, Recreation and Tourism, Baton Rouge, LA.

**Hawkins, N. W., South, S., Charles, T., and Walden, M. B.** (1989) *Can You Dig It? A Classroom Guide to South Carolina Archaeology,* South Carolina Department of Education and South Carolina Institute of Archaeology and Anthropology, Columbia.

**Higgins, P. J. and Holm, K. A.** (1985) Introduction. In *Archeology and Education: A Successful Combination for Precollegiate Students,* Holm, K. A. and Higgins, P. J., Eds., Anthropology Curriculum Project, University of Georgia, Athens.

**Holm, K. A.** (1985) Preparing teachers to introduce archaeology into the curriculum. In *Archeology and Education: A Successful Combination for Precollegiate Students,* Holm, K. A. and Higgins, P. J., Eds., Anthropology Curriculum Project, University of Georgia, Athens.

**Judge, C.** (1989) South Carolina classroom archaeology syllabus. On file with Margaret Walden, Social Studies Consultant, Department of Education, Columbia, SC.

**Lipetzky, J.** (1982) *DIG 2,* Interact, Lakeside, CA.

**McNutt, N.** (1988) *Project Archeology: Saving Traditions,* Sopris West, Denver.

**Parren, L. K.** (1987) A teacher's guide to 12,000 years of Vermont's past, Vermont State Archaeologist's Office, Montpelier.

**Rogge, A. E. and Bell, P.** (1989) Archeology in the classroom: a case study from Arizona, Archeological Assistance Program Technical Brief 4, U. S. Department of the Interior, National Park Service, Washington D.C.

**Smith, K. C., Ed.** (1990) *Pathways to the Past: Educator's Guide to Resources in Archaeology,* Museum of Florida History, Tallahassee.

**Thomas, G.** (1967) *Archeological Methods: A Programmed Text,* Anthropology Curriculum Project, University of Georgia, Athens.

**Tirrell, P. B.** (1983) Archaeology for elementary and secondary students. In *Anthropology and Multicultural Education: Classroom Applications,* Moses, Y. T. and Higgins, P. J., Eds., Anthropology Curriculum Project, University of Georgia, Athens.

# THE ARCHAEOLOGIST AS GLOBAL EDUCATOR

Phyllis Mauch Messenger and Walter W. Enloe

## INTRODUCTION

Archaeology is the stuff of our childhood fantasies about exotic peoples, places, and times. The subject matter of archaeological exploration seems almost limitless, with discovery, intrigue, and foreign locations often thrown in. To many, archaeology would seem to be the perfect career. Yet archaeologists often are not succeeding in communicating what they do, why and how they do it, and why it might be important. And it can be argued that they "do not take enough notice of the perceptions of the past held by the public" (Stone 1989:195). The current focus on cultural heritage resource preservation is a key factor motivating archaeologists to look for opportunities to improve their performance in the area of public education, especially in the schools. This article will attempt to offer paths of thought along which those interested in studying the nature of humankind in a variety of times and places — which certainly includes archaeologists and educators — might meet.

Archaeologists and educators share common areas of interest and have much to offer one another. The archaeologist seeks to create interest in the study and support of archaeology, including the preservation of cultural heritage resources. The archaeologist realizes a need to reach students in K–12 classrooms, ideally offering more than a "dog and pony" show. The educator wants to help students gain an understanding of who we are and how we fit in the world (a "global perspective"), in part by studying human responses to change over time. The educator seeks to help students understand the commonalities of being human and to respect the rich diversity of human culture. The educator seeks to gain access to community resources, integrating enrichment activities into the curriculum in a meaningful way.

In order to understand and integrate these goals, let us look at the growing field of global education and at anthropologists' analysis of the role of anthropology/archaeology in it. We will build a profile of the "archaeologist as global educator," and a parallel profile of the "archaeologist and child as active learner and explorer," with examples of activities and approaches that illustrate the possibilities of using global education as a framework for archaeology in the schools, and using archaeology and cultural heritage education as powerful tools for global education.

## GLOBAL, INTERNATIONAL, AND MULTICULTURAL STUDIES

There is a growing movement in U.S. elementary and secondary education to address, appreciate, and understand the multicultural nature of our population. In many areas this is a mandated addition to the curriculum. Multicultural education addresses the reality that countries such as the U.S. are a plurality of peoples, that, in fact, "we are the world," and that we must help our children respect the commonalities of being citizens of one country while respecting the varieties of cultural differences within it. We are not so much a melting pot as a multi-ingredient salad or a cultural mosaic.

The movement toward globalizing or internationalizing curricula recognizes our increasing global interdependence and the need to understand the world and our place in it. For many educators, "global" is synonymous with "international" and encompasses a variety of diverse

157

educational goals and strategies: area studies and foreign languages; multicultural and intercultural education; international relations and foreign policy studies; international development studies; and single issue perspectives on a global scale, such as environmental or war-and-peace issues. Global education also has been defined as either world issue and problem studies or world-centered approaches to education (i.e., the world as an interdependent system). A more integrating (as well as historic) definition of global is "interactive and systemic," suggesting spherical completeness and comprehensiveness. An interactive whole understood synchronically and diachronically (that is, historically or developmentally, and presently or in process) may refer to the world, humanity, a particular culture or village, or the local community or classroom. More specifically, we use the term global to convey the concept of the planet as an interactive whole (Gaia or spaceship earth) and the human species as an interactive whole (human family, global village).

We recognize that the last half century has brought rapid and sweeping changes, uniting humanity through technological breakthroughs in transportation and communication, causing it to become, in Martin Luther King's terms, more of "a neighborhood" linked by technology as well as by global problems, such as global warming, pollution, and uneven distribution of resources. On numerous occasions, Dr. King argued that unless we learn to see ourselves as a "brotherhood" ("humanhood" or humanity) and resolve our global problems, "we will perish together as fools" (Washington 1986:117–122). Similarly, human scientist and psychoanalyst Erik Erikson contends that human beings are the only living species that tend toward "pseudo-speciation." Through gender, race, or cultural background, we tend to segregate; we tend to rate as superior or inferior; we tend to differentiate our single, organic whole — the human species (Erikson 1968:41–42). A global perspective in education, then, will be informed by the concepts of an interactive system, the whole world, the whole of organic life (including humanity), and the whole of human culture.

A number of educators have elaborated the basic characteristics of a school curriculum that is global, addressing the need to understand the world, its cultures, and our relationship to them. Archaeologists should find it useful to reflect on how their perspectives on a particular culture illustrate or encompass the components of these conceptions, as well as how an understanding of anthropological concepts and processes could enrich the global classroom. In current thinking about social studies, in general, and global education, in particular, we find an increasing emphasis on an historical perspective to current issues: evaluating human responses to change and seeing patterns and systems in particular geographic contexts, rather than looking at isolated events. The goal is to provide a context or foundation for social participation. It is possible to envision the eventual formulation of a new interdisciplinary area of human studies. Recent academic developments have established human science as a recognized rubric within which the traditional social sciences, including archaeology, interface with biology (Piaget 1972). With the interdependency of the human sciences and the humanities, a more complete approach to the study of human beings can be formulated that will foster human attitudes and skills that transcend the school house and are essential capacities that aid the lived experience of students as a whole.

Global educator Lee Anderson delineates a set of global citizenship competencies in terms of self-perspective and self-awareness. Archaeologists will recognize these as issues and questions they deal with in their research and teaching, particularly the fourth point. Anderson's themes are (1) a capacity to perceive oneself and all other individuals as members of a single species of life whose numbers share a common biological status, a common way of adapting to their natural environments, a common history, a common set of biological and psychological needs, common existential concerns, and common social problems; (2) a capacity to perceive oneself, the groups to which one belongs, and the human species as a whole as a part of the earth's ecosystem; (3) a capacity to perceive oneself and the group one belongs to as participants in the transnational social order; (4) a capacity to perceive oneself, one's community, one's nation, and one's civilization as both "cultural borrowers" and "cultural depositors" who both draw from and contribute to a "global band of human culture" that has been, and continues to be, fed by contributions by all peoples, in all geographical regions, and in all periods of history; and (5) a self-conscious capacity to perceive that the world system and its component elements are objects of perception, beliefs, attitudes, opinions, values, and assumptions on our part as well as the part of others (Anderson 1979).

Educator Willard Kniep, of the American Forum — Global Perspectives in Education, sees the need for holistic strands across subject areas and through grade levels in order for a curriculum to be global (Kniep 1988). These strands are addressed through broad school-community collaboration, inquiry, and consensus on these two essential questions. What is the nature of the contemporary world? What skills, attitudes, and knowledge do students need to be responsible and reasonable participants for the future in a world we know to be increasingly complex, changing, and interdependent?

This growing orientation toward educating for local and global citizenship and, correspondingly, the need to reevaluate the changing role for education in a changing multiboundary, transnational world, is no better formulated than through the perspective of the foremost American educational reformer, John Goodlad. He has proposed that the total system worldview of economist Kenneth Boulding (1985) is a novel paradigm approximating "the way things are" and providing a guidepost for school renewal and curriculum restructuring. Goodlad has adapted Boulding's world model to provide an appropriate systems model for global studies. Goodlad categorizes various methods of study and subject matter through which students expand their localized view of the world into the wider context of global systems (Goodlad 1988:19 also see 1984). His systems (and some of the methods and subjects he lists) are (1) the world as a physical system (the physical sciences, technology), (2) the world as a biological system (e.g., zoology, ecology), (3) evaluative and belief systems (studies in the bases of choice and decision making, e.g., religion, economics), (4) communicative and expressive systems (the means and ways of human communication and expression), (5) the human species (studies in the traits and characteristics of human beings, e.g., history, the arts, religion, archaeology), and (6) the global village — social, political, and economic systems (how humans collectively manage their lives, e.g., anthropology, economics, ecology, archaeology). While archaeology is central to the last two, methods and subject matter related to archaeology are found in all areas of Goodlad's vision of the scope of school-based curricula for expanding students' worldviews.

Global educators have developed the framework for preparing young people for life in a world increasingly characterized by pluralism, interdependence, and change. As political leaders and citizens add to the voice calling for global education, its attainment becomes more of a reality. And those, including archaeologists/anthropologists, who can make an informed contribution to our understanding of the human species and the global village will be valued in the education community. This vision is edging toward reality. Take, for example, the 1989 report of the National Governor's Association, which argues that education must prepare young people for an increasingly globalized world:

> Times have changed. Revolutionary advances in science, technology, communications and transportation have brought nations and peoples together. World trade and financial, economic, and political

developments have transformed disparate economic systems into a highly interdependent global marketplace. Today, the nations that inhabit the planet are often more closely linked than neighboring states or villages were at the turn of the century.

Yet these important changes are not reflected in the way many U.S. schools prepare students for citizenship. In educating students, the languages, cultures, values, traditions, and even the location of other nations are often ignored. Schools and universities reflect the same lack of global understanding that pervades the nation, from government and business leaders to school children.

## ANTHROPOLOGY/ARCHAEOLOGY IN A GLOBAL CURRICULUM

The framework developed by global educators insists upon the inclusion of an anthropological perspective. The extensive potential contribution of archaeology to this curriculum, through both content and methods, provides a challenge and an opportunity to the archaeological community. By understanding the philosophy and goals of global education, archaeologists can begin to work with educators to provide a valued component of the educational experience.

Where do we begin? In 1989 the Curriculum Task Force of the National Commission on Social Studies in the Schools issued a report that urged the teaching of social studies in every K–12 grade to ensure development of qualities crucial to citizenship, including the ability of students to see themselves as part of the larger human experience, to understand the diversity of world history and cultures, and to grasp the critical values and analytical perspectives appropriate to the analysis of the human condition. One of the contributors to the report was anthropologist Jane J. White, co-chair of the Task Force on Teaching Anthropology in the Schools for the American Anthropological Association (AAA). Her discussion of the contributions anthropology can make to the social studies curriculum includes a number of points that archaeologists wanting to argue the relevancy of archaeology to global education should keep in mind. Many of her points address those outlined above by Kniep, Goodlad, and Boulding. White states, "The central goal of anthropology is to explain why groups of people are different from each other . . . [and to] try to explain each group's way of life in terms of their own perspectives." We would add that an authentic global perspective builds upon human commonalities to explicate more fully human differences. Anthropology has a wealth of big ideas — culture, evolution, adaptation, cultural contact, technological change. Studying them helps students organize data and perceive patterns. White quotes Clifford Geertz: "The aim is to draw large conclusions from small, but very densely textured facts; to support broad assertions . . . by engaging them with complex specifics" (Geertz 1973:21–28). White sees the application of anthropological processes — analyzing artifacts, documents, art and narrative, and daily life accounts — as adding depth, intensity, and variety to work in social studies.

White cautions that teachers must move beyond a "touristy," or strange lands and friendly peoples, approach to cultures, through the use of case studies to give a complex picture. This will "help students confront, in intellectually honest ways, the sometimes threatening concept of cultural differences. If the challenge is met, then students will have moved one step closer toward becoming true world citizens" (White 1989:36).

The anthropological perspective is a major component of the historical cultures approach to world studies, as described by Paul Bohannan, past president of the American Anthropological Association (AAA) and of the African Studies Association, in a handbook looking at five approaches to world studies curriculum (Woyach and Remy 1989). This approach focuses on the dynamics of cultural change within history, especially responses to challenges to the environment. By looking at the achievements of different cultures in meeting challenges, why societies have faltered, and speculating on what might have been, students are led to a new understanding of our problems today and the premises that may cloud our eyes. This approach emphasizes the urgent need for cross-cultural understanding and helps us express and assess the premises of our own and other cultures. Having the perspective of different times and places helps us achieve those goals.

Bohannan discusses the importance of the concept of cultures as the "stuff" that makes people of different times and places different from one another. The birth, development, and death of different cultures is the very substance of human history. Looking at the two manifestations of culture as "artifact" and "mentifact" aids in the ever difficult task of defining culture, says Bohannan. We would add that active enquiry by students, activities describing and interpreting one's own culture, and otherwise empowering children as archaeologists and ethnographers will enhance that understanding.

## THE ARCHAEOLOGIST AS GLOBAL EDUCATOR

How can the archaeologist combine the demands of global education, the promise of anthropology, and the needs of the child into an educational experience that the archaeologist can facilitate? We have adapted Selby and Pike's profile of a global teacher to indicate how and where the archaeologist's skills and expertise can be applied.

According to Selby and Pike (1988:chap. 4), the global teacher is globalcentric, looking at broad systems. We would add, the archaeologist looks at the past, on both the small and the large scale, to see how global conditions, trends, and developments have changed over time.

The global teacher is concerned about culture and perspective, wanting to present a coherent understanding of cultures studied. "Cultures are portrayed as neither monolithic nor unchanging" (Selby and Pike 1988: chap. 4). In-depth study of cultures is emphasized to encourage respect for diversity and promote tolerance and appreciation of other perspectives and world views. The archaeologist can offer deep treatment of a single culture at a single moment or over time, and in comparison to other cultures. An archaeological comparison of our material culture with that of another culture may remove the exotic quality often associated with differences and, in the process, will contribute to respect for the culture and its objects, as well as the process for studying them.

The global teacher is future oriented, conveying that humans can influence the future by their actions; it is not predetermined. Students develop skills to cope with an accelerated rate of change. The archaeologists' portraits of cultures deal with change and adaptation, often through a great depth of time. Their histories suggest how past human actions affected nature and cultural development: both their own and that of other groups.

The global teacher is a facilitator helping students learn how to learn. Rather than only presenting a long lecture full of complicated facts, the archaeologist has the opportunity to help students understand how we know what we know about a culture. Students can be presented with clues and the opportunity to experience moving from evidence to hypothesis. The archaeologist should have the confidence to admit that we don't have all the answers (or necessarily the right ones) and encourage self-esteem by letting the child take chances, too.

The global teacher believes in human potential, recognizing that students are eager to discover and relish a challenge. This educator "knows that students who are put in contact with what they perceive to be real issues and problems are intrinsically motivated" (Selby and Pike 1988:chap. 4). The archaeologist can seize on the enthusiasm for discovery and the fascination with the exotic image of the archaeologist to encourage students to understand the methodic and scientific side of archaeology. The issue of site protection, for example, can be powerfully presented if students are offered positive actions that they can take as a group, as individuals, or with their families. A simple negative message of "no, don't touch, let the professionals do it" is not productive. Instead, positive actions, such as adopting a site (or project or archaeologist), learning more about preservation, or understanding how to report collections or sites, what should be reported, and to whom, are important.

The global teacher is concerned with the development of the whole person, accepting "that there are diverse and synergistic dimensions to human learning, including the abstract, the concrete, the experiential, the analytical, the rational, the intuitive, and the emotional" (Selby and Pike 1988:chap. 4). The archaeologist can lead students through the variety of learning styles involved in archaeological investigation. Simple materials, such as old magazines or phone books, can be used to look for commonalities and differences, changes in types of ads, products that appear or disappear, the appearance of last names reflecting the introduction of new immigrant groups, and other characteristics. Students might begin with publications from their own year of birth, moving backward or forward to other significant dates, to develop a sense of change between time markers.

The global teacher employs various teaching/learning styles in the classroom, including action research, group discussion, experiential units, role plays, simulation games, and direct and hands-on experience. The archaeologist can offer a range of activities, including group exercises in measuring, quantifying, and estimating; hands-on exploration of cultural material; and role playing in another time and place. Some activities can take place during the visit or residency of an archaeologist. Others can occur before or after, guided by handouts or discussions between teacher and archaeologist. Students might be asked to create a personal geography of a special place, describing or drawing it, and letting their peers try to determine its location, meaning, and identity. Or they might bring an object from early childhood and let others analyze its significance.

The global teacher believes in lifelong learning and sees himself or herself as a perpetual learner. Students are encouraged to ask good questions and understand that our answers and solutions are impermanent. The archaeologist knows from experience that our understanding of people and events is evolving and can facilitate a student's understanding of the same process. This is especially apparent in the study of past cultures as research technologies improve. In addition, the increasingly recognized contributions of indigenous groups and developing cultures/nations in studying, explaining, and owning their own past has led to an enrichment and deepening of our understanding of the human past and its continuity with the present (e.g., Layton 1989).

The global teacher tries to be congruent, seeking to keep the medium and the message in harmony, as well as one's own professional and personal life. The archaeologist who respects and admires past cultures must be willing to show respect for the beliefs and needs of contemporary cultures. A valuable exercise in developing empathy and understanding involves archaeologists and students assuming roles of different individuals or representatives of various countries in a round table discussion of rights to cultural objects (see Messenger 1989:chap. 14). Another discussion might be based on an actual event in their community, such as the desecration of a public monument or cemetery vandalism.

The global teacher is rights respectful, with a goal of shifting the focus of power and decision making in the classroom. The goal is autonomy and empowerment of the individual, encouraged by a system of feedback and evaluation. The archaeologist can contribute to this process by helping students understand the dynamic processes of group investigation, discussion, and give and take, which comprise good archaeological investigation — cooperative learning at its best.

The global teacher seeks fundamental interdependence across the curriculum, with continuity in aims, objectives, and teaching and learning strategies, through subject matter and grade level. Ideally, the archaeologist's contribution would include interaction and discussion with teacher groups to discuss the integration of archaeology at different learning levels. How and where are cultures, systems, and areas of the world currently introduced in the curriculum? What are alternative strategies? The archaeologist can offer the types of presentations to be developed, seeking a dialogue with teachers on how to introduce new topics, either by the archaeologist or by the classroom teacher, into the curriculum. One avenue to such group discussions is through district or state teacher workshops. For example, a state social studies conference might feature a session led by an archaeologist on "archaeology and the study of the past across the curriculum," or "current research in archaeology/anthropology." This sort of approach might also be developed within one globally minded school or through a college of education or state department of education.

The global teacher is a community teacher who recognizes opportunities for holistic education offered by the local community. The archaeologist often represents a set of resources, including archaeological societies, museums, historical societies, colleges or universities, and local heritage sites and interpretive centers. Connected with an archaeologist, in one way or another, is often a cadre of archaeology students, volunteer excavators (sometimes senior citizens), and other professionals from the related institutions. Often these individuals and institutions can be called upon to serve as additional resources in the classroom or in providing field-trip opportunities. For example, senior citizens who have worked as volunteer excavators might work with a class on an extended project after an archaeologist has visited the class.

## ARCHAEOLOGIST AND CHILD AS ACTIVE LEARNER AND EXPLORER/SCIENTIST

How do we make archaeology meaningful to a child's experiences? Children work from the present backward. They find it difficult to make a leap of understanding from their own environment to other situations distant in time and space. A 1986 survey of a multicultural group of school children in Great Britain elicited such views of history as: "I don't see how it could help you now. Nowadays is so different," or "You're in this world now. The past is gone" (Emmott 1989:25). Children often find social studies, including archaeology, boring as it is usually presented. When archaeological studies begin in a context distant from a child's personal meaning system, it is usually handless, inactive, and unengaging. The following discussion will offer perspectives on bridging the gap between here and there, now and then.

If we wish to teach children something about global citizenship, about the past, or about respect for cultural heritage, we must actively seek to make those concepts relevant to their classroom, community, and home. And we should encourage their participation in meaningful activities that address a variety of learning styles (see Gardner 1983). In Piaget's terms, we are simply suggesting that we aid the active lived experience of children (Piaget 1972). Increasingly, we know that learning is an active, constructive, meaning-making process. "The medium is the message." How we teach must reflect the natural development and experience of our students. If we want children to understand the world as an interdependent entity whose development requires active collaboration, we cannot simply tell them about it by "covering the material." We must teach them in ways in which learning is cooperative, active, engaging, and full of hands-on meaningfulness. We must take seriously that children are not primarily passive receivers of information, a mode that is so characteristic of much of our schooling practice. They are human scientists: creators, explorers, discoverers, interpreters, and meaning makers.

Hilda Taba, the great researcher and teacher educator, outlined the ideal teacher-learner/ learner-teacher 20 years ago for the Foreign Policy Association's conference on international-izing the K–12 curriculum. This work offers a framework of the active global learner within which we can place the kinds of activities and interactions that archaeology can contribute (Collins 1982).

Taba's active learner develops certain kinds of knowledge, including organized sets of concepts, ideas, and/or generalizations that enable him or her to put masses of data in order. The active learner can process information; that is, analyze data, form generalizations, ask pertinent questions, make inferences, and use data to hypothesize, to predict causal change, and as a useful model for inquiry, for analysis, and for probing problems. The active learner is a self-learner and has the intellectual tools and desire to do his or her own data processing and keep on learning. Well-organized visits to archaeological sites or labs, along with preliminary visits by archaeolo-gists to schools for discussions with teachers and classes, can offer this sort of active learning opportunity. A key to the success of such a project is the availability of a staff person to carry out the planning of activities and the creating of work sheets, artifact boxes, and other learning tools, as well as maintaining the stability of a project to continue over a period of time (e.g., Shaw 1989:5–9).

The active learner has a genuine sense of participation, involvement, and commitment. Activities developed out of an encounter with archaeology might include creating an archaeo-logical record of the students' own class or school, doing experimental archaeology or ethnoarchaeology by growing a garden using certain techniques or crops, making pottery with appropriate tools and materials (such as shells, pebbles, and corncobs, to smooth the clay), or making a scrapbook of news items related to archaeology. (See Hawkins 1987, for further discussion.)

The active learner can face change without trauma: that is, can grasp, take hold of, influence, and control in a constructive manner the change processes underway. The active learner has a capacity to transcend his or her own ethnocentric skin, seeing equivalents in values and universals in the human condition, and possessing the sensibilities that are necessary to live in a pluralistic world. The active learner can handle community, national, or international situations objectively: that is, can treat other peoples' (nations') feelings or value patterns as "facts" or "givens" in a situation. The active learner has a sense of the complexity of issues, both local and global. Students might begin a personal exchange of artifacts of their own culture with students from other cultures, whether it be Minnesota and Japan or California and Tennessee. These "culture boxes" help students confront what they value, and try to see the objects they choose as someone from another culture might see them. Teachers and students can create culture boxes of a place they have visited, of a rural or urban contemporary American family, or of the culture of their school community (Enloe 1990).

The active learner has loyalties, realizing that loyalty is not a finite quality and that one can be loyal to a range of people or institutions or ideas, simultaneously. Emmott's discussion of the British survey of school children looked at children's attitudes about their own varied cultural backgrounds. Most of the children claimed they would pass on more about all aspects of their cultures than their parents did, which the children identified as one reason for learning about the past. They emphasized language, myths, religion, music, and art, in that order. Emmott notes that

89% of the children surveyed found family history interesting, and suggests designing projects aimed at creating individual family histories by interviewing grandparents and retirees. This active enquiry would help "create a sense of the personal meaning of the past and its effect on ordinary people's lives" (Emmott 1989:42). This version of archaeology in our own back yard would be a valuable lesson on the topic of history, preceding the classroom visit of an archaeologist who would talk about family histories of a more distant culture.

## CONCLUSION

It is clear that the archaeologist is well positioned to step into the roles of active learner and global teacher, offering a broad perspective on cultures and change over time. Done with care and thoughtfulness, we can present a positive, active message to children that encourages them to understand and respect other cultures, past and present; respect what remains of them, just as they respect themselves and the world around them; and participate in the quest for understanding. By valuing the process and results, we will share in the ownership/stewardship of the past and actively work to preserve it.

By sharing ownership, we do not lose our right to archaeological resources as scholars and researchers, but we gain a broader base for stewardship of cultural heritage resources. Developing a stronger cultural norm for preservation may take several generations, but it is not beyond our grasp. The public schools are a logical place to begin.

## REFERENCES CITED

**Anderson, L.** (1979) *Schooling and Citizenship in a Global Age,* Social Studies Development Center, Indiana University, Bloomington.

**Boulding, K.** (1985) *The World as a Total System,* Sage, Beverly Hills, CA.

**Collins, T. H.** (1982) *Getting Started in Global Education,* National Association of Elementary School Principals, Arlington, VA.

**Enloe, W.** (1991) Cultural Information Exchanges, Minnesota Department of Education, St. Paul, MN (forthcoming).

**Emmott, K.** (1989) A child's perspective on the past: influences of home, media and school. In *Who Needs the Past? Indigenous Values and Archaeology,* Layton, R., Ed., Unwin Hyman, London.

**Erickson, E.** (1968) *Identity, Youth, Crisis,* Norton, New York.

**Gardner, H.** (1983) *Frames of Mind,* Basic, New York.

**Geertz, C.** (1973) *The Interpretation of Cultures,* Basic, New York.

**Goodlad, J.** (1984) *A Place Called School,* Houghton Mifflin, New York.

**Goodlad, J.** (1988) A new look at an old idea: core curriculum. In *Next Steps in Global Education,* Kniep, W., Ed., American Forum, New York 15–23.

**Hawkins, N. W.** (1987) *Classroom Archaeology: An Archaeology Activity Guide for Teachers,* Division of Archaeology, Baton Rouge, LA.

**Kniep, W.** (1988) *Next Steps in Global Education,* American Forum, New York.

**Layton, R., Ed.** (1989) *Who Needs the Past? Indigenous Values and Archaeology,* Unwin Hyman, London.

**Messenger, P. M., Ed.** (1989) *The Ethics of Collecting Cultural Property: Whose Culture? Whose Property?* University of New Mexico Press, Albuquerque.

National Governors Association (1989) America in Transition: The International Frontier. A Report of the National Governors' Association, The American Forum for Global Education, *Access,* 85.

**Piaget, J.** (1972) *Science of Education and the Psychology of the Child,* Viking, New York.

**Selby, D. and Pike, G.** (1988) *Global Teacher, Global Learner,* Stroughton, London.

**Shaw, R.** (1989) Combining archaeology and education — an example from England, *Archaeology and Education,* 1(1).

**Stone, P. G.** (1989) Interpretations and uses of the past in modern Britain and Europe. Why are people interested in the past? Do the experts know or care? A plea for further study. In *Who Needs the Past? Indigenous Values and Archaeology,* Layton, R., Ed., Unwin Hyman, London.

**Washington, J. M., Ed.** (1986) *A Testament of Hope — The Essential Writings of Martin Luther King, Jr.,* Harper & Row, San Francisco.

**Woyach, R. B. and Remy, R. C.** (1989) *Approaches to World Studies. A Handbook for Curriculum Planners,* Allyn and Bacon, Needham Heights, MA.

**White, J. J.** (1989) Anthropology. In *Charting a Course: Social Studies for the 21st Century,* a report of the Curriculum Task Force of the National Commission on Social Studies in the Schools, 31–36.

# MARKETING ARCHAEOLOGICAL RESOURCE PROTECTION

### Harvey M. Shields

## INTRODUCTION

Marketing archaeological resource protection may appear confusing to archaeologists and historic preservationists, who generally receive little or no training in business administration. The two most definitely relate, in that marketing can provide a unique and, hopefully, more successful way of organizing and implementing a concerted archaeological resource protection program. To better understand this relationship, think of marketing as an alternate paradigm by which one can observe, analyze, and affect a dynamic social process. Before proceeding any further, I must digress for a moment in order to overcome any prejudices that you, the reader, may have. Many of you have a background in the social sciences rather than business. Marketing, as you all surely know, comes out of the discipline of "business administration." This will, hopefully, not taint what is to follow.

## MARKETING

Philip Kotler (1984:4) defines marketing as "a social process by which individuals and groups obtain what they need and want through creating and exchanging products and value with others." There are many concepts wrapped up in this definition that need to be developed separately. Needs and wants are two key marketing concepts. People need many things in order to live. Items such as air, food, and water are basic to human survival and are thus required. People also have strong preferences for other goods and services. Some embellish on basic needs, while others revolve around more abstract concepts, such as recreation and education. Marketing does not create needs and wants; these pre-exist. Marketing acts to influence wants by pointing out how a good or service may fulfill a desire.

The attraction that some people have to archaeology, archaeological sites, and artifacts relates to these basic desires. It may have something to do with the desire of human beings to understand themselves and their origins, or it may have to do with an appreciation for art as manifested in artifacts. Whatever the cause, there is no doubt that some people want to deal with "things archaeological."

Another marketing concept is the product. A product is a good or a service that satisfies the needs and wants of individuals. Actually, all goods are really vehicles for a service. For example, a car provides a transportation service, a hammer provides the service of driving a nail, and a refrigerator provides the service of food preservation. The marketer's job is to convey clearly to the consumer what service is being realized by the product so they can identify the desire to be fulfilled.

The discipline of archaeology provides a wide variety of services. For example, it answers questions about human origins and lifeways. It also is the vehicle that produces artifacts to be viewed, appreciated, and/or possessed. The product may be packaged in the form of a dig, a museum, a movie, or, for some, a "tastefully" arranged wall-hanging of arrowheads.

Another set of related marketing concepts are value and satisfaction. Here, value is used as the relative rating of a product in providing for, or satisfying, one's need or want. The better a product does that, the more value it has. In an archaeological context, value may be ascribed on the basis of age, association with an historic figure, or monetary value. Satisfaction of the "archaeological desire" can be obtained by a range of options, from viewing or excavating a site or object to actual possession of a site or object.

The concepts of exchange and transaction are key economic and social concepts necessary to an understanding of marketing. People can obtain an item by producing it themselves, taking it from someone else, begging for it, or exchanging it for something they have (usually for money). The discipline of marketing implies the latter method. Exchange represents the transaction of obtaining a desired product by offering something of value in return and having it accepted. This is a processual concept rather than a static one and fits nicely within the range of social science theory.

Even the archaeological product is involved in the exchange of value and satisfaction. This may be as direct as a collector exchanging tens of thousands of dollars for an Anasazi pot or as abstract as a museum exchanging knowledge for a donation or volunteer work.

The final concept of concern to us is that of market. "A market consists of all the potential customers sharing a particular need or want who might be willing and able to engage in an exchange to satisfy that need or want" (Kotler 1984:12). Whereas economists consider a market as including all buyers and sellers, a marketer sees it as encompassing the entire industry and the buyers. However, the term "market" may be used in a variety of other ways. A market may refer to a specific group of buyers, as well as the all-inclusive system described in the definition above. Thus, one must be sure of the context of the word when inferring its meaning.

For archaeology, the market consists of those people who share the want or desire for "things archaeological" and are willing to enter into exchanges to satisfy those needs. By "things archaeological" I include the process of archaeological recovery of data, the knowledge obtained from this process, the recovered artifacts, and the storage and interpretive facilities (e.g., museums). The market involves all people with this want or desire. The fact that the activities of some of these people are detrimental to the archaeological resource is of no concern at this point in defining the market. It will have great importance later, however, when applying marketing techniques to the protection of the resource.

Defining the market brings us full circle back to marketing. In a crude sense, marketing is the anthropology of buying. Thus, it may be seen as a dynamic social process that can be observed, analyzed, and affected. The way one does this is referred to as marketing management.

## MARKETING MANAGEMENT

Marketing management ". . .consists of analyzing market opportunities, researching and selecting target markets, developing marketing strategies, planning marketing tactics, and implementing and controlling the marketing effort" (Kotler 1984:61). It is the process by which one delineates the market, understands it, and, accordingly, develops and implements a plan to accomplish the organization's goals.

### The Mission Statement

The first step in the process of marketing management is to develop a mission statement that clearly identifies the purpose of the organization or the effort about to be undertaken. This may sound easy enough, but the clear articulation of the mission statement can make all the difference between success and failure. It is the mission statement that provides both direction and a touchstone to determine if the product is doing what it is supposed to do. If the mission statement is too broad, it will not provide sufficient direction. If it is too narrow, it will choke off fruitful activities.

In the case of archaeological resource protection, the content of the mission statement will depend on the nature of the organization undertaking the effort, its philosophy, goal, and the background of the people making up the organization. For one group this might be "to educate the public about the value of archaeology," for another, "to physically protect archaeological sites under our management," for yet another, "to deter pothunters from plundering sites." In all likelihood, a single organization will not be able to carry out the mission "to protect all archaeological sites." Attempting such a broad mission would, more than likely, diffuse the effect of precious dollars. In any case, development of a mission statement is a key concept that forms the basis for decision making in the process outlined below.

## Situational Analysis

The next step in marketing management is to conduct a situational analysis. This amounts to doing the necessary background research on the context within which one is trying to operate. The context, or environment, can be broken into two areas: the macro- and microenvironments. The macroenvironment concerns the world around us and how it impinges on the market of concern. It takes in aspects such as demographics, national and international economic trends, the physical environment, technology, politics, and society. The microenvironment looks at the infrastructure relating to your activity and/or organization. It would include the organizational structure, supply of resources, middlemen, consumers, competitors, and groups that are interested in and may affect the conduct of the organization's activities. Any marketing effort must understand and take into account these factors.

The archaeological environment is a complex one. At the macroenvironmental level, an assessment must be made of the population at large and how demographic trends may relate to archaeological resources. For example, one effect of the "baby boomer" phenomenon is the likelihood of increased travel by this group as they enter their prime income-producing years. This may lead to more visits to archaeological sites, resulting in more impacts upon them. Economics and politics are important to examine. If the economy is generally healthy, there is a great possibility of private and/or public support of archaeological projects. Politics is always of concern, given the raft of federal and state historic preservation laws that help or hinder protection of archaeological resources. Society and its attitudes toward archaeology also are important to gauge in this process, as they are key to knowing how far or how deep educational efforts might have to go.

An analysis of the microenvironment must look at the archaeological organization: whether it is a museum, university, or government agency. The structure of the organization may be a help or a hindrance to the effort under consideration. In the archaeological context, the supply of resources may take in a variety of forms, including the availability of sites to excavate, the availability of money to excavate sites and preserve artifacts, the type and number of museum exhibits, and the number of dealers of artifacts. Consumers are also important to your analysis. How are consumers defined? Are they readers of archaeological reports, visitors to sites or museums, donors to your organization, or customers in a gift shop? Competitors, in the archaeological context, is an interesting idea that has received little thought. Certainly, there are competitors for visitors to museums, there are other archaeological projects that are competitors for funding, and there are even competitors for the recreational time of the people you want to visit a site or museum. It is a competitive world, even for archaeology.

These are examples of some of the items that should be included in a situational analysis of archaeological resources. In other words, the situational analysis must look at everything related to the resources and your organization. Only by seeing where you are, can you know where to go.

## Researching and Selecting Target Markets

A crucial realization in researching and selecting a target market is that not everyone is interested in what your organization offers. Unfortunately, many archaeologists and historic preservationists have a tendency to assume that everyone is interested in archaeology and history. This simply is not true. Just as everyone is not interested in attending symphony concert performances or watching "Wall Street Week" on public television, there is a limited market for "things archaeological."

A rule of thumb in marketing is the "80-20 rule." This common-sense theorum dictates that 20% of the market does 80% of the consuming. The rule leads to a concept called "target marketing." It dictates that marketing activities be directed to the 20% rather than the 80%. This results in more effective use of dollars and other resources in marketing your product. It is a particularly practical approach to take in this era of limited public and private support for just about any activity. Attempts to reach 100% of the market with a single marketing campaign simply are not very effective in reaching the primary consumers.

The next step in marketing management is to define who your market is. You need to get an idea of the group of consumers in which you are interested. Is it all people who are interested in "things archaeological?" Is it only those people who visit archaeological sites? Is it the people who traffic in illegal artifacts? Is it the people who "pothunt" sites? In other words, what group do you seek to reach with your activity? Clearly defining your market is crucial to the rest of the marketing management process.

Once the group of consumers that you are interested in has been defined, you must determine what they look like. This means understanding them demographically, attitudinally, geographically, and behaviorally (see Pokotylo, this volume, for a discussion of public attitudes about archaeology). It is also necessary to understand their perceptions about the product and the benefits they receive from its use. The point is to look at the consumer in great detail, both as an individual and as a member of a society.

Part and parcel of understanding your market is estimating its size. This provides a dimension to the effort one must undertake to sell the product. Preliminary results from a recent representative survey of 15,000 U.S. households by Longwoods International, Inc. (1989, 1990) revealed that 50.3% of people who traveled during the past 12 months visited an historical site. This proportion provides some indication of the total market for "things archaeological."

Finally, you need to know how best to reach your market. This includes knowing which media they use the most, i.e., television, radio, or print. What are their favorite programs in the broadcast media, or their favorite periodicals in the print media. Only by knowing this information can you place your message where it will do the most good.

Once this research about your target market is completed, you will have the ability to segment your market. The 80-20 rule applies to a market as much as it does to the universe of all consumers. That is, a few segments of your total market will do most of the consuming. There are a number of ways to segment a market. It can be done on the basis of demographics, such as age or income. It can be done on the basis of geography, such as zip code, state, county, city, or census districts. For purposes of archaeological resource protection, as in most endeavors, it may be best to segment the market on the basis of interest. This is the one sure way to reach the target group, regardless of demographics or place of residence.

Based on the study of consumer's interests, you can begin to develop segments. Segmenting the target market is analogous to developing artifact typologies. They can also be derived in the same way. Marketers usually use a variety of statistical clustering techniques and/or factor analyses. Archaeologists should be very much at home in determining market segments. If the goal is to reach the pothunter, they can be studied and one can come to understand them. Chances are that much pothunting is of the casual sort and could be easily affected by an informational and educational campaign targeted to that group and directed at deterring their activities. The hard-core pothunter of your nightmares can also be addressed through such a research effort. If nothing else, the information gained through a survey would provide law enforcement officials with a profile of these people. Whoever you pick as your target market should relate to the mission statement for your activity/organization.

In all likelihood, the specific information for use in marketing archaeological resource protection is simply not available at this time. Original research must be done. Just as archaeologists conduct background research before beginning an archaeological survey or excavating a site, market research must be obtained before the start of a protection effort. In the long run, it will save funds and ensure that the effort will be as successful as possible.

## Developing a Marketing Plan and Strategy

Most organizations, especially bureaucratic ones, are familiar with the planning process. It is very much the same for marketing as it is for any other activity for which one is used to planning. Development of a marketing plan and strategy are necessary steps to the successful realization of one's mission.

There are many ways to construct a plan, and I will not belabor that point here. The point is to make a plan and be sure that it combines the knowledge gleaned from the situational analysis and that it applies to the mission of the effort. As with all plans, it must contain a series of goals and objectives, with detailed action plans to make sure that each step of the plan is implemented. Subsequent to this, you will be able to estimate how much money will be needed to accomplish the plan.

There is one part of this process that is unique to marketing. This unique aspect is called the marketing mix. It often is confused with the totality of marketing. While it is not the whole, it is perhaps the heart of marketing management. The marketing mix consists of the "4 Ps": product, price, place, and promotion. These are the variables over which marketers have control and represent the means by which they realize their goals and objectives.

The product is a concept that we have touched upon earlier. It is the good or service that is being offered. Identifying the product is based on the answer to the question: What is the buyer really buying? (Kotler 1984:463). As stated earlier, every product is really a service, even ones that seem to be rather tangible. When a consumer buys an automobile, he is really buying transportation; or in the case of a sports car, perhaps he is buying status or a youthful image. What the marketer does is sell the benefits of the product, not its features. The core product must be converted into a tangible product that may have up to five characteristics: a level of quality, features, styling, a brand name, and packaging (Kotler 1984).

What does this have to do with archaeological protection? It has everything to do with developing a concerted marketing effort directed at creating change. The product concept can apply to "things archaeological." Of course the delineation of its characteristics would be different, depending on what the mission of the organization was. For instance, let us say that public education is the mission, and the goal is to make pothunters aware of the national value of archaeological resources, as a means of deterring casual looting. The level of quality would relate to the great value of the archaeological resource to our society and the nation. Features would include the resource's physical nature and condition (e.g., is it above or below ground; does it contain burials, ceramics, or projectile points?). Styling is quite obvious. It would relate to the many types of archaeological sites that exist (e.g., is it a rock shelter, a pueblo, or a big-game hunting kill site?). A brand name used to evoke a specific place would be a well-known site such as Mesa Verde or Cahokia Mounds. Packaging relates to the presentation of the message (e.g., using broadcast media spots by famous people associated with archaeology, such as Harrison Ford). The point here is that the product must be thought through and not assumed to be self-evident. It can be presented in a variety of ways, any one of which can send a different message that may appeal to, rather than turn off, a targeted group.

Price is a variable that also is related to archaeological resource protection. What are you going to charge for your service? What is the price that the public would be willing to pay if these resources are allowed to perish? Of course, price also refers to what the public may pay through donations of time and money or through appropriations to government agencies. In whatever format, pricing is something one must consider in this process. In determining the price, one must look at a variety of factors (Kotler 1984). What is the objective of the price? Is it for survival or for profit? What is the demand for the product? Even in archaeological resources protection, there is a demand equation for this service. A high demand would enhance an already high intrinsic value. What are the costs involved in producing the product? This would include costs associated with excavations, museum storage, and interpretation, as well as the commercial value of artifacts. It would also include the cost of law enforcement or public service announcements. Understanding costs would help an organization to set a price.

Price can be determined by simply looking at actual costs, but they can also be determined by looking at the competition. In this day and age, many worthwhile causes look to the public for support in accomplishing their own goals. What kinds of donations are competitors getting? How are they assessing the value of their product for the public? Examining all these factors will help in setting the price variable, however one wants to use it in the cause of archaeological resource protection.

The concept of place refers to the distribution channels used to deliver the product to the consuming public. In the case of a service like archaeological protection, how is the service made available and accessible to the public? The distributional channel for an educational message could be the broadcast or print media. It might also be a network of community museums. In the case of law enforcement, distribution of that service is through the activities of the members of the law enforcement establishments.

Finally, there is the promotional variable. This amounts to getting the word out and actually communicating the benefits and features of your product to the targeted markets. Promotion is not a single activity, but a mix of four major tools: advertising, sales promotion, publicity, and personal selling (Kotler 1984). Advertising consists of paid announcements in a variety of media. Sales promotion consists of short-term incentives to encourage the purchase of a product. Publicity concerns the placement of information about the product into the news media. Personal selling involves face-to-face interaction with groups or individuals for the purpose of selling the product.

All of these can be applied to the protection of archaeological resources. Other than law enforcement, most people think of advertising as the primary means of promoting their product. As you can see, there are other possibilities, many less costly. Publicity is free except for the time needed to prepare press releases, hold press conferences, or deal with the media. In some instances, the use of a sales promotion may be more effective. In archaeology this may relate to letting people actually dig at a site. This would enable them to see the cost and effort, in human terms, that goes into the recovery of archaeological information. Personal selling in archaeology may amount to giving lectures in front of local avocational archaeology societies or even talking with collectors.

Now that you have developed your marketing mix and devised tactics to implement that strategy, you need to evaluate the whole process. It does not do much good to do all that work and not be able to judge whether it was successful or not. This may seem like it might not be worth the time or expense, but it will be to the groups that supply the money for your projects. If you can clearly demonstrate improvement of the situation, they are more likely to continue providing funds for the effort. In addition, such an evaluation effort lets you know where to make improvements in the program. It provides the feedback mechanism so important to a dynamic system designed to achieve its goal.

## CONCLUSION

The discipline of marketing is one way for an organization to approach the protection of archaeological resources. It provides a way of visualizing the issues and addressing them in a coherent and logical fashion. The effort to protect the world's archaeological resources takes every bit as much time and work to produce success as it does to produce a successful archaeological research project. Marketing provides a method by which the protection effort, in whatever form, can be organized, implemented, and controlled. Its use will be well worth the effort.

## REFERENCES CITED

**Kotler, P.** (1984) *Marketing Management: Analysis, Planning, and Control,* Prentice-Hall, Englewood Cliffs, NJ.
Longwoods International, Inc. (1989, 1990) Travel USA (ongoing research on the travel behavior of U.S. citizens). Contact Dr. Bill Siegel, 2161 Yonge St., Suite 200, Toronto, Ontario, Canada M4S 3A6.

# AVOCATIONAL ARCHAEOLOGY GROUPS: A SECRET WEAPON FOR SITE PROTECTION

Hester A. Davis

## INTRODUCTION

The size, nature, purpose, and structure of avocational archaeological groups in the U.S. vary tremendously. This variation, particularly in organizational purpose and goals, reflects the divergent interests of the members relative to archaeology, artifacts, research, site protection, Native Americans, and local history.

Before we discuss this variation, however, it is important to set down some definitions so that readers will understand what is meant in this article by "avocational archaeologists." The term has often been used synonymously with the term "amateur archaeologists," and presumably is to differentiate these people from "professional archaeologists," on the one hand, and "artifact dealers" and "grave robbers," on the other. And then there are "collectors" and "relic hunters:" those who do not profess to be "archaeologists," as the term is usually used, but who are quick to point out that they do not destroy sites, as do grave robbers and vandals.

There is, perhaps, another way of looking at the semantics of this universe of people: there are archaeologists and there are nonarchaeologists, and the basic distinction is that of attitude toward the resources. Archaeologists consider sites and artifacts as sources of information; nonarchaeologists consider sites as sources of artifacts. Since this is not a discussion on the ethics of archaeology, let me say that I will be using the term avocational and amateur synonymously and that I consider these individuals to be archaeologists, as opposed to nonarchaeologists, as defined above. Since there are archaeological organizations in which avocational archaeologists do not participate, I will also be talking of those organizations in which avocational archaeologists are the leaders, organizers, and perpetuators. I will *not* be considering the organizations of dealers, traders, and collectors of artifacts, of which there are also a great many.

In order to understand the potential for avocational organizations to aid in site and resource protection, perhaps a review of their variety is in order. The greatest difference is probably in size of membership. There is, for example, the Archaeological Institute of America (AIA), with membership in the thousands and two major publications, one a quarterly scientific journal and the other directed to the general public, with a circulation of over 100,000. At the other end of the membership scale, there are probably hundreds of small organizations, often with 50 or less members, such as local chapters of state or regional societies. There are state-oriented societies, regional groups, county and city organized societies; there is an organization of avocational societies called the Eastern States Archaeological Federation (ESAF); and there is, as of this writing, a proposed organization of avocational archaeological societies that would affiliate with the Society for American Archaeology (SAA).

Almost all of the groups with which this article is concerned have generally similar goals and purposes: to hold meetings for discussion and exchange of information, to promote archaeological research, to help professional archaeologists, and to provide information to the public; and many have "a determination to help preserve archaeological sites, materials, and traditions" (Lubensky 1988:6). Each of these organizations achieves or strives for these goals differently: some, of course, with greater success than others.

To follow through with our particular interest in the goal of site protection, there are three areas that need addressing: (1) what "site protection" involves relative to actions by organized groups of interested people; (2) what avocational societies have done in the past to protect sites; and (3) what such groups could do in the future. Let me add here that I am using the term site protection to mean the physical protection of an archaeological site from disturbance (by plowing, erosion, vandalism, looting, and other nonarchaeological land-disturbing activities).

## HOW CAN ORGANIZED GROUPS PROTECT SITES?

Again, by "site protection" I mean both the physical protection of sites and the protection of the information that sites contain. This protection can, in addition, be both direct and indirect. There are, it seems to me, several ways in which groups can actively become involved in protecting sites. One of the most direct actions a group could take would be to purchase sites or arrange for conservation or preservation easements on sites. This could be done tangentially, through active support of the Archaeological Conservancy, the one entity in this country designed specifically to purchase threatened archaeological sites (see Michel, this volume, for a discussion of the Archaeological Conservancy).

A second kind of direct action is for an organization or its individual members to become site stewards, taking personal or group responsibility for the protection of a site (or sites) that is actually owned by someone else (see Hoffman, this volume, for a discussion of site stewardship programs).

And finally, there is protection of site information through data recovery. This kind of direct protective action requires that archaeological organizations arrange for their members to be trained in scientific excavation techniques, appropriate laboratory work, analysis, and report writing. If they take on the responsibility for data recovery, these organizations must also arrange for permanent curation of the artifacts and associated information.

Less direct but, in the long run, equally important activities for site protection come to mind as well. First, organizations should continually educate their individual members about the nature of site and the dangers to them; these members can then, in turn, influence those who own sites (which in a few cases may be one and the same). Organizations can sponsor local and statewide educational programs for the public, such as an "archaeology week" (see Lerner, this volume, for a discussion of Arizona Archaeology Week). They can be a source for civic club programs, for school assemblies, for county and state fair booths — all designed to provide the widest possible education to citizens about "saving the past for the future."

Finally, there is the possibility of active support for protective legislation, whether local, state, or national, since legislation can be oriented toward general protective measures for state property or for unmarked graves and can include protection or purchase of individual sites by state and federal governments (see Neumann, this volume, for a discussion of legislative involvement in archaeological site protection).

## WHAT HAVE ARCHAEOLOGICAL ORGANIZATIONS BEEN DOING?

What is the record of avocational organizations in pursuing these kinds of protective activities? The best record is in educating the membership in a preservation ethic. Since there are organizations for those who want to buy, sell, and trade, if an individual remains a member of an avocational society, which by our definition has restrictions about members buying, selling, or trading artifacts, it means that person is interested in the research/scientific goals of the organization. By personal experience, I am aware of many people who joined the Arkansas

Archeological Society because they collected "arrowheads" all their lives and who subsequently soaked up the preservation ethic and made it their own. This does not necessarily mean they will cease to collect artifacts from the surface of disturbed sites, but it does mean they catalogue their collection, they report sites being dug by pothunters, they participate in training programs so that they can do research on their own, and they actively support, if not lobby, for protective legislation. They often see that their society does, too.

Most state archaeological organizations have both avocational and professional archaeologists as members, and many of their organizational activities are oriented toward "science," toward helping professionals when there are emergencies, volunteering for laboratory work, reporting sites, and cataloguing collections. Some societies have also developed standard programs that members can borrow to provide talks to the public and to school children. Colorado and Arizona have led the way in combining efforts of several organizations in sponsoring statewide archaeological awareness programs.

Training and certification programs have developed in the past 20 years that again combine the time and talents of the avocationals and professionals. In Texas, the Texas Archeological Society contracts with a professional archaeologist to direct the 9-day training program for society members. In Arkansas, the Arkansas Archeological Survey provides the professional leadership for both a training program and a formal certification program for members of the Arkansas Archeological Society. These, and over a dozen other similar or adapted programs, mean that many states have a cadre of people with some knowledge of scientific techniques, which can be used in conjunction with professional projects and/or student crews, or that small local groups can conduct scientific salvage excavations on their own. In many instances, these programs have become vital in efforts to save both sites and information that otherwise would have been lost for lack of knowledgeable people.

This brings us to the other area in which avocational societies have been active: support of protective legislation. This is largely a recent phenomena (as it is with professional organizations, for that matter), but some of the older societies have an admirable record, particularly on the state level. Chapman's description (1985:244) of actions by the leadership of the Missouri Archeological Society in the 1950s and 1960s in this regard is an excellent example. He also recognizes (1985:245) that it took both avocational and professional organizations to get the Archaeological and Historic Preservation Act (PL 93-291) of 1974 passed through Congress. It should also be pointed out, of course, that some state *historical* societies have long been prime movers in the protection and even purchase of archaeological sites; the Ohio Historical Society immediately comes to mind.

Most recently, many state archaeological societies have become involved with Native Americans and professional archaeologists in trying to work out mutually agreeable ways in which burial sites can be protected from grave robbers through state legislation.

To the best of my knowledge, however, avocational archaeological societies have not gone into the business of protecting sites through purchase. The reasons for this are multifarious, not the least of which is that it would mean a money-raising campaign. But the principal one is undoubtedly because purchase means ownership and management, and most avocational archaeological organizations are neither set up to do this nor are their members really oriented to this kind of responsibility.

I have observed a phenomena concerning local or even state archaeological organizations (as opposed to historical societies and, more recently, historic preservation groups), which might account for this lack of orientation toward raising money and taking group responsibility for management. It is my impression that archaeological society membership is largely made up of "ordinary citizens." I would wager that there are more rural route postmen interested in archaeology than there are chief executive officers with similar archaeological interests.

Local and state archaeological organizations are all volunteer; none that I know of have any paid staff, even part time. Often an organization's address changes as its officers change, so there is no permanent mailing address. Their energies, as a group, are taken up in publications, in annual or chapter meetings, and, if possible, in providing some way for members to have field experience. Archaeological societies (avocational *and* professional, it seems) do not run major fund-raising campaigns, nor do they have funds for an advertizing blitz to put across their message about site protection. A case in point is from my own experience: my own local Washington County (Arkansas) Historical Society *owns* two historic houses in Fayetteville, purchased through major donations and a fund-raising campaign to save them; the statewide Arkansas Archeological Society, in 5 years, has yet to raise $20,000 for a research fund, much less purchase a threatened site.

Archaeological societies have worked most successfully at the grass roots level (e.g., the individualistic nature of the stewardship programs). Many can mobilize volunteers for an emergency salvage of a site being destroyed (after all, that means doing real archaeology) more easily than they can mobilize a volunteer force to lobby their state legislators.

In general, then, the history of really active efforts directed at site protection per se by avocational archaeological groups across the country is not much to write home about (or to summarize in a publication on the subject). But the *potential* is tremendous. All it will take is a lot of hard work, time, money, and strong and committed leadership from a few professional and avocational archaeologists working together.

## THE SECRET WEAPON

The greatest potential for greater site protection is through the statewide avocational archaeological groups. The *secret weapon* held by these organizations is their ability to influence their own members, politicians, landowners, teachers, school children, and even pothunters. By their very numbers and the fact of their organization, avocational archaeological societies should be real *advocates* for site protection, in the most contemporary use of that term.

Advocacy has become a powerful tool in the fight for a better environment. However, convincing avocational organizations to actually take on politically active programs may take some innovative approaches. As implied earlier, archaeologists often seem to be oriented toward activities that lead to direct personal satisfaction: excavation, handling artifacts, having their name appear on reports, etc. Contributing to and/or becoming personally active in programs with less direct personal reward (lobbying for legislation, for example) may require some study of how the Sierra Club and the Audubon Society have been so successful in getting so much of the nation's population willing to march on Earth Day to help save the environment.

Ideas for programs, activities, and legislation could, and probably should, be communicated to state and local groups from the national archaeological organizations, particularly the SAA through its "Save the Past" initiative (see Reinburg, Judge, this volume) and also from the American Society for Conservation Archeology (ASCA), whose whole orientation is supposed to be toward site and resource protection. The state organizations can then pass this information on to chapters or other local groups (including historical societies and historic preservation organizations).

This country is attuned to advocacy groups. One would think that members of archaeological organizations would more often be seen on the evening news lying down in front of the bulldozers. How many archaeological groups do you know who organize press conferences on the state capitol steps to speak out, complete with banners and posters, for stopping destruction of the past? Not many, I would wager, although there have certainly been some success stories of organized efforts to stop, or at least delay, destruction of individuals sites and maybe even of projects. However, generally (perhaps excluding many groups in California), avocational organizations are not rabble rousers. They have gone about their advocacy, if at all, on a case-by-case basis as an individual local crisis arises. Since this seems to be the habit if not the nature of archaeological organizations (to say nothing of archaeologists), then this approach needs to be taken advantage of in organizing avocationals to work toward the common goal of site protection (see Bense, this volume, for a discussion of public involvement in archaeological site protection).

There is, of course, already an activity that gives individual satisfaction and that can be promoted on the state level and on the local level, with members, with landowners, and even with the general public. The stewardship concept for protection of individual archaeological sites is tailor-made for this kind of program. National organizations, it seems to me, need to become advocates themselves, not just for saving sites on public land, but for saving sites anywhere. They need to get out a heavy blitz of information to state societies about the concept, provide flexible ideas for how to set up such a program so individual groups can adjust a program to their own circumstances, provide guidelines on dos and don'ts, and, in every way possible, indicate that the *crisis is upon us* and that each individual archaeologist has a personal, moral, and ethical responsibility to be a steward for at least one site. Given that there are probably between 25,000 and 50,000 individuals who are members of avocational organizations (an estimate made about 10 years ago from membership of those organizations in ESAF), there could be a major impact on site protection.

## CONCLUSION

Avocational archaeological groups have the greatest potential for making a real difference in which sites and how many sites are protected in the future. All archaeologists, in my use of the term, must coordinate, communicate, organize nationally, and become proprotection. Legislation protecting unmarked graves must hit hard on the looters and vandals; ordinances at the local level must become commonplace. The names and faces of archaeological organizations speaking out for less wanton destruction must be on educational television and the evening news.

There are probably four or five times as many avocational archaeologists as there are professional ones. There are probably dozens more avocational archaeological organizations than there are professional ones. Since their interests are supposed to be the same, they must all become strong active advocates for site protection, from the individual site where the shopping center is going in, to the national historic landmarks still in private ownership.

None of these thoughts are new. Almost 10 years ago, George Frison said,"...their [archaeological resources] value must be established through education of the public.... Here the avocational groups can make their greatest contribution ....When enough people become concerned about our cultural resources, legislative indifference to their protection and proper management will not be tolerated" (Frison 1984:190).

In point of fact, many people, both professional and avocational, have been saying that we who are interested in preservation must act in unison. However, the leadership for springing this secret weapon upon the nation must come from the national archaeological organizations.

## REFERENCES CITED

**Chapman, C. H.** (1985) The amateur archaeological society: a Missouri example, *Am. Antiquity,* 50(2), 241–248.
**Frison, G. C.** (1984) Avocational archaeology: its past, present, and future. In *Ethics and Values in Archaeology,* Green, E. L., Ed., Free Press, New York, chap. 21.
**Lubensky, E. H.** (1988) Objectives and programs of archaeological societies. Paper presented at the Ann. Meet. Soc. for American Archaeology, Phoenix.

# PRESENTING THE PAST: A CONFERENCE SERIES AIMED AT PUBLIC EDUCATION

## Peter S. Wells

## INTRODUCTION

The most important way to protect archaeological resources is to raise the consciousness of the public about the existence and significance of the remains of the past. We need widespread public awareness and support to develop comprehensive programs for the protection of monuments on a nationwide scale. We must also develop ways by which we can utilize archaeological resources to educate the public about the human past.

The Center for Ancient Studies at the University of Minnesota, with the cooperation of several other institutions (including federal agencies), has organized a series of conferences on the subject of presenting the past to the public. Our direct goal has been broader than protection in the immediate sense. I wish here to discuss these conferences: why we began them, what we accomplished at them, and how they contribute to this theme. The views I present here are my own; other participants might represent the conferences in other ways.

## BACKGROUND

Archaeology is a subject of vast potential popular appeal. Newspapers, magazines, and television regularly carry reports of new discoveries and new interpretations. All archaeological excavations in populated areas have streams of interested visitors. Many people are intrigued by the idea of discovering physical remains of past human activity, whether they consist of dishes used by people living a few generations ago or projectile points left by hunters millennia in the past.

As professional archaeologists, most of us could be doing more to make the results of our work available to public audiences as well as to scholarly ones. Many individuals have been engaged in this enterprise for a long time — presenting public lectures, on both local and national levels; working with television production companies to make documentaries that deal with archaeology; writing for popular journals; conducting site tours for the public; and involving volunteers in archaeological fieldwork. But most members of the profession could do much more along these lines, for the benefit of the public and the field of archaeology.

During my first year as director of the Center for Ancient Studies at the University of Minnesota in 1986, I discussed with Tom Trow, cultural liaison officer for the College of Liberal Arts at the university and an alumnus of the center, the idea of organizing a conference that would focus on what professional archaeologists and historians do to present their work to public audiences. We formed a planning committee comprised of individuals from different institutions in the Twin Cities who were involved in such efforts. The committee included Christy Caine of the U.S. Forest Service, state archaeologist for Minnesota; Leslie Denny of the Department of Professional Development and Conferences Services of the University of Minnesota; Clark Dobbs of the Institute for Minnesota Archaeology; Louise Lincoln of the Minneapolis Institute of Arts; Phyllis Messenger of the Institute of International Studies at the University of Minnesota; Orrin Shane of the Science Museum of Minnesota; and Nicholas Westbrook of the Minnesota Historical Society. After several initial discussions, we found that we all shared the common perception that this subject was of immediate concern to a great many people, locally and nationally, but that little was being done to confront the issue systematically and broadly.

The aim of the conference we decided to plan was threefold. First, we wanted to learn as much as possible about what was currently being done in the U.S. to inform the public about archaeology and to involve the public in the process of doing archaeology. Second, we wanted to use that information to formulate working plans for future action. Third, we wanted to discuss what could be done in the short term to improve communication between the profession and the public.

## THE CONFERENCE

The planning process for the first conference was long and complex. The subject is immense, as we quickly learned, and we wanted to touch upon it on local, national, and international levels. This first conference was conceived as an informational meeting to provide a means for the sharing of information about what was being done in different places and to begin discussion of what could be done on a broader scale. To this end, we defined several categories of professionals that we wanted to invite. We needed individuals who had developed well-known and highly successful programs in public archaeology. We also wanted to invite representatives from abroad, since perspectives from other countries are always valuable in suggesting different questions and solutions. We felt that good representation of local Minnesota efforts was important, both because archaeologists in Minnesota have been active in this field and because we wanted our local audience to be made aware of the efforts being made here in the state. Finally, we wanted to involve members of the local Indian community as representatives of some of the peoples studied by archaeologists.

We designed the first conference (1987) in two parts directed toward two different, but overlapping, audiences. The first we called the professional program, and it was intended principally for people whose professional positions entailed presenting archaeology to the public. The title of this part of the conference was "Perception and Presentation of the Past." It ran for 3 days. This part included a series of case studies in the presentation of archaeology and its results to the public. Sets of papers were followed by formal discussion initiated by scheduled discussants and carried further by audience participation. The second part of the conference, entitled "Presenting Our Past," was designed for a public audience. It was meant to accomplish two aims: to provide a local public audience with an overview of the issues with which we were concerned and, at the same time, to present to this audience some results of archaeological research. This public program took place on a Friday evening and all day on Saturday.

The presentations and formal discussions in both the professional and public programs were of high quality and raised many topics of concern to the participants. Most satisfying for the planners of the program, however, was the level and quality of audience participation. The lively discussion and debate that followed the papers indicated the high level of interest in the subject on the part of a wide range of professionals. Two field trips to local archaeological and historical sites provided case studies for on-site consideration, as well as informal settings in which people could continue discussions initiated during the sessions.

It was clear from the enthusiasm shown by participants in the conference that the issue was important to people involved with public archaeology on many different levels in the late 1980s. Conference participants included personnel from federal agencies; from state, county, local, and university museums; from state and local historical and archaeological organizations; and from academic departments at universities. Most were directly involved in the planning and implementing of public programs in archaeology. It became clear that many people were grappling with the same issues and that all could benefit by sharing experiences and ideas. We often observed that different individuals and groups were working on the same problem, without being aware that others were involved in very similar efforts.

As a result of the strong demonstration of interest in this issue and the enthusiasm of the participants at the first conference, we decided to plan a second one for the next year, 1988. Several federal agencies agreed to help sponsor the second conference, including the National Park Service, the Soil Conservation Service, the Bureau of Land Management, and the Tennessee Valley Authority. The National Park Service also played a major role in the planning of the second conference.

Whereas the first conference had been a very general one aimed at presenting cases for discussion and opening dialogue about presenting archaeology to public audiences, the second conference (1988) was more tightly focused. The title was "Presenting the Past: Media, Marketing, and the Public," and the theme was the use of media and marketing in the presentation of archaeological sites, materials, and information. Speakers addressed the role of newspapers, television, and other media in disseminating information about archaeology. Others spoke on the use of volunteers from the public in excavating and protecting archaeological sites, and about lecturing to public audiences. In addition to the lecture presentations, we organized workshops in which small groups could discuss particular themes with individuals knowledgeable in the subject.

The third conference (1989) focused on public education, specifically the presentation of the past in schools and museums. The title of this program was "Presenting the Past to the Public: History and Archaeology in Schools and Museums." We invited speakers to discuss specific projects they had initiated in presenting archaeology and history in museum and school contexts. Others addressed broader issues of curriculum development and the politics of education and public awareness. A public program associated with this conference was entitled "Confronting Columbus: Contact and Cultural Diversity in America." In this program, speakers addressed the question of presenting subjects bearing on cultural diversity in the past, with particular reference to the upcoming commemoration of Columbus' voyages. We were fortunate to have the Honorable Bruce Vento of the U.S. House of Representatives, chairman of the Subcommittee on National Parks and Public Lands, as the first speaker in this public program.

## DISCUSSION

The principal result of the three conferences in 1987, 1988, and 1989 was the demonstration that a large number of individuals throughout the U.S. and Canada, working in many different federal, state, local, and private agencies, are deeply concerned with how we present the past. Many people made substantial commitments of time and effort to participate in the conferences. There have always been archaeological and historical sites and museums whose staffs have made major efforts to communicate with the public — Plymoth Plantation, Colonial Williamsburg, and Sturbridge Village come to mind as outstanding examples in North America, but hundreds more could be mentioned. What is new, I think, is the groundswell of concern that we have seen through these conferences, for improving communication with the public and for involving the public more fully in the future of the past. This concern has been shown by the participation of numerous individuals and by many letters and telephone calls we have received requesting information about the programs.

In order to assure the protection of our archaeological and historical sites so that they survive for the enlightenment of future generations, we need to continue our efforts at bringing the public into the discussion about presentation, in all contexts. Major questions that have emerged from the conference are discussed below.

How can we involve members of the public in the early stages of archaeological discovery? We can develop programs through which volunteers can assist archaeologists map, survey, and excavate sites. One of the best ways to instill an appreciation for the informational value of archaeological sites is to involve people in archaeological excavations. Only a small minority will have the time and sufficient interest to actually work at archaeology, however. For others, the organization of site tours during excavations is an important means of showing people why archaeological sites are important and why they must be treated properly. The public needs to be informed about significant new discoveries and thereby encouraged to learn more about the archaeological record. We need to develop systematic ways of cooperating with the media in order to disseminate such information. Yet, as several conference speakers noted, information must be made public carefully and with appropriate education; we do not want inadvertently to stimulate the looting of archaeological sites.

How can the public be involved in later stages of archaeology? Sites can sometimes be preserved as they are revealed by excavation, with appropriate signs, maps, explanations, and, in some cases, parks constructed to enclose the remains. Museum displays can be developed to show what materials have come from a site and what we can learn through proper excavation and analysis.

Most important is the need to educate early. Many professionals that attended our conferences agreed that the key to developing a broad-based appreciation of archaeology and history is education at the primary school level. If we can develop means to teach school children why the archaeological and historical remains are important — what kinds of information we can learn from them through proper research techniques — then we shall succeed in raising the awareness level of the general public on an unprecedented scale. Only then will it be possible to generate widespread support for protection of archaeological resources (see Rogge, Smartz, McNutt, and Hawkins, this volume, for discussions of archaeological education and children).

The next conference, planned for 1991, will focus on the development of curricula for schools. This theme emerged in the concluding discussion at the 1989 conference as the critical issue for the immediate future.

## CONCLUSION

In closing, I should like to make a few general observations about the process and outcome of the three conferences. We found that it was valuable to have speakers from a wide range of different backgrounds and institutions. It was instructive to hear about large-scale and well-known programs, but equally important to hear from people involved in smaller, local community efforts. The latter often provided a perspective unfamiliar to many of the participants. Many common themes emerged from varied experiences where we did not necessarily anticipate them. Many participants remarked that they were interested to learn that numerous others around the country were facing the same issues and dilemmas.

Perspectives provided by people working in other countries were valuable. European archaeologists have been facing these issues for a much longer time than we in the New World have. In Britain and Germany, for example, countries from which several of our speakers came, issues of public access to archaeological and historical sites, and protection of those sites, have histories of many centuries in some cases. Stonehenge is the most familiar example — a site of great cultural importance to our understanding of Neolithic northwest Europe, and also one severely threatened by public overuse. Christopher Chippindale, a participant in the 1988 conference, has documented (1983) the long and complex history of the public presentation and official protection of this most famous of monuments.

The three conferences have been successful in bringing together many people concerned with the presentation and protection of archaeological sites and materials. The discussions have been productive, and we now need to develop our ideas into specific plans for public education.

## ACKNOWLEDGMENTS

I thank especially the planning committees and the participants in the three conferences, for their dedicated work and their excellent presentations. Both groups have now grown much too large to name all of the individuals here. The Department of Professional Development and Conference Services, Continuing Education and Extension, University of Minnesota, has supported all three conferences; Leslie Denny and Steven Weiland have been particularly helpful. The Minnesota Humanities Commission supported the public portions of the 1987 and 1989 conferences. The National Park Service and the Soil Conservation Service helped sponsor the 1988 and 1989 conferences; Frank McManamon, George Smith, and Diane Gelburd have been especially supportive. The Bureau of Land Management and the Tennessee Valley Authority helped sponsor the 1988 program. I thank all of these institutions for making this conference series possible.

## REFERENCES CITED

**Chippindale, C.** (1983) *Stonehenge Complete,* Cornell University Press, Ithaca, NY.

# PROTECTING THE PAST FROM A MUSEUM

## David S. Brose

## INTRODUCTION

Today human action is global in scale, leaving relatively little of the earth unaffected (see Messenger and Enloe, this volume, for a discussion of global education). The dimension of change accelerates, and by the end of the century, more than 5 billion people will be alive. Along with many natural habitats, the places of the past disappear at a rapid rate. In a free society the public must be clearly informed of the value of understanding and preserving the past if it is to choose wisely among future options. Making such information available must be one goal of any successful strategy to protect the past.

It should be pointed out that while archaeology is not the only profession whose goal is to interpret and preserve the past, I shall confine my remarks to what it is that archaeologists have done, and should be doing, to further those goals. And, while not even a large proportion of archaeologists operate from a museum, it is to museum archaeology that my remarks are directed. My title is equivocal because museums have not had an unequivocal role in protecting much beyond scattered pieces of the past. In this brief review I hope to indicate not only how and why this has been the case, but why and how it is changing.

## PUBLIC EXPOSURE

Public awareness of archaeology occurs in various ways. Reasonably accurate and understandable information can be found by attending lectures at universities or libraries, by watching educational or public television, by visiting museums or archaeological and historic sites, or by reading scholarly or semipopular books and journals that deal with the discoveries of prehistoric or early historic societies. These presentations usually explain to their audience that from the materials they recover from the ground, archaeologists not only study ancient and exotic cultures, but that such investigations can shed new light upon America's own past. Many of these presentations cautiously stress the fact that excavation must be done carefully, that good archaeology takes training, and that proper analysis and restoration of artifacts and environmental samples also takes time and money. Sometimes it is even made clear that the records and documents, as well as the artifacts from archaeological excavation, must be given equal long-term care. At those few reconstructed archaeological sites open to the visitor, they may see earthworks and mounds of various shapes, or buildings and artifacts of various eras, and they are occasionally reminded that these carefully protected ancient monuments are fragile.

Nonetheless, to most of the public, doing archaeology is as arcane as doing astrophysics. Although fascinated, few of even that small segment of the public that knows what archaeology is, believe there could be any personal role for them in the interpretation and preservation of prehistoric or historic archaeological sites. At almost no university, library, or historic site is such a role offered to the public. A museum is the archaeological purveyor most likely to offer the public an involvement with its archaeology program. This leaves the museum archaeologist as the individual best able to convince the public that the sites of the past are endangered and that the public can and should protect them.

## THE VARIETIES OF MUSEUM EXPERIENCE

It is true that the focus on differing aspects of the past is not the same in the archaeological presentations of differing types of museums. No doubt this is because there have been differing types of archaeology. Unlike many disciplines, archaeology did not begin with clearly defined objectives, and only recently have there been many generally accepted field or laboratory procedures. There is still nothing like an accepted theoretical framework within which these goals and methods articulate. The history of what kinds of archaeology have actually been done in the past demonstrates the rather haphazard interactions of techniques, problems, overall strategy, and results, thus indicating the eclectic development of modern archaeology. Archaeology has been practiced as art, as technique, as narrative, and as science. Little wonder, then, that archaeological objects and information are presented in art museums, historical societies, museums of history, and in science museums, both natural and unnatural. And less wonder that the focus of such presentations often ignores the potential for preserving the places of the past from which archaeological objects and information come.

There has always been archaeology presented in the guise of historical particularism. Whether as classic art or as an extension of ancient history, this is the study of the recovered object, whether sherd or site, which is seen to be of unique antiquarian interest. Frequently, museum exhibits of such art objects from nonindustrialized societies touch only briefly, if at all, upon the material conditions affecting the artists or the society, or upon their contact with other cultures. But this idealist approach misses much that is significant in understanding human experience and much that is significant in understanding the art object itself.

The original meaning of a "masterpiece" was the journeyman's proof of having mastered his craft. The acceptance of its arrangements of matter and form marked the transition of an individual from one status to a new and higher status. Though usually functional, the masterpiece was frequently dedicated to the most powerful secular or sacred individuals accessible to its maker. Thus, far more than mere aesthetic content, a masterpiece carried a strong social message, one which often reflected it's maker's perceptions of political or ceremonial realms beyond his own experience. As the physical expression of a *rite de passage,* the masterpiece combined, at differing levels, nearly all components of social information.

Now, however difficult it may be to disentangle these levels of past social information, it is incumbent on every museum to stress that cultural objects can only be artistic masterpieces when the integrity of their past is knowable. A focus upon aesthetically pleasing objects from the past is no excuse for a museum to avoid informing its visitors that even an artistic masterpiece once existed in some past context. Recognition of the embedded social contexts of ancient art reveals the hypocrisy of those museums who have attempted justifications for purchasing archaeological loot.

Archaeology is not only presented to the public in museums of art. With the introduction to archaeology of a geological perspective and with the growing understanding of stratigraphy and seriation, there came greater appreciation for the temporal dimensions of the past. The stress on anthropological and general systems frameworks led many museum archaeologists to justify their work as a study of the processes of cultural change through time. The range of objects studied varied from the most particular to the most general, and the spatial and temporal dimensions also varied. Recent literature on cultural resource management is filled with examples of how and why scientific museum collections from archaeological excavations are valuable scientific and historical data. This is not surprising, as most archaeologists in such museums received their training as social scientists or as historians of science and technology.

   Such scientific museum archaeologists promoted research and created exhibits reconstructing the dynamic interactions of cultural, environmental, and technological change. Typical museum exhibits revealed how the study of pottery and flint artifacts or human and nonhuman bone from carefully excavated archaeological sites could reveal cultural migrations, prehistoric health, or ancient manufacturing techniques and trade networks. As in so many other aspects of the archaeological record, the variability within societies was a focus of many carefully planned museum displays that juxtaposed diverse eras, habitats, and cultures to illustrate the relationships among environment, social ecology, and material culture.

   Too often, however, scientific archaeology museum exhibits that illustrated the importance of environment and economy in past societies ignored the role of willful individual or social actions. Such museum exhibits suggested to the visitor that not only were geographic settlement and political systems a response to the economy, but that material conditions constrained all social choices both in the past and in the present. The public message promoted by too many archaeologists in science museums was that the prehistoric and historic sites themselves were merely valuable to the extent that they were supply houses from which the archaeologist alone might systematically acquire the specimens and raw data upon which science operated. Their continued preservation beyond that end was ignored.

   In the cultural historical exhibits of some museums, archaeology offered yet a different message to the public. Not only the basic economic and social systems, but the shapes and decorative treatment of tools or objects of industrial design, the styles or art and architecture, and even mythological cycles were presented as the complex result and the subtle agents of change through time and across space. In the best of such exhibits, the visitor was informed that technology provides the means by which societies articulate with and understand environmental and cultural interactions. For if all human societies are aware of their interaction with the environment, both history and technology reflect a society's view of its role within their "ecological niche." Perhaps this is easiest to see in those cultural historical programs and exhibits that bring museum visitors some appreciation for the archaeology of American industrial society. Within a mile of almost every museum, one can find the stores and factories, the hospitals, colleges, and theaters that represent the physical manifestations of our own historical cultural values. These are artifacts of the population and technology acting on the environment. They are also present nearby, thus presenting new opportunities for the museum archaeologist.

   For example, at the Cleveland Museum of Natural History, a Martha Holding Jennings Foundation scholarship program has permitted over 2000 elementary, junior high, and high school students and their teachers a unique opportunity to participate in the excitement of professional archaeological excavation and discovery. Since its beginning, this program reflected the museum's belief that involving students and public in the archaeological exploration of their own history is critical to preserving significant archaeological sites of all periods (see Smartz, this volume, for a discussion of involving the public in archaeology in Toronto, Canada).

   Field archaeology does not occur in a vacuum. All participants are shown why and where we dig and how what we have previously learned influences the strategy of the next field season. And then with careful and close supervision, the students spend from half a day to 4 days actually digging on a real archaeological site. An integral part of the archaeological experience is the students' training in laboratory analysis, research report preparation, and the design and evaluation of archaeological exhibits. The results of their work are presented to other school groups when they visit the Archaeology Laboratory in conjunction with their field experience.

During these tours, students are taught the types of artifacts found in the site contexts and how they were used and modified by the people who once used them. Students are made aware of the full range of archaeological research activities, as they watch and listen to museum technicians explain their work.

All of the participating schools are fully aware that they have been engaged in real archaeological investigations rather than in some prearranged educational game. They have not only performed all aspects of archaeological excavation, they have contributed significantly to acquiring the information that allows us to understand much of the past and have found the experience exciting and rewarding. They are all anxious to protect not only the archaeological site at which they worked, but other sites at which we may yet learn more. As the citizens of the future, they are advocates of protecting the past.

Such historical archaeological excavation can result in exciting exhibits, revealing new social, ethnic, and economic information about a community. Excavated artifacts can reveal the variety of activities carried out and the daily life of the occupants of specific households. They can illustrate the history of an ethnic group or a company, and its place in the economic life of a community, in ways that can easily be communicated to the museum visitor. Texts and graphics can use photographs and drawings of the archaeological excavations, early artists' or photographers' views, maps, atlases, copies of contemporary advertisements, and city directories and census data, to tie the artifacts and structural remains found to real and specific people. Because such archaeological museum exhibits can reveal new facts about the historical actions of individuals and groups, they can show museum visitors that conscious behavior is both the consequence and modifier of human experience and the environment through time.

Such presentations can inform the public that, like all human societies, the growth of our population and our technology had results that seldom were planned or directed. The consequences to archaeological sites of undirected population and technological pressure can be shown, as can the fact that our ability to understand the magnitude of archaeological site destruction has come long after the destructive changes were initiated. In many cases, modern technology has the potential to identify future consequences or to mitigate problems of the past. While for some sites this understanding comes too late, for many threatened historical properties, public awareness can still be critical.

## THE MUSEUM ARCHAEOLOGISTS' RESPONSIBILITY

Every rural or urban neighborhood in every state in the country has its own history. Beneath forests, fields, buildings, streets, and parks lies the material evidence of America's growth. In the 19th century, over 100,000 archaeological sites were reported across America. Each site was a unique record of the past. Many sites were destroyed by erosion or by farming, some by highway, canal, and railroad construction. More were lost to industrial or urban development. Many were looted, and some were vandalized. Although thousands of previously unknown archaeological sites have been discovered, many of these, and tens of thousands more, have disappeared. The loss of this heritage accelerates.

Museums have been in the forefront of the movement to show the public that archaeology has become an important way to study this fragile record of centuries of cultural and environmental change in our country. Museums have long tried to reveal the significance of the structures, the artifacts, and the information from the past. Museum exhibits and educational programs may properly inform visitors that they cannot successfully excavate archaeological sites on their own, although they may be able to teach visitors to recognize and report archaeological sites, and entice visitors to participate in their excavation and interpretation. If museum archaeologists have shown the public how they use a vast range of modern techniques, not many have emphasized that even modern technology cannot create an historic site that has been destroyed.

Most museums, of any type, have internal divisions that loosely correspond to activities such as save, store, study, show, and speak. No other institution combines this diversity of activities with a constant stream of visitors and volunteers of all ages. Not only in different types of museums, but even within a single institution, archaeologists in various departments have sometimes been divisive in their approach to preserving the integrity of the past as something more than a collection of objects or information. To date, few museum archaeologists have overcome this insularity. But time is short.

## CONCLUSION

As museum archaeologists, we must take time out from our research and our curation to inform visitors that the past is under siege by the present. We alone have the opportunity to show what has been lost and what can be done to preserve or salvage what remains. Beyond our technical skills in field research or laboratory analysis, in conservation or education, museum archaeologists must call on architects, designers, educators, and publicists to convince visitors that their interest and their energy are needed to preserve historical and archaeological sites from destruction. If we will not find ways to convince the public to save what archaeological sites remain, we will find eventually little of the past, outside of museum cabinets, for the education and the appreciation of the future.

# CLEARINGHOUSES FOR ARCHAEOLOGICAL EDUCATION AND LOOTING: LEAP AND LOOT[*]

### Patricia C. Knoll

## INTRODUCTION

LEAP (the Listing of Education in Archaeological Programs) and LOOT (a listing of prosecuted cases of looting and vandalism of archaeological resources) are two computerized archaeological clearinghouses that are intended to assist in the identification of relevant information about educational products and programs, and about prosecutions of archaeological looters. The clearinghouses have been developed by the National Park Service, Archaeological Assistance Division, in cooperation with federal, state, and local agencies throughout the country. The purpose of this article is to describe the background and intent of these clearing-houses, how they work, and examples of their use.

The necessity for this article can be illustrated by an event that took place in a New Mexico national forest. In the fall of 1985, a U.S. Forest Service law enforcement officer was on patrol. As part of his duties, he stopped to see if there were any recent disturbances at a prehistoric archaeological site where looting had taken place. He noticed a vehicle parked on the road near the site and requested a license check from headquarters. As he made his way to investigate, he noticed an individual coming toward him from the direction of the site. The officer suspected that he may have been a looter, as there was evidence of fresh dirt on his hands and clothes. When asked if he had been digging in the nearby archaeological site, the suspect responded that he had, but that he didn't know he was doing anything wrong. He reported that while on a hike with his son a few weeks earlier, they had come across the site with a large looter's hole in it and began to dig, looking for artifacts. The officer informed him that he may have broken the law and that he had to return any artifacts he had taken. When asked if he had dug at the site before, the suspect replied that he had dug there on two other occasions in the same hole. He also admitted that he knew that he was on national forest land, but again stated that he didn't know he was doing anything wrong.

This is a classic problem regarding archaeological resource looting and vandalism. People (campers, hikers, weekend enthusiasts, hobbyists, etc.) are actively removing pieces of the past and don't think, believe, or know that there is anything wrong with what they are doing.

Incidents of looting and vandalism of archaeological sites are increasing. One of the major problems is that people are not aware of what archaeological resources are, of their importance, or of laws protecting them from unauthorized disturbance. They do not realize that picking up an artifact or using a metal detector to find Civil War period objects is affecting archaeological resources, or that on federal and Indian land and in many states these activities are illegal.

The popularity of movies such as the "Indiana Jones" series have romanticized archaeology and brought it to the attention of the public. This heightening of awareness can be very positive; however, problems arise when people do not realize that their own explorations can permanently damage archaeological sites. They are not aware that artifacts and other remains removed from their context lose most of what they can tell about the past. In addition, since many people tend to collect the most attractive types of artifacts, such as projectile points and ceramics, the loss

---

[*] Portions of this article have been previously presented in Knoll and Knudson's introduction to Knoll (1990).

of the artifact or even an entire class of artifacts can greatly diminish what can be learned about the site as a whole. One solution to this problem is better public education through a variety of materials and methods that will attract the public's attention toward a positive response.

In August 1985 and July 1986 Jerry L. Rogers, the associate director for cultural resources of the National Park Service, and Bennie C. Keel, then departmental consulting archaeologist, hosted interagency meetings to discuss improving implementation of the Archaeological Resources Protection Act of 1979 (ARPA). Participating in those meetings were cultural resource and law enforcement personnel from a wide variety of federal agencies. One of the primary concerns raised by the participants was the problem of archaeological looting and vandalism on public lands. One suggestion that the participants made in an effort to combat this problem was to organize a clearinghouse of information about federal archaeological activities, particularly public education efforts and antilooting initiatives.

## THE LISTING OF EDUCATION IN ARCHAEOLOGICAL PROGRAMS (LEAP)

Following up on these suggestions, the National Park Service hosted an interagency meeting of federal archaeologists and historic preservation officers, in September 1986, specifically to discuss archaeological public awareness initiatives. Participants at this meeting again expressed the need to establish a clearinghouse for information on public awareness programs, projects, and products used to inform the public about archaeology. The Archaeological Assistance Division of the National Park Service agreed to establish and maintain the clearinghouse.

An initial round of data collection was accomplished through an invitation from the assistant secretary for Fish and Wildlife and Parks to all federal agency heads with archaeological programs, requesting their participation in the clearinghouse. They were asked to complete an information form on each of the agency's archaeological projects or programs that included a public awareness effort. The Archaeological Assistance Division staff also publicized the existence of the clearinghouse and requested information through informal contacts, presentations at meetings, newsletters, and journal announcements. The result of this initial compilation of data was named the Listing of Education in Archaeological Programs (LEAP) Clearinghouse.

The original objective of the LEAP Clearinghouse was to improve the sharing of information among public agencies, and potentially others (states, academia, and museums), about efforts to make the results of archaeological programs or projects more readily available to the general public. This objective has since expanded to include any public or private group interested in promoting its archaeological educational activities.

The LEAP Clearinghouse contains, but is not limited to, information on:

1.  Projects or programs (including the cooperative efforts among agencies) to protect archaeological resources and to educate the public about these resources
2.  Projects or programs with avocational organizations and volunteers involving archaeological survey, testing, excavation, or interpretation
3.  Projects or programs with museums, academic institutions, historical societies, etc., for exhibits or displays about archaeological resources
4.  Brochures, posters, videos, radio and television coverage, and other products of these efforts

The LEAP Clearinghouse is intended as a reference for federal, state, and local agencies, museums, societies, educational organizations, and individual archaeologists, that are seeking

## 2.5  SCHOOL EDUCATION PROGRAMS

---

### Alaska

---

**Agency:** Bureau of Land Management

**Project/Program:** Public School Presentations

**Contact:**    Robert E. King
                Alaska State Office
                Bureau of Land Management
                6881 Abbott Road
                Anchorage, AK 99507
                907-271-5510

The Anchorage District Office of the Bureau of Land Management (BLM) has an informal program entitled "Science in Schools." The BLM provides, upon request, specialists to give programs on various natural and cultural resources topics at local area schools.  Archeology has been discussed as part of these presentations.

**Date of Information:** 5/87

---

FIGURE 1.  LEAP Clearinghouse product record.

information on existing projects, programs, and products to increase public awareness of archaeology.

To date, more than 430 responses have been received from 13 federal agencies and 70 state and local governments, academic institutions, museums, societies, and private foundations and companies, resulting in approximately 1300 individual entries of various products used in public education activities. With a dBASEIII Plus program originally designed by Edward Friedman, then of the Minerals Management Service, and later modified by a consultant/computer programmer, the entries (records) may be queried for summary information under the categories of agency, state, and specific product. The product-specific portion cites title (of product), sponsoring agency or institution, contact person (address and telephone), and a narrative summary of the product. The brief narrative contains information about the project or program to which it relates, its organization, production, use, distribution, availability, etc. (Figure 1).

An initial LEAP report has been published that summarizes the nearly 1300 individual records in the clearinghouse (Knoll 1990). Information in the report has been organized into chapters by major product categories:

1.  Posters
2.  Brochures
3.  Exhibits/displays
4.  Public participation programs
5.  School education programs
6.  Audios/videos/films
7.  Broadcasts
8.  Press articles
9.  Popular publications
10. Community outreach

Product subcategories provide additional methods and materials under the main category. For example, "public participation programs" includes the subcategories of "volunteer programs" and "tours;" "school education programs" includes the subcategories of "curriculum" (elementary, middle, secondary, adult) and "classroom presentations."

Under each product, individual organizations (federal, state, local, or private) are listed by the state in which the archaeological project or program occurred. For additional easy reference, there are indices organized by agency, product category and title, and project/program title.

A few examples of how the LEAP Clearinghouse can be used are as follows:

1.  A federal archaeologist is about to begin a large project that will take several years to complete. Due to limited personnel, the archaeologist is interested in the possibility of establishing a volunteer effort to assist in the excavation and laboratory aspects of the project. Using LEAP, the archaeologist can refer to the chapter on "public participation programs" for information and personal contacts. Likewise, the "agency index" can be used to find examples of what the archaeologist's own agency has done regarding volunteer efforts, or what other federal agencies have developed in the same state. The other chapters, in and of themselves, also are ways to inform the public of the project's progress and results.

2.  A state agency is interested in developing an "archaeology day" or "archaeology week." The "project/program index" in LEAP can provide examples of successful public awareness events such as Arizona Archaeology Week, Utah Archaeology Week, or Colorado Cultural Resources Awareness Week. The pages listed under Arizona Archeology Week, for instance, direct the user to the chapters on "posters," "press articles," "broadcasts," "public participation programs," "exhibits/displays," and other products developed and used to promote this event.

3.  A sixth-grade teacher in Colorado is preparing to teach a unit on American Indians and would like to incorporate archaeology into the class. The teacher is interested in any materials relating to basic archaeology, past or present projects in the state, and lesson plans from other teachers. Each chapter in the LEAP Clearinghouse can provide the teacher with a variety of sources for information. For example, the chapter on "posters" includes "Save the Pieces of the Past" by the Bureau of Land Management, and "Protect Our Past" from the U.S. Army Corps of Engineers. "A Place in Time" and "Your Fragile Legacy," two videos available for viewing, are listed in the "audios/videos/films" chapter. The chapter on "school education programs" provides information about curricula for elementary, middle, secondary, and adult education. The "Cultural Resources/Indian Lifeways Learning Station" for middle school students by the Bureau of Land Management or the "Archeology Activity Workbook" developed by the New York State Historic Preservation Office may be excellent projects to use. In addition, the product category index contains sections on "classroom presentations" and "tours," which might lead to a guest speaker from the Bureau of Land Management (BLM) on Indian rock art in Colorado, or a field trip to Craig Sandrocks. Contact names and addresses are provided for each product so that the teacher may check if these materials and services are available.

Additional editions of the LEAP summary report will be produced either as updates or as supplemental inserts, on a schedule commensurate with the level of new information received. The clearinghouse will be maintained as long as users supply information and updates and find the summaries useful. The possibility has been discussed that in the future, the query capabilities of the clearinghouse data base may be used for telephone requests for the most up-to-date information. Information may be submitted to the LEAP Clearinghouse by any federal, state, and local government, academic institution, archaeological or historical society, museum, private foundation, or company, that has utilized outreach methods and materials to promote an archaeological project or program to the public.

## THE LOOT CLEARINGHOUSE

Another result of the federal agencies' conference in the summer of 1986 and subsequent Public Awareness Working Group meetings (a committee chaired by the National Park Service, Archaeological Assistance Division) was the establishment of the LOOT Clearinghouse.

The looting of archaeological sites has been recognized as a problem since the late 19th century when the avarice of private collectors of antiquities made looting a profitable business. This occurred in Egypt, Greece, the U.S., and elsewhere and still occurs today. Preliminary analyses of available quantitative data on archaeological looting in the U.S. show that there are 10 to 15 times the number of reported incidents of looting and vandalism as compared to the number of arrests made or citations given (see King, McAllister, and McManamon, this volume, for further discussion on the extent of archaeological looting in the U.S.). Even fewer of those cases are prosecuted and result in criminal convictions or civil penalties. The number of reported incidents has increased in each of the years for which data are available (fiscal years 1985–1987), while the number of prosecutions remains about the same. Improved information collection may be the basis for increases in the numbers of reported incidents, but this does not mitigate what seems to be the general trend — very few incidents are discovered in time to apprehend the looters or vandals, much less prevent damage to the archaeological sites.

Many solutions to the problem have been proposed, and a wide attack on the problem is necessary (Judge and Bruen 1990). One of the most important efforts is to improve incident documentation and information exchange on prosecution cases. A major objective of such efforts is to improve coordination of law enforcement and archaeological resource protection on a regional, interagency basis. The LOOT Clearinghouse is designed to be this kind of information exchange.

The objective of the LOOT Clearinghouse is to provide a central place for those seeking information about cases in which looting or vandalism of archaeological resources on public lands have been prosecuted. It is intended for use by federal, state, and local agencies who also may request information and advice on how to pursue ARPA cases. In order to gather information about looting and vandalism cases, a form was developed to systematically collect these data. The form requests information on arrests, indictments, trials, pleas, judgements, sentences, fines, and forfeitures. These summary records are currently maintained in a data base accessed by an in-house word-processing system. At this writing, there are approximately 70 cases in the data base, dating from 1936 to the present. The Archaeological Assistance Division is working with cultural resource and law enforcement officials in public agencies on appropriate means of distributing this information. An excellent example of what the LOOT Clearinghouse can do follows.

In March 1989, U.S. Forest Service archaeologists and law enforcement officers began to notice new evidence of looting to known and undocumented archaeological sites in a northern California national forest. Patrols and surveillance efforts were increased, including the use of electronic sensing equipment, in hope of apprehending the looters. More than 2 months of weekend surveillance and evidence gathering eventually succeeded. While in route to conduct surveillance at a newly discovered, but frequently looted site, an officer noticed fresh tire tracks on the trailhead leading to the site. He followed the tracks of the suspects and observed them in the process of digging, sifting dirt through a wire-mesh screen, and setting aside artifacts. The officer photographed the two suspects and then radioed for backup. When later confronted by officers, the two men said they didn't know that they were on government property. One man said he had never dug before and was just collecting arrowheads for school. Both men were arrested for vandalizing and looting the site of a prehistoric Indian village. They were charged with destruction of government property, conspiracy, and excavating an archaeological resource without a permit, a violation of the Archaeological Resources Protection Act of 1979 (ARPA).

During the course of the investigation, law enforcement officers found maps belonging to the suspects, with locations of archaeological sites on federal land marked. They also found equipment that had been used so much in digging that they were worn out, and extensive private collections of prehistoric projectile points and other tools, beads, and some human remains. One suspect moved most of his collection from his home and hid it so that it would not be confiscated by police. The two men pleaded guilty to all charges and were subsequently convicted.

Since this was the first ARPA case in California, the judge was not familiar with the types of sentences applied in such cases. He postponed sentencing until the prosecution could provide information about other ARPA cases. The special agent from the national forest involved in the case notified the Archaeological Assistance Division and the LOOT Clearinghouse to request the data. The agent needed to know how many ARPA cases had been prosecuted, how many of those cases were felonies, and the type of sentence given for each case in terms of prison time, forfeitures, and fines. The information was available in the LOOT Clearinghouse and was provided to the agent, prosecutor, and judge. Both men were sentenced to 60 days in jail, 1 year of supervised release, a $1000 fine, forfeiture of the all-terrain vehicles used in the crime, and forfeiture of significant portions of their private collections.

The LOOT Clearinghouse also provides case statistics to be included in the Secretary of the Interior's annual report to Congress on federal archaeological activities (Keel et al. 1989) and has contributed to other official inquiries about looting and vandalism. The clearinghouse will be maintained as long as users find the case studies useful and information continues to be supplied.

## CONCLUSION

The goals of the LEAP and LOOT Clearinghouses are to ultimately make an impact in the battle against looting and vandalism, through information exchange. The clearinghouses are in the beginning stages and have only just begun to acquire the large quantity of data that are known to exist about archaeological education and awareness programs, and looting and vandalism cases. They seem to be helpful in providing needed information in these areas, but require more cooperation and coordination to be successful. The clearinghouses also can be considered prototypes for similar information-gathering efforts that can lead to better understanding of, and more solutions to, these archaeological issues.

## ACKNOWLEDGMENTS

The author kindly wishes to thank Dr. Francis P. McManamon, Dr. Elizabeth A. Crowell, Dr. Robert Schumacher, and John S. Knoll for their valuable comments and support in this debut endeavor.

# REFERENCES CITED

**Judge, J. and Bruen, B., compilers** (1990) *Save the Past for the Future: Actions for the '90s,* Wildesen, L., Ed., Society for American Archaeology, Washington, D.C.

**Keel, B. C., McManamon, F. P., and Smith, G. S.** (1989) *Federal Archeology: The Current,* Program, National Park Service, U.S. Department of the Interior, Washington, D.C.

**Knoll, P. C., Ed.** (1990) *Listing of Education in Archeological Programs: The LEAP Clearinghouse, 1987–1989 Summary Report,* National Park, U.S. Department of the Interior, Washington, D.C.

# ARCHAEOLOGICAL RESOURCE PROTECTION TRAINING

## Richard C. Waldbauer

## INTRODUCTION

Since the passage of the Archaeological Resources Protection Act in 1979 (ARPA), and particularly since the 1984 publication of the uniform regulations that implement ARPA, federal agencies have dramatically improved their programs to protect archaeological resources. These improvements have included better monitoring of sites, better reporting on incidents of looting and vandalism (see Knoll, this volume), and increased prosecutions of looters and vandals.

Nevertheless, it is the experience of federal agencies that enforcement of the law only in a judicial way is unlikely to yield effective, long-term results. Admittedly, uneven and sporadic judicial actions against violators of ARPA may contribute to the problems in perceiving the law as an effective deterrent. But law enforcement program managers have also determined that any effective deterrent must be based upon a general understanding of what archaeological resources are and why they should be protected. ARPA provides for this educational aspect of law enforcement when it requires actions "to foster and improve the communication, cooperation, and exchange of information between private individuals,...federal authorities..professional archaeologists, and associations of professional archaeologists." ARPA also recognizes that these kinds of actions must have appropriate, coordinated objectives so that the results will contribute most effectively to site protection. The Secretary of the Interior is specifically charged with providing coordination.

Late in 1988 the educational component of ARPA received further emphasis via an amendment to the law (Public Law 100-588) that directed federal land managers to establish programs "...to increase public awareness of the significance of the archaeological resources located on public lands and Indian lands and the need to protect such resources." A second amendment (Public Law 100-555) will ensure that education about archaeological resources protection is based upon sound information, by requiring "documents for the reporting of suspected violations of [ARPA] and establishing when and how those documents are to be completed by officers, employees, and agents of their respective agencies."

There are two important education objectives that must be accomplished for archaeological resource protection to be effective. First, education is needed in order for law enforcement and cultural resources personnel to properly carry out the criminal and civil penalty responsibilities of archaeological resource protection laws. Without efficient law enforcement, the deterrent effect of statutory sanctions, such as prison sentences and fines, is diminished. Second, the range of training opportunities must have appropriate, coordinated objectives, especially since education is needed to improve public awareness of archaeological resources as places and things that must be protected. Efficient enforcement of archaeological resource protection laws is hampered or given low priority when the public does not perceive protection of archaeological resources as socially important.

## EDUCATION FOR LAW ENFORCEMENT AND CULTURAL RESOURCES OPERATIONS

Education for law enforcement and cultural resources personnel has become increasingly effective since 1984 as training objectives have been better defined. To enforce protection laws, individuals must know what the law is, what is being protected, what the separate duties of law enforcement and cultural resources management are, and how individuals in these two functions need to interact with one another to insure that their efforts yield effective, efficient results.

## Levels of Training for Law Enforcement and Cultural Resources Personnel

### Field Operations

Currently there are three levels of training opportunities available. The most intensive level is training that applies to field operations. Several agencies offer these in varying formats, often in cooperation with another agency whose primary responsibility is law enforcement.

The most intensive course at this level has been offered through the Federal Law Enforcement Training Center (FLETC) in Glynco, GA, since 1983. As part of the Department of the Treasury, FLETC principally serves 63 federal organizations to teach common areas of law enforcement skills to police and investigative personnel. They also provide support services for participating organizations to conduct advanced training for their own law enforcement personnel. The National Park Service, U.S. Park Police, Fish and Wildlife Service, and Forest Service each have offices at FLETC that provide on-site representation.

FLETC's "Archaeological Resources Protection Training Program" is conducted by the Enforcement Techniques Division. A senior instructor manages the program and maintains the highly regarded curriculum content. It is scheduled in two or more regional locations each year as a 40-hour course with an archaeologist, a judicial expert, and a law enforcement officer as instructors. It has consistently provided the most up-to-date skills required to identify, investigate, and prosecute archaeological resource crime.

There is particular emphasis in the course on the different roles of law enforcement officers and cultural resource specialists, and the course is noted for its powerful demonstration of the need for these people to interact while still preserving their separate duties and professional functions. The course concludes with a vivid practical exercise in casework. Since 1988 the frequency with which the course is offered has increased dramatically, as several federal agencies have requested special "export" versions to be held in specific regions. Since its inception, this training has been offered nearly 25 times to more than 750 participants.

Federal agencies with law enforcement staff conduct periodic "refresher" courses, typically on a regional basis and as a way to address regional needs. Agents not only upgrade their personal law enforcement qualifications through such courses, but also gain new skills. Archaeological protection is frequently a topic during refresher courses, and it is essential that course coordinators have access to current teaching materials and skilled archaeology instructors.

Organizations other than federal agencies also are concerned with effective training in field operations and federal archaeological resources protection. Often, state agencies or local law enforcement jurisdictions conduct casework involving federal lands, on behalf of federal agencies or in cooperation with federal agents. Indian tribal police are concerned with protecting archaeological resources on Indian lands. These organizations develop their own coursework, participate in federal agency courses, or seek technical assistance for training materials from federal agencies.

### Program-Oriented Training

The second level is program oriented. That is, the educational objectives of these courses are designed to provide introductory guidance or strategic overviews of archaeological resource protection, so that managers gain an understanding of what their programs should contain, who should operate them, and how results can be measured. Agency cultural resources management courses usually contain a component on site protection, to familiarize managers with agency policy and procedures in this regard.

However, in 1988, for the first time, training at this level was offered on a nationwide basis. This was a 12-hour course that is now titled "Overview of Archaeological Resource Protection Programs" and sponsored by the National Park Service Archaeological Assistance and Employee Development Divisions. It was made possible as part of a special appropriation by a concerned Congress, which moved later in that year to amend ARPA. The course was held nine times, tuition-free, for classes of up to 50 people. In 1989 it was held 13 times, and one of those courses coincided with the Society for American Archaeology annual meeting in Atlanta, GA. By the end of 1990, the course had been offered 33 times and reached nearly 1000 participants.

### Self-Teaching and Generalized Materials

The third level is geared for individual instruction, particularly through self-teaching or self-paced materials. This kind of training emphasizes brief, concise topics and skills for wide-ranging audiences that include seasonal agency employees as well as the general public. The materials tend to be widely available upon request. Videotapes and films, such as the well-known "Thieves of Time," produced by the U.S. Forest Service, are designed to provide introductory instruction.

A new videotape, titled "Assault on Time," has been produced by the Media Support Division of FLETC in cooperation with the Fish and Wildlife Service, National Park Service, Bureau of Land Management, Forest Service, and Department of Defense. It provides the most current introductory information, in videotape format, skillfully illustrating the wide variety of archaeological resources and poignantly portraying how important they are to people.

The Soil Conservation Service has produced a set of self-paced training materials to train its employees in the agency's cultural resources program. There are eight modules, which are an excellent combination of slides, cassette tapes, and instructional manuals.

### Coordinated Objectives for Education

The second component of archaeological resources protection training concerns appropriate, coordinated objectives, especially when the efforts are directed at improving public awareness. Development of training objectives for public awareness has not kept pace with that for field enforcement. Too often failure to define objectives, especially the audiences to be reached and purposes for educating them, results in minimal impact and confusion among the participants. Nevertheless, there are several successful programs that are geared to educating the general public about archaeological resources and fostering the awareness that site protection is socially important. These are discussed in detail elsewhere in this volume.

It is important to discuss public awareness from a training objectives standpoint because to be effective, the public must be able to perceive a consistent policy conducted within a coordinated program and based upon complementary materials.

### Policy and Coordination

Training courses must be marketed, and staff must understand that training will help them carry out their responsibilities and agency missions. As federal agency archaeology programs have improved, there has been clearer policy guidance about the importance of archaeological resources protection.

On March 20, 1990, Secretary of the Interior Manuel Lujan announced a national strategy for archaeology that included improved interagency efforts to fight looting (Lujan 1990). One of the ways for this policy to be disseminated is through interagency coordination activities, such as the Law Enforcement Group facilitated by the National Park Service, Archaeological Assistance Division. Its members consist of federal agency chief law enforcement officers, or their representatives, and meets regularly to address archaeological protection issues, exchange information on agency activities and training, and gain insight on professional approaches. Results of these meetings are then distributed throughout the respective agencies, particularly regarding training available to agency personnel.

Coordination of training is accomplished also between the National Park Service and Federal Law Enforcement Training Center. As the agencies that conduct the two most widely offered courses, field enforcement skills training (FLETC) and program management training (NPS), it is critical that these education programs not conflict in dates or locations as well as content. As a result of improved coordination in marketing and organization, the respective courses began to reach about four times more participants by late 1989.

These kinds of accomplishments contribute to policy dissemination throughout agencies because initiatives and prioritization of funding and staffing commitments can be tied to specific activities with foreseeable results. For example, the National Park Service determined that field training of its law enforcement officers for archaeological protection could be a major priority in fiscal year 1991, given that the FLETC program would be widely available.

### Complementary Materials

Policy and coordinated programs provide agency staff with a useful organizational structure upon which to base education activities such as public awareness. Instructional materials provide the means to conduct those activities, particularly when seasonal or collateral duty personnel must be trained and the basic message of archaeological protection must be conveyed. To be effective, these materials must be complementary and demonstrate the role of protection within the national archaeological preservation program.

Production of complementary materials requires the kind of coordination that takes place on a national level, as described above, as well as regional coordination. Examples at the national level include the archaeological protection bookmarks (designed by the Fish and Wildlife Service in 1987 and printed as part of the "Take Pride in America" campaign), an instructors' handbook sponsored by seven federal agencies, the FLETC videotape "Assault on Time," and the "Protecting the Past" book.

Regional coordination occurs in many ways, and one such example is the Forest Service Region 6 task force on archaeological protection (Davis 1989:10). National forests partook in the task force and cooperated to produce a training videotape suitable for use throughout Region 6. Another example is the laminated field guide distributed to officers trained by the U.S. Army Corps of Engineers, Portland District (Freed 1988:3). This handy pocket guide complements their brochure and poster, "Preserving Our Cultural Heritage," distributed to the public and asking visitors to help protect cultural resources within Corps of Engineers lands.

## CONCLUSION

Training in archaeological resources protection must ensure that programs achieve goals meaningful within the general concern for archaeological preservation. While law enforcement activities themselves require that effective instruction in archaeological resources crime, laws and regulations, field operations, and casework is provided to law enforcement and cultural resources personnel, there must also be continued public awareness that destruction of archaeological resources diminishes the nation's cultural heritage. When these two objectives are achieved, the laws are an effective deterrent, and the public benefit of archaeological preservation is realized.

## REFERENCES CITED

**Davis, C.** (1989) Archaeological protection efforts: Forest Service, *Fed. Archeol. Rep,*. 2(2), 10.

**Freed, R.** (1988) Corps of Engineers Archaeological Protection Program, Portland District, *Fed. Archeol. Rep.,* 1(3), 3.

**Lujan, M.** (1990) Memorandum; Secretary of the Interior to Under Secretary, Solicitor, Assistant Secretaries, all bureau heads, Department of the Interior, Office of the Secretary, March 20, 1990.

Public Law 100-588.

# *Chapter 5*

## *ARCHAEOLOGICAL SITE PROTECTION PROGRAMS*

"What we need is nothing less than a national commitment to protect what the German poet Rainer Maria Rilke called the 'stored humanity of place'." (Ronald L. Fleming, New York Times, 1987)

"No battle plan ever survives contact with the enemy." (ancient military proverb)

# OPERATION SAVE: AN INTEGRATED APPROACH TO PROTECTING THE PAST

Lynell Schalk

## INTRODUCTION

Over 100 years ago, Abraham Lincoln told the nation, "Public sentiment is everything. With it, nothing can fail. Without it, nothing can succeed." Those involved in various national efforts to halt the looting and destruction of our nation's cultural legacy can fully appreciate Mr. Lincoln's perspective. Many believe that saving the archaeological record is not merely a governmental responsibility and that programs to heighten citizen awareness, concern, and involvement are critical. Operation SAVE is one such program.

## BACKGROUND

With the passage of the Archaeological Resources Protection Act in 1979 (ARPA), anticipation was high amongst those concerned about archaeological protection. Congress believed the deficiencies of the 1906 Antiquities Act had been remedied. Archaeologists were satisfied that this new law with its stiffer penalties would heighten public awareness and act as a strong deterrent. The law enforcement community anticipated enforcing what they now hoped would be an enforceable law.

These expectations were not fully realized, however. Delayed promulgation of implementing regulations for over 4 years hampered prosecutorial efforts and frustrated the criminal justice community. Juries were confused by the complexities of the new statute and forced to listen to long hours of archaeological expert witness testimony. As a result, jurors often lost interest. All of the defendants who opted to go to trial during this interim period were either acquitted or convicted of only misdemeanor crimes. Defendants quickly learned that refusal to plea bargain with government prosecutors often resulted in exoneration.

But these prosecutorial failures were not merely related to a lack of regulations. Public ignorance and apathy were also hard at work. Federal agents and prosecutors realized that enforcement of this new law resembled the nation's "War on Drugs." Apprehension of violators and seizures of artifacts were making little inroads in halting the demand for illicit artifacts. Public attitudes were apathetic at best — and often sympathetic toward the "supplyside."

This realization probably became most evident in the Pacific Northwest in May 1982 when two men were acquitted by a federal jury after an exhausting 5-day trial in a stuffy courtroom in Medford, Oregon. Charged with felony violations of the Archaeological Resources Protection Act and other statutes, the two defendants walked out of the courtroom exonerated of all charges. The judge even ordered the government to return the men's artifacts and digging implements. This included sifting screens, shovels, respirators, eye protectors, artifact containers, and a briefcase marked on the bottom as property of the U.S. Government.

This case came about when a Bureau of Land Management (BLM) special agent apprehended three men in an ancient rockshelter site on public lands in a remote valley of southern Oregon late one spring afternoon in 1981. The site was unsigned and unfenced. Confronted at the site by the agent, the men lied about their identities and denied any ownership or knowledge of the freshly dug hole at the site or the digging equipment hidden under some brush in the back of the cave. They argued with the agent that surface collection of arrowheads was legal under the new law, yet denied they were doing anything more than just hiking. Later when the defendants stood trial, they testified that they believed that no one owned this land or cared about it, or it would have been better protected by the BLM. When one of the men's fingerprints was lifted from the inside of an artifact container and the government presented this as evidence, the defense attorney argued that his clients were only surface collecting for arrowheads. When the government introduced site material and a projectile point that had been recovered from one of the stashed sifting screens, the defense attorney accused the case agent of placing the arrowhead in the screen to incriminate his clients. Their defense for lying about their identities to the agent when apprehended was that the lone officer was visibly wearing a firearm and they were afraid to identify themselves.

After 3 days of exhausting testimony under extensive cross-examination by the defense, the government rested its case, assured that the evidence was solid. The defense then brought forth a string of witnesses who testified that they, too, had dug in this site over the past 20 years. Of course, all of them were clear in their explanations that this was done many years before; therefore, the 5-year statute of limitations had run out on their crimes. The defense argued that the site was already totally destroyed by the time the defendants got there. One defense witness wore a large obsidian spearpoint bolo tie during his testimony. Another witness identified himself as a Forest Service employee and a para-archaeologist. He brought in a plastic fishing tackle box full of ancient pieces of sandals, matting, and cordage, all of which he readily admitted to removing from the rockshelter while employed by the Forest Service (The judge allowed him to keep this federal property after his testimony, although the U.S. Attorney later ordered the BLM and Forest Service to recover the artifacts. The artifacts were eventually recovered, but the federal employee filed a lawsuit. He later lost his suit). During the defense attorney's closing argument, the jury was told:

> It's the professional archaeologists and the government experts and the agents of the government and the police and law enforcement community against the people who go out and dig and explore and want to learn about archaeology on their own. That's the way the case has come down.
> This is a big case, and all the archaeologists are looking at this case to see what's going to happen. And frankly, it's a premature case. Frankly, they should have waited for regulations and they should have told these guys, 'Hey, next time you're going to be in a lot of trouble. You've gotten fair warning now, but stay out of there.' And what would really have been fair is to post it, because it's a new law. Who knows about it? Who has notice of this change or of the definition of resource? Are we all supposed to have knowledge of the thousands of laws that Congress passes every day because its published in the Federal Register? That's the burden the government wants to impose on this individual. But they don't want to accept any responsibility for preserving that site.

This trial made it perfectly clear that public attitudes were contributing to the government's inability to protect the nation's archaeological heritage. The government and its employees were the ones who had been put on trial.

But juries were not alone in their lack of understanding and appreciation for the new law. Prosecutors, judges, land managers, even law enforcement officers, and archaeologists were not as aware and supportive as they should have been during the early part of the 1980s. And more importantly, a significant special interest group was generally being ignored by everyone — the Native American community. Their ancestral sites were being desecrated. Ancient skeletal and mummified human remains were being publicly displayed and openly sold in the national market. The American public was only being told about the scientific values of archaeology, so important to the archaeological community. But outraged Indian voices were not being heard.

The time was right for a new direction: an integrated and cooperative effort to increase protection of the archaeological record. Out of this was born Operation SAVE. Operation SAVE, which stands for "Save Archaeological Values for Everyone," emphasizes three areas: (1) public education initiatives, (2) archaeological protection training, and (3) increased enforcement operations.

## OPERATION SAVE

In December 1986 the BLM Law Enforcement Staff in the Oregon State Office proposed a three-part agency program to heighten citizen awareness and enforcement of the Archaeological Resources Protection Act in the Pacific Northwest. The framework was laid in the 1986 State of the Union address when the President of the U.S. called upon all Americans to "take pride in their outstanding public lands and historic sites that belong to everyone." Shortly thereafter, the Secretary for the Department of the Interior launched the "Take Pride in America" campaign. In July 1986, in a letter written to the Attorney General, the Secretary asked the Department of Justice to assist in "...spreading awareness of the importance of crimes against our heritage throughout the criminal justice community. It is important that we prosecute these crimes and impose appropriate penalties which will serve as examples to deter potential offenders."

Realizing that a successful protection effort would depend on agency support at all levels of the organization, the plan was presented to the BLM state director in Oregon and his management team. There was immediate and unanimous acceptance of the proposal. From this, Operation SAVE became the bureau's regional program and, later on, an agency prototype program for increasing archaeological protection efforts on the nation's public lands. A small and workable committee was formed, consisting of a law enforcement officer, an archaeologist, and a public affairs officer. Meeting regularly, but informally, the team made assignments and periodically assessed progress. Costs for the program were absorbed in existing budgets. Most of the first year's work was initially carried out by the three committee members. In the subsequent years, participation has expanded to all levels of the organization.

### Public Education Initiatives

Operation SAVE was launched on July 7, 1987, with a news release. This release generated numerous media inquiries. Announcement letters were sent to the U.S. Attorney's office, the governor, archaeological societies, and the Washington office. The committee members participated in a number of joint television and radio interviews. This prompted follow-up interviews at the district level and media field visits to protected archaeological sites. Coinciding with the public launching of Operation SAVE, Oregon Governor Neil Goldschmidt signed a proclamation on July 1, 1987, declaring "Archaeological Resources Protection Week."

After a logo was selected for the program, posters and stickers were produced. The logo depicts a prehistoric Wishram Indian rock art design that appears on artifacts and rock faces throughout the Columbia River region. Before the posters were printed, permission to use the design was obtained from the Yakima Nation Tribal Council. The Yakimas only condition was that the design was not to be used for commercial purposes. After printing, the posters and stickers were widely distributed throughout the Pacific Northwest, including placement at public libraries, state police offices, tribal offices, BLM campgrounds and reception desks, post offices, professional organizations, universities, state park offices, museums, senior citizen centers, and places of business. On each poster and sticker is listed a toll-free number (1-800-333-SAVE) for reporting archaeological crime. The posters are also frequently provided to landowners living adjacent to public lands and various public land user groups.

The toll-free crime reporting line is intended to encourage the public to report archaeological crime. The line rings directly into the law enforcement office in the BLM's Oregon State office. Since its installation, the bureau has received numerous calls from the public and informants reporting suspected violations. Callers also frequently ask questions regarding archaeological protection laws and Operation SAVE, as well as request posters and other materials. The staff has also received a number of calls from outside the region during the past 4 years. The staff takes the information and refers the calling party to the appropriate authorities.

Operation SAVE also promotes as many public presentations on archaeological protection as possible by bureau employees. Particular attention is given to requests from schools, museums, local archaeological groups, scout troops, and tribal organizations. Speakers emphasize that regardless of one's level of personal appreciation for archaeological values, it is against the law, and the law is being enforced on the federal lands.

## Training

Archaeological protection training is Operation SAVE's second area of emphasis. During its first year, Operation SAVE sponsored and supported training courses for an estimated 412 federal, state, and local agency employees from over 100 agencies (for additional information on training see Waldbauer, this volume). The agency also provided instructors for three 40-hour interagency sessions of the Federal Law Enforcement Training Center's Archaeological Resource Protection Training Program (ARPTP), two interagency courses in Washington, D.C., entitled Archaeological Protection Issues for Managers; three interagency classes in Oregon and California on "Archaeological Protection Training for Field Employees;" and a number of other training sessions held throughout the Pacific Northwest and other areas on the West Coast. Native Americans were given priority in enrollment in the ARPTP class, due to their increasing concerns for protection of their ancestral and sacred sites. More recently, an interagency meeting was held with the Warm Springs Indians to discuss the handling of burial remains recovered during criminal investigations. Field trips have been given to the Coquille, Lower Umpqua, and Siuslaw Indian tribes. At the request of the Siletz tribe, a one-day training session was held to discuss coordination and integration of bureau programs and tribal site protection concerns. As time and staffing allows, Operation SAVE also tries to provide instructors for sessions held outside the region. One such session was given in Victorville, California for 20 new law enforcement rangers stationed in the California Desert Conservation Area. The new officers were given training in archaeological protection statutes and site recognition. There have also been a number of requests from Pacific Northwest universities asking for instructors to lecture on archaeological protection and the bureau's cultural resource management program. The committee tries to respond to as many of these requests as time allows.

## Enforcement Operations

The third major area of emphasis in Operation SAVE is increased law enforcement operations. Under the direction of the BLM Law Enforcement Staff, state and district office archaeologists have assisted bureau law enforcement personnel in several proactive surveillance and site-monitoring operations. In the spring of 1987, teams of BLM special agents, rangers, and archaeologists in Oregon and California conducted an interstate aerial detection and surveillance operation — the largest such program in the history of archaeological enforcement. The three-state border area of Oregon, California, and Nevada was covered. Six BLM districts participated in the operation. The teams encountered 16 violations of state and federal law, 14 of which were archaeological violations. Officers seized 70 illegally taken surface artifacts and issued a number of written warnings regarding surface collection of artifacts. While conducting the operation, archaeologists took advantage of the cooperative opportunity to explain the prehistory of the region to the individual law enforcement officer they were teamed with. The officers used the opportunity to raise the awareness level of the archaeologists regarding the criminal justice system and law enforcement constraints. And most importantly, the two groups learned how to work together and even developed an esprit de corps. As a result of these enforcement operations, the public was beginning to realize that the laws were being enforced. Even surface collection of artifacts would no longer be tolerated. The illegal collector was effectively put on notice.

The BLM also intensified their investigations of archaeological crime. In the first year, two subjects were convicted in federal court, and over 300 artifacts were forfeited. Three more subjects were convicted in state court for burial desecration. Another subject was indicted following an interagency investigation (In 1988 he was convicted and forfeited several thousand artifacts, served 4 months of a 2-year prison sentence, was given 5-years probation, and ordered to serve 400 hours of community service). Oregon is presently one of three states with a significant number of archaeological prosecutions occurring each year.

Operation SAVE also emphasizes assistance to other agencies and tribal organizations in their investigative efforts. Over 100 agencies were assisted during Operation SAVE's first year. As a result, the BML is seeing increased awareness and enforcement by other agencies and, therefore, more awareness by those who illegally collect and deal in artifacts.

Now into its fourth year, Operation SAVE has moved from a reactive to a proactive response to archaeological crime. This effort is expected to result in a significant decline in the illicit artifact market in the Pacific Northwest within the next few years.

## CONCLUSION

Since its first year, Operation SAVE has continued to reach as many people as possible. Frequent contacts are made with the news media. In 1989 the committee members and district archaeologists worked closely with an investigative reporter. A series of articles later appeared in the *Bend Bulletin* regarding the looting and trafficking of archaeological sites in the region. Operation SAVE posters continue to be widely distributed. Posters have even been shipped to Thailand, China, the Soviet Union, and Canada. One committee member annually lectures at a cultural resource law class at the Lewis and Clark Northwestern School of Law. In eastern Oregon the BLM has added more rangers to increase surveillance and patrols of archaeological sites. The aerial surveillance program continues, having expanded to a multistate and multiagency operation. An archaeological exhibit is now set up annually at the Oregon State Fair where Operation SAVE posters and other program information are widely distributed to fairgoers. In 1989 a visiting archaeologist from Thailand was escorted throughout western Oregon by two committee members to view the archaeological looting and trafficking problem in the Pacific Northwest and the Operation SAVE approach to protecting the past.

After 4 years, Operation SAVE continues to be an unfunded program and no additional federal employees have been hired. Its success has been the result of employees' personal commitment and a willingness by all participants to work together for a common objective. The hallmark of Operation SAVE has been its integrated approach. In the past, archaeologists generally generated most of the public education programs. It was also the archaeologists who monitored sites, discussed site protection and the values of archaeology with the public, and developed cultural resource protection plans. With minimal staffing in cultural resource programs, these efforts were generally one-person efforts.

Working under these conditions, some archaeologists occasionally became involved in areas outside their expertise. In fact, it was a committee of archaeologists who wrote the ARPA criminal regulations. It was a task force of archaeologists in the state of Utah who proposed changes in the criminal laws. At times, these various committees were making proposals contradictory to effective law enforcement. Archaeologists were proposing laws and regulations that the criminal justice community perceived as constraining or even self-defeating to their investigative and prosecutorial efforts. A few archaeologists even publicly criticized enforcement efforts. Law enforcement officers and prosecutors were rarely consulted, and in most regions of the country, few officers showed any interest in archaeological enforcement. There was also some division between archaeologists and Native Americans. Indian groups were outraged at the continuing disrespect by some archaeologists in their treatment of their people's sacred sites and ancestral remains. Indian values appeared to be secondary to scientific values. The common thread of concern for archaeological protection was failing to pull these various factions together. It became evident that successful protection and enforcement efforts would require a united effort.

Operation SAVE is hopefully serving to bring these diverse groups together, for the first time, in a unified and coordinated effort to save the nation's past. Through Operation SAVE, the citizens of this country are made aware that the archaeological statute passed by Congress in 1979 is being enforced. Citizens are expected to respect the law, particularly if they are given notice that the law is being enforced. Operation SAVE is a program that is giving notice.

# PROTECTING THE PAST, PROTECTING THE PRESENT: CULTURAL RESOURCES AND AMERICAN INDIANS

Roger Anyon

## INTRODUCTION

While the protection of the past appears to be a simple concept, both the "past" and the nature of its "protection" are culturally defined. Many issues of critical relevance to American Indians are often ignored, or merely implied, in discussions about archaeological resources protection. To Indians, archaeological resources are only part of the realm of cultural resources for which protection and preservation is a serious concern; cultural resources represent not only the past but also the present; they are a legacy derived from hundreds of generations of ancestors.

For a western-trained scientist, protection of the past is a difficult proposition. The material record created in the past is now transformed into the archaeological record. The archaeological record is an unbiased present-day phenomenon; it can be measured, observed, and analyzed. The past, on the other hand, is what we make it; it is our interpretation of the archaeological record. The crucial problem for scientific archaeology is to develop methods to evaluate interpretations of the past.

Since the arrival of Columbus, non-Indians have acquired title to nearly 2 billion acres of land in the U.S. alone, all of which was once controlled by Indians (National Park Service 1990). Today Indians have title to about 2% of these lands. Millions of archaeological sites scattered throughout the U.S., on non-Indian and Indian lands, represent the unwritten record of Indian achievements, histories, and cultures. For centuries Indians have witnessed their cultural heritage under siege from foreign cultures. They have survived policies of removal from their homelands, assimilation, and termination. Even after the right of Indians to self-determination within a pluralistic society was recognized in 1975 with the passage of the Indian Self-Determination and Education Assistance Act, an important part of their cultural heritage remains under assault. Looters and vandals continue to destroy ancestral homes, camps, religious sites, burial grounds, and other cultural resources.

The complete protection and preservation of cultural resources is a common goal shared by Indians, archaeologists, legislators, and many other citizens. It is important, however, for non-Indians to understand that while Indians share a common goal to protect and preserve cultural resources, their needs and ultimate objectives may differ. When laws and regulations to protect these resources are written, enacted, and applied, Indian perspectives have often been over-looked.

Federal, tribal, and state laws protect cultural resources on federal, Indian, and state lands. Cultural resources on private lands, however, are unprotected for the most part. At present only 27 states protect unmarked burials through state legislation, but they provide no protection for other cultural resources on private land. A number of tribes have enacted their own ordinances and tribal codes to provide not only for protection of cultural resources on tribal lands, but also for site protection on other lands, for example in traditional use areas where they have allowed non-Indians to settle. Protection for all cultural resources, on a national level, is clearly inadequate. To provide adequate protection will require a comprehensive integration of multiple cultural viewpoints about the importance of cultural resources, as well as more inclusive laws than presently exist at the federal, state, and tribal levels.

In this article I explore some of the differences between Indian and non-Indian cultures, values, pasts, and presents, in terms of perceptions about cultural resources (including burials, which to Indians are an integral part of the cultural resource protection issue). It is important that these differences be addressed if Indians and non-Indians are to develop mutually agreeable and workable solutions to protect, preserve, and manage cultural resources. I also provide a brief review of how some tribes are using the law to assert their role in protecting their cultural heritage.

I am a non-Indian, but I have spent a number of years living and working as the tribal archaeologist for the Zuni tribe on their reservation in New Mexico. Although non-Indians can never expect to gain a complete understanding of a particular Indian culture and world view, it is important that we attempt to understand Indian viewpoints concerning cultural resources. After all, it is the archaeological record of the American Indian that comprises the vast majority of archaeological sites in the U.S., and it is this resource that the vast majority of archaeologists working in North America study.

## DIFFERENT CULTURES, DIFFERENT VALUES

The Indian view of cultural resources is, in general, much more holistic than that of non-Indians. While non-Indians are primarily concerned about protecting and preserving archaeological sites, Indians view archaeological sites as part of the larger realm of cultural resources that cannot be separated from those resources. "From a Tribal perspective, preservation is approached holistically; the past lives on in the present.... Historic properties ... include not only the places where significant events happen or have happened, but also whole classes of natural elements ... (National Park Service 1990:7)."

Tribal law and codes emphasize this holistic approach to cultural resources (see Rogers, this volume, for a discussion of model tribal laws). For example, the Warm Springs Tribal Code explicitly incorporates this view of cultural resources needing protection and adequate management, including those sites that are "ancient and contemporary cultural use sites and materials ... those associated with traditional foods and other natural resources, other sacred sites as designated by the Tribes, habitations, and historical events and personalities. It is recognized that these are an invaluable, irreplaceable, and endangered tribal resource" (Warm Springs Tribal Code Chapter 490.001).

Indians wish to preserve archaeological sites as a part of their efforts to preserve cultural resources, because these sites are an integral and irreplaceable part of their cultural identity and their history as a people. These resources are the heritage of Indians; with no written records of their past, these resources are their history to which they retain their links through legends and myths about the land and its people. Archaeologists and concerned non-Indians, on the other hand, wish to preserve and protect archaeological sites primarily to protect a nonrenewable data base that holds part of the record of human adaptive evolution. Indians are often dismayed at the restrictive values placed on definitions of cultural resources by non-Indians. It simply does not make sense to them that only a portion of their cultural history should warrant protection.

Another, more fundamental point of importance for Indians is the issue of land ownership and the protection, or lack thereof, for cultural resources. Non-Indian concepts of private land ownership and individual property rights, as they extend to cultural resources, are appalling to most Indians. Why does the use of the land through it's current legal ownership apply to the cultural resources within that land? (See Fowler, this volume, for a discussion of the legal structure of historic preservation law). Why should only the cultural resources that happen to lie on lands controlled and owned by federal, Indian, or state governments be protected under laws such as the National Historic Preservation Act (NHPA) and the Archaeological Resources Protection Act (ARPA)? Whether cultural resources are on federal, Indian, state, or private lands is not a point of relevance to Indians, as Weldon Johnson of the Colorado Indian Tribes has stated "Our starting point in our cultural resources program is that we never did give up ownership of cultural resources off the reservation." (National Park Service 1990:21).

A number of tribal ordinances reflect this expectation that off-reservation cultural resources, under any land ownership, should be afforded equal protection as those resources on lands with protective legislation. The Navajo Nation Cultural Resources Protection Act and the Warm Springs Tribal Code, among others, call for such protection. Other tribes from a variety of areas and different cultural backgrounds, including the Hopi, Zuni, Seneca, Chemehuevi, Paorch Creek, Cherokee, Lummi, and the Praire Band of the Potawatomi, have also demanded full protection for cultural resources on private land.

Situations such as that at the ancestral Zuni site of Heshodan Imk'osk'wa graphically illustrate the absurdity of pretending that land ownership boundaries have any relevance when the protection of cultural resources is at stake. This site lies partially on and partially off the Zuni reservation. With full protection of the law, the portion of this site on the Zuni reservation remains intact, whereas the privately owned portion of the site has been looted with impunity (Nichols et al. 1989).

It is ironic that the American concept of individual rights, to do as one pleases on ones land, a right often touted as being the reason that looting Indian cultural resources is acceptable, has many other restrictions that are apparently for the health and welfare of the nation. If an endangered species, for example the bald eagle, nests on private land, it has the same protection as it would if it had nested on federal land. The landowner may not destroy or harm the bald eagle or its nest, despite his or her ownership of that land. Land owners are not permitted to exercise their individual rights to do as they please in this case; they must obey the law, private land or not. The bald eagle, symbol of the U.S., is well protected on private land. Indian cultural resources, symbols of a long and proud Indian heritage, are not protected on private lands. Of even greater irony is that a renewable resource like the bald eagle (through breeding) is given full protection, whereas nonrenewable cultural resources are provided no protection at all from the whims of private landowners (for a discussion on archeology and the Public Trust concept see Knudson, this volume).

Even under the provisions of current federal legislation that specifically ensures the protection of some cultural resources, the need to provide accountability for different cultural values is not adequately addressed. Given that most of the cultural resources protected under the NHPA and ARPA are ancestral or in-use Indian resources, the roles of tribes, under federal laws and regulations, are inadequate. Tribes are allowed only a consulting role or given the power to make recommendations. Whether or not Indian concerns are actually taken into account in the final decision about the disposition of cultural resources depends upon the individual land manager. Managers that take Indian consultation and recommendations seriously often ensure that the Indian concerns are addressed in the final decision. If, on the other hand, the land manager does not see any need to address Indian concerns, then these concerns are ignored. For Indians this can lead to serious problems if the protection afforded a resource is inappropriate or inadequate.

## DIFFERENT PASTS, DIFFERENT PRESENTS

To Indians and non-Indians the past and present are perceived in different ways. Under NHPA, properties should be minimally 50-years old to qualify as being significant, while under

ARPA the cut off is at 100 years. Many Indians, however, do not distinguish the past and the present in such concise and arbitrary terms. To Indians, for whom time is often not the linear concept it is to most Americans, the past can be the present, and the present the past. Consequently, although the past and the present may be separated in the law, these legal non-Indian definitions of past and present and what constitutes an historic property can be perplexing to many Indians. Take for example two instances of perceptions about the role and use of two historic properties, as defined under the law, that are important cultural resources to the Zunis.

The site of Kia'makia is located to the south of the present day Zuni reservation. To archaeologists, this pueblo was occupied sometime during the 13th and 14th centuries and abandoned before the arrival of Coronado in 1540. Archaeologists believe Kia'makia should be protected for its potential to provide significant data to the discipline. For the Zunis, however, Kia'makia is not only a ruin, it is where the Kia'nakwe lived and where Cha'kwena corralled all game animals. After the Zunis defeated the Kia'nakwe in battle, they opened the corral and freed the game. Since that time, game have roamed the face of the earth (Stevenson 1904:36–39). When Stevenson visited the site in the early 1900s, the spring and water hole at Kia'makia were surrounded by hundreds of Zuni prayer sticks. On a recent visit to the site, the prayer sticks mentioned by Stevenson were not observed, but for the Zunis their visit to the spring was of great significance. They began to recall and tell the legends of Kia'makia, the Kia'nakwe, and Cha'kwena. Future religious visits to the site are planned. To the Zunis, Kia'makia is as important in the present as it is a location of their past history.

At the pueblo of Zuni itself, Indian and non-Indian perceptions of the past and present are not entirely congruous. While the Zunis value their past as an integral and important part of their culture, they do not wish to become a society viewed by outsiders as a living museum. The protection of in-use historic properties, such as Zuni Pueblo, can therefore become problematic. At Zuni the present day needs of the tribe can sometimes be at odds with the expectations of non-Indian historic preservation efforts.

The pueblo of Zuni has been occupied for hundreds of years and has become a modern town atop a complex archaeological site, a site that continues to evolve in the present. Over the past 100 years the architecture of the pueblo has undergone drastic changes. What was once a compact five-story pueblo has been modified into a more diffuse series of one-story structures surrounded by suburbs. During the last century the essential integrity of spatial structure within the pueblo has been maintained, even though Zuni vernacular architecture has undergone massive changes (Ferguson et al. 1990). Zunis want to have modern homes and continue to live in the pueblo. Here the fundamental needs of shelter and housing for the Zuni people often conflict with the non-Indian ideals of historic preservation. Historic preservation ideals are for the pueblo to retain its historic character, but these ideals are sometimes applied in such a way that Zunis feel as if they have little control over the continued growth and development of their own pueblo. This is not meant to imply that the goals of historic preservation and the goals of modernization at Zuni are incompatible, but rather that the two different cultural perceptions of historic preservation are not necessarily the same. Preservation of the historic character of the pueblo is important to the Zunis, but they feel that historic preservation concerns of both Zunis and non-Zunis must be accommodated by a dialogue in which both parties are treated as equals.

The pressure from historic preservation agencies for Zunis to retain the pueblo as it once was, is echoed in the questions of many tourists who visit Zuni. Tourists arrive in Zuni expecting something quite different from the present-day town. They usually begin a conversation by asking where the pueblo is, and then are disappointed to find that the five-story 19th-century pueblo is not in existence today. The tourist perception of what Zuni should look like is conditioned, to a large degree, by history as presented at many of the protected and preserved archaeological sites in the Southwest. At these sites visitors see exhibits and receive literature showing late 19th-century pueblos, implying that Zuni, for example, is some kind of living museum. Thus, non-Indians often expect the present to look like the past and are surprised when this is not the case. To the Zunis, the present does not have to look like the past because the past lives on in the every day actions of the Zuni people. The essential cultural difference is that non-Indians want to see the past to know it, whereas to Indians, the present embodies the past, and thus they do not necessarily have to see their past to know it.

The ways in which the past is used to interpret the present also play a vital role in molding cultural perceptions. That every culture, at different times, perceives its past and the past of other cultures in its own idiosyncratic way is well established. Today we see the great moundbuilder debate of the late 19th century (Willey and Sabloff 1980:34–43) as a parochial view that is an unfortunate legacy of our intellectual past. But is this debate just an unfortunate part of our intellectual past? Present-day visitors to Anasazi archaeological sites in New Mexico are often presented with the mysterious disappearance of the Anasazi as being a focus of archaeological research in the area. The abandonment of the spectacular pueblos in Chaco Canyon and other locales is presented as a mystery. Interpretive signs and exhibits ask, "What happened? Where did the Anasazi go?" Even if mention is made that modern pueblos are populated by descendants of the Anasazi, the tourist is provided with photographs of 19th-century pueblos. It is with these questions of Anasazi disappearance in mind that the tourist arrives in Zuni. Asking a Zuni where the Anasazi went is simultaneously comical and insulting. The Zunis are direct descendants of the Anasazi and are fully aware that Anasazi archaeological sites are those of their ancestors. They often fail to understand why anyone should ask so strange a question. An Anasazi mystery fabricated by mostly non-Indians is just as mysterious to the Zunis as is the fable itself to the visitors. This type of fabricated past forces us to consider, once the past is protected and preserved, how it should be presented to the public. Whose past and whose present is being protected?

## TRIBAL CULTURAL RESOURCE PROTECTION STRATEGIES

"What a tribal program is about is a tribe establishing standards and policies in controlling its own cultural resources rather than letting someone else do that" (Alan Downer, Navajo Nation Historic Preservation Officer, quoted in National Park Service 1990:13).

Given the varied cultural values, traditions, and resources of Indian tribes, it is not surprising that they have developed different methods for protecting their cultural resources. It is precisely because of these differences that the need for cultural resource protection and management lies at a local level within a framework provided by federal legislation. The NHPA provides the mechanism through which tribes may develop their own standards and procedures for protecting cultural resources, and some tribes are beginning to implement their own historic and cultural preservation offices. This process will be one of adjustment, by both Indians and non-Indians, due to greater Indian involvement in cultural resource issues. Here I outline some of the different strategies implemented by several tribes to take control of their cultural resources. This discussion is far from exhaustive; it is meant to provide a brief overview of the range of strategies being applied by tribes in the U.S.

As I have noted above, the protection, preservation, and management of cultural resources are issues of great importance to Indians. This can, however, mean different things to different tribes, just as much as it means different things to Indians and non-Indians. To some Kootenai tribal members, these concepts mean leaving the cultural resources alone and keeping archaeologists away from resources on the reservation (Pat Lefthand, quoted in National Park Service 1990:47). To the Hopi of Arizona, these concepts have been treated as a basis for working with the state and archaeologists to study ancestral ruins and develop them as a park for public education and enjoyment (Adams 1989).

Tribes have successfully used the provisions in NHPA and ARPA to develop tribal involvement in the protection of ancestral cultural resources on their reservations. On many reservations a combination of NHPA and tribal ordinances have been used to prevent destruction of tribal cultural resources. Any development projects that have not assessed impacts to cultural resources cannot be activated, and projects that do start without assessing this impact are often shut down by tribes until they do comply with the law.

For the past 15 years the Zuni tribe of New Mexico has owned and operated its own archaeology program. After seeing outsiders doing archaeology on its reservation for decades, the tribe decided that it should exert control over cultural resources management issues and formed its own archaeology program in 1975. Since then the Zuni Archaeology Program has been involved in all aspects of cultural resource management; research, inventory, and curation of cultural materials; public interpretation programs; and training and development for tribal members (Anyon and Zunie 1989).

Both the AkChin in Arizona and Koniagmiut of Kodiak Island in Alaska have used archaeology projects to initiate tribal cultural resource programs. For the AkChin, the successful litigation of water rights led to an agricultural development project that led directly to tribal involvement in cultural resources management. Under the NHPA and ARPA, archaeological research led to the discovery of prehistoric ancestral ruins on the AkChin lands being developed for agricultural purposes. This experience provided the impetus for the tribe to establish its own ecomuseum where the community itself controls the prehistoric resources removed from the ground. The museum also provides for the protection and use of these resources for the benefit of tribal members (Charles Carlyle, personal communication 1989). For the Koniagmiut, the experiences of working with students from Bryn Mawr College at the excavation of an ancestral archaeological site, although fraught with initial problems (Pullar 1987), have proved to be extremely rewarding for both the tribe and archaeology students. The tribe has increased its own involvement in the project and has used this as a springboard for developing cultural resource management issues.

For the Navajo Nation the provisions in the NHPA have created the conditions for the development of a tribal Historic Preservation Office. This office has been instrumental in the passage of the Navajo Nation Cultural Resources Protection Act and the negotiations for the tribal office to take over the responsibilities of the State Historic Preservation Offices (Arizona, New Mexico, and Utah) for tribal lands within those three states. An initial project undertaken by the Navajo Nation Historic Preservation Office was a pilot study, at selected chapters (the unit of local government on the Navajo Nation), into Navajo perceptions about cultural resources (Kelley and Francis 1988). One of the more interesting results of this study is that many Navajos regard prehistoric Anasazi sites as an aspect of the natural landscape. This is quite a different perception than that held by the Hopis and Zunis, who regard Anasazi sites as ancestral cultural resources.

The Navajo Nation has also linked the provisions of the NHPA with those in the Self-Determination Act and has recently contracted with the Bureau of Indian Affairs to take over cultural resources management work on the Navajo reservation from this particular federal agency. For all tribes, the initiation of an independent tribal historic preservation office and the self-determination contracting of cultural resources work are major precedent-setting steps towards tribal management of cultural resources on tribal lands.

## CONCLUSION

The protection, preservation, and management of cultural resources are issues of great importance to Indians. It is, however, important for archaeologists, legislators, and the public to understand that different cultures, whether they be Indian or non-Indian, have different concepts and values that they bring to protecting the past. The archaeological record is a present-day phenomenon that must be protected. It is this present day phenomenon that is the key to different cultural pasts.

The archaeological record is an essential part of the Indian cultural heritage. It is also the fundamental data base of archaeologists. For Indians, the record embodies aspects of their cultural past and their cultural present; it is an affirmation of their long and close ties to the land. They are sure of their cultural past and see the archaeological record as their ancestral cultural resources and a record of the past they know. For archaeologists with scientific training, the archaeological record embodies the unknown, the data to unlock the cross-cultural patterns of human adaptive evolution. Both Indians and archaeologists see the same archaeological record, and both have equal and valid needs of that record.

To successfully promote the goal of protecting cultural resources, it is essential that all parties are treated as equals. The goal of cultural resource protection should continue to be met through federal statutes such as the National Historic Preservation Act. Federal statutes should, however, be amended to provide complete protection of all cultural resources throughout the country, regardless of current landholding legalities. If the goal of federal statutes is to protect this nonrenewable record of the national heritage, then the law should provide equal protection for all of this heritage, not just those parts on certain landholder's property. The idea of declaring all archaeological resources as a part of the national patrimony is nothing new; it is the law in many other countries throughout the world. While federal legislation should provide more inclusive protection for all cultural resources, it should also provide greater latitude for the development, enactment, and application of tribal laws, to allow even stricter protection of the resources at a local level.

The protection of cultural resources is a common goal of different cultures, each with its own agenda about why it is protecting the past. It is a goal that can only be met through equal participation of all relevant parties. This participation must be met not only through the law, but also through direct and honest communication in which the views of each culture are accepted as having equal validity. It is the acceptance of multiple viewpoints that is the key to accomplishing the goal we have set.

## REFERENCES CITED

Adams, E. C. (1989) The Homol'ovi Research Program, *Kiva,* 54(3), 175–194.
Anyon, R. and Zunie, J. (1989) Cooperation at the Pueblo of Zuni: common ground for archaeology and tribal concerns. *Pract. Anthropol.,* 11(3), 13–15.

**Carlyle, C. L.** (1989) Personal communication. Route 2, Box 27, Maricopa, AZ.

**Ferguson, T. J., Mills, B. J., and Seciwa, C.** (1990) Contemporary Zuni architecture and society. In *Pueblo Style and Regional Architecture*, Markovich, N. C., Preiser, W. F. E., and Sturm, F. G., Eds., Van Nostrand Reinheld, New York, 103–121.

**Kelley, K. and Francis, H.** (1988) Zuni and Navajo Use of the Navajo "New Lands," paper presented at the American Anthropological Assoc. Ann. Meet., Phoenix.

National Park Service (1990) Keepers of the treasures: protecting historical properties and cultural traditions on Indian lands, Government Printing Office, Washington D.C.

**Nichols, D. L., Klesert, A. L., and Anyon, R.** (1989) Ancestral sites, shrines, and graves: Native American perspectives on the ethics of collecting cultural properties. In *The Ethics of Collecting Cultural Property. Whose Culture? Whose Property?* Messenger, P. M., Ed., University of New Mexico Press, Albuquerque, 27–38.

**Pullar, G. L.** (1987) The Kodiak Island Project, paper presented at a Conf. Native Americans, Native American Lands and Archaeology, Heard Museum, Phoenix.

**Stevenson, M. C.** (1904) The Zuni Indians: their mythology, esoteric fraternities, and ceremonies, 23rd Annual Report of the Bureau of American Ethnology 1901-1902, Government Printing Office, Washington D.C.

Warm Springs Tribal Code (no date) *Chapters 490, Protection and Management of Archaeological, Historical, and Cultural Resources,* Confederated Tribes of the Warm Springs Reservation of Oregon.

**Willey, G. R. and Sabloff J. A.** (1980) *A History of American Archaeology,* 2nd ed., W. H. Freeman, San Francisco.

# THE ARCHAEOLOGICAL SITES MONITORING PROGRAM AT THE BIG SOUTH FORK NATIONAL RIVER AND RECREATION AREA, 1986 TO 1989

Tom Des Jean

## INTRODUCTION

The Big South Fork of the Cumberland River flows northward along the Upper Cumberland Plateau. This formation is a part of the Appalachian Plateau Physiographic Province and represents a true peneplain, or "a broad area of slight relief shaped by erosional processes." The swiftly moving waters of the river have scoured deep gorges into the usually resistant 250 million-year-old Pennsylvanian sandstones of the plateau formation. This cutting action has produced literally thousands of rockshelters and "bench" or terrace areas. These locations have been occupied by prehistoric and historic peoples living in this area for the past 10,000 to 12,000 years.

The Big South Fork National River and Recreation Area (BISO) was created by Congress (Public Law 93-251) in 1974 "...for the purposes of conserving and interpreting an area containing unique cultural, historic, geologic, fish and wildlife, archaeologic, scenic, and recreational values...for the benefit and enjoyment of present and future generations." At present there are 848 known archaeological sites recorded within the BISO boundary (Figure 1), many of which have been looted for the artifacts they contain. Only 10% of this National Area has been surveyed, but if the remaining lands possess sites at the same density as the areas already surveyed, then the National Park Service (NPS) is congressionally mandated to protect a huge archaeological resource that may well exceed 8000 sites.

An archaeological sites monitoring program was one step toward developing site preservation at the Big South Fork National River and Recreational Area (Faust 1986). The program was funded by the U.S. Army Corps of Engineers (COE), which presented a very generalized scope of work to assess and manage the effects that trail development and trail use in the National Area had, and continues to have, on the cultural resources at BISO. The program was then developed and conducted by the Southeast Archaeological Center (SEAC) of the NPS, from December 1986 through March 1989.

This 2-year program was divided into three developmental phases: phase I (6 months), phase II (6 months), and phase III (1 year). The phases are discussed further in the research- design section. A research design was developed for the monitoring program, which outlined archaeological site impact data collection. The research design also proposed monitoring various trails, to define and isolate different types of impacts. Baseline-data collection for this program included monitoring control areas in order to gauge variations in impacts from area to area.

The development of the monitoring program anticipated some logistical adjustments and technical problems that could only be overcome through field trials. Procedural changes were made throughout the first year of monitoring activities, in order to streamline and "fine-tune" baseline-data collection. Following these modifications, the final phase of this study was completed. This article presents a monitoring program "template" that can be modified for use in other areas.

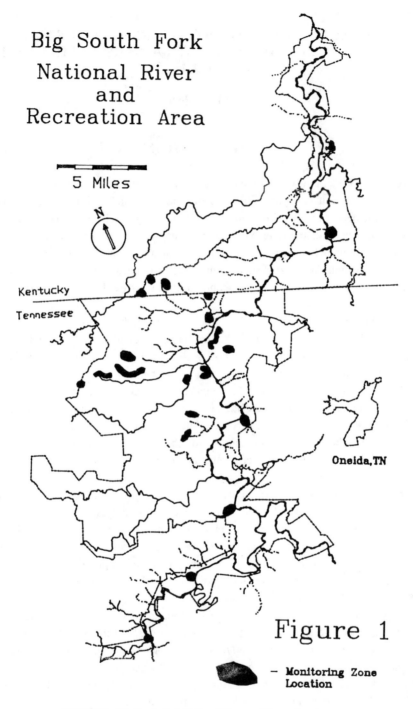

FIGURE 1.  Big South Fork National River and Recreation Area.

## RESEARCH DESIGN

The goal of the archaeological sites monitoring program was to understand and define various types of site impacts (natural and human) and to develop a model for cultural resources monitoring in the BISO area of the Upper Cumberland Plateau. To accomplish this, the research design followed a chronological set of operational steps and objectives described below.

The three phases of the archaeological sites monitoring program contained specific and overlapping objectives. The three primary objectives were

1.   To develop a park archaeological sites monitoring program by:

      a.   Collecting archaeological baseline data
      b.   Developing monitoring procedures within a limited area
      c.   Testing monitoring procedures with park staff within a limited area
      d.   Modifying monitoring procedures where needed
      e.   Expanding the monitoring program to other areas within BISO

2.   To evaluate the monitoring program with respect to:

      a.   Estimating person hours required to obtain baseline data per site
      b.   Estimating person hours for various park staff to monitor different types of sites
      c.   Identifying zones that are having adverse impacts
      d.   Determining the frequency of monitoring needed with respect to site types, types of impacts, and zones
      e.   Identifying types of impacts that occur on sites

3.   To report results and recommendations concerning:

      a.   Changes and/or modifications to the monitoring program
      b.   Identifying zones, areas, or sites needing monitoring
      c.   Estimating person hours required to monitor these areas or sites
      d.   Recommending methods for eliminating the effects of adverse impacts to archaeological sites at BISO

Two secondary objectives were also defined as part of the monitoring program:

1.   To increase the knowledge concerning the archaeological resources at BISO through the monitoring program by:

      a.   Surveying new areas of the park
      b.   Surface collecting of sites

2.   To increase the public awareness concerning the park's nonrenewable archaeological resources through:

      a.   Education programs at schools
      b.   Interpretation programs for the public at the park
      c.   Assistance to the park's law enforcement activities

Phase I of the monitoring program addressed, primarily, items 1a, 1b, 2a, and 3a. Phases II and III addressed the remaining objectives. The secondary objectives were collateral duties that were done by the monitoring program archaeologist or BISO interpretation staff, whenever opportunity or occasion permitted.

# DATA COLLECTION

Baseline-data collection, as indicated in the above discussion, required a lot of trial and error in the field. The basic procedure was to locate rockshelters in the three zones (hiking trails, horse/jeep trails, and remote areas) described in the research design and to define every rockshelter by length, height, depth, size category, color, aspect, presence/absence of artifacts, presence/absence of digging, photographs, locational description and field sketch, and a locational map. A permanent metal tag was then attached to every rockshelter that was recorded. All of this data was collated onto 5" × 8" field index cards and then entered into a "dbase file."

Once an area had been recorded, seasonal visits were made to all of the tagged sites in that area, and any new disturbance was noted on the monitoring cards. The locational cards and photographs worked well, but there were a few sites in steep, jagged, and densely overgrown terrain that were not able to be relocated for a year. Other sites located in monitoring areas of rugged terrain were overlooked and only identified long after the program had been in place.

Discerning evidence of new looting from old looting activity was easier as monitoring became more frequent and as the person monitoring became more familiar with each site in the data base. It also became easier to recognize various clues about site disturbances. It would be a very helpful technique to be able to read computer "bar code dates" that are now found on most product labels discarded at sites during illegal digging. Often the trash left by looters did contain readable product expiration dates that provided a *terminus ante quem* (time before which) for disturbances. Additionally, sun bleaching of labels and plastic, the growth of mold/lichen on backdirt piles, the rounding of the sharp edges of backdirt piles, rainfall and erosion, blown-in leaf litter, and the disappearance time for footprints gave some indication of the time since disturbance.

The rates of change for many of these signs differ for every disturbed rockshelter site. An example of this is that shallow footprints or handprints will disappear within a matter of a few hours to a day in rockshelter soils containing high-to-moderate amounts of nitrates. Erosional processes also vary considerably from rockshelter to rockshelter, and this tends to obscure episodes of "new digging."

Many of the disturbed rockshelter sites were so impacted that discovering clues to indicate recent looting activity was very difficult. One idea proposed to address this situation was to "sweep" rockshelter sites so that it would be easier to identify new looting activity. An assistant was hired for 3 months to accompany the monitoring program researcher and "sweep" these heavily disturbed sites, leaving a smooth surface that would reveal any new impacts. This technique worked well and helped to determine 32 new impacts and to speed up the monitoring process.

Determining types of impacts involved identifying human vs. animal disturbances. This was not always easy to do, but the presence of animal denning materials, animal feces, and other animal signs were adequate to differentiate those sites recently disturbed by animals. Most of the time, the presence of human garbage was enough to indicate that the observed disturbance was not of natural origin. Also, the size of disturbances varied from minimal amounts, in the case of animal activity, to unusually large and deep craters or numerous small impacts that resulted from human activities.

Rockshelter locations were initially investigated using a three-zone research design. This design proposed monitoring archaeological sites within stratified zones. The zones were defined as; zone I — hiking trails, zone II — horse/jeep trails, and zone III — remote areas. It became

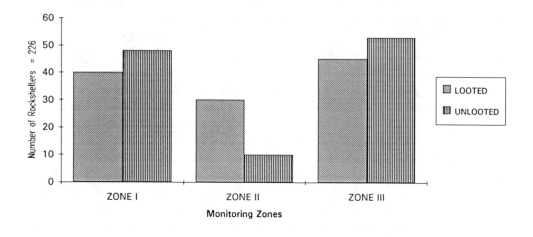

FIGURE 2. Looted vs. unlooted rockshelters by monitoring zone.

clear early in phase II that no prehistorically occupied rockshelter was immune to impacts. Even the "remote zone" sites have been, and continue to be, looted (Des Jean 1987a:8–9). While evidence was collected indicating that disturbed rockshelter sites along the more heavily used trails suffered a slightly lower rate of looting compared to other zones, no zone or area in BISO has remained free of intensive site looting or site destruction (Figure 2). This fact is not unique to the Big South Fork area. Lack of easy access is not a consideration to dedicated relic collectors, and this fact has been noted by other researchers in numerous areas of the country (Lightfoot and Francis 1978:89; Ison et al. 1981:29; Lyneis et al. 1980:152; Williams 1978:Table 33).

Verification of this factor at BISO convinced the monitoring program archaeologist to modify the program's research design and eliminate the stratified zones originally defined (Des Jean 1987b). Rockshelters were then logged in as either on or adjacent to jeep roads or trails (100 m either side), or not on or adjacent to jeep roads or trails. This modification still provided the data that answered questions that the funding agency (COE) wanted addressed (impacts to rockshelters on trails), and it provided the control information (nontrail rockshelter impacts) with which to interpret that data. Data continued to be collected on all of the sites logged into the data base from the beginning.

One other modification to the research design was to eliminate the use of BISO staff participation in monitoring activities. This was an optimistic goal that, because of the shortage in staffing, was never really able to be implemented. There were, however, several individuals from all of the BISO divisions who reported observing new impacts. One exception to staff participation in this program was a biology researcher who was able to monitor a prehistorically occupied rockshelter site associated with his year-long monthly sampling regimen. After more than 2 years of data collection, the monitoring program has identified a number of patterns in looting behavior, not previously recognized.

# RESULTS

The monitoring program archaeologist recorded 226 rockshelter locations and made an average of 5 visits per site during the 2-year program. The number of visits ranged from only one visit at some rockshelters to a maximum of 13 visits to rockshelter #RS22. This latter site, Muleshoe rockshelter, was the one closest to BISO headquarters and the one used in an interpretive tour to illustrate to the public the effects of looting and vandalism.

Out of the 226 rockshelters that have been recorded in the monitoring program data base, 139 (62%) were identified to be prehistoric archaeological sites. Looting activity is evident at 128 (92%) of these sites. This is similar to the 95% looting impact rate given for the Daniel Boone National Forest (DBNF), which has a common boundary with BISO (Ison 1989).

The 11 archaeological sites in the monitoring program data base that have not been looted are either intact due to roof-fall, have very difficult access and/or low visibility, are of small size, have low artifact densities, or all of the foregoing. Since the beginning of the monitoring program, 208 incidents of looting have been recorded. Most of these were past episodes, but 86 incidents of looting were relatively new, and 32 of these were repeat-looting incidents occurring between monitoring visits. Eight other rockshelters suffered digging impacts made by animals.

There were 109 rockshelters monitored that had no artifacts evident. Only 18 of these had been looted, and many of these were in the small (<20 linear meters) category. It appears, then, that the one critical element that looters use to determine site location is the presence of *chert debitage*. Usually this material is visible in the dripline of a rockshelter, but the 18 "tested" sites indicate that some looters do understand that not all prehistoric rockshelter sites will be immediately evident. The 91 rockshelters that have had no disturbances will be dropped from future monitoring activities. Also, archaeological sites that have had no new impacts for a year or more can be monitored on a yearly basis following the season of greatest looting activity, which in BISO is during the fall.

It was initially assumed that more archaeological site looting would be evident along the federally constructed trails where heavy public use occurs. It was also assumed that remote areas where few roads or trails are located would have the least amount of looting. Figure 3 demonstrates that these ideas are not correct. While the hiking trail areas, zone I in the original monitoring program research design, have suffered a tremendous amount of site looting, more impacted sites were found along zone II, the horse trails and jeep roads. This fact was also found to be true for jeep trails, by Lightfoot and Francis (1978:89), on U.S. Forest Service lands in Colorado.

A direct relationship has been reported to exist at BISO, and elsewhere, between rockshelter site looting and the linear distance to jeep or secondary roads (Ferguson et al. 1986:232; Wylie 1989), but monitoring program data do not appear to reflect this very strongly. This may be due to the fact that there are a number of unrecorded roads in the area that serve to provide looter access. The same thing is evident in the National Forest (DBNF), according to Ison et al. (1981:29), who found that "...accessibility is no problem because of numerous unrecorded roads and undeveloped trails." Another reason that this relationship appears to be weak is because of the intense site looting that occurred during TVA trail construction at BISO, where unsupervised workers, some of them avid relic collectors, worked for 5-years, from 1981 to 1985 (personal informant 1987).

Remote areas of BISO, zone III, evidenced more looting impacts numerically, but in the zone II areas no archaeological rockshelter sites were found that were not looted. Both zones I and III, at least, possessed some nonlooted prehistoric rockshelter sites. New disturbances continue to occur along hiking trails, but to a lesser degree than in other areas of BISO. The explanation

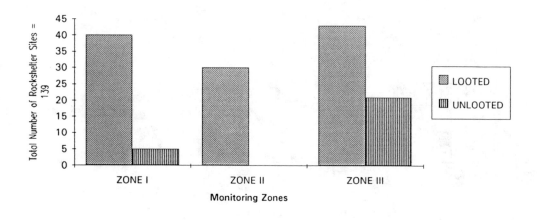

FIGURE 3.   Looted vs. unlooted rockshelter with artifacts by monitoring zone.

for slightly lower site looting along frequently used hiking trails may be found in a looters reluctance to dig in areas where discovery would be more likely.

Regardless of accessibility or location, rockshelter sites suffer from repeated looting. The one evident fact is that "proximity to roads will have a powerful influence on the **degree** of disturbance which can be expected" (Ferguson et al. 1986:239). This has been observed to be the case during the monitoring program: remote location offers little protection from repeated site looting.

Another statistic that was thought to have some significance in documenting looting behavior is that of rockshelter size. It was thought at the outset of this study that the larger rockshelters would indicate selectively greater evidence of impacts. This, however, was not the case: a fact also documented by the University of Tennessee Survey (Ferguson et al. 1986:234). Rockshelters were divided by opening length into small (1–20 m), medium (>20 m–50 m), and large (>50m) sizes. The medium-sized rockshelter sites exhibit about twice as much impact as both large and small rockshelter sites (Figure 4). This may be due to a selective bias of looters for rockshelters larger than 20 m in length and because there are fewer prehistorically occupied small rockshelters. It may also be a result of fewer prehistorically occupied large (>50m) rockshelters that are able to be dug into (Figure 5).

Many of the large- category rockshelter sites have a great deal of roof-fall that prevents them from being looted. Ison, Norville, and Pollack (1981:28, 30) noted this fact, too, in a study done in the Red River Gorge area of the DBNF, where it was reported that while roof-fall does protect some sites, looters will attempt to break up roof-fall boulders to dig under them for artifacts. One collector interviewed by the monitoring program archaeologist stated that he takes a block and tackle back to particularly good sites in order to remove roof-fall.

Earlier findings of this study indicated that the hunting season (fall) accounted for most of the looting of archaeological resources in the National Area (Des Jean 1987b:10). This situation has not changed, but new evidence indicates that looting activity is now occurring in the summer at higher levels than anticipated (Figure 6). This summertime looting activity may be the result

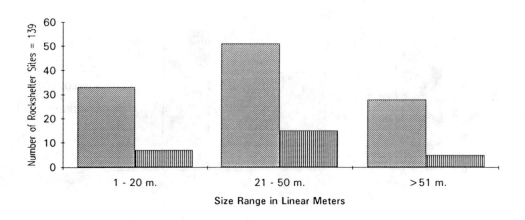

FIGURE 4.  Looted vs. unlooted rockshelter sites by size.

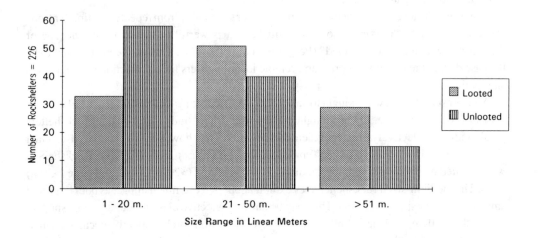

FIGURE 5.  Looted vs. unlooted rockshelters by size in linear meters.

of a continually rising rate of visitation (Figure 7). The Red River Gorge study at DBNF (ISON et al. 1981:24) found that as visitation increased, so too did looting impacts, at the rate of 10% for both developed and remote sites. The increase observed in summertime looting may also be due, in part, to the fact that the monitoring program data base was not adequately set up during the previous year (1987) to predict seasonal trends by 1988. Impacts that occur during hunting season, based on current data, still account for the majority (53%) of known sites looted in BISO (Des Jean and Wilson 1989:5).

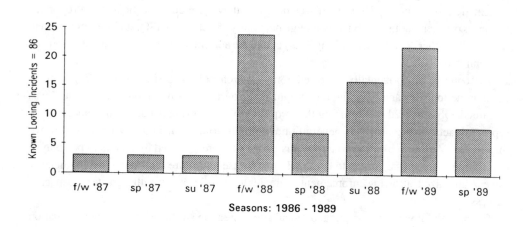

FIGURE 6.  Looting incidents and approximate seasonality.

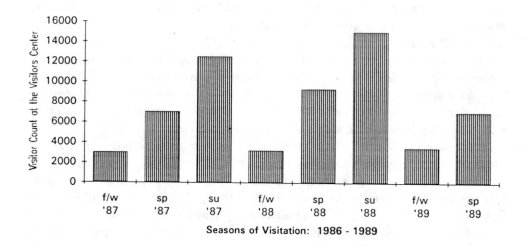

FIGURE 7.  Seasonal visitation rates, Big South Fork NRRA.

## ASSESSING THE MONITORING PROGRAM

The three primary objectives of the monitoring program were accomplished or modified as the program developed. Most of these procedures worked well, but a few problems that were encountered and a few successes that were noteworthy will be discussed. Objectives (1c, 2a, and 2b) concerning staff participation in monitoring activities were unworkable because of limited personnel and Big South Forks's large and dispersed cultural resource base. While no real systematic monitoring by BISO staff was possible, they were enthusiastic and did report 13 instances of recent looting activity. Although not totally effective at BISO, staff monitoring may work well in other areas where staffing is larger and the cultural resources are better defined and concentrated.

The concept of horizontally stratified zones of archaeological site impacts (2c), used in guiding the logistics and planning the monitoring program, was not applicable here and was discarded. Objective 2d (determining the frequency of monitoring needed with respect to site types, impacts, and zones) was generally not difficult to do, but in a few cases, did prove impossible. Various reasons account for this: some sites are assumed by looters to be "played out," while other sites continue to be dug. In a few cases, sites are repeatedly and predictably looted/vandalized, allowing enforcement strategies to come into play with a greater prospect of success.

The one useful variable for archaeological site protection strategies was the determination that site looting was a seasonal activity geared to greater visibility as a result of leaf fall and vegetation dieback in the fall. The fall season also coincides with snake hibernation and the hunting season: the latter providing a time to be in the woods and the opportunity to search in many areas without worrying about snakes, which are numerous on the Upper Cumberland Plateau.

Secondary objectives included increasing the knowledge of cultural resources in the Big South Fork area and increasing public awareness. Secondary objective 1 called for surveying new areas of the park and for surface collection of sites to help define a cultural chronology for this area of the Upper Cumberland Plateau. As a result, the monitoring program identified approximately 150 new archaeological sites, and collections made at these sites have helped to establish a more reliable cultural chronology.

The other secondary objective was for the monitoring program archaeologist to provide education programs at local schools, to help develop interpretation programs at BISO, and to help law enforcement personnel in archaeological site-protection efforts. A number of programs were developed to educate the public, using school "chalk and talk" programs, a cultural hiking trail, an area "dig box" activity, and posters and activity hand outs for children.

Primary objective 3d and secondary objective 2c concern recommendations for eliminating effects of adverse impacts. Suggestions were made to reduce looting impacts through law enforcement measures, using up-to-date data supplied by the on-going monitoring program. This was done, with the result that four suspects were apprehended in the act of looting an archaeological site. These suspects later pleaded guilty to a misdemeanor under the Archaeological Resources Protection Act. This conviction was one of the first made in the eastern U.S. for the looting of a prehistoric site.

## CONCLUSION

The applicability of various protection strategies has been discussed extensively at BISO and has resulted in an archaeological resources protection plan (Des Jean 1988b). The plan outlined a number of strategies that rely on information developed from an ongoing archaeological sites monitoring program. These suggestions include law enforcement methods involving remote sensing, increased backcountry patrolling, increasing warning signs, and increased seasonal protection; management strategies, including focusing protection efforts in critical zones, selective protection of critically significant sites, and closing public access to critical areas; maintenance strategies involving rerouting roads and trails and erecting barricades to prevent looting in critical rockshelter sites; and interpretation efforts to increase public education programs.

Information gathered during the monitoring program indicates that there are three types of looters: (1) opportunists, (2) those that collect for personal acquisition, and (3) those who collect for profit (Des Jean 1988a:6). Ison, Norville, and Pollack (1981:30–32) also identified three classes of looters/vandals: unintentional (opportunists), relic collectors (acquisition), and commercial looters (profiteers). Law enforcement, interpretation, and education strategies may have to be tailored to the characteristics of each class of looter in order to effectively combat the impacts resulting from this activity.

In addition to the deterrence provided by increasing law enforcement, public education is the other necessary approach to the protection of the archaeological resources on our public lands. The Red River Gorge Study (Ison et al. 1981), the Little Colorado Planning Unit Study (Plog 1978), and this monitoring program study have all come to the same conclusions: that law enforcement and public education are the most important deterrents to archaeological site destruction (Ison et al. 1981:34), and that "education is the most important means of protecting archaeological resources" (Lightfoot and Francis 1978:34). Educating the general public on the elementary, middle school, high school, and adult level will instill a degree of appreciation and understanding for the value of cultural resources. Hopefully, this will prevent unchanneled interest in prehistoric peoples from becoming a frenzy of site destruction and relic collecting. The dividends from such public education programs, though, will not be observed for years. Of course, for some looters, education will have little effect. For those, the only deterrent is the criminal justice system.

## REFERENCES CITED

Des Jean, T. (1987a) Monitoring archaeological site impacts. Paper presented at the 44th Ann. Southeastern Archaeological Conf., Charleston, SC.

Des Jean, T. (1987b) Monitoring Program Interim Report: following the completion of phase I of the Archaeological Sites Monitoring Program at Big South Fork National River and Recreation Area. National Park Service, Southeast Archaeological Center, Tallahassee, FL.

Des Jean, T. (1988a) Big South Fork National River and Recreation Area Archaeological Resources Protection Plan for FY88 through FY92. National Park Service, Southeast Archaeological Center, Tallahassee, FL.

Des Jean, T. (1988b) Looting activity: a folk tradition of the Upper Cumberland Plateau, Lamar Briefs No. 11:6-7, Watkinsville, GA.

Des Jean, T. and Wilson, R. C. (1989) Vandalism behavior in the national parks: diagnoses and treatment. Paper presented at the 53rd Ann. Meet.of the Society for American Archaeology, Atlanta.

Faust, R. (1986) Archaeological Resources Status Report, Big South Fork National River and Recreation Area. National Park Service, Southeast Archaeological Center, Tallahassee, FL.

Ferguson, T. A., Pace, R. A., Gardner, J. W., and Hoffman, R. J. (1986) Final Report of the Big South Fork Archaeological Project: survey, testing and recommendations, U.S. Army Corps of Engineers, Nashville District.

Ison, C. (1989) Oldest Indian site in Kentucky. *Lexington Herald-Leader,* (Lexington, KY), July 12, 1989.

Ison, C., Norville, C., and Pollack, D. (1981) Vandalism of rockshelter sites in Red River Gorge, Kentucky: an assessment, Department of Anthropology, University of Kentucky, Lexington.

Lightfoot, K. G. and Francis, J. E. (1978) Management information and recommendations. In *An Analytical Approach to Cultural Resource Management: The Little Colorado Planning Unit,* Plog,     F. C., Ed., Anthropological Research Papers No. 13, Arizona State University, Tempe.

**Lyneis, M. M., Weide, D. L., and Warren, E.** (1980) *Impacts: Damage to Cultural Resources of the California Desert,* Department of Anthropology, University of Nevada, Las Vegas.

**Plog, F.** (1978) *An Analytical Approach to Cultural Resource Management: The Little Colorado Planning Unit,* Anthropological Research Papers No.13, Arizona State University, Tempe.

**Wylie, J.** (1989) Archaeological protection efforts. Federal Archaeology Report, Washington, D.C., August 1989, 2(3), 5.

**Williams, L. R.** (1978) Vandalism of the resources of the Rocky Mountain West. Cultural Resources Report No. 21, USDA, U.S. Forest Service, Southwestern Region, Albuquerque, NM.

Public Law 93–251.

# SIGNING AS A MEANS OF PROTECTING ARCHAEOLOGICAL SITES

John H. Jameson, Jr. and Marc Kodack

## INTRODUCTION

This article discusses the effectiveness of signing as a tool for protecting archaeological sites. The signing data are drawn largely from the results of a nationwide questionnaire that was sponsored by the U.S. Army Corps of Engineers Waterways Experiment Station (WES). For convenience and consistency, we have centered our discussion on the comments and answers from National Park Service (NPS) personnel, who comprised nearly half of the questionnaire respondents and whose responses appear to be representative of the whole. We include a brief description of an available field study: a before-and-after scenario from the Anthony Shoals site in southeastern Georgia.

The posting of formal, written signs has probably been an important form of communication for many thousands of years. Perhaps it is with some degree of irony that modern-day archaeologists and resource managers employ signing as a communication technique in order to protect and preserve the remains of former lifeways, the "signs" of the past.

In the following discussion, we present an assessment of signing as a method or means of protecting archaeological sites from looters and other resource abusers. We draw, to a limited extent, on our own experiences and observations, but have relied heavily on data collected in response to a nationally distributed questionnaire (Kodack 1990a; 1990b; 1990c). We have used these data to draw a number of conclusions about the utility of signing as a site-protection tool. This assessment of signing is by no means an exhaustive or complete analysis and should be considered preliminary.

## PREVIOUS ASSUMPTIONS

Many archaeologists, including the authors, have long held certain assumptions about signing that are common within the field of cultural resource management (General Accounting Office 1987:46–47). These preconceived notions on the value and usefulness of signing were based on limited personal experiences with signs, on conversations and communications with colleagues, and on what were considered to be common sense ideas in the application of various signing strategies and conditions. Briefly stated, these assumptions were that: (1) it is better to have signs than not to have signs, except in remote or less obtrusive areas where signs may draw unwanted attention; (2) signing may help in a majority of cases, but it is more effective when accompanied by monitoring and enforcement activities; and (3) signs, whether placed on a site or on a nearby access road, should contain a warning about what laws will be broken, what specific actions are against the law, and information on possible penalties.

The creators of the U.S. Corps of Engineers Waterways Experimental Station (WES) questionnaire shared these ideas and assumptions, but hoped to establish a more objective basis for evaluating the nature and overall effectiveness of signing within the field of cultural resource management (Paul Nickens, personal communication 1990).

235

# A NATIONWIDE QUESTIONNAIRE

The U.S. Army Corps of Engineers administers many archaeological sites and features that occur near and adjacent to the nation's navigable waterways. The Corps has recognized that, as part of its protection responsibilities, a proactive program of management of these archaeological materials is needed. As part of this program, with the purpose of measuring and analyzing the expressed experiences of the nation's archaeological resource managers, a questionnaire was designed and distributed by WES. The questionnaires were sent out in early 1989 to federal, state, and local agencies throughout the U.S. The authors believe that the Corps' nationwide questionnaire can be thought of as a test of the common assumptions about the "whys," "hows," "whats," and "whens" of signing.

The questions in the nationwide questionnaire were divided into three parts. In part 1 respondents were asked for an opinion on how strongly they agree or disagree with statements on the effectiveness of signs, the location of signs, what the message on a sign should say, and what archaeological materials should be signed. In part 2 other protection strategies supplemental to signing, such as law enforcement and interpretation, were addressed. Part 3 could be used by respondents for additional statements.

As mentioned above, the questions in part 1 asked the respondents for an opinion on how strongly they agreed or disagreed with general statements on the nature and effectiveness of signing. The possible choices for answers included one of the following: "strongly agree, agree, neither agree nor disagree, disagree, and strongly disagree." In this analysis the "strongly agree" and the "agree" answers and the "strongly disagree" and the "disagree" answers have been combined in an attempt to determine how the majority of people are leaning in their answer to a question. By combining these answers, a clearer indication of the general opinion about a question is possible. Because the "neither agree nor disagree" answers represent the absence of any leaning, one way or the other, on a statement, these responses have been eliminated from the analysis.

# AN ANALYSIS OF NATIONAL PARK SERVICE RESPONSES

Nearly half (47.7%) (n = 203) of all the questionnaires that were returned were answered by NPS personnel. Because their responses appear to be representative of the responses as a whole, and for sake of convenience and consistency, we have chosen to focus our discussion on the NPS material.

In the course of tabulating the data in the questionnaire, we noticed that the total number of responses varied for each question. Consequently, the total number of responses for each question is occasionally less than the total number of respondents. In the following discussion, in order to allow the reader to follow this variation and level of participation for each question, we have given the corresponding number (n =) of responses for each question or statement addressed in the questionnaire, when that information was available.

## Overall Effectiveness of Signs

The first section of part 1 of the questionnaire addressed general topics and sought to measure the opinions of respondents on the overall effectiveness of signing at archaeological sites. It contains four basic opinion statements:

- Signs can be used as an effective protective strategy at sites (n = 172). Ninety percent of the respondents to this statement agreed, while 10% disagreed. The overwhelming majority think that signs are, or can be, a successful method in trying to protect the large numbers of archaeological sites and resources.
- Signing contributes to vandalism or casual collecting (n = 150). Of the participating respondents to this statement, 45% agreed and 55% disagreed. The majority opinion was that, although identifying these materials by signing may draw attention to them and have an unintentional negative affect, *overall*, signs are useful in protecting archaeological materials from looting and vandalism, but this is not the normal expectation.
- Signing is more protective if placed off site than on site (n = 129). Forty-four percent agreed, while 56% disagreed; a majority of the respondents believe that signs should be placed directly on site.
- Signing will be most effective if employed with other protective strategies, e.g., interpretive exhibits, visitor center, fence, patrol or control of access (n = 196). With only 1% disagreeing, there is virtually unanimous agreement that the most effective way to use signs is for signing *not* to be the sole protection strategy.

## Sign Messages

The next section of part 1 posed the following question, followed by a list of possible alternatives messages: "Once a decision has been made to sign archaeological materials, what kind of message should be on the sign?"

- Nonspecific, e.g., "Off Limits" or "Do not Disturb" (n = 144): 33% agreed; 67% disagreed.
- Specific, e.g., "Archaeological Site — Do Not Disturb" (n = 151): 66% agreed; 34% disagreed.
- Interpretive, e.g., "This is an important Mississippian mound group..." (n = 167): 87% agreed; 13% disagreed.
- Warning, or threatened sanction, e.g., "Archaeological Site — Protected by Law," and giving penalties (n = 162): 90% agreed; 10% disagreed.
- Bogus, e.g., "poison ivy" or "Hazardous Waste" (n = 160): 23% agreed; 77% disagreed.
- Combination of one of more of the above formats? (n = 159): 94% agreed; 6% disagreed.

"Which combination?" (n = 147).

- Nonspecific/interpretive      1%
- Nonspecific/warning      3%
- Nonspecific/bogus      1%
- Specific/interpretive      14%
- Specific/warning      2%
- Interpretive/warning      41%
- Interpretive/bogus      1%
- Warning/bogus      1%
- Other      36%

Although messages with interpretive or warning language were endorsed, the combination of these two messages is considered most effective. A third message theme, one specifically identifying the archaeological material, could be integrated with, and incorporated into, the interpretive/warning sign. The only message theme that was not strongly endorsed was one presenting false information to the visitor via a bogus message.

In the questionnaire response narratives (part 3), a number of opinions on sign messages were expressed. Many respondents stated that sign messages that refer to the legal penalties for disturbing or destroying archaeological resources need to be updated to reflect the Archaeological Resources Protection Act (ARPA) and *not* the mostly superseded 1906 Antiquities Act. This is important because the ambiguities in the 1906 Act, specifically the reference to "object of antiquity," make successful prosecutions under the act highly unlikely, as has been borne out by court case histories. The lowering from $5000 to $500 in the dollar-value threshold for a felony in the assessment of damages to an archaeological resource should help to discourage looting and vandalism and to increase the number of successful prosecutions. Signs used to mark the boundaries of a NPS park unit (this could be applied to other federally managed lands, as well) should include some warning about the removal or disturbance of both archaeological and natural materials. All signs should be free standing or attached to a modern device such as a fence or railing, if possible. Signs should not be attached to trees, historic buildings, and other landscape features, in order to avoid the paradox of placing signs with a resource protection message in a manner that results in further damages to trees, buildings, or other features.

## Visibility of Archaeological Materials

The next section of the questionnaire addressed the subject of whether sites in remote or inconspicuous areas should be signed.

- Only large or highly obtrusive resource sites which are receiving impacts should be signed (n = 173): 57% agreed; 43% did not agree.
- Generally, unobtrusive sites should not be signed (n = 173): 75% agreed; 25% disagreed.
- Sites located in remote areas with only periodic or little surveillance should not be signed (n = 169): 68% agreed; 32% disagreed.

The respondents felt that the ability of a visitor to see archaeological materials should be considered when signing these resources. Those sites that are highly visible, prehistoric or historic, and have been subject to past looting or vandalism should be prominently signed to prevent further attacks. Those resources that are much less noticeable to the casual observer or are located in areas infrequently visited should not be signed. The reduced visibility and inconspicuous location of these sites has brought a measure of protection that would be diminished by the placing of an identifying sign.

## The Need to Investigate Specific Signing Strategies

The final question in part 1 asked whether controlled case studies are needed:

- Do you think it would be useful to investigate, under controlled conditions at select archaeological sites, specific signing strategies in order to evaluate their relative effectiveness? (n = 197): 95% said "yes," only 5% said "no."

A large majority of these respondents would like to see a field program designed so that their opinions could be verified or negated.

## Experiences with Past Signing Projects

The 12 questions or inquiries in part 2 of the questionnaire asked for descriptions of specific signing projects and opinions on how effective these projects have been. Some questions are similar in format to part 1, and these answers have been summarized by category. For other, more open-ended questions, a greater variety of answers were possible.

- Type of resource signed (n = 99): historic, 54%; prehistoric, 29%; both, 17%. Respondents indicated that both prehistoric and historic resources have been signed, although almost twice as many historic sites have been involved in signing efforts.
- Location and context of signed resource. A combination of off-site and on-site projects are reported, with the majority of signs placed on site. However, because entire Park Service units can be archaeological resources, all signs placed within the boundaries of that unit are, by definition, "on site." When signs are present, they are integrated into park interpretive efforts. Signs are positioned at trailheads and along trails, in developed and backcountry areas, along shorelines, near camp sites, along roads and park boundaries, at looted/vandalized sites, and as a part of wayside exhibits.
- Impacts and reasons for signing. One of the more common visitor impacts described is the climbing or walking on prehistoric or historic structures, which destroy the structures by increasing erosion or disturbing the physical integrity. Hikers and children taking short cuts create unwanted "new" trails across structures and features. Acts of looting/vandalism include graffiti and illegal excavation of artifacts. Signs were erected to prevent these kinds of destructive activities, whether they are intentional or not. While many signs are erected for interpretive purposes, not all signing projects are specifically targeted at archaeological materials.

The respondents further commented that park visitors include local or regional residents who are regular users, persons from elsewhere in the U.S., and foreign nationals on vacation. The number of visitors who annually visit these NPS areas ranges from several thousand to several million. Although the specific objectives of these transient visitors are unknown, most do not intentionally disturb or destroy archaeological sites.

- *Wording of sign message.* The following are examples of messages listed:

  "Protect Your Past, Help Preserve the Past for the Future..."
  "Walking on Mounds Causes Erosion — Please Stay Off — Thank You"
  "NOTICE, Please Help Us Protect America's Resources..." (includes description of legal penalties)
  "Help Protect this Historic Hill, Use Walks"
  "The Past Belongs to the Future, But Only the Present Can Preserve it..."
  "Do Not Approach Rock Art Panel Past This Point"
  "Use of Metal Detectors Prohibited"
  "In Order to Protect the Park's Historic Resources, No Recreational Activities are Permitted on this Site. Sunbathing, Ballplaying, Picnicking, Car Polishing and Other Recreational Activities are Permitted Only in the Recreational Field"

"Caution: Relic Hunting is Against the Law"
"No Hunting or Trapping. Protected Area, All Natural, Historic & Archaeological Features are Protected By Law..."
"Pets not allowed on trails or in ruins"

Respondents reported that many sign messages are interpretive and are specific to the unit in which they are located. Some signs are selected from the "NPS Sign Manual." Both Bureau of Land Management and U.S. Forest Service antiquities signs have been used.

- *Sign location and method of placement.* Respondents stated that signs are located both off site and on site. Signs are either free standing, supported by stakes or posts, or they are attached to a man-made or natural object such as a building, tree, gate, or fence.
- *Was sign used in conjunction with other protective strategies?* (n = 96): 89% answered "yes"; 11% answered "no." *If yes, what were they?* In order of preference, these other strategies were listed: (1) interpretive programs, (2) patrols, (3) physical barriers, and (4) visitor center/museum.
- *Number of signs used per cultural resource.* Most signing efforts have used between one and four signs per site. The most common number of signs used is one per site.
- *Available guidance in planning and implementing the signing effort.* In most cases described, no guidance was available for a signing project. Most local efforts relied on staff experience and common sense. A minority of persons have received guidance from archaeologists, NPS law enforcement personnel, NPS Regional Office personnel, the "NPS Sign Manual," or the NPS Harper's Ferry (Mather) Center.
- *What changes in impacts have you noticed after signing?* (n = 83): large increase, 4%; some increase, 7%; no change, 27%; some decrease, 31%; large decrease, 6%; not determined, 25%. The use of signs does not usually increase on-site looting/vandalism; no change or a decrease in adverse impacts takes place when signs are used. This supports the above responses on the overall effectiveness of signs.
- *Has the sign itself been vandalized?* (n = 89): yes, 62%; no, 38%. *If yes, in what manner?* The respondents stated that little creativity has been shown in persons who damage or destroy signs. Pistol or rifle shots are the most common form of vandalism, with burning, graffiti, breaking, scratching, and stealing occasionally occurring. The most determined method reported was the use of a blow torch to remove a sign.
- *Do you have a scheduled or formalized monitoring strategy for determining and evaluating the success or failure of the signing effort?* (n = 93): yes, 16%; no, 84%. *If yes, briefly describe the strategy.* Respondents stated that most evaluations are conducted while the staff is on patrol. The frequency of patrols varies from daily, to bi-weekly, monthly, or yearly. One respondent reported a program of evaluation that documented the presence and location of artifacts along an historic trail. These artifacts were mapped in place and not removed, while an initial artifact map helped in assessing the state and presence of artifacts over time. This respondent highly recommended the use of similar field experiments for other park units.
- *What kind of documentation is available describing the signing effort?* Very few references were noted by the respondents. The handful that did mention a reference stated that the sign project is included in some type of management plan or sign plan.

To summarize the NPS experience with signing projects, it can be stated that signing must be one part of a preservation and protection program and that signs need to be supplemented by other kinds of strategies, such as law enforcement, interpretation programs, visitor center and/or museums, and physical barriers.

**Other General Comments**

As stated above, part 3 of the questionnaire could be used by respondents for general comments. One theme that occurs repeatedly throughout these comments is the strong feeling that archaeological materials that currently are unsigned and are not being adversely impacted should remain unsigned. If signed, unwanted attention might be directed towards these resources. The total number of signs that are used should be balanced between their purpose, or "mission," and the visual impact to the surroundings where these signs will be placed. Too many signs would be an intrusion on the natural, prehistoric, or historic setting.

The use of signs is generally supported and is felt to work well with larger, more visible kinds of archaeological materials. Additional protection measures, such as law enforcement and regular monitoring, should also be used in conjunction with signing.

One commentator presented a good summary of the issues to be considered when designing signing projects: "Signing of cultural resources can be an effective deterrent to negative human impacts. There can be no absolute rule by which managers may sign or not sign a particular resource. The management variables which the manager must consider include:

1. The significance of the resource (which may change with area management or national policy, availability of scientific data, the needs of the scientific community, etc.)
2. Agency policy and guidelines
3. Area development and management needs
4. A history of vandalism, pothunting, and souvenir or relic hunting
5. Kinds of problems that the signs are to solve (legal warning, public interpretation, public education, etc.)
6. Level of or immediacy of threat to the resource
7. Remoteness/accessibility of the site either to looters, vandals, or law enforcement patrols

One question that should always be asked is, 'Will signing the resource increase the threat of damage?' Once that question is answered, it is only necessary to determine the management approach to the resource, kind of verbiage, appropriate placement of the sign, etc."

## SIGNING EXPERIENCES OUTSIDE THE NATIONAL PARK SERVICE

In general, the non-NPS respondents, including State Historic Preservation Offices (n = 34) and various other federal, state, and local agencies, mirrored the opinions expressed by the NPS respondents: signing coupled with other methods can be an effective way to monitor and deter looting/vandalism against archaeological resources. Sites that are highly visible are probably the best candidates for signing, as the signs may help to discourage vandalism and looting. Signing sites that are not threatened by looting/vandalism should be avoided to prevent the signs from acting as a beacon, drawing unwanted curiosity to the site. Public education on archaeology and why it is important to protect archaeological resources is pointed out as the only real solution to looting/vandalism. Some distinctive aspects of the non-NPS responses are summarized below.

- U.S. Bureau of Land Management (BLM) (n = 58). When compared with the NPS responses, BLM officials place more emphasis on law enforcement efforts, which may be a reflection or result of the BLM multiple land use mission; archaeological resource preservation or protection must be balanced against other "competing" resources, such as minerals exploration, forest management, and cattle grazing. A point that is stressed in the BLM responses is that it is important to install identifying signs for federal lands and their accompanying archaeological sites for successful prosecution under ARPA and other statutes.

- U.S. Army Corps of Engineers (Corps) (n = 45). The Corps answers parallel the NPS answers more closely than BLM. Concern for law enforcement is common, but a concern for interpretation is also present. Signs with both warning and interpretive messages have a better chance of deterring looting/vandalism or unwanted behavior than signs that possess only a warning message.

- U.S. Forest Service (FS) (n = 57). The FS answers emphasize law enforcement somewhat more than the NPS, but not as much as BLM. Sign messages should be both interpretive and warning.

## SIGNING AT THE ANTHONY SHOALS SITE

The results of the WES questionnaire indicate that signs are an essential element in any strategy to protect archaeological sites. However, no objective field studies have been available that can confirm this observation. In an attempt to measure the effects of signing at a previously unsigned site, observations were made over a 2-year period at the Anthony Shoals Site (9 Ws 51), located in southeastern Georgia. The site, which has suffered from severe looting for a number of years, is comanaged within the Broad River Wildlife Management Area by the U.S. Army Corps of Engineers and the lessee, the Georgia Department of Natural Resources, Game and Fish Division (DNR) (Jameson 1990).

At Anthony Shoals, despite specific lease stipulations for resource protection, the Corps (and not DNR) has assumed the active management responsibilities for protecting it from rampant looting/vandalism. The site, approximately 4 hectares (10 acres) in size, is composed of a relatively large, multicomponent prehistoric occupation that is located on the flood plain of the Broad River. It is easily accessed by a county-maintained dirt road and by water on the south bank of the adjacent river. Exposed and easily spotted artifacts and features are numerous. The site was initially inspected by Corps archaeologist John Jameson in May 1987, who reported several freshly dug pot holes. Following a Corps-sponsored program of archaeological testing in 1987, an archaeological contractor recommended a three-pronged approach to the long-range management here: stepped up site monitoring, data recovery in a small portion of the site that is exposed on the surface, and restoration of looted areas to their original contours (Wood and Smith 1988). With no funding, as yet, allocated to carry out these recommendations, efforts by the Corps to curb the rate of looting/vandalism have been limited to using posts as roadblocks placed on site along the unpaved access road, slightly increased monitoring of the site by Corps rangers, and signing.

Because the area remains accessible by both land and water, these efforts have had marginal success. Revisits to the site by the senior author (Jameson) in March 1989, shortly after the signs had been installed, and again with Marc Kodack in May 1990, show that significant looting is still occurring, but at a reduced rate. The March 1989 visit uncovered evidence of some minor surface scratching, indicating that, at least at that time, the *rate* of destruction at the site had abated. However, the May 1990 visit recorded renewed looting/vandalism in the form of several freshly dug pot holes and a large backhoe-excavated area within the access road. One of the two on-site posted metal signs, which had been installed at eye level on wooden posts approximately 500 feet apart and adjacent to the intrusive access road, had been removed. At two points along the access road, the posts had been pulled out of the ground. Notwithstanding the more recent observations of damage, the present rate of destruction still appears to be less than in 1988 and earlier.

It is difficult to assess at this time whether the signs *alone* have contributed as a deterrent to looting. However, due to the very minimal monitoring that has been conducted (less than one visit per month) and the failure of the installed road barriers, signing has probably played the most significant role. Nevertheless, for the signing effort to be more than marginally effective, it must be accompanied in the future by more intensive monitoring and law enforcement efforts.

## THE IMPORTANCE OF SIGNING FOR LAW ENFORCEMENT

The criminal prosecution of the looters at Anthony Shoals and other sites located on federally controlled properties may well hinge on the presence or absence of warning signs. Recent court cases have demonstrated that the presence of warning signs is a key element in almost all successful prosecutions under ARPA. Although the Archaeological Resources Protection Act (ARPA) is a general intent law (meaning that a person cannot plead ignorance of the law as an excuse for not abiding by the law), some defense attorneys attempt to convince federal judges that ARPA is a specific intent law, where ignorance of the law can constitute a successful defense. The issue is further confused by misinformed or inexperienced judges. In a recent court case in Utah, for example, a judge incorrectly instructed a jury that ARPA is a specific intent law, thus possibly jeopardizing the outcome of future court cases in that state (Martin McAllister, personal communication 1990).

Understanding the importance of on-site or near-site signing, most prosecuting attorneys, before taking or pursuing an ARPA case, invariably ask if the resource in question was signed; the specific vs. general intent argument becomes moot when the site is signed. Other protection statutes, such as 18 U.S.C. 641 (theft of government property) and 18 U.S.C 1361 (destruction of government property), which have been used in the prosecution of looters, are also much easier to enforce when the site is signed (McAllister, personal communication 1990; General Accounting Office 1987:53).

In some cases, warning signs posted off site on access roads, trails, and other conspicuous places have assisted law enforcement. At Big South Fork National River and Recreation Area, for instance, an ARPA warning sign was undoubtedly the key to the successful prosecution of the looters. Visitor information centers, campground bulletin boards, and other public notice areas are good locations for signs that convey the ARPA warning message. In addition to signs, public-use brochures, exhibits, tour guides, interpretive talks, and even hunting licenses are all good media for the posting of warning messages (McAllister, personal communication 1990).

Signs are most effective for law enforcement when they contain the following combination of messages: a cultural history or interpretative message describing the importance of the archaeological resource and why the resource is fragile and irreplaceable, plus information on possible fines and imprisonment, and ending with an "up" note to "enjoy but do not destroy your cultural heritage." For purposes of law enforcement, people react more positively when there is an interpretive message, importance message or restoration message. This will have a positive effect on all but commercial looters, who are not interested in archaeological protection. In some instances, commercial looters have been known to actually steal and use signs to promote the risk factor, thus enabling them to demand a higher price for the looted relics. However, most artifact and relic hunters *do* care and will react positively when the right message is given (McAllister, personal communication 1990).

# THE NEED FOR CONTROLLED CASE STUDIES

A major finding of the WES questionnaire was the strongly expressed need for case studies on a wide variety of signing conditions and scenarios. The use of signs to protect archaeological resources is apparently open to question because of the lack of controlled field studies. A program of field experiments to gather data on signing is essential to moving away from qualitative impressions.

# A PROPOSED FIELD EXPERIMENT DESIGN

Kodack (1990c) has outlined a proposed experimental design for a field experiment on signing at archaeological sites. He proposes that a controlled field experiment be composed of four basic elements: (1) site creation and field setup, (2) development and use of pseudosite variables, (3) a monitoring program, and (4) development and distribution of a field questionnaire.

## Site creation and field setup

As a case example, Kodack suggests that a flintknapper manufacture artifacts and flakes for the creation of a "lithic scatter" site. Restricting the materials to stone would eliminate the longer periods of time needed to manufacture other artifacts, such as pottery or textiles. Once the artifacts and flakes have been manufactured, they can be quickly positioned in the field.

Each artifact would then be photographed and drawn prior to placing it in the field, to provide a record of the artifact. The location for this "pseudosite" would be checked to insure that the area does not contain real archaeological materials. Once all the artifacts are in position, a permanent site benchmark would need to be created and installed. This benchmark would serve as the reference point for mapping the artifacts.

## Development of pseudosite variables

Important variables that could directly influence the success of the experiment are the visibility and density of the stone materials. "Visibility" is defined as a measure of how easily the surface materials can be seen by someone passing (walking) by. Visibility is affected by the kind of material the stone artifacts are manufactured from, the density of the surrounding vegetation, and the nature of shadows (time of day). The lithic raw material chosen for manufacturing the artifacts should be of a type that occurs naturally and is commonly found on real sites in the area, so the material itself will not draw attention to the pseudosite. Since the density of the stone materials will also affect their visibility, Kodack would use three different density scenarios to determine what effect density has on visibility.

The physical placement of the pseudosite with respect to visitor traffic is another potential variable that would be a major factor in the "discovery" of the site. For purposes of comparison, sites could be placed in high visitor-use areas (100 or more people per day), medium-use areas (50 to 100 people per day), and low-use areas (1 to 50 people per day). In addition, a pseudosite might be placed in a remote location, off vehicular and pedestrian trails, to test the effects that infrequent or negligible visitor use would have on the archaeological materials.

Sign placement should be tried both on site and off site. Off-site placement of signs should be at least 30 m away from the site. Different sign messages and combinations of messages should be tried both off site and on site. These messages could be rotated from one pseudosite to another through time. Kodack suggests keeping constant the sign size, material, and height above the ground, so the effect of the message will not be influenced by these variables. All signs should be free standing to allow for maximum flexibility in their field placement.

## Monitoring the program

The monitoring frequency (daily, weekly, biweekly, or monthly) is the most critical part of the experiment. Insuring that the observations provided by the monitoring are accurate is the most difficult aspect of this experiment. Kodack suggests that at least a biweekly frequency be tried at the start of the experiment, to be decreased to a monthly rate if impacts are not visible, or increased to a weekly rate if too many impacts are occurring. Monitoring should consist of an overall assessment of the conditions of both the sign *and* the pseudosite.

Photographs of the sign and site should be taken, with verbal descriptions of any impacts. Remeasurement of the artifacts on the surface would be necessary to provide an interim catalog of what artifacts are present vs. those that are missing. Caution should be applied to insure that any "missing" artifacts have not been inadvertently buried by humans (as a result of human foot traffic), animals, or natural processes, such as wind and erosion.

The true measure of the effectiveness of a sign at the end of the experiment will be the observation of the number of artifacts still present (provided they are not buried or have not been so widely dispersed as to be unrecoverable). To determine this, a systematic examination of the surface should be carried out. The recorded observations for the current state of the materials can then be compared to the position of the artifacts on the original site map. Some minor excavation of the original area where the artifacts were placed may have to be done to determine if any of these artifacts have been buried. If all the artifacts are present and are not widely dispersed due to unintentional human foot traffic, the selected sign and/or sign message used will be considered effective.

## Distribution of a field questionnaire

The field experiment should be coupled with a questionnaire targeted to local residents and transient visitors. To insure the integrity of the field experiments (visitors' and local residents' behavior towards signs might be affected by their participation in a sign questionnaire), the collection of the questionnaire information should be performed in a separate location. For example, if the field experiment was set up in Zion National Park, the collection of the questionnaire data might be conducted in Grand Teton National Park.

Modifications to the suggested field experiment would be needed for areas with other kinds of materials and structures. Although the field testing of signs targeted at protecting archaeological resources is possible, these tests must be regularly monitored if the effectiveness of the signs is to be assessed.

# CONCLUSION

From the foregoing discussion on archaeological signing, we can conclude the following:

1.  Signs are usually an effective means of protecting archaeological sites, especially when the sites are larger and more conspicuous. Signs can be one part of a plan that seeks to manage archaeological resources for the benefit of public visitors and simultaneously provide protection of these resources. Those sites that are currently undergoing impacts from looters and vandals and are readily visible might be the starting point for any new signing programs.
2.  All signs should be used in conjunction, or in combination, with other forms of protection, such as law (ARPA) enforcement and routine monitoring.
3.  Sign messages should present the visitor or public land user with information that interprets the archaeological material, but also describes the legal protections that have been enacted and the associated penalties that can potentially be levied on violators.
4.  There is a pressing need for controlled case studies in future assessments of the effectiveness of signing. Objectively designed field experiments, such as outlined in this article, are needed.
5.  There is a current lack of government-wide or agency policy that addresses the specific issues in the signing of archaeological sites. As was pointed out by the NPS respondents, the current "NPS Sign Manual" is inadequate because it does not provide any justification or discussion of why and how we should be signing archaeological materials; no official guidance was available to any of the questionnaire respondents.

# ACKNOWLEDGMENTS

The authors wish to thank Paul Nickens of WES, the principal questionnaire developer, for allowing us to use the WES questionnaire data.

# REFERENCES CITED

General Accounting Office (1987) Cultural Resources: Problems Protecting and Preserving Federal Archaeological Resources, United States General Accounting Office Report to Congressional Investigators, GAO/RCED-88-3, Gaithersburg, MD.

Jameson J. H., Jr. (1990) Co-management of vandalized sites; opportunities and problems. In Coping with Site Looting: Essays in Archaeological Resource Management, Ehrenhard, J. E., Ed., Interagency Archaeological Services Division, Southeast Regional Office, National Park Service, Atlanta.

Kodack, M. (1990a) A summary of the National Park Service responses to a questionnaire on the signing of archaeological sites. Unpublished manuscript submitted to the Waterways Experiment Station, U.S. Army Corps of Engineers, Vicksburg, MS. Copy on file at Interagency Archaeological Services Division, Southeast Regional Office, National Park Service, Atlanta.

Kodack, M. (1990b) Comments on part 3 of the Sign Questionnaire answered by non park service respondents. Unpublished manuscript submitted to the Waterways Experiment Station, U.S. Army Corps of Engineers, Vicksburg, MS. Copy on file at the Interagency Archaeological Services Division, Southeast Regional Office, National Park Service, Atlanta.

Kodack, M. (1990c) An outline for a field experiment to test the effectiveness of signing of archaeological sites. Unpublished manuscript submitted to the Waterways Experiment Station, U.S. Army Corps of Engineers, Vicksburg, MS. Copy on file at the Interagency Archaeological Services Division, Southeast Regional Office, National Park Service, Atlanta.

Wood, W. D. and Smith, C. A. (1988) Archaeological evaluation of the Anthony Shoals Site, 9Ws51. Southeastern Archaeological Services, Inc., Athens. Copy on file at the Environmental Resources Branch, U.S. Army Corps of Engineers, Savannah District Office, Savannah, GA.

# PROTECTING SITES AT THE LOCAL LEVEL: THE RESPONSIBILITY AND THE LEGAL AUTHORITY TOWNS HAVE TO PROTECT THEIR ARCHAEOLOGICAL RESOURCES

## Betsy Kearns and Cece Kirkorian

## INTRODUCTION

Most archaeological sites lie undiscovered and unrecorded, thus both unappreciated and unprotected by the community whose cultural heritage they represent. They are especially vulnerable to the ravages of neglect and development activity. Communities can prevent the loss of their archaeological heritage by acknowledging and acting upon their responsibility to protect it. Indeed, many communities across the U.S. have implemented ordinances, regulations, and permit systems that act as an "archaeology alarm system" so that potentially valuable sites can be properly examined and professional archaeological management plans can be made as part of local decision-making processes.

By 1985 two town governments (Greenwich and Westport) in the state of Connecticut, in a pioneering attempt to preserve their archaeological resources, had instituted consideration of historical and archaeological factors as a function of their planning and zoning permit application processes. Both communities experienced frustration and difficulty in assembling data on local protection alternatives for cultural resources, and in interpreting Connecticut's enabling statutes, as they researched and drafted their archaeological preservation regulations. In order to encourage other towns to take similar, legally defensible action and to provide the technical guidance heretofore unavailable to town governments, the Connecticut Historical Commission/State Historic Preservation Office (SHPO) published, with the assistance of the Department of the Interior, National Park Service, our guide, the *Archaeological Resource Protection Handbook* (Kearns and Kirkorian 1987). Intended for statewide distribution to town planning boards, the *Handbook* presents various methods for local preservation action and examples of how communities throughout the country have successfully implemented preservation goals. Since 1987, 14 more Connecticut towns have instituted archaeological protection measures, and at least seven more communities are in the process of adopting such measures. The *Handbook,* in part through the distribution efforts of the state archaeologist, has been a catalytic force for these actions. The following discussion is based on the book, which was distributed to all of the nation's SHPO offices. Contact your state office in this regard.

## PROTECTION METHODS AVAILABLE TO MUNICIPALITIES

### Fee Simple Absolute

The municipal ownership of a site, with conservation control deeded in perpetuity, is called "fee simple absolute" and is the only way to ensure permanent protection. All others must be considered temporary measures, since they are dependent upon and subject to diverse and competing agendas. If a town decides to purchase land with archaeological resources, there often are ways to obtain at least partial funding, such as matching-grant sources at the state level. The drawbacks to this method are that state or local funds may be insufficient to purchase more than one archaeological site in a town. Second, not all archaeological sites warrant the cost of purchase; and third, there are only a limited number of sites readily available for outright acquisition at any given time.

## Conservation Easement

An easement is defined as an interest or right in property that is less than the full, or fee simple, interest. A property owner may be willing to donate land containing archaeological resources because of altruistic motives or because of the tax benefits of a charitable contribution. An easement is conveyed by a legal document and is written in deed form and filed with the official recorder of deeds. For tax purposes, conservation easements are typically assessed as the difference between the fair market value of the property before and after the grant of the easement. Acceptance of easements that guarantee the nondevelopment of parcels of land is consistent with many local "master plan" objectives.

The benefits of a conservation easement vs. "fee simple absolute" acquisition include reduced town maintenance responsibility and liability for the land. Conservation easements involve the ownership of only those rights necessary to protect specific resources, and the uses of the site that do not conflict with the easement remain vested in the landowner. In the drafting of an easement contract, it is vitally important that the guidance of both an attorney and a professional archaeologist be sought; each easement transaction will involve unique conditions specific to the resource and the property in question.

Once a town decides to actively encourage private preservation action, it should initiate a publicity campaign to increase the awareness of conservation easement donations, including legal and tax benefit information, and to apprise local law and real estate associations of the easement option. Various public conservation-minded organizations active in the community (e.g., the Trust for Public Lands and the Nature Conservancy, Inc.) may be eager to develop coordinated plans for easement donations and management control.

## Zoning Regulation

Subdivision regulations often stipulate that development on parcels beyond a certain size include an "open space set aside." The mandatory dedication of "open space" lands through subdivision review provides local officials with an opportunity to preserve archaeological resources. Without placing undue hardship on a developer, a town can work with the property owner to overlay the percentage of the development parcel that must become parkland, with areas that are archaeologically sensitive. Passive recreational activities, e.g., nature and exercise trails, can be planned for this open space.

Cluster zoning, where the area of individual lots is reduced while the total number of dwelling units for the project remains the same, is gaining popularity in some areas. The land not used for house lots and driveways in cluster zoning is used for recreational purposes or kept as common open space. If such zoning is allowed, the local community and a responsible developer could take advantage of it to include any known or predicted areas of historic and prehistoric resources in the undisturbed common land, while directing construction activity to less sensitive portions of the development parcel.

# LOCAL PRESERVATION ORDINANCE IS THE MOST EFFECTIVE

## How to Draft a Preservation Ordinance

In order to protect archaeological resources, a town or county government may develop an explicit mechanism within the framework of their established planning and zoning regulations, which will guarantee consideration of archaeological factors. The most comprehensive and successful method of protection is an ordinance that mandates the preconstruction identification and consideration of design alternatives with regard to archaeological resources. A town can request a developer/property owner to supply a professional assessment of a parcel's archaeological sensitivity at the time other reports (e.g., wetlands analysis or traffic studies) are required. Consideration of archaeological resources should be integrated into local project review procedures so as not to burden the private developer with an overextended review period.

When designing an ordinance that considers archaeological resources, as in creating any law, special care must be taken to ensure that it incorporates the full intent of the concern, does not conflict with laws already in place, and provides a reasonable and manageable working process for the people and actions it directs. Of concern to town counsels is the possibility that a local regulation may be challenged in court, with resulting time and monies required for defense. Federal and state courts have uniformly upheld state and local land-use programs as legitimate attempts to control environmental and growth-related problems. Many states have granted towns or similar local governmental entities the authority to legislate protection of historic resources; and in turn, state and federal courts have upheld a wide variety of environmental and historic preservation-related public objectives and regulatory approaches, so long as they are fair and equitable.

Regardless of the source of an ordinance, whether the result of a voter-referendum action or not, the outcome of cases taken to court is usually based on the integrity and preciseness of the local law and its manner of enforcement. The jurisdiction of any local administrative authority must be understood; town actions to regulate federal and state-owned/administered land uses may often be preempted. Of primary concern is local alignment with state enabling statutes. To eliminate the potential for litigation on conflicting provisions, the language of the proposed law should precisely reflect the powers bestowed on local governments. A clearly worded "grand-father" clause can minimize the threat of litigation. Avoiding the potential for litigation altogether is not realistic, but when it does occur, the courts will often place the burden of proving compliance with the statute on the applicant rather than the regulatory body.

Court reversal of locally established ordinances is often based on the grounds of (1) denial of equal protection, (2) denial of due process, or (3) uncompensated taking. To ensure the acceptance of an archaeological protection ordinance and to minimize the potential for an adverse court decision, a regulatory body should take the following three specific precautions: (1) everyone with a legitimate interest in the outcome of a permit decision should be afforded an opportunity to participate in the review process, (2) the administering body should develop "substantial evidence" on the record of its proceedings, and (3) the regulatory body should explicitly follow its own regulations in every detail.

## How to Implement a Preservation Ordinance

Integrating the consideration of archaeological resources into the local review process should entail a well-designed program for the review of archaeological reports, for the determination of the relative significance of archaeological sites, and for the enforcement of preservation guidelines. A town ordinance that mandates that preconstruction identification and consideration of design alternatives regarding archaeological resources be undertaken on private land (as well as town land) may require either the creation of or the designation of an appropriate town agency/staff to coordinate implementation of the ordinance. Ideally, the coordinator should be an archaeologist on the municipal payroll. Many cities, such as Philadelphia, New York, Alexandria, Baltimore, Boston, and Wilmington, have established the position of city archaeologist. In other cities (e.g., Tucson), an "on call" contract with an archaeologist assures the town of a professional consultant on an as-needed basis.

Alternatively, there exist several creative strategies for obtaining technical archaeological assistance. The state archaeologist and the state historic preservation officer (SHPO) (this is a combined office in some states) should be tapped for as much guidance as possible. Federal agencies that might encourage involvement with the public/neighboring communities and their staff archaeologists might be able to assist local municipalities. A local government could divide the review and enforcement responsibilities between an individual who manages the daily office procedures and a part-time professional archaeologist who provides technical archaeological review. If qualified, a regular town planning and zoning, or conservation, commission staff member could be assigned the ordinance-related duties. Alternatively, an established historic district commission has state-empowered general advisory authority and might assume the coordinator role for the town. Several smaller communities could jointly employ a professional archaeologist, perhaps on a part-time basis. A nearby university or college could be a source for professional assistance on a limited budget. But unless a rigorous review process is instituted and upheld, the purpose of an archaeological preservation ordinance will not be attained.

## How to Ensure Quality Archaeological Assessments

Specific guidelines for the level of documentary research and field investigation necessary to satisfy the town review board should be established and distributed to all interested parties (developers, contract archaeologists, review board). A concerted effort should be made to place an archaeologist or other well-qualified personnel on the town planning and zoning commission, since judging archaeological survey data may be one of the most difficult tasks of the local review board. Guidance may be requested from other agencies, such as the SHPO, the state or county archaeologist (e.g., in Pima County, AZ), or an appropriate archaeological organization (e.g., the New York Archaeological Council and the Arkansas Archaeological Survey). Professional archaeologists at nearby museums/colleges/universities may act as consultants to local governmental boards. Some states (e.g., Minnesota) have historical societies with established archaeological programs, which might provide review assistance.

Archaeological work mandated on the local level can also contribute importantly to regional and state resource management. State historic preservation plans must consider *all* significant cultural resources. The SHPO needs to be kept abreast of local archaeological surveys so that its planning decisions can accurately reflect the current inventory of the state's resources. The local ordinance should require that copies of archaeological reports be forwarded to the appropriate SHPO and office of the state archaeologist.

Obviously there is the probability that a locally required archaeological survey will discover prehistoric or historic artifacts. A local museum or historical society is often not the proper repository for an archaeological collection, since curatorial demands, storage requirements, and research activities can become too burdensome for a small organization. Town officials should actively encourage the donation of recovered materials to a state-designated repository.

## OTHER ARCHAEOLOGICAL PROTECTION STRATEGIES

The time required to draft and enact an archaeological ordinance can be lengthy, and it may meet with resistance from the local development community. Negative perceptions can be reduced if local citizens are exposed to municipal review and approval as a normal process. An initial public relations endeavor could be the proposed integration of archaeological considerations into an established architectural or historical design review committee. Certain municipalities (e.g., Wichita Falls, TX) with extensive historic districts have included archaeological protection as one of the considerations of impact during the district review process. The Certified Local Government program, in place throughout the country and administered by the SHPOs, also provides a mechanism for archaeological consideration.

If a town or county government wishes to institute measures to protect archaeological resources prior to, or instead of, an ordinance, there are several possibilities. For example, earth mining can cause major disturbance to subsurface resources. A model "Earth Removal Bylaw," formulated by the Massachusetts Southeastern Regional Planning District (Taunton, MA), includes a "Provision for the Safeguarding of Historic and Archaeological Resources." The California Environmental Quality Act enables local governments to regulate private land through discretionary permits. Larkspur, CA took advantage of this act and passed a law (1977) prohibiting the excavation or disturbance of any archaeological site, without an investigation permit.

Another approach is relevant to those states having coastlines. Under federal and state coastal zone management (CZM) policies, local planning and zoning agencies may have the authority to enact a plan review process when alteration/development is proposed for parcels in the coastal zone. Archaeological resource protection should become an integral factor in local CZM decision making.

Some states, such as Florida, have enacted protective legislation for archaeological resources on locally designated landmark properties. In Dade County, FL, a nine-member preservation board is responsible for designating sites, districts, and archaeological zones, that are significant in the county's history. Any proposed alteration to such a designated property cannot proceed without a permission certificate issued by the board (Dade County Ordinance No. 81-13).

## MEASURES FOR A RESOURCE-THREATENING EMERGENCY

When a town has not incorporated protective regulations into the planning and zoning review process, it has limited options if its cultural resources are threatened. Even if a town desires to establish an archaeological protection regulation, the required public hearing and approval process for such a regulation may take a considerable amount of time. Established archaeological programs in both Boston and Charleston took 2 years to implement. During such a lengthy process, the threatened archaeological resources must be evaluated and protected on an emergency basis.

If a planning and zoning review board is confronted with the undeniable need for archaeological protection and it has not yet instituted preservation regulations, it can still often require an archaeological assessment of the threatened parcel, through the mechanism of "other documents." In standard review regulations is the category of "other documents," which can be requested of the applicant whenever such data is deemed necessary for an informed judgement.

## CONCLUSION

Towns and cities have a responsibility to their cultural resources heritage. Historical and archaeological sites, often threatened by development proposals, are integral to the "public good." Accepting this responsibility and acting on the legal authority granted by the state legislature, municipalities can control the destruction of local archaeological sites through a variety of measures.

## REFERENCES CITED

Dade County, FL, Ordinance No. 81-13.
Greenwich, CT. Pursuant to Section 6-266(a)(19) of the Greenwich subdivision regions, Guidelines for Archaeological Impact Statement Submission. Conservation Commission, Greenwich, CT.
**Kearns, B. and Kirkorian, C.** (1987) *Archaeological Resource Protection Handbook*, Connecticut Historical Commission/State Historic Preservation Office, Hartford.
Larkspur, CA. Larkspur Municipal Code 15.42, Ordinance 571-1977, Archaeological Investigation Permit.
Massachusetts Southeastern Regional Planning District (MARPD) Earth Removal Bylaw, Tauton, MA.

# STEWARDS OF THE PAST: PRESERVING ARIZONA'S ARCHAEOLOGICAL RESOURCES THROUGH POSITIVE PUBLIC INVOLVEMENT

Teresa L. Hoffman

## INTRODUCTION

In the face of increasing pressures upon the global environment, it comes as no surprise that the archaeological remains of our cultural heritage are at greater risk. This is particularly true in the U.S. where the tangible evidence of our nation's collective ancestry is not always afforded protection on private land as it is in other nations, and where sites on public land are increasingly vulnerable to impacts from the growing numbers of citizens seeking recreation in the great outdoors. How we choose to respond to these changing conditions, and to influence the manner in which people relate to the prehistory and history of our nation, will have a major impact on the future survival of those resources.

Recognizing that people generally do not respond favorably to negative messages couched in legal terms, Arizona archaeologists have taken a positive approach to the issue of site looting and vandalism. Encounters with archaeological sites are seen as opportunities for offering information and positive messages about the value of these resources. There is also a growing ethic that it is a duty to provide access to these resources, rather than taking steps to keep the public away. This is particularly evident for the Federal Government, as reflected in the 1988 amendments to the Archaeological Resources Protection Act (P.L. 96-95), which call for each federal land manager to "...establish a program to increase public awareness of the significance of the archaeological resources located on public lands and Indian lands and the need to protect such resources." Also, it is clear that resource avoidance is not always possible or desirable. In some cases, increasing site access provides a measure of protection by enhancing visibility and providing a sense of "presence," although the degree of access must be considered. In northern Arizona, the Coconino National Forest has had success in curbing looting and vandalism, by placing interpretive signs and guest registers at several sites experiencing increasing pressures (Pilles 1989). The interpretive sign provides information on the site and requests cooperation in its preservation. The guest register also provides some interpretive material and indicates that the "patrolling ranger" can be contacted for more information. Although there may actually be no regular patrol by a ranger, the implied presence of a site monitor has a beneficial effect.

## ARIZONA'S SITE STEWARD PROGRAM

The Arizona Site Steward Program, an organization of volunteers, developed as a statewide, cooperative response to curb site destruction, gather information, and provide positive opportunities for public involvement. These objectives are met by placing Stewards in the field at specially selected resources. The public land managers of Arizona and a Native American tribal government sponsor the Steward Program. Stewards are selected, trained and certified by the State Historic Preservation Officer (SHPO) and the Archaeology Advisory Commission and, in general, most Stewards are not professional archaeologists. They are interested and concerned citizens who share an appreciation and respect for our rich cultural heritage and choose this avenue to contribute to its preservation. It is no coincidence that many Stewards are members of the two avocational archaeology organizations in the state, the Arizona Archaeological

Society (AAS) and the Arizona Archaeological and Historical Society (AAHS). The following "Statement of Purpose" outlines the basic program tenets from the *Arizona Site Steward Program Handbook for Volunteers* (Bashaw 1990:1).

## Statement of Purpose

In recognition of the fact that prehistoric and historic archaeological materials are irreplaceable national cultural resources, the Arizona Site Steward Program works toward the following goals:

1.   To preserve in perpetuity major prehistoric and historic archaeological resources for the purposes of conservation, scientific study, and interpretation
2.   To increase public awareness of the significance and value of cultural resources and the damage done by artifact hunters
3.   To discourage site looting and vandalism and the sale and trade of antiquities
4.   To support the adoption and enforcement of national, state, and local preservation laws and regulations
5.   To support and encourage high standards of cultural resource investigation throughout the state
6.   To promote better understanding and cooperation among agencies, organizations, and individuals concerned about the preservation of cultural resources
7.   To enhance the completeness of the statewide archaeological inventory

The current focus of the program is primarily on items 1–3 and 6, at this relatively early stage of operation.

## Program Development

The Site Steward Program is strongly rooted in the history of the growth of public archaeology in Arizona, and tied to the Arizona Archaeology Advisory Commission. A brief synopsis of this history is provided here, while a detailed explanation can be found elsewhere (Hoffman 1988; Hoffman and Lerner 1986, 1988, 1989; Rogge 1989; also see Lerner, Rogge, this volume). The Commission was created in 1985 by the Arizona Legislature to act as an advisory body to the SHPO. Early in its development, the Commission adopted the position that deterring looting and vandalism through informational and educational activities should be a high priority, and many proposals for programs that would accomplish these goals were considered. However, the most fruitful approach appeared to be a statewide program of volunteer Site Stewards who would monitor the condition of archaeological sites. There had been increasing interest in establishing a volunteer program of this type. In 1982 two short-lived efforts involving avocational archaeologists from the AAS and the AAHS were tried in southern Arizona for specific sites on state land. In addition, the U.S. Forest Service and the Bureau of Land Management have used volunteers to patrol sites on their lands. However, until the recent efforts of the Commission, no attempt had been made to coordinate such activities or to determine needs and priorities for site patrols on a statewide basis.

At the Commission's first meeting on December 6, 1985, then-Governor Bruce Babbitt indicated his interest in the Texas Archaeological Stewardship Network and suggested that the Commission investigate the feasibility of a similar program to protect Arizona's resources. The

Commission made the Steward Program a top priority and formed the Law Enforcement Committee to pursue this.

At its first meeting on January 25, 1986, the Law Enforcement Committee began its efforts and soon discovered that volunteer initiatives to identify and protect cultural resources were rare. Only six formal programs could be identified. In 1972 British Columbia had formed a similar program, and Saskatchewan, Ontario, Australia, and South Carolina had apparently attempted such programs, as well as Texas. Currently, active programs are in place only in British Columbia, Australia, and Texas. The state of Texas and the province of British Columbia were approached to obtain information on their programs. During the spring of 1986, the committee prepared a proposal to develop a Steward program in Arizona. The Commission formally approved this proposal on June 5, and press releases immediately were distributed statewide to recruit volunteers. By August 7, a statewide coordinator and 13 region coordinators had been selected from 22 applicants, and on October 1, a general meeting of the Stewards and Commission was held to organize the program.

Throughout the next year and a half, a draft handbook and initial training program were developed, and the program was given a trial test on the Coconino and Tonto National Forests. Issues of liability and insurance were resolved through federal and state volunteer agreements (Pilles 1989:42). In addition, an intergovernmental agreement (IGA) defining and formally creating the program was developed and signed by the SHPO, Arizona State Parks; the Bureau of Land Management; the State Land Department; the USDA Forest Service, Southwestern Region; and the Hopi Tribe. The IGA served to define the purpose and organization of the program, and assigned responsibilities for program administration, operation, and support to each of the participating parties. The final IGA was filed in March 1988 with the Arizona Secretary of State, and by midyear the program was functioning on a statewide basis.

## Program Organization

As a result of signing the IGA, the program was formalized and the stage was set for defining the roles of everyone involved. As currently organized, the main players in the Site Steward Program are (1) the signators of the IGA, (2) the Archaeology Advisory Commission and the Site Steward Committee, (3) the statewide coordinator, (4) the region coordinators, and (5) the Site Stewards. The role of each of these and how they integrate is discussed below. The SHPO provides administrative support for the program from its offices, including a computerized system to track progress in terms of personnel training, volunteer hours, and site monitoring results.

### Role of the SHPO

With oversight responsibility for the entire program, the SHPO selects and trains volunteer coordinators, formulates procedures for administration and training, creates and oversees the conduct of a training program, and oversees public information statewide. In addition, the SHPO reports annually on the activities and accomplishments of the Site Steward Program to the participating parties and the public. The majority of these activities are done in coordination with the statewide coordinator who works out of the SHPO offices.

### Role of Land Managers

Each of the land managers develops a list of prioritized sites for monitoring and executes volunteer agreements with Site Stewards working on their respective lands. Law enforcement contacts are identified, and the reporting procedures to be followed are outlined. Ideally, each agency has a coordinator, or coordinators, for Site Steward activities on its lands. This coordinator, as well as other archaeologists within the agency, participates in both field and classroom training for Stewards and usually takes Stewards and/or region coordinators out on the initial site visits. The coordinator is the land manager's representative and often nominates sites for monitoring and works closely with the region coordinator and Stewards to develop local procedures for scheduling monitoring, establishing priorities, site recording, protection and maintenance, and local program support.

Each agency works together to monitor program activities. This is done primarily under the auspices of the Site Steward Committee, which contains at least one representative of each signatory of the IGA. At least annually, the signatories of the IGA are to evaluate the effectiveness of the Site Steward Program, make recommendations, and acknowledge superior performances.

### Role of the Commission

As an advisory body to the SHPO set in Arizona statute, the Commission initiated the Steward Program and reviews the recommendations of the statewide coordinator for region coordinators, receives reports on current program activities at each meeting, delegates one member to sit on the Site Steward Committee, and reports on the Site Steward Program to the Governor, Legislature, and others as part of its annual report. Commission members are appointed by the Governor. They receive no compensation for their services, nor do they have a budget, so support of the program is limited.

### Role of the Site Steward Committee

This committee is composed of representatives of each signatory to the IGA, as well as a member of the Commission and the statewide coordinator. These meetings are open to all Stewards and the public as well. The committee reviews program procedures, standards, and overall operations; makes recommendations to the SHPO; is directed to report annually to the signatories on the efficiency and effectiveness of the program; and recognizes outstanding performances by program participants. In practice, the committee has met infrequently, on an as-needed basis.

### Role of the Statewide Coordinator

The statewide coordinator is responsible for coordinating and implementing the statewide Steward Program through periodic program monitoring; scheduling of regular meetings with region coordinators, Stewards, and land managers; volunteer recruiting and program promotion; scheduling of training; processing certification requests; publication of a quarterly newsletter; maintenance/update of appropriate computer and paper files; updating of the *Handbook for Volunteers;* and communication of policies and procedures to participants. As part of the data gathering portion of the program, the statewide coordinator works with Stewards in producing annual and quarterly reports on the status of the statewide program, based on information gathered from regions throughout the state and on ongoing collection of program data. The result is a well-coordinated and integrated program that meets the needs of program participants and sponsors.

Over the past several years, this voluntary role has been ably filled by Jack Bashaw, a retired physician, whose endless energy and commitment have been instrumental in the implementation of the program. His hard work and dedication to the program clearly indicates that this position required a greater commitment of support from the program participants than a volunteer could be reasonably expected to provide. Although the SHPO has provided a "home" and administrative support for the program, and the Bureau of Land Management has donated $3000 to assist in program management, obtaining sufficient funding to support a paid position has proven to be difficult. The SHPO has requested a full time statewide coordinator position, entitled "Resource Protection Specialist," and funding in its state budget, for the past 2 years. The position was recently approved, and the SHPO filled this position in May 1991.

### Roles of Region Coordinators and Stewards

Recognizing that most site monitoring would be done on a regional basis, the program was designed to operate at the local level. Initially, 12 regions were identified, but as the program grew, it soon became apparent that smaller, autonomous areas were needed to maintain effective communications and dissemination of materials for site patrols. By the spring of 1990, 28 regions, covering most of the state, had been created.

Each region coordinator serves as the local contact for Steward activities in his/her region, serving as the liaison between the statewide coordinator, land manager and individual Stewards. Region coordinators work closely with land managers to determine site monitoring priorities, establish patrol routes, recruit volunteers to serve as Site Stewards, often conduct the 8-hour training programs, ensure that site patrols are conducted by qualified Stewards, and assume overall responsibility for operation of the program at the regional level. As mentioned above, this person is approved for the position by the Commission and appointed by the SHPO on an annual basis. Initial and subsequent nominations are made by the statewide coordinator, with input from local land managers and Stewards.

Stewards are volunteers certified by the Commission and appointed by the SHPO. The initial appointment is probationary for one year, with subsequent appointments, at the recommendation of the region coordinator, for 2 years. The basic duties of the Stewards include monitoring historic and prehistoric archaeological sites; recording site condition; and reporting evidence of looting, vandalism, or other damage to the responsible land manager. Stewards may also get involved with other, related activities, as defined in the volunteer agreements they sign with each land managing agency.

## Training Requirements for Stewards

The sponsors of the Steward Program have been consistent in their desire that the program be a flexible one that meets the needs of both land managers and Stewards, and this wish has carried over into the training and other components of the program. The training is designed to provide candidates with (1) introductions to the program purpose and sponsors, (2) basic outdoor skills for their own safety, (3) sufficient information to allow them to identify and evaluate site conditions, and (4) a sense of ownership in the accomplishments of the program in preserving and protecting the cultural resources of the state. This latter point is particularly important and is a constant challenge to maintain. Because Stewards are volunteers, they can be expected to stay in the program only as long as it is interesting and rewarding for them. Part of maintaining that interest is to keep training time and paperwork to a minimum. The training course that a candidate must pass to be a certified Steward consists of roughly 3 hours in the classroom and 5 hours in the field with an archaeologist. The core program includes the following topics:
- Organization and administration
- Antiquity laws
- Recognition of sites and features

- Identifying and dealing with looting and vandalism
- Health and safety hazards on patrol
- Conduct of patrols
- Collecting and recording information
- Map and compass review
- Working with regional law enforcement agencies

Throughout training and introduction to the program, it is strongly emphasized that law enforcement is not a focus of the program. The role of the Steward is to deter looting and vandalism, through monitoring and education, not law enforcement activities.

## PROGRAM ACCOMPLISHMENTS AND DIRECTIONS FOR THE FUTURE

The Site Steward Program is a dynamic initiative that is still growing and adapting to changing needs and conditions. It has proven effective in assisting land managers in protecting archaeological resources on public lands, in gathering baseline information on site condition and the extent of looting and vandalism, and in offering meaningful opportunities to the interested public for participation in archaeology. By mid-1990, at least 354 Stewards had been trained and certified, over 7200 hours of Steward service had been logged, and at least 205 archaeological sites were being monitored. The program has strengthened relations between avocational and professional archaeologists and forged new ties between archaeologists and the public. As volunteers, Stewards have credibility in convincing people about the importance of archaeological resources. The results of this, and other public archaeology programs in Arizona, has been heightened public sensitivity to cultural resources, which has been expressed in a variety of ways.

For instance, an increase in citizen activism and advocacy for archaeological resources has been noted. The most recent example occurred in north central Arizona where a private developer who owned property containing a significant Sinagua pueblo and associated burials had leased the land to a pothunter prior to construction of a housing development. Over 200 citizens, including members of local Native American tribes, turned out in protest and blocked the path of the bulldozer. This display of public outrage received state and national attention and has subsequently convinced the landowner to reconsider his approach and to establish a dialogue with the interested parties. In mid-1991, the Archaeological Conservancy signed a 1-year option to purchase the site known as Sugarloaf Ruin. Another benefit of this demonstration of public concern was that it drew the attention of state legislators, leading to revival and passage of burial protection bills that had previously languished.

Site Stewards also played a role in the recent conviction of a site looter/vandal in northern Arizona on a state park. Steward monitoring of sites on the park had created a set of baseline maps and site condition information that proved valuable in making a case for site damage against several individuals caught red-handed in the act of looting/vandalism at one particularly important archaeological site. Although the outcome was only a single misdemeanor conviction, without the work of the Stewards this case might never have been brought to trial.

The Steward Program continues to achieve recognition and was recently awarded one of the highest honors for historic preservation in the state of Arizona. In May 1990 Arizona Governor Rose Mofford presented the Governor's Award for Historic Preservation to Jack Bashaw and the Arizona Site Stewards in the organization category. The award recognized the role of the Site Stewards in preserving and protecting the state's cultural heritage. The program was also recognized in Governor Mofford's 1990 State of the State address as an example of volunteerism in protecting our cultural resources.

As we look to the future, with increasing program growth and the collection of a higher level of site looting/vandalism data, it should be possible to evaluate this site information and direct site protection efforts more effectively. The Steward Program also provides a firm basis for establishing a wider network of partnerships with other agencies and organizations in the public and private sector. A broader base of support should allow expansion of program efforts to include more of the goals outlined in the "Statement of Purpose" at the beginning of this article.

## CONCLUSION

The Site Steward program is only one component of a broad-based public archaeology initiative in Arizona, and the key to its success has been cooperation between the many organizations who are concerned over the future survival of our cultural heritage. By working together on this, we have significantly increased our chances of accomplishing our shared objectives.

## REFERENCES CITED

Bashaw, J. (1990) *Arizona Site Steward Program Handbook for Volunteers,* State Historic Preservation Office, Arizona State Parks, Phoenix.

Hoffman, T. L. (1988) Arizona Archaeology Week: expanding public awareness through a federal and state partnership. *Cult. Resour. Manage. Bull.* 11.

Hoffman, T. L. and Lerner, S. (1986) The use and abuse of archaeological sites: educating the public. Paper presented at the 1986 Society for American Archaeology Symp. "The Carrot, Not the Stick," sponsored by the National Association of State Archaeologists.

Hoffman, T. L. and Lerner, S. (1988) Arizona Archaeology Week: promoting the past to the public, *Natl. Park Ser. Tech. Bull.* 2.

Hoffman, T. L. and Lerner, S. (1989) Arizona Archaeology Week: promoting the past to the public. In *Fighting Indiana Jones in Arizona: Proc. 1988 American Soc. Conservation Archaeology,* Rogge, A. E., Ed., Portales, NM, 31–37.

Pilles, P. J., Jr. (1989) The Arizona Archaeology Advisory Commission and the Site Stewards Program. In *Fighting Indiana Jones in Arizona: Proc. 1988 American Soc. for Conservation Archaeology,* Rogge, A. E., Ed., Portales, NM, 39–44.

Rogge, A. E., Ed. (1989) *Fighting Indiana Jones in Arizona: Proceedings of the 1988 American Society for Conservation Archaeology.* Papers from the Symposium held at the 53rd Ann. Meet. Soc. for American Archaeology, Phoenix. Portales, NM.

P.L. 96-95 (1988).

# THE FEDERAL GOVERNMENT'S RECENT RESPONSE TO ARCHAEOLOGICAL LOOTING

Francis P. McManamon

## INTRODUCTION

In his recent, critically praised, and popular book *A Thief of Time* (1988), Tony Hillerman provided his readers with a view into the seedy world of looters, full of stolen backhoes, falsified documents, violence, and antiquities trafficking. This is the reality of archaeological looting throughout the U.S., not just in Hillerman's Southwest. The looting of archaeological sites robs all Americans of an irreplaceable part of their national heritage. The information about the past that looters destroy reduces the extent to which we can ever understand how people lived in the past and what motivated them. Archaeological sites do not regenerate; they cannot be restored or replanted like wetlands or forests. The objects sought by commercial looters are rare works of art that should be held in trust and interpreted.

Official concern by the Federal government for the preservation of important archaeological properties began during the 19th century in response to the destruction and looting of Indian ruins in the West. The nature of official concern has expanded beyond a concern with archaeological looting on federal land; however, the fight against looting remains a concern of primary importance to many federal archaeologists, law enforcement officials, and managers. In the next section the development of the Federal Government's involvement with archaeological preservation is described briefly. The following section describes more recent federal responses to the problem of archaeological looting.

## A BRIEF HISTORICAL BACKGROUND OF FEDERAL ARCHAEOLOGY

The first archaeological investigations in this country were conducted by individuals and private organizations more interested in knowing something about the people who lived in America before European contact than in recovering artifacts as art objects. This is considerably different from what was happening at the same time in other parts of the world. In Greece, Italy, and Egypt, for example, many archaeological sites were being looted for the valuable objects they contained, with little or no effort to learn about the people who made them.

The early interest in excavating sites for scientific reasons and publishing the results had a major influence on the development of archaeology in this country and on federal involvement in archaeology.

In 1784 Thomas Jefferson excavated an Indian mound on his Monticello plantation in order to determine its construction and use; his description of the work and his analysis of it were published in his *"Notes on the State of Virginia"* (Jefferson 1984). The importance of Jefferson's work is that it was undertaken to answer research questions, used careful excavation techniques to recover data, drew conclusions, and was published, all of which were to become part of modern archaeology (Willey and Sabloff 1974:36–38). From this and other early beginnings, interest in understanding and preserving archaeological sites grew, archaeology developed as an academic discipline and science, and efforts to preserve American archaeological resources resulted in a body of federal legislation that today guides many archaeological activities conducted in this country.

In addition to Jefferson's early work, mounds near Cincinnati were examined in 1793, and the results were published by the Historical Society of Ohio. During the mid-1800s, public concern for historic sites, such as Mount Vernon, stimulated movements to preserve sites associated with individuals and events important to the country's short but dynamic history (Hosmer 1965). During the late 1800s there was a similar concern for Revolutionary and Civil War battlefields. Private organizations and individuals were the primary sponsors of archaeological activities in this country through most of the 19th century, but this was to change as a result of the Federal government efforts to map the West.

In the late 1800s the Federal government sent expeditions to map the West. As a result, numerous spectacular archaeological sites were documented in the American Southwest. In addition to reporting on the ruins, the extensive looting that had already taken place at prominent sites, such as Pecos, Mesa Verde, and Casa Grande, was noted. Expeditions organized by the U.S. Geological Survey and the Smithsonian Institution's Bureau of Ethnology, both established in 1879, and private expeditions such as the Hemmenway Southwest Archaeological Expedition (1886 to 1888), collected an enormous amount of archaeological data (Hinsley 1981). Increasing research by academic institutions and museums added to this. Using this information, influential citizens and members of Congress were able to establish legislation and funding in 1889 to protect and repair Casa Grande, a large prehistoric adobe ruin in Arizona (Lee 1970:20).

During the late 1800s and early 1900s, concern for American antiquities grew in both private and governmental sectors. Reports and warnings from individuals and professional organizations, such as the American Association for the Advancement of Science, the Anthropological Society of Washington, and the Archaeological Institute of America, increased public awareness of the destruction of archaeological sites, which contributed to the passage in 1906 of the Antiquities Act (Lee 1970). This far-reaching statute made federal officials responsible for protecting archaeological sites as public resources and prohibited looting and vandalism. With passage of this act, archaeological sites on approximately one third of the country's land were, at least nominally, afforded protection. The 1906 act also gave the President the power to establish national monuments in areas of outstanding scientific and historical value (Rothman 1989).

The Antiquities Act provided a mandate for federal agencies administering public lands to preserve archaeological sites on those lands. During the 20th century, concern for the preservation of all kinds of archaeological and historic properties has produced many statutes that affect the treatment of archaeological sites. The scope of federal involvement in archaeology and the effects of federal activities beyond public lands increased substantially during the massive public works program of the 1930s. The majority of legislation addressing archaeological concerns has been enacted since that time. (Interested readers will find more detailed accounts of the development of federal archaeology and historic preservation in Hosmer 1965, 1981; King et al. 1977; King and Lyneis 1978; as well as Fowler, Friedman, Cheek, Neumann, Rogers, and King, in this volume.) In particular, the National Historic Preservation Act of 1966 has had important and positive effects on archaeological preservation (Advisory Council on Historic Preservation 1986; Stipe and Lee 1987).

In 1979, in response to an apparent failure of the Antiquities Act to protect archaeological sites, preservationists successfully lobbied for enactment of the Archaeological Resources Protection Act (ARPA) (Friedman 1985a; also see Cheek, this volume). This statute expanded the provisions of the 1906 act by establishing major criminal and civil penalties for violations of that act, establishing procedures for issuing permits for archaeological testing and excavation on public lands, and requiring various interagency program reporting and coordination activities. In 1988, amendments to ARPA improved the ease with which felony prosecutions could be developed using that statute, made the intent to loot an equally punishable crime, and added requirements for federal agencies to undertake inventories of archaeological resources, develop public education programs, and standardize formats for reporting looting incidents.

## FEDERAL EFFORTS AGAINST LOOTING: THE RECENT ACTIONS

Since the 19th century, the breadth of federal concern for archaeological preservation has grown to include consideration of the impact of modern life upon archaeological properties nationwide. However, the expansion of areas of concern has not reduced the attention that has focused on the looting problem.

During the late 1970s, rampant and growing looting and vandalism of archaeological sites in the southwestern U.S. once again provided the impetus for legislation to improve site protection (Friedman 1985b). Between the late 1970s and mid-1980s much effort went into development and passage of ARPA and the approval of regulations to implement the statute (see Cheek, this volume, for a discussion of the history of ARPA).

The appearance of ARPA and its uniform regulations, however, proved to be only a new beginning point. Even before the uniform regulations were developed, activist archaeologists, law enforcement personnel, and like-minded advocates of archaeological preservation had begun to analyze the looting problem and share experiences, in efforts to help in the fight against looting (Green and Davis 1981). This period also witnessed the completion of the most detailed investigation of archaeological looters and vandals that had been conducted to date (Nickens et al. 1981; see King 1982, for a summary of the results of this investigation).

Despite this level of attention, the looting problem has continued, fueled, perhaps, by regional economic downturns that limited the availability of legitimate economic activities in some areas and by the skyrocketing prices of American antiquities on the national and international art markets. The archaeological community, primarily through the Society for American Archaeology (SAA), but with the active participation of other archaeological and historic preservation organizations, has developed a program to highlight the looting problem (see Reinburg, Judge, this volume). Federal agencies have participated actively in this program, contributing both funds and staff expertise.

Additional actions have been taken by federal agencies and Congress in response to the problem. The next section describes and comments upon these recent actions. These actions are considered in light of the three areas of concern identified for the Taos Working Conference on Preventing Archaeological Looting and Vandalism (Society for American Archaeology 1990): (1) understanding the problem; (2) combating the problem; and (3) preventing the problem.

### Understanding the Problem

Recent efforts by Congress and Federal agencies to better understand the looting problem have involved Congressional hearings, improved quantitative information about the extent of the looting and the effectiveness of protection, and initial research efforts to collect information on the nature and extent of looting.

In October 1985, at the instigation of New Mexico's Senator Jeff Bingaman, the Senate Subcommittee on Public Lands, Reserved Water, and Resource Conservation of the Committee on Energy and Natural Resources held a hearing, chaired by Senator Pete V. Domenici of New Mexico, in Albuquerque (Senate Committee on Energy and Natural Resources 1986). Reading the testimony and statements provided at this hearing, one senses a rising level of frustration with the inability to quantify, or even reach consensus on, the magnitude of the looting problem. Some witnesses believed that while looting occurred, it was not substantial and was controlled. Others questioned such views, noting that in their experience, no substantial sites in New Mexico had not been looted or vandalized (Senate Committee on Energy and Natural Resources 1986:136–142). Perhaps in reaction to the lack of clear information from the hearing, in December 1985 Senators Malcom Wallop of Wyoming, Bingaman, and Domenici asked the General Accounting Office (GAO) to investigate the extent to which organized looting of archaeological sites on Federal land was occurring. GAO (1987:1) agreed, in consultation with the senators to undertake an investigation, but to focus its efforts on the Four Corners area of the Southwest.

Federal agencies also were becoming more concerned with understanding the looting problem. In July 1985 the Departmental Consulting Archaeologist, Bennie C. Keel, organized an interdepartmental meeting of Federal agencies to discuss greater cooperation and coordination in Federal archaeological activities. Agreement was reached to provide a common set of quantitative information governmentwide on a variety of archaeological topics. One of the important areas identified by the group for better quantitative information was the looting and vandalism of archaeological sites. Since then, these quantitative data have been collected, described, and analyzed as part of the Secretary of the Interior's "Report to Congress on Federal Archeology" (e.g., Keel et al. 1989). In the dry world of government statistical reporting, these quantitative data supplement the vivid and personal accounts of looting in Tony Hillerman's fiction and the personal testimony of the Congressional hearings. Reported incidents of looting on Federal land (Figure 1) have risen steadily in the years for which statistics are available: 430 incidents in fiscal year 1985, 627 in fiscal year 1986, and 657 in fiscal year 1987 (also see King, McAllister, this volume). Reported incidents are only the tip of the iceberg. Many archaeological sites are in remote areas, many are unknown even to the Federal agencies that are charged with managing them, and Federal agencies have limited resources for systematically monitoring the condition of sites that they do know exist.

Figure 1 also shows that Federal law enforcement efforts against looting have a steady but low level of success. Reported arrests or citations of looters indicate that only a small percentage of violators are being stopped or subsequently apprehended: 15% during fiscal year 1985, 7% in fiscal year 1986, and 10% in fiscal year 1987. Reported prosecutions through the criminal justice system also are steady, but low in number and percentage of reported incidents: approximately 5% for fiscal years 1985 and 1986 and 4% for fiscal year 1987.

Agency officials also recognized the need for more detailed information about looting incidents and prosecutions. They agreed to cooperate by assembling a clearinghouse for information about prosecutions of looters. This information would be shared among law enforcement, U.S. Attorney office, and agency archaeological staffs to assist in future operations against looters and in preparing cases for prosecution of looters. (See the article by Knoll in this volume for further details on the looting clearinghouse, LOOT.)

Congressional and Federal agency activity during recent years has focused substantial attention on efforts to understand the problem better. Although the attention and understanding have improved, much remains to be better understood. The SAA's (1990) report *Save the Past for the Future: Actions for the '90s* lists pages of recommendations for information that is needed to achieve a better understanding of the looting problem.

To more precisely understand looting, agency archaeologist and law enforcement officials are developing more focused studies of this activity and its results. In southwest Utah the several

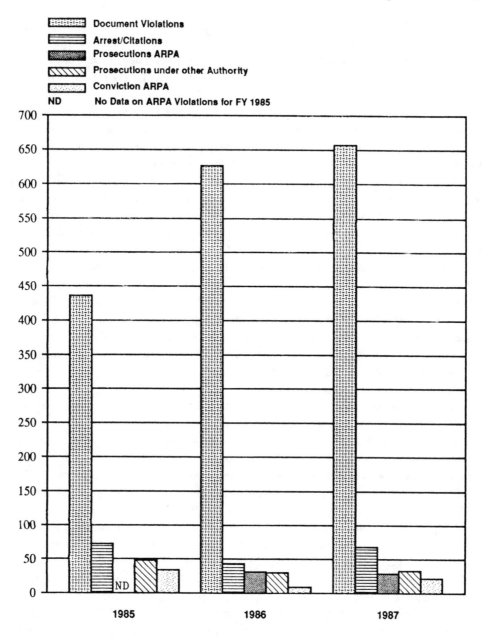

FIGURE 1.  Looting and vandalism statistics, fiscal year 1985, 1986, and 1987.

federal and state offices are cooperating on such a study (Wylie and Nagel 1989). In Arizona, at the Tonto National Forest, a similar project is getting underway (Wood, personal communication 1990).

## Combating the Problem

The agency statistical and clearinghouse information was quickly put to use, along with quantitative information from the Four Corners area that GAO had compiled in its investigation (General Accounting Office 1987), to improve the legal means of combating looting. The governmentwide data were cited broadly by the House Subcommittee on General Oversight and Investigations of the Committee on Interior and Insular Affairs. The chairman of the Subcommittee, Representative Sam Gejdenson of Connecticut, held an oversight hearing on the theft of Indian artifacts from archaeological sites at Cortez, CO, on October 19, 1987 (House Committee on Interior and Insular Affairs 1988a,b).

The GAO report (1987) made a series of recommendations on how to improve enforcement of ARPA and reduce looting of archaeological sites. The GAO recommendations addressed each of the three topics listed above: better understanding of the problem through improved documentation of looting incidents, better prevention of the problem by improving inventories of archaeological sites so they could be more effectively protected, and better combating of the problem through more attention by law enforcement officials through data analysis and undercover operations. Senators Domenici and Bingaman incorporated several of these recommendations into a bill (S. 1985) that they introduced on December 22, 1987. This bill called upon the Secretaries of Agriculture, Defense, and the Interior and the chairman of the Tennessee Valley Authority to develop plans and a schedule to survey their lands for archaeological sites and to develop documents for reporting looting violations. Senator Domenici already had introduced, on June 3, 1987, a short bill (S. 1314) to reduce the "felony threshold" for ARPA violations from $5000 worth of damage to a $500 damage level. In the House, Representative Gejdenson introduced H.R. 4068, based upon the results of his hearings and the report analyzing them (House Committee on Interior and Insular Affairs 1988a,b; also see Neumann, this volume, for a discussion of ARPA and the legislative process, and Cheek, this volume, for further discussion of the ARPA amendments).

The House Subcommittee on National Parks and Public Lands, chaired by Representative Bruce F. Vento of Minnesota, held hearings on H.R. 4068 on June 14, 1988. Following the hearings, negotiations between the Subcommittee staff and Representative Gejdenson resulted in an amended version of H.R. 4068 that incorporated the intent of S. 1314 and added a requirement that Federal land managers establish programs to increase public awareness of the significance of archaeological resources (House Committee on Interior and Insular Affairs 1988c). This bill was passed by the House on July 26, 1988.

On September 22, 1988, the Senate Subcommittee on Public Lands, National Parks, and Forests held a hearing on S. 1314, S. 1985, and H.R. 4068. At the hearing, representatives of several Federal agencies strongly supported the provisions of S. 1314 and H.R. 4068, but pointed out that the requirements in S. 1985 already existed under other Federal laws (Senate Committee on Energy and Natural Resources 1988). The Subcommittee reported favorably on S. 1985; it was passed by the Senate on October 11 and by the House on October 13. The Subcommittee also reported favorably on H.R. 4068, with one amendment of the House version. The Senate passed this on October 14. In the last days of the 100th Congress, Representatives Vento and Gejdenson agreed to the Senate amendment to H.R. 4068, which was reconsidered and passed by the House in its amended version on October 19 (Congressional Record 1988).

Congressional action in the 1988 amendments to ARPA reflect an understanding of possible long- and short-term solutions to the problem of archaeological looting. Short-term solutions required some basic improvements in the ability to prosecute under ARPA. The inclusion of the "attempt" wording in the amendments, for example, fixed one immediate technical problem for ARPA. The more serious problem that law enforcement officials were having in establishing a

$5000 damage level in order to obtain a felony conviction was hindering the use of ARPA in prosecuting looters. This was another immediate problem that the 1988 amendments eliminated. Easier felony prosecution of looters on Federal and Indian land, indeed, seems to be occurring. Successful prosecutions of looters since the passage of the 1988 amendments, in Tennessee's Big South Fork National Recreation Area, California's Lassen National Forest, on Corps of Engineers property near Lewiston in Idaho, and at Bonneville Reservoir in Washington, indicate that U.S. Attorneys have been able to prosecute more effectively.

The National Park Service (NPS) LOOT clearinghouse proved useful to the U.S. Attorney's office in the Lassen National Forest case. NPS provided information about sentences in similar cases, to assist the prosecutors in developing recommended sentences to present to judges. NPS was informed by a U.S. Attorney's office that the LOOT information was very helpful in justifying its recommendation to the judge.

Combating the problem has also involved greater efforts in law enforcement by field offices. Congress added $500,000 to the NPS fiscal year 1990 appropriation and $250,000 to the Bureau of Land Management (BLM) fiscal year 1990 budget to fight archaeological looting on their lands. The NPS funds have been used to increase the number of field law enforcement personnel trained in archaeological resource protection (the FLETC 40-hour course), to purchase and install electronic monitoring devices at endangered sites, and for other law enforcement operations. The Administration also provided additional funding for archaeological law enforcement by the BLM in fiscal year 1991.

National Park Service and Federal Law Enforcement Training Center (FLETC) training courses also have helped. The 12-hour Archaeological Protection Training Course was held by the NPS in 13 locations in 1989. Nearly 350 individuals enrolled. Mainly, the attendees were from Federal agencies (278), but 54 state and tribal officials attended, 3 from Saskatchewan, and 10 individuals from private organizations (also see Waldbauer, this volume, for further discussion of archaeological resource protection training).

## Preventing the Problem

The new sections of ARPA emphasizing Federal agency inventory programs, more rigorous reporting of looting violations, and the development of public education programs are designed to address long-term needs in fighting looting. Better information about where archaeological resources are located so that they can be protected more efficiently and their condition can be monitored is clearly necessary for more effective resource protection. More comprehensive and detailed reporting of incidents and greater ability to share these data among agencies are needed to improve the effectiveness with which law enforcement personnel can combat looters.

More general awareness through public education is needed to persuade Americans that looting diminishes our common heritage and the legacy that they leave to their children and grandchildren. More public programs are needed to provide Americans who want to "do" archaeology with legitimate opportunities to participate in professionally supervised field, laboratory, and curatorial work. Each of these areas is part of the long term solution to reducing the looting problem. Federal agency archaeology programs will continue to spearhead many of these efforts.

# CONCLUSION

Careful readers will have noted that the descriptions of recent Federal actions to fight looting include many references to actions and programs that are ongoing. We have witnessed a series of recent landmarks in the fight against looting. Among these are the GAO report (1987), the congressional action leading to the 1988 ARPA amendments, the development of quantitative data on the problem (e.g., Figure 1), and the publication of the SAA's action plan to fight looting (1990). More important than these achievements, however, is the large number of actions that are underway. These include efforts to better understand looting, through closer monitoring of site locations and conditions, more attention by law enforcement officers to discover and apprehend looters through field operations and electronic monitoring, and a wide range of educational efforts by headquarters, regional, state, and local office archaeologist. The looting problem continues, but Federal agencies are making progress in their efforts to stem the tide.

# REFERENCES CITED

Advisory Council on Historic Preservation (1986) *Twenty Years of the National Historic Preservation Act,* Advisory Council on Historic Preservation, Washington, D.C.

Congressional Record (1988) Archaeological Resources Protection Act of 1979 Amendments, *Congressional Record-House* H. 10465-H. 10466, October 19, 1988.

Friedman, J. L. (1985a) Introduction: a drama in three acts. In A History of the Archaeological Resources Protection Act: Law and Regulations, Friedman, J. L. Ed., *Am. Archeol.,* 5(2), 82–119.

Friedman, J. L., Ed. (1985b) A history of the Archaeological Resources Protection Act: law and regulations. *Am. Archeol.,* 5(2), 82–119.

General Accounting Office (1987) *Problems Protecting and Preserving Federal Archeology Resources,* GAO/RCED-88-3, General Accounting Office, Washington, D.C.

Green, D. F. and Davis, P. (1981) *Cultural Resources Law Enforcement: An Emerging Science,* second ed., Southwestern Region, National Forest Service, Albuquerque, NM.

Hillerman, T. (1988) *Thief of Time,* Harper and Row, New York.

Hinsley, C. M., Jr. (1981) *Savages and Scientists: The Smithsonian Institution and the Development of American Anthropology, 1946–1910,* Smithsonian Institution Press, Washington, D.C.

Hosmer, C. R., Jr. (1965) *Presence of the Past,* Putnam, New York.

Hosmer, C. R. (1981) *Preservation Comes of Age: From Williamsburg to the National Trust, 1926–1949,* University of Virginia Press, Charlottesville.

House Committee on Interior and Insular Affairs (1988a) *Theft of Indian Artifacts from Archaeological Sites,* Oversight Hearing, Committee on Interior and Insular Affairs, Serial No. 100-27, Government Printing Office, Washington, D.C.

House Committee on Interior and Insular Affairs (1988b) *The destruction of America's Archaeological Heritage: Looting and Vandalism of Indian Archaeological Sites in the Four Corners States of the Southwest,* Committee Print No. 6, Government Printing Office, Washington, D.C.

House Committee on Interior and Insular Affairs (1988c) *Amending the Archaeological Resources Protection Act of 1979 to Strengthen the Enforcement Provisions of that Act, and for Other Purposes,* House of Representatives, Report No. 100-791, Part 1, General Printing Office, Washington, D.C.

Jefferson, T. (1984) Notes on the State of Virginia. In *Thomas Jefferson: Writings,* Library of America, New York, 123–325.

Keel, B. C., McManamon, F. P., and Smith, G.S. (1989) *Federal Archeology: The Current Program,* 20402-9325: S/N 024-005-010-572, National Park Service, Department of the Interior, Washington, D.C.

King, T. F. (1982) The pothunter as an ally, not an enemy, *Early Man,* summer, 1982.

King, T. F., Hickman, P. P., and Berg, G. (1977) *Anthropology in Historic Preservation,* Academic Press, New York.

King, T. F. and Lyneis, M. M. (1978) Preservation: a developing focus of American archaeology, *Am. Anthropol.,* 80, 873–893.

Lee, R. F. (1970) *The Antiquities Act of 1906,* National Park Service, Washington, D.C. (Available through the National Technical Information Service, U.S. Department of Commerce, Springfield, VA. 22161; Publication No. PB88-200837).

**Nickens, P. R., Larralde, S. L., and Tucker, G. C., Jr.** (1981) *A Survey of Vandalism to Archaeological Resources in Southwestern Colorado,* Cultural Resources Series No. 11, Colorado State Office, Bureau of Land Management, Denver.

**Rothman, H.** (1989) *Preserving Different Pasts: The American National Monuments,* University of Illinois Press, Urbana and Chicago.

Senate Committee on Energy and Natural Resources (1986) *Management of Archaeological and Paleontological Resources on Federal Land,* Senate Hearing 99-463, Government Printing Office, Washington, D.C.

Senate Committee on Energy and Natural Resources (1988) *Improving the Protection and Management of Archaeological Resources on Federal Land,* Senate, Report No. 100-569, Government Printing Office, Washington, D.C.

Society for American Archaeology (1990) *Save the Past for the Future: Actions for the '90s,* Society for American Archaeology, Office of Government Relations, Washington, D.C.

**Stipe, R. E. and Lee A.** (1987) *The American Mosaic: Preserving a Nation's Heritage,* U.S. Committee of the International Council on Monuments and Sites, Washington, D.C.

**Willey, G. R. and Sabloff, J. A.** (1974) *A History of American Archaeology,* W. H. Freeman, San Francisco.

**Wylie, J. and Nagel, B.** (1989) Quantifying and modeling archaeological looting: the Utah Interagency GIS Project, *Fed. Archeol. Rep.,* 2, 3, 9–12.

**Wood, S.** (1990) Personal communication.

# SAVE THE PAST FOR THE FUTURE: A PARTNERSHIP TO PROTECT OUR PAST

Kathleen M. Reinburg

## INTRODUCTION

"Its a crisis."

"It is increasing at an epidemic rate."

"We are losing our sense of who we are."

"If something isn't done soon, we will have no archaeological data base in ten years."

These are just some of the comments made over the last several years pertaining to the increase in theft and vandalism at archaeological sites. While this problem has been a concern to archaeologists and land managers for decades, the epidemic spread of these criminal actions was first graphically brought to the public's attention in 1986 in "Raiders of the Sacred Sites," a *New York Times Magazine* article by Derek V. Goodwin. The interest generated by this article led to several far-reaching official reports. The first of these was the 1987 General Accounting Office report "Cultural Resources: Problems Protecting and Preserving Federal Archaeological Resources." This was followed by the 1988 U.S. House of Representatives Interior Committee, Subcommittee on General Oversight and Investigations report, "The Destruction of America's Archaeological Heritage: Looting and Vandalism of Indian Archaeological Sites in the Four Corners States of the Southwest." The statistics in these reports were mind boggling. To cite just a few:

- Ninety percent of known sites on federal lands in the Four Corners area of the American Southwest, including over 800 sites on Fish and Wildlife Refuge lands alone, have been looted or vandalized.
- Nearly all of the known Classic Mimbres sites in southwestern New Mexico have been looted.
- A 1000% increase in looting and vandalism has been reported on the Navajo reservation between 1980 and 1987.
- Underwater sites, like historic shipwrecks from California to Florida, have been damaged or destroyed by treasure salvors searching for gold.
- Revolutionary and Civil War battlefields have been destroyed by relic hunters looking for guns, bottles, and other objects.

## THE SAVE THE PAST FOR THE FUTURE PROJECT

In 1988 the Society for American Archaeology (SAA), during its annual meeting, raised the question: What was the nation's largest association of professional and avocational archaeologists devoted to the discovery, interpretation and protection of the archaeology of the Americas going to do to save the nation's archaeological heritage? It was clear that the time was right to take positive action. The public was becoming aware of the problem. Articles were beginning to appear in local and national papers. Congress was also conscious of the problem as indicated by the release of Congressional reports, the appropriation of specific funding for archaeological resource protection and enforcement of protection laws, and the introduction of two major amendments to the 1979 Archaeological Resources Protection Act (P.L. 96-95). People were beginning to recognize that archaeological sites and the resources they contain are time capsules of the past, and like endangered species, once destroyed, they are gone forever.

The "Save the Past for the Future" project was developed to (1) understand why archaeological looting and vandalism occur, (2) determine ways to reduce looting and vandalism, (3) provide opportunities for public education, and (4) devise strategies to improve protection of America's archaeological heritage.

By working towards these goals, archaeologists would also be presenting to the public the fact that America's historic and prehistoric archaeological resources constitute an important and fascinating national scientific and recreational resource. In addition, "Save the Past" would explain why preventing further destruction of important archaeological resources is vital to our ability to understand the past, present, and future. The Executive Committee of the Society for American Archaeology approved the project.

## FORMING A PARTNERSHIP

Realizing that the professional community could not solve this problem alone, the SAA sought the support of federal agencies, national and state organizations, and private foundations. A planning committee was formed, composed of individuals with a wide range of experience and expertise, to guide the project. It consisted of experts in the areas of archaeological resources, law enforcement, land management, legal and legislative issues, public relations, and education.

Management of the project for the first year was provided by Loretta Neumann, project administrator; Kathleen Reinburg, project director; Annetta Cheek, planning committee chair; and James Judge, conference director. Financial support for the project was provided by federal agencies, professional societies, organizations, and foundations, including the Bureau of Land Management, the Bureau of Reclamation, the Forest Service, the National Park Service, the Army Corps of Engineers, the Minerals Management Service, the Dimick Foundation, the Fish and Wildlife Service, the National Conference of State Historic Preservation Officers, the National Oceanic and Atmospheric Administration, the National Trust for Historic Preservation, the Soil Conservation Service, the National Parks and Conservation Association, and the Society for Historical Archaeology.

## SPECIAL SESSION IN ATLANTA

After nearly a year of behind-the-scenes planning, the project was kicked off by a special session during the SAA meetings in Atlanta, GA in April 1989. "Our Vanishing Past: The Willful Destruction of a Nation's Heritage" included presentations by experts in the areas of archaeological site protection, prosecution, and legislation.

Presentations included "The Magnitude and Dimensions of the Looting Problem" by Thomas King, which looked at looting of sites from an inter-national perspective, stimulated by an insatiable market and ineffective laws (see King, this volume). "Protecting the Resources: The Broad Perspective," by Sherry Hutt, dealt with learning lessons from the last 10 years of resource protection legislation and the need to make site protection an agency priority. "Visual and Verbal Images of Looting," by Elizabeth Bruen and W. James Judge, presented dramatic documentation of the loss of sites across the country, due to looting and vandalism. "Archaeology, Looting and the Public," by Brian Fagan, raised the issues of public perceptions that revolve around romantic images of the past, and strategies for improving communication between the profession and the public. "Where to From Here? The Role of the Profession in the Looting Problem," by Jeremy

Sabloff, challenged the profession to understand the extent and effect of looting in order to develop protection strategies. A panel of experts in legislation, land management, and archaeological research synthesized the papers.

## THE TAOS WORKING CONFERENCE

To fully understand the extent of looting and vandalism, recognize the realities of why people do these things, and develop concrete actions and solutions, the SAA sponsored a working conference in May 1989 (see Judge, this volume, for additional discussion of the Taos conference). Held at the Fort Burgwin Research Center in Taos, NM, the conference brought together over 70 national experts in a variety of related fields: archaeologists from academia, federal and state government, and the private sector, along with law enforcement experts, social scientists, politicians, Native Americans, and other citizens concerned with the problem of archaeological looting and vandalism.

Three concurrent workshops, each chaired by an expert in the field, were held. Each workshop was charged with examining the specific topic, developing achievable recommendations, and researching funding sources. The first workshop, "Understanding the Problem," was chaired by Chris Christensen, a research social scientist for the U.S. Forest Service in Alaska. Their charge was to delve into sociological questions of deviant behavior, research, and hard data needs to better understand how to address archaeological site damage and evaluation of tangible and intangible resource loss. Before solutions can be implemented, the problem must be fully understood. The second workshop, "Preventing the Problem," was chaired by Shereen Lerner, Arizona's state historic preservation officer. The participants of this workshop dealt with public involvement and participation as a means of site protection. The group discussed various types of programs that exist: their successes and failures having recognized that involving the public in positive and rewarding programs will serve as a deterrent to site destruction. The final workshop, "Combating the Problem," was chaired by Martin McAllister, who developed the Archaeological Resources Protection Act training courses for federal agencies. This group looked at the criminal aspects of archaeological site destruction. They evaluated current federal, state, and local laws; enforcement and prosecution history; and possible legislative changes to correct inaccuracies. This workshop dealt with what is called the "commercial looter."

While at Taos, the conference attendees unanimously endorsed and adopted the following as the mission statement of the "Save the Past for the Future" project:

> ...The consensus of this conference is that archaeology in the 1990s must change from our traditional perceptions. We can no longer afford to remain academics in isolation. Archaeology must now include all aspects of the archaeological community — academics, amateurs, environmentalists, historic preservationists, etc. — in order to properly serve the entire community and provide a coalition that can effect and achieve the objectives we believe need to be done if we are to save the past for the future.

At the close of the week, over 250 recommendations were developed, and many of these are already being implemented by the SAA, various federal agencies, and other organizations.

## ACTIONS FOR THE '90s

The *Actions for the '90s* report is the compilation of the recommendations and actions from the Taos conference and includes excerpts from selected papers from both the Atlanta and Taos sessions. The report, and the subsequent actions that have taken place since the conference, reveals that those who are aware of the value of our diminishing cultural record can make a major contribution to preserving that record. The following are the major findings and recommendations included in the report.

## SUMMARY OF MAJOR FINDINGS

### Information Must Reach the Public

Americans need and, indeed, deserve to know about their heritage and the history and prehistory of the nation. Professional archaeologists in government, private practice, and academia must explain, in articulate and compelling terms, why archaeology is important, the public benefit derived from archaeology, and how looting and vandalism damage that public benefit.

### Education and Training Must be Improved

Educational outreach programs must be developed to inform and sensitize the public, and be targeted to members of special groups such as Native Americans, attorneys, law enforcement personnel, students, and the media. Training for government personnel dealing with cultural resources must emphasize archaeological values and ethics, proper methods, legal requirements, and enforcement procedures.

### Laws Must be Strengthened

Existing laws, regulations, and government programs must be revised both to increase penalties against professional looters and to provide effective deterrents to hobbyists. Appropriate federal, state, tribal, and local laws must be enacted to improve protection for burials, submerged sites, and sites on private lands. Tax incentives and conservation easement programs must be provided for site protection on private lands.

### Protection Efforts Must be Increased

Archaeological resources on federal, state, and local government lands are not being adequately protected, and new mechanisms are needed to protect sites on private lands as well. Substantially more money and staff are needed to improve protection efforts by federal land-managing agencies. Agencies at all government levels must enlist the general public and Native Americans in archaeological resource protection.

### Agencies Must Improve Coordination

Cooperative agreements must be negotiated among federal land-managing agencies and between agencies and states, for the protection of archaeological resources. Agencies must develop ways to share both personnel and information. Coordination efforts must include Native Americans, professional societies, and other preservation organizations.

### More Research is Needed

Not enough hard data is available about archaeological looting and vandalism. Field research must document where and when looting occurs, the primary types of sites targeted, and how different types of sites are looted. Research is needed on how the trafficking network operates and what tangible (monetary) and intangible (research) losses result from looting and vandalism. Behavioral research must help determine the causes of looting and vandalism, the motives of different types of perpetrators, and the most effective deterrent strategies.

### Alternatives Must be Provided

The interested public must be provided with alternative ways (ethical and legal) to participate in archaeology. This includes opportunities to participate in local avocational societies, volunteer projects or "Earthwatch"-type study activities, site steward programs, and opportunities to make financial contributions that aid archaeological research and protection.

## ACCOMPLISHMENTS SINCE TAOS

It has been an exciting time since the closing of the Taos, Fort Burgwin conference. The conference participants did not just return to their jobs. These dedicated people began working to implement the Taos recommendations. The following are some of the many accomplishments that have occurred since May 1989.

- The SAA promoted $500,000 in the fiscal year 1990 appropriations for law enforcement efforts to protect archaeological resources on national park lands. The funds were spent on undercover efforts, surveillance equipment, manager level resource protection training, offering Archaeological Resources Protection Act (ARPA) training to field agents, and more public education efforts such as Alaska Archaeology Week.
- The Departments of Agriculture and Interior law enforcement divisions developed a Memorandum of Agreement (MOA), which was signed by the two Secretaries on February 27, 1990. The MOA allowed cooperative efforts and exchanges of law enforcement personnel.
- The SAA designated a Public Education Task Force, formed initially as an ad hoc public education group in Taos. The task force developed an action plan for public involvement in archaeological site protection, which was adopted by the SAA. In April 1990 this task force was made a standing SAA committee.
- The September 1989 issue of the *SAA Bulletin* included a special 8-page report on the Taos conference. These were widely distributed to members of Congress, federal agencies, and public access areas such as interpretive centers.
- The Bureau of Land Management produced several public service announcements (PSAs) on site protection. One featured popular author Tony Hillerman *(Thief of Time)*, another featured author Jean Auel *(Clan of the Cave Bear)*.
- The Forest Service revised its regulations (36 CRF) to make it illegal to possess an artifact on forest lands. The National Park Service has a similar regulation.
- Work began on developing an international symbol for signs indicating that it is illegal to disturb archaeological resources. This is similar to the international "No Smoking" signs consisting of a cigarette within a red circle with a slash through it.

- An archaeological protection information booth was staffed at the 1989 National Boy Scout Jamboree. Over 11,000 Boy Scouts stopped by the booth, took a short quiz on archaeological resource protection, and were given buttons, brochures, and archaeological site protection theme book marks. A similar booth was organized for the 1990 Earth Day exposition on the National Mall in Washington, D.C.
- Information data bases were developed for media, interested persons, and contact persons.
- Press kits were developed to be used by local persons interested in local media contact.
- An antilooting plenary session was held during the 1990 SAA meeting in Las Vegas.
- Special executive summaries of the *Actions for the '90s* report were produced and widely distributed.

## HOW TO HELP

There are many ways to get involved. Archaeologists can help by documenting looting and vandalism, including taking photographs of such activity and sending copies of slides and photographs to the SAA, for use in public education efforts; writing articles for professional journals and newsletters; writing letters to the editor of newspapers, magazines, and other publications; participating on radio or television talk shows; giving talks at local schools, civic organizations, and other local groups; and inviting groups to see an excavation first hand (see Milanich, this volume, for a discussion of archaeology and the media).

There are many ways the public can get involved, too, such as visiting archaeological sites and volunteering to help (information may be available from local historical societies, museums, universities, and local federal land managing agencies). The state archaeologist's office and the State Historic Preservation Office may also have information and ideas. Archaeologists from the local archaeological societies or universities might be invited to speak to civic groups, scout troops, youth clubs, or schools.

## CONCLUSION

The success of the "Save the Past for the Future" project and the future of the nation's heritage depends on the continuation of the successful partnership that has been forged between the public and private sectors, among professionals and others concerned about this issue, both inside and outside the government. Each sector has added a necessary element that none could have accomplished as effectively alone. The *Actions for the '90s* report contains many recommendations. Some will need substantial funding and institutions in order to be implemented. But many others are appropriate for an individual to do. We have taken an important first step, but it is only the first step. The future of our heritage depends on everyone becoming involved.

## REFERENCES CITED

Goodwin, D. V. (1986) Raiders of the sacred sites, *New York Times Magazine,* p. 65, December 7, 1986.

Society for American Archaeology (1990) *Save the Past for the Future: Actions for the '90s,* Society for American Archeology, Office of Government Relations, Washington, D.C.

General Accounting Office (1987) Cultural resources: problems protecting and preserving federal archaeological resource, U.S. General Accounting Office, Washington, D.C.

U.S. House of Representatives Interior Committee (1988) The destruction of America's archaeological heritage: looting and vandalism of Indian archaeological sites in the Four Corners States of the Southwest. Subcommittee on General Oversight and Investigations Report, Washington, DC.

# SAVING THE PAST FOR OURSELVES: THE SOCIETY FOR AMERICAN ARCHAEOLOGY TAOS ANTI-LOOTING CONFERENCE

## W. James Judge

## INTRODUCTION

There are two basic goals of this article. One is to present a brief overview of the Taos Conference and its results, and the other is to examine where those results might lead us in the future.

The Taos Anti-Looting Conference was sponsored by the Society for American Archaeology (SAA) and held at the Fort Burgwin Research Center near Taos, NM, May 7–12, 1989. It was attended by 72 people representing a wide variety of disciplines, all in some way related to the field of archaeology or historic preservation. Most (70%) of those attending were federal employees.

In organizing the conference, the looting and vandalism problem was divided into three segments — understanding, preventing, and combating — and a workshop was devoted to each of these segments during the week-long session.

Three chairpersons, each experts in their field, were selected to lead the workshops: Chris Christensen, Sherry Lerner, and Martin McAllister. Prior to the conference, each chair was asked to define a number of key issues relevant to their respective workshop topics. These issues were then distributed to the participants so they could come to the conference prepared to discuss them.

## THE CONFERENCE

Once at the Fort Burgwin Research Center in Taos, participants worked intensively on discussing the issues and developing recommended courses of action. Following the conference, issues and recommendations were circulated to the participants for review and then compiled by the workshop chairs. Some 50 issues resulted in 237 recommendations, which Bliss Bruen and I summarized in a report to the SAA. Leslie Wildesen later compiled the issues and edited the recommendations into a final report *(Actions for the '90s)* that was released at the 1990 SAA annual meetings in Las Vegas.

To put the results in perspective, I think it important to review the purpose of the Taos Conference, which was intimately related to the goals of the larger antilooting project (see Reinburg, this volume) of which it was a part. The project itself was prompted by a growing awareness of the rapid increase in looting and vandalism of sites in this country, and its goals were simply to understand why such activities occur and determine ways to reduce them. Within this framework, the conference attempted to examine in detail the underlying causes of looting, to search for ways of preventing it in the future, and to seek better means of curtailing it now. In my view, we were successful in addressing the three issues, although each of us who attended the conference has his or her own perception of that success. The following summary may be tempered by more pessimism than others would allow.

First, there is a need for much more data on looting and vandalism; we simply cannot understand the problem fully, based on the information currently available to us. Second, we need to spend more money on public education and law enforcement. We need more personnel involved in each, we need to train them better, and we need more programs. Third, and most important in my view, we need a major paradigm shift in American archaeology, in which we consciously and systematically engage the public to join us in the challenge of defending the past. Engaging the public as partners in our discipline must become a fully integrated, even honored, component of our professional lives (see Chapter 4, this volume, for articles on public involvement in archaeology).

It would be nice if 20 years from now we were able to say that archaeological site looting and vandalism was reduced to a minimum. But what is the most effective way to achieve that goal? Do we need more brochures, more workshops, more training, more law enforcement, more legislation, more T-shirts, or all of these? In 1972 our colleague Bob McGimsey issued a clarion call to action in the form of his book *Public Archeology* (see McGimsey, this volume). "Archaeologists . . . cannot expect others to preserve the nation's heritage if we, who . . . are best qualified in the field, do not assume a role of positive leadership and public education" (1972:4). I would certainly not belittle McGimsey's effort, which was exemplary and remains so today, but looting and vandalism have not abated in the last 20 years. So what is the answer? How can we be more effective? How can we actually implement the results of the Taos Conference? Let us return again briefly to the issues.

First, the solution to the issue of combating the problem is fairly clear cut. We need more law enforcement and more enlightened judges, and probably always will. I am not dismissing this as a trivial issue, but it is one that can be solved with better technology and more money (not necessarily more legislation). The solutions to the other two workshop issues are less transparent. To understand the problem, we need more basic research into the social and economic causes underlying looting and vandalism. Neither the magnitude nor the dimensions of the problem are clearly understood, nor are its true effects on the research and interpretive potential of the archaeological record. Some might argue with this view, holding that the magnitude is great and the effects are devastating, but I am referring here to more precise, refined knowledge. What kinds of sites are looted and what time periods are favored? Of the sites looted, what percentage has been destroyed and what kinds of features are targeted? What things are left behind and what are ignored? And more importantly, precisely how does this destruction actually jeopardize the research and interpretive potential of the archaeological data base? (See Nickens, this volume, for a discussion of the destruction of archaeological site data.) Which research interests are affected and which are not? What are the values of the looters and how do they compare with those of the archaeologist? One individual in southeast Utah stated that although he felt right about looting trash mounds for burial goods, he would never destroy a wall. For him, architectural features are sacred; trash mounds are not. We need much more information on the fundamental motivations and value systems of those who loot for profit, as well as the more casual vandal.

On the surface, a feasible approach to preventing the problem seems to be fairly clear cut: simply educate the public in a manner yet undefined, but somewhat akin to Smokey the Bear, and looting will decrease to a minimum. Yet we need to do more than simply say we will spend more money to educate the public. We must develop a comprehensive and systematic plan, as our colleague Brian Fagan reminded us of during the 1989 SAA meetings. The recently formed public education committee is an excellent start, but it should be part of a broader, more inclusive plan with specific goals. My perception is that this vital component of the antilooting effort is currently missing, and I would urge the SAA, in partnership with the relevant state and federal agencies, to initiate such a plan. Without a plan that prioritizes the multitude of recommendations emerging from the conference and sets out means of implementing them, 20 years from now people will still remain confused about why they should not loot. Without the why, the effort will be largely ineffective.

Assuming effective implementation of the Taos Conference recommendations, how will the success of the antilooting project be measured in the long run — by the number of buttons sold, or by the degree of change of our own professional attitudes and values? T-shirts and other marketable objects are very effective stage setters — they grab the public's attention. But once we have their attention, do we really have something of substance to say to them? Let's not lose the opportunity by not having a message ready. To give them something of substance, we might begin by examining our own archaeological value system, again as Fagan counsels us. Right now this value system holds that we must preserve the archaeological record because the sites contain an "invaluable wealth of scientific information." But the only reason they contain the wealth is because we, the archaeologists, define it as such. Does not this constitute archaeological self-perpetuation: in effect, saving sites because they are there? Leaving the power to define that "wealth of scientific information" solely in the hands of a small community of scholars whose careers depend on it is not justifiable. Biologists go to great lengths to explain the horror of species extinction by reference to the need to preserve genetic diversity. We are obliged to do no less. We need to preserve our dwindling data base, but equally, we need to comprehend why it is important to others that we do so. Unquestioned loyalty to our cause may result in unsubstantiated loyalty to our cause.

Biologists do not try to save the snail darter because it is there, or a rainforest because the canopy is pretty and holds secrets we do not understand, or a riparian habitat because it is someone's esoteric research project. Instead they seek reasons all can understand and are equally affected by, such as the need to reduce atmospheric $CO_2$ or the need to preserve habitat and thus genetic diversity, and then they publicize those reasons. Biologists arm their defense with relevant, concrete data understandable to the public. I am not sure we do the same.

We need to put the creative forces, which normally drive our research, to work on the issue of transmitting our messages to others. Yet we do not always recognize or agree on what those messages could or should be. At a recent dissertation defense I attended, a respected colleague suggested that we turn the discussion from "methodological issues to questions of substance." This dismissal of archaeological method obscures its intrinsic value and educational potential. In fact, from the public's perspective, questions of method may well be archaeology's issues of genuine substance. People are fascinated by the means we use to extract information from the unwritten record. This may be our real gift, that which we can pass on to benefit others most. Were we to arm every man, woman, and child with our powers of observation and interpretation, we would indeed leave a formidable legacy, that of a truly ethical and valuable intellectual process.

Most archaeologists would have us offer something more than method, however, and would turn instead to our quest to explain human behavior or understand cultural process. Yet it is not clear to the layman why archaeologists, rather than historians or cultural anthropologists, have been chosen to forge an attempt to understand human behavior. A review of the literature reveals that this basic topic of archaeological relevance is studiously avoided by our colleagues. Either archaeologists do not know, or do not want to know, if what they do is important to anyone else. Should not we at least question whether what we spend 60 million dollars per year doing is perceived as important to the taxpayer?

At the most fundamental level, one finds it extremely difficult for professional archaeologists, trained in the modern paradigm, to answer the question "Why archaeology?" in a manner acceptable to the layman. In his excellent introductory text, S. J. Knudson provides a nice analogy of what it is like to do archaeology: putting together a large jigsaw puzzle without a picture and with half the pieces missing (Knudson 1978:3). Yet we still wonder why it is so important to put the puzzle together and, for that matter, who the puzzle is for. I do not believe archaeologists are making conscientious efforts to address such issues.

Another colleague, Joe Tainter, suggests that we "interest the public in what we do, rather than doing what we think the public will find interesting. The challenge is to make certain that the archaeology each of us practices is linked clearly to the broader goals of understanding human society and history. Too often our specialized studies seem to lose sight of the broader goals of the discipline, and that is where archaeology becomes vulnerable to misunderstanding" (personal communication 1988). I agree fully with Joe, yet I am not sure how many others do. According to the member survey reported in the *SAA Bulletin,* the members did not particularly want to encourage membership by avocational archaeologists, nor did they want a general interest magazine published by the SAA, nor would they themselves be willing to fund a public information program (Roveland 1988:3).

It would seem very important, if not crucial, that the public become informed. A recent article in *American Scientist* (Hively 1988:439–444) discussed the issue of scientific literacy within the American populace. "The middle-aged adults of the year 2010 are already in high school. Unless they are locked up until they learn more science, about 95% will be scientifically illiterate." Will this be a problem? Hively quotes Jon Miller, of the Public Opinion Laboratory: "Public indifference has limits. The 'nonattentive' do not determine policy, but sometimes they exercise a veto. They are, after all, a majority" (1988:444).

Right now we archaeologists are dealing with an interested and highly tolerant public. Unless we address that interest directly, though, they can become highly intolerant of our activities. If the expenditure of public funds on archaeology impinges on the public's pocketbook in ways they perceive as unjustifiable, they will perceive we are doing archaeology only for ourselves, and the ultimate veto will be exercised by those who, through no fault of their own, are archaeologically illiterate.

## CONCLUSION

If archaeology is to avoid the veto, it must become relevant in the eyes of those who do not understand it, yet continue to pay for it. In what context and at what level should this relevance be expressed? I offer the following quote for consideration: "Modern civilization, more than any which has gone before, is living visibly and dangerously beyond its means. The power and knowledge at our disposal are being used, as never before, to drain the treasures of the past and borrow from the future. We are flowering for the sake of the immediate present, and at an accelerated speed. . . . The past, so dark, dim, and different can be forgotten; the future will take care of itself" (Sears 1971:19). A very timely observation, this plea for recognition of the value of the past was issued over 50 years ago by Paul Sears, one of the most literate and socially responsible ecologists of our times.

I suggest we define and adhere to issues of global concern (see Messenger and Enloe, this volume, for a discussion of archaeologists as global educators). Science and scientists should feel morally and ethically obligated to rationalize their work by addressing globally relevant issues, and archaeologists should not be exempt. Thus, if the future of humanity depends on the achievement of global sustainable growth, archaeologists should provide examples of such growth from the past and demonstrate what life was like under sustainable conditions (in balance with the available resources) and what happened when a path was chosen that no longer allowed the balance to be sustained.

Perhaps, then, the most relevant aspect of archaeology as a science lies not in its ability to discover laws or offer multivariate explanations of human behavior, but instead in its potential to raise the level of awareness of the public to the value of knowing and appreciating the diversity of the past and, more importantly, realizing the adaptive advantage of that knowledge. The richness of a culture is measured by its diversity, and the success of a culture is engendered accordingly by that richness. Documentation of the diversity through archaeological research is the mechanism of achieving this. It keeps it culturally alive, even nourishes it.

In a book about forests written 20 years ago, Richard Ketchum noted that "for most of human history, man's involvement with nature was both intimate and complete. The primitive's wisdom was his accumulated knowledge about the environment of which he was a part; his skills were techniques of adapting to the natural surroundings. Only in fairly recent times has man removed himself from the partnership nature requires, ignoring its incalculable blessings and forgetting the terrors it can hold" (1970:7).

It is that accumulated knowledge of the environment that is important for us to maintain as the modern world tears us further and further from intimate contact with it. Preserving the diversity of cultures, past and present, and informing the public, our constituency, about it will allow the transformation of that cumulative store of knowledge into a collective wisdom of incalculable value to future generations. In this manner, archaeology becomes both globally and immediately relevant, and following public perception of this relevance, looting and vandalism of our sites will become a more manageable problem.

## REFERENCES CITED

Hively, W. (1988) Science observer: a special report on scientific literacy. *Am. Sci.*, 76(5), 439–444.
Ketchum, R. M. (1970) *The Secret Life of the Forest*, American Heritage Press, New York.
Knudson, S. J. (1978) *Culture in Retrospect*, Rand McNally, Chicago.
McGimsey, C. R., III (1972) *Public Archeology*, Seminar Press, New York .
Roveland, B. E. (1988) Looking forward: the society and its future, *Bull. Soc. Am. Archaeol.*, 6, 5.
Sears, P. B. (1971) *This is Our World*, University of Oklahoma Press, Norman.
Society for American Archaeology (1990) *Save the Past for the Future: Actions for the '90s*, Society for American Archaeology, Office of Governmental Relations, Washington, D.C.

# THE ARCHAEOLOGICAL CONSERVANCY AND SITE PROTECTION

## Mark Michel

## INTRODUCTION

In 1979 a small group of conservationists and archaeologists formed the Archaeological Conservancy in an attempt to develop an effective program to permanently preserve important archaeological sites on private land. The effort came from our successful drive to enact a new federal site protection law, the Archaeological Resources Protection Act of 1979, which was designed to protect sites on federal lands from looters, a continuing and growing problem.

Pleased as we were with this success, we knew only too well that the vast majority of archaeological resources in the U.S. are on private land, subject to the whim of the owners. While publicly owned sites have been seriously impacted by looters, those on private land have been devastated, mainly by development, modern agriculture, and professional looters. Since the first Europeans arrived, these sites of antiquity have been obliterated, and the process continues virtually unabated.

Yet even today neither the Society for American Archaeology nor the Federal Government has any program whatsoever for the systematic protection of archaeological resources on private lands.

No one has any idea of what still exists, but the few estimates that are available are appalling. For example, in 1880 the Bureau of Ethnology estimated there were 20,000 burial mounds in the Ohio and Mississippi River valleys. It is estimated that less than 200 survive today, and those on private lands are still without protection. Just within the past 3 years, at least four important Anasazi ruins in the Mesa Verde area that were located on private land have been totally destroyed by looters.

## ARCHAEOLOGICAL LOOTING

One of the effects of the Archaeological Resources Protection Act of 1979 has been an increase in looting on private lands. As a result, legal looting on private lands has correspondingly increased. Professional looters buy looting rights or sometimes even sites themselves. One old trick used in the Southwest has been to buy a site at a high price, but with little or no down payment, then loot the site and default on the mortgage. In the well-known Slack Farm (Kentucky) case, several men reportedly paid the owner $10,000 to dig up artifacts at this Mississippian period cemetery.

Whereas other countries have taken possession, or at least control, of their antiquity, two factors make that unlikely in the U.S. First is the very powerful American impulse of the sanctity of private land (see Fowler, this volume, for a discussion of the legal basis for archaeological site protection in the U.S.). No other nation in the world gives such prominent protection of private property rights. Secondly, there is the reality of the dominant group in our society, i.e., persons of European stock, being unrelated, either racially or culturally, to the nation's prehistoric archaeological remains. As one state senator told me when I explained that we should protect our national heritage, "Son, it may be part of your heritage, but it ain't part of mine." Not surprisingly, the two largest archaeological organizations in the U.S. deal with European and Middle Eastern archaeology.

While legislation to regulate the digging of archaeological sites may pass court review, no one that I know believes ownership of the resource rests anywhere but with the owner of the land. To do otherwise would violate the Constitutional prohibition of taking property without just compensation. A prohibition on digging on private land may do likewise.

## THE ARCHAEOLOGICAL CONSERVANCY

It was with this in mind that the Archaeological Conservancy was founded with the premise that the most effective way to preserve archaeological sites on privately owned land was to own them. This was not an entirely new idea. Various land trusts around the nation had been doing that for years. The most successful is the Nature Conservancy, which now boasts 500,000 members and preserves over 1000 acres of land per day: mostly land containing rare and endangered species. Since 1951 the Nature Conservancy has acquired more than 5 million acres in 50 states.

It is not a new idea for government either. The U.S. Fish and Wildlife Service acquires thousands of acres to protect habitat. The National Park Service has acquired land for more than 100 years, including archaeological sites. It is not a new idea for archaeological sites either. Beginning with Serpent Mound in the 1890s, the Ohio Historical Society has acquired and protected a number of important sites in that state, but virtually none since the 1920s.

It is a thoroughly American idea. If you want to protect or control some land, then the most effective way to do that is to own it. If you have fee simple ownership, then you hold the cards. If a highway department wants to put a road through your site, then they have to take you to court and prove their need. If a looter trespasses on your property to steal some valuable artifacts, then he is committing a felony. It is something that everyone in America understands.

The other guiding principle of the Conservancy is the belief in "conservation archaeology." Archaeology is perhaps unique among scientific disciplines in that it destroys its own research base in the course of doing research. Thus, yesterday's archaeologist, no matter how competent, missed many clues. But it is very difficult, if not impossible, to go back and do it again once a site is excavated. Modern technology has many applications for archaeologists, and it is important that information remain *in situ* for new techniques and new insights. The Conservancy is like a museum, only instead of storing artifacts on shelves, we store them in the ground.

Beginning with start-up grants from the Ford Foundation and the Rockefeller Brothers Fund, the Conservancy began to acquire sites in 1980. The first step was to evaluate and prioritize the sites. Actually, much of the data was readily available. Each state has a state historic preservation officer (SHPO), established under the Historic Preservation Act of 1966. We began our selection process by asking the SHPOs to develop a list of 20 or so of the most important sites in his or her state, in need of protection. Professional archaeologists from the academic community are consulted as well. Once that list is complete, we field check the sites to see what condition they are in today. Often, no one has been to check on these sites for many years, and more than once we have unhappily found an important site to no longer exist.

We then apply practical tests to the list. How endangered is the site? How much time does it have left? Are there similar sites available? How difficult is the project? What is the attitude of the owner? How much is it going to cost?

One of the first states in which we began to operate was Ohio. We got excellent support from the SHPO and archaeological community, and we wanted to build on the past accomplishments in preservation of the Ohio Historical Society. The SHPO provided us with a list of about 20 sites, and we began to work. Many of the great moundbuilder sites of Ohio were gone, destroyed by urban development or modern agriculture, making the preservation of those that remained even more important.

Our first target was the famous Hopewell Mounds Group, the type site of the Hopewell culture. This provides a very good case study. The site itself consists of a D-shaped earthen enclosure covering 111 acres, with an attached square enclosure covering an additional 18 acres. The outside walls are 3-miles long and made of earth and stone. Inside the enclosures are up to 40 mounds. Extensive research has taken place there on three separate occasions since 1845.

These excavations discovered the fabulous artifacts that made the Hopewell culture famous: huge caches of pearls, copper, and obsidian; exquisitely carved pipes and mica cutouts; grizzly bear teeth, and conch shells. These materials were collected from across the continent and brought to the Hopewell site and eventually placed in burial mounds. Yet despite all the attention given to the Hopewell site, perhaps the most famous archaeological site east of the Mississippi River, nothing had been done to preserve it. In fact, it had been almost forgotten since 1925.

Consultation with leading experts drew a consensus that despite the extensive research done at the Hopwell site, perhaps as much as 90% remained untested. I'll never forget my first visit in the spring of 1980. There it was, the fabulous Hopewell site: impacted by 200 years of farming, crossed by a county road and the B & O Railroad, marred by a high voltage transmission line; but there it was, still intact. Mounds were still clearly visible in the dormant fields. The earthen enclosure was plowed down in places, but largely undisturbed in others, still clearly visible from the ground and from the air.

Suburban development was getting perilously close to the Hopewell site, now less than one-half mile away. Rural residential developments occur throughout the East along any county road, and a county road bisects the site. Fortunately, the owners, a young engineer and his mother, were sympathetic to preservation. They had considered a subdivision, but were pleased with the alternative we gave them. Shortly, the Conservancy had an agreement to buy 124 acres of the site for about 60% of the fair market value, or $165,000. The sellers were able to take the balance as a tax deduction.

This agreement covered most of the site, but three smaller parcels, with a combined total of about 40 acres, remained. The Conservancy then began efforts to raise the funds to pay for the site over the next 3 years. This was the first test of the Conservancy's ability to raise substantial funds to acquire and permanently preserve endangered archaeological sites.

It quickly became apparent that a lot of education was needed before funds could be successfully raised. No foundation or corporation had previously contributed funds to preserve an archaeological site. The work of land trusts, like the Nature Conservancy, helped pave the way, but only to a limited degree. After the 3-year period, the funds were in hand and the first acquisition completed. We continue to seek to acquire additional small pieces of the site and expect to close on two in 1990.

The principal and interest for the acquisition had come to about $185,000. Of that sum, $25,000 came from the "Acquisition and Development" portion of the federal Historic Preservation Fund, which is administered by the National Park Service and the SHPO in each state. When the Conservancy was founded in 1979, it was assumed that a substantial portion of acquisition costs would come from this matching fund. But those hopes were dashed by a reduction in such federal funding under the Reagan Administration.

By 1981 the federal matching funds had disappeared in the government's drive to reduce federal domestic spending. The state SHPO offices were threatened with federal fund cutoffs as well, and turned their attention to maintaining their offices. The decrease of federal funds removed a significant and seemingly dependable source of funds from the efforts to preserve

America's prehistoric past. Only in 1990 did federal funds for acquisition and development begin to reappear, and in only very small amounts.

The reduction of federal funding for dozens of domestic programs placed the burden of maintaining these services on state and local governments. It was anticipated by the Federal Government that the "private sector" would make up the difference. However, this was not the case. Foundations and corporations were swamped with proposals for funding from all sorts of organizations, including government agencies. The overall net result was a decrease in funding for historic preservation as well as for other programs.

Thus, funding for private-site protection, which had seemed promising in 1980, became extremely difficult by 1981. Yet the Conservancy continued to identify, acquire, and preserve sites in an ever-expanding area of the U.S. By the end of 1989, it had completed 60 projects in 11 states. The book value of the property reached $3 million.

Today the Conservancy has about 8500 contributors from across the nation. Two thirds of the 60 parcels acquired were purchased — usually at bargain prices. The other third were donated to the Conservancy, whose staff is trained in real estate and tax matters. Archaeological sites tend to be small and often relatively inexpensive to purchase. The vast majority of Conservancy preserves are under 100 acres, and seldom do acquisition costs exceed $100,000 for a single project.

The Conservancy does not pay for archaeology. Occasionally an owner of an important site will have great expectations for the "buried treasure" value of his property. Our first task is to explain the nature of the archaeological resource while, at the same time, impressing on the owner the national significance of the property.

This may seem like a paradox, but it is the key to successful negotiations. The commercial potential of a site is offset by the cost of recovery and the resulting damage to the property. In the end, if an owner is not interested in preserving a site, it is unlikely that it will still be there.

The Conservancy's Board of Directors sets goals and priorities on the basis of need. It was determined that the remains of the Caddo culture in Texas, Oklahoma, Arkansas, and Louisiana were in great need of preservation due to the ravages of landleveling and looting. A Caddo project was launched in 1986 with the goal of acquiring, as quickly as possible, a good sampling of Caddo culture sites. Packaging a number of sites together in one project saves time and money. It is just as difficult to raise funds to save five sites as to save one, and a lot less time consuming. Five Caddo sites in Texas and Oklahoma have been acquired, and several more are in various stages of negotiations.

Once a site has been acquired, the Conservancy stabilizes it and prepares a 100-year management plan that governs research. Volunteers play a large role in both stabilization and preparation of the management plan. At a preserve in southeastern Colorado, more than 50 volunteers, some from as far away as Denver, spent a long weekend stabilizing ancient walls and filling in pot holes with sterile soil. Near Santa Fe, volunteers built a diversion dam to protect important ruins from a meandering stream.

Preventing looting is one of our biggest concerns. We fence most of our preserves in order to visually and legally establish boundaries. No fence will keep a looter off a site, but if a looter knows that if he is caught inside our fence he will go to jail, he will think twice about it. We then set up a regular patrol system, mainly using volunteers. From this point, most archaeological preserves need little care. In the East we like to keep preserves in grass and prevent dense brush from overrunning the site. This is usually accomplished with an agreement with a neighboring farmer to cut hay or graze cattle on the preserve. A well-trimmed preserve prevents erosion and deters looters, who have little cover and who are deterred by a "cared-for" appearance.

The first decade of the Archaeological Conservancy proved that private acquisition works. We have demonstrated that archaeological sites on private lands can be preserved in the U.S. by using the oldest American tradition, ownership of the land.

In the next decade we plan to expand this program. Field offices have already been opened in Santa Fe, Sacramento, and Indianapolis. New offices are planned for Atlanta and Washington. Thematic projects now include Chaco outliers, Mesa Verde cultural centers, Caddo ceremonial centers, Hopewell and Adena sites of all kinds, Sacramento Delta villages, and many more. In the next few years we plan to add even more, as funds are available.

With this demonstrated success, it is now time for professional archaeologists and the Federal Government to adopt a national program for the preservation of archaeological sites found on private lands. At the current rate of destruction, only a short time remains before much of these priceless resources are destroyed forever. Not every archaeological site can be purchased or turned into a permanent preserve, nor should they. Only those with the most depth and most potential for sustained research need be given this highest form of protection. Lesser degrees of protection can be afforded to less important sites. Archaeological easements can be used for some, and owner protection programs on a voluntary basis for others. Kentucky has embarked on such a program, where private owners pledge to protect sites on their land.

## CONCLUSION

Clearly it is time for the federal and state governments to join in the permanent preservation of the nation's prehistoric legacy. Archaeological sites are usually small and relatively inexpensive to purchase. The average private site can probably be bought for only about $40,000. At this rate 1000 sites, or an average of 25 per state, could be purchased for only $40 million. It would take 10 years to accomplish that, or a mere $4 million per year. Various states have already begun to invest in their cultural heritage, with innovative programs to establish archaeological preserves.

The fiscal impact of managing a national preserve system could be lessened by joining a partnership of private organizations, state governments through the SHPOs, museums, and universities. Once established, preserves are relatively easy to maintain and protect.

Some skeptics would say that this is only a fraction of the resource. But it would be a large fraction of the sites with good integrity and ample depth for sustained research purposes. Besides, what is the alternative: to continue to stand by and do nothing while the best of America's prehistoric past is destroyed?

Preserving the remains of America's prehistoric legacy is a race against time. Every day more of these sites are destroyed, and along with them, the information that would someday tell of the great cultures of prehistoric America. Our experience confirms that the most effective way to preserve these privately owned resources is to set them aside as permanent preserves (see Kearns and Kirkorian, Knudson, McAllister, Rogers, and Grant, this volume, for further discussion on protecting sites on private property). It is a big job, and we need all the help we can get.

# Chapter 6

## THE FUTURE OF PROTECTING THE PAST

"If you wish to know the nature of man, you must take his testimony in all times and places. The future is the next witness." (Anonymous)

# THE FUTURE OF PROTECTING THE PAST

Bennie C. Keel

## INTRODUCTION

It is difficult to discuss the future without reference to the past and present. It is in comparison that changes can be evaluated, successes and failures identified, and new directions charted. We are at a critical point in American archaeology. What we do in the next decade about the problem of the dwindling archaeological resource base will affect the future of the profession. There are many important issues facing the profession today; how we deal with them will define our future as a science.

This article discusses the historical background of archaeological resource protection in the U.S. and where it is going and, in my opinion, where it needs to go. I am pleased to have the opportunity to provide my perspectives, observations, and, of course, my bias on this important topic. I think that the present volume will greatly assist in providing future direction for protecting the past.

## HISTORIC OVERVIEW

The historical development of archaeological resource protection in the U.S. has been described in several articles in this volume (Domenici, McGimsey, Knudson, Fowler, Friedman, Cheek, Neumann, and Rogers and Grant). The efforts directed at archaeological conservation, which began in the late 1800s, demonstrate a long commitment by private citizens, professional organizations, and the Federal Government. As a result, numerous laws have been passed designed to protect the past for the future. Without those efforts, I believe little of the past would be left, and American archaeology as we know it today would be considerably different.

I do not wish to review in detail the historic development of the federal archaeological laws; others in this volume have covered that ground. Nonetheless, I do think that it is important for us to examine why these laws were necessary and how the implementation and administration of these laws have, on occasion, drifted away from the course their supporters and authors charted. If for no other reason, such an examination should demonstrate the care we should demand in crafting statutory language.

The Antiquities Act of 1906, for example, was enacted after several attempts to halt the wanton destruction of prehistoric sites in the Southwest. It also provided for the creation of national monuments from public lands and the issuance of permits to insure that the excavation of publicly owned sites was carried out properly. Within a short time, lands were being withdrawn for other than archaeological reasons. The way the act was written allowed this. Knowledgeable people would argue that such lands were worthy of protection for reasons other than their archaeological value, but I am certain that the extent of use of the act to protect nonarchaeological values was not anticipated by its authors or supporters. (For a detailed treatment of executive order withdrawals and the establishment of national historic monuments, see Rothman 1989.) The creation of a couple of hundred national monuments, as is being done by the exemplary efforts of the Archaeological Conservancy, should not be minimized (see Michel, this volume, for further discussion of the Archaeological Conservancy). The issuance of permits became a *pro forma* exercise because of a variety of circumstances. Law enforcement of the criminal sanctions of the act was a failure — less than 25 prosecutions occurred under the act.

In 1979, almost three quarters of a century later, Congress passed the Archaeological Resources Protection Act of 1979. This legislation was required to stop looting and vandalism in the Southwest. The niceties that distinguish these two statutes will be omitted here, but the fact of the matter remains that both laws had the same purpose — to halt unauthorized destruction of the archaeological record.

It is interesting to note that historic preservation legislation of the 1960s and mid-1970s focused on planned federal undertakings, not illegal actions by looters and vandals. What was the reason for this focus? Had looting and vandalism dropped to tolerable levels? Was planned development perceived as the greater threat to the national archaeological data base? Or was American archaeology sophisticated enough to recognize that it was easier to cope with identifiable institutions responsible for archaeological resource destruction than the faceless hordes of pothunters?

The Reservoir Salvage Act of 1960, based on the need to rescue archaeological data from the development of a national water resource program, provided a small appropriation to the National Park Service to support its efforts as well as the River Basin Surveys program located in the Smithsonian Institution. This program's predecessor had been the rescue work, statewide surveys, and restoration projects that were conducted during the Great Depression, under the Historic Sites Act of 1935 and various economic relief legislation of that era.

During this 22-year period between 1966 and 1988, more federal archaeological laws were enacted (or amended) than in the preceding century and a half. The Moss-Bennett bill amended the Reservoir Salvage Act of 1960 in the most startling manner; it provided a "built-in" funding source independent of the annual Congressional appropriation process for archaeological rescue work. This "built-in" funding source was the authorization for agencies to transfer up to 1% of authorized construction funds to the Secretary of the Interior to assist the secretary in carrying out the act. Subsequently, this provision was interpreted to mean that agencies were authorized to spend up to 1% for archaeological recovery work themselves. Consistent with the National Environmental Policy Act of 1969 and the National Historic Preservation Act, the amended act covered all federal undertakings, not just reservoir developments.

The Archaeological and Historic Preservation Act of 1974, or the "Moss-Bennett Act," as the amended Reservoir Salvage Act is popularly known, was directly responsible for the geometric growth in archaeological, or "cultural resource management," jobs in the Federal Government, academia, and the private sector.

Carl Chapman once told me that he and the others who were intimately involved with writing the Moss-Bennett law assumed that the federal agencies would use the assistance authority to transfer funds to the Secretary of the Interior (National Park Service) to carry out the act's requirements. With the additional funds, they assumed the National Park Service would establish an entity (Interagency Archaeological Services) similar to "national archaeological surveys" in other countries. He, and perhaps others, saw the act being implemented through close cooperation between the National Park Service and universities and museums across the country, in much the same manner as the River Basin Survey program of the 1960s. Although efforts were made (both within and outside of the National Park Service) to create this kind of organization, they were unsuccessful. The failure to establish an organization capable of implementing the act has been attributed to two complementary factors. First, National Park Service senior management was not in a position to allot the necessary positions from its personnel ceiling. Second, agencies were somewhat reluctant to transfer funds to the Secretary of the Interior, but were even more reluctant to transfer the conduct of a program that had the potential for immense impact on their construction programs. In simple terms, the Corps of Engineers, Department of Transportation, Department of Agriculture, and other federal agencies were not about to minimize their control over their projects and funds by transferring archaeological responsibility to another agency, especially a conservation agency such as the National Park Service.

Much has been written regarding the unexpected administrative structure that developed to carry out the act within the federal bureaucracy. As a result of this unanticipated institutionalization of the program across the Federal Government, the Department of the Interior, and specifically the National Park Service, has been criticized. For a number of reasons, I believe that the institutionalization of archaeological programs in major federal agencies is much more desirable than a centralized program in a single agency.

The development of individual agency archaeological programs has created more archaeological jobs than a central operation would have. The creation of archaeological programs across the government has insured that archaeological concerns are routine day-to-day considerations in other aspects of agency operations. Fulfilling archaeological responsibilities is viewed as part of the agency mission, not as a requirement to be met by the use of consultants as needed. An old-time bureaucrat once told me that when agencies employ consultants to conduct their business, it means that the agency isn't committed to that segment of their business; they perceive it as a temporary inconvenience.

Within the federal system, the chaos that might be expected from a multitude of agency archaeology programs has largely been avoided through the leadership of the National Park Service, the Advisory Council on Historic Preservation, and the Society of Professional Archaeologists. Various regulations and guidelines developed by the National Park Service and the Advisory Council through the open rule-making process have insured consistency in requirements, procedures, and professional qualifications. The Society for Professional Archaeologists has preformed an immeasurable service through its certification program and grievance process, which would have been impossible by federal agencies.

It is also important to recognize that the actions by other academic disciplines, professions, and segments of the public were the primary stimuli that led to the enactment of other broader historic preservation laws: the Historic Sites Act of 1935 and the National Historic Preservation Act of 1966. Noteworthy, also, is the inclusion of heritage resources in the National Environmental Policy Act of 1969 as a consideration in the development of federal undertakings. The National Transportation Act of 1966, the Archaeological Resources Protection Act of 1979, and the Abandoned Shipwreck Act of 1988 were enacted to deal with other specific threats to archaeological resources. The purpose and scope of these statutes are described elsewhere in this volume.

Federal legislation, in particular the Archaeological and Historic Preservation Act of 1974, was directly responsible for the geometric growth in archaeological, or "cultural resource management" (CRM), jobs in the Federal Government, academia, and the private sector (see McGimsey, this volume, for a personal perspective on the development of CRM in the U.S.). This resulted in a tremendous increase in the archaeological data base and a commensurate increase in our understanding of the history and prehistory of this country.

Historically, the archaeological profession and its allied public have sought to preserve and conserve archaeological resources through the legislative process. Despite the common admonition contained in the bulk of preservation statutes, that these efforts are for the "benefit of the American people," the vast majority of the actions undertaken under the laws were for the benefit of archaeology and its practitioners. This situation has improved and can continue to improve if the actions described in this volume are implemented.

Gordon Willey and Jeremy Sabloff (1973) have provided a historical description of the evolution of intellectual development of American archaeology. Little of their account considers the administrative constraints in which the discipline grew. For the present purpose, it is sufficient to note that virtually all growth in the discipline in the U.S. has been influenced by federal law in one way or another. I am unsure whether federal requirements had more effect on intellectual growth of the discipline, or vice versa. It may be more accurate to consider the interaction as symbiotic. Despite suggestions to the contrary, the Federal Archeology Program has always reflected the current trajectory of American archaeological theory. This is how it should be, and I suggest that this is how it will continue to be. It is my impression that much of the criticism directed at the Federal Archeology Program is based on myopic, altruistic perceptions.

By the last decade of this millennium, there seems to be sufficient legal authority in place to deal with archaeological properties in the federal domain as well as in many states and some local jurisdictions. Like the Internal Revenue Code, historic preservation legislation has needed, and will continue to need, fine tuning (e.g., the 1980 amendments to the National Historic Preservation Act of 1966, and 1988 amendments to the Archaeological Resources Protection Act of 1979).

## PRESENT CONCERNS

It may seem ironic that the current, most pressing threat to the national archaeological data base is the same threat identified a century ago — looting and vandalism. This problem will not go away. The legal means to protect archaeological properties are in place. The effective use of these means has yet to be fully recognized. Additionally, and for a major portion of the nation (the eastern U.S.), the majority of sites are situated on private lands. Many of the states and a few county and municipality governments have passed laws and ordinances modeled on federal statutes. These, too, have avoided the constitutional issues regarding government interference with private property rights. The treatment of unmarked graves is the only area that has been consistently considered. In this area both archaeologists and Native Americans agree that the looting of graves by pothunters should be stopped.

Many archaeologists must do as I have: face the fact that in the majority of situations, the treatment of Native American skeletal remains has been, in a large part, insensitive at best and racist at worst. Native Americans are concerned not only with current practices of recovery of additional skeletal material, grave goods, and sacred sites, but with collections curated in institutions across the country (see Anyon, this volume, for further discussion of Native American concerns regarding archaeological resources). In establishing the National Museum of the American Indian, Congress has directed the Smithsonian Institution to set in motion a process by which these materials can be turned over to the tribes. In November 1990, Congress extended its concern with the human remains issue with the passage of the Native American Graves Protection and Repatriation Act. To be sure, some portion of these collections have immense scientific importance, but other portions have little or none. We must pay more attention to the rights and desires of the legitimate Native Americans and do our best to find a way out of this morass.

The Taos Conference and special sessions at the Society for American Archaeology annual meetings in Atlanta (1989) and Las Vegas (1990) are clear examples of the major national professional organizations confronting the problem. The cooperation between the various interest groups that these meetings have generated is laudatory.

None of the articles in this volume call for new major legislation. Thus, if new legislation is not the answer to the dilemma, where lies our hope? It should be clear to even the most casual reader that our hope for better archaeological data preservation is to be found in the distillation of the sound and practical ideas and concepts found in this volume and by adopting the sound methodological approaches that have worked in various venues across the country.

## FUTURE DIRECTIONS

Clearly, the Taos Conference addressed many of the questions regarding the scope and causes of looting and vandalism, and provided a long list of proactive efforts that should ameliorate the problem. The call for additional research regarding the scope and causes of looting and vandalism should not go unheeded, but most important consideration must be given to research priorities. These priorities must be established by the Society for American Archaeology. While the society can not dictate research activities, it does stand a great chance in influencing the profession and the government in the sequence and levels of effort to accomplish the necessary research. Given that there is a national consensus regarding the magnitude of the problem and the real world constraints of limited personnel (with other duties to accomplish) and limited available money, it is incumbent that duplication of efforts are avoided.

Harvey Shields (this volume) has offered a paradigm for attacking this problem, which should be given the most serious consideration. We must avoid the idea that the integration of archaeology into public education, media bombardment, the use of volunteers in archaeological projects, the development of site stewardship programs, law enforcement, and the other salutary suggestions will stop *all* looting and vandalism. Clearly they will not. Even the threat of immediate execution did not deter all tomb robbers in dynastic Egypt.

Our grand strategy must obtain the "biggest bang for the buck." Our planning and execution must be integrated both horizontally and vertically. The articles in this volume clearly indicate that several fronts must be attacked simultaneously. The challenge is to identify the appropriate strategy and tactics. The wisdom of experience provided in the articles in this volume that focus on specific fronts must be heeded. Federal and state laws and local government ordinances dealing with the criminalization of acts related to the archaeological data base must be developed with input from law enforcement professionals, representatives from the judicial system, and Native Americans as well as archaeologists and politicians. Kris Rogers' (this volume) experiments in developing model legislation are excellent resources to guide such efforts.

Clear thinking has to be given the area of education. I am uncertain that enough attention has been given to devising a national archaeological education strategy. Its seems that a clear distinction needs to be made between the strategy and tactics to be used for each of the population segments we need to reach. We also need to develop greater precision in defining the goals of education: what elements of archaeological education are common to all sectors of the population and what elements are specific to particular sectors. If the outcome of our educational effort is to develop the idea and acceptance of the public trust theory for heritage resources management (Knudson, this volume), the approach will be different from educational efforts aimed at improving the observance of current laws. A different approach will also be necessary in educating individuals who wish to participate in site stewardship programs or field projects.

Clearly, raising the sensitivity of the general public regarding the increasing loss of archaeological properties is a job that can best be accomplished by the popular media. Public awareness of the loss of a heritage resource is usually the first step in efforts to rescue the property, or the data it contains, at the local project level. Infrequently, the larger problem has not been described in these local efforts, but this is changing.

The inclusion or integration of archaeological information in public school curricula will take a different tact. Clearly, to be successful it will take a tremendous amount of individual commitment, time, and energy. No matter how important we believe our cause, it is as Gene Rogge (this volume) points out: archaeology is just one more crusade that competes for the attention of the public school system. It is likely that much of the effort required of individual archaeologists working in this area can be reduced by the preparation of curriculum materials at the national or state level. More progress is possible if the prepackaged material is developed and used as it is in other public school study areas. Given the limited resources for this kind of foray, the approach should be in general and global terms rather than *emphasize* local or regional matters (see Messenger and Enloe, this volume, for a discussion of archaeologists as global educators).

## CONCLUSION

The challenge we face in affecting the future of archaeological resource protection is one of coming to grips with an unfamiliar area. For the most part, we have no experience in grass-roots movements, yet many archaeologists are convinced this is where the solution to our current dilemma lies. The public trust theory regarding the wisest use of heritage resources must be developed. This seems to be the only viable long-run mechanism to deal with the protection of the entire archaeological data base in a nation with such strong concepts of private property.

## REFERENCES CITED

**Rothman, H.** (1989) *Preserving Different Pasts: The American National Monuments,* University of Illinois Press, Urbana and Chicago.
**Willey, G. R. and Sabloff, J. A.** (1973) *A History of American Archaeology,* W. H. Freeman, San Francisco.

# EPILOG

"It was early morning, very early, when I walked out to a shell bank exposed by the ebb tide at the mouth of Lostmans River in the 10,000 Islands Archaeological District, Everglades National Park, Florida. The morning air was uncommonly still, and only the smell of the salt air seemed to interrupt the quietness. As the sun climbed up over the eastern sky and lit the waters in the Gulf of Mexico, the rays of light flashed like static electricity through the mangrove. The effect was mesmerizing, and I don't recall knowing exactly when the eagle landed beside me; it was marvelous. The bird was riveting, and its piercing glare resembled that of the Wishram Indian guardian spirit *Tsagaglalal*. As we stared back at each other, I had the tingling sensation that I could see countless centuries of human prehistory reflected in her eyes. The air seemed to faintly hum with the distant sounds of voices, desires, and lives of people long vanquished by time" (John Ehrenhard).

This book has been a cooperative endeavor by people dedicated to providing information concerning various archaeological resource protection issues in order to increase the awareness of, and appreciation for, our nation's heritage. The authors in this diverse group of professionals have all contributed to the principle that we are all archivists of the nation. As you close this book, remember that each of us does have a moral and ethical responsibility to educate our fellow brothers and sisters and provide them with a viable framework for understanding and protecting our portion of the human experience. May *Protecting the Past* give you counsel in your endeavor to give future generations a chance to see *Tsagaglalal* in the eye of the eagle.

It is altogether fitting and proper that the first Americans have the last word in this book concerning protecting the past for the future.

"We know that the white man does not understand our ways. One portion of the land is the same to him as the next, for he is a stranger who comes in the night and takes from the land whatever he needs. The earth is not his brother, but his enemy, and when he has conquered it, he moves on. He leaves his fathers' graves, and his children's birthright is forgotten....

When the last redman has vanished from the earth, and the memory is only the shadow of a cloud moving across the prairie, these shores and forests will still hold the spirits of my people, for they love this earth as the newborn loves its mother's heartbeat. If we sell you our land, love it as we've loved it. Care for it, as we've cared for it. Hold in your mind the memory of the land, as it is when you take it. And with all your strength, with all your might, and with all your heart — preserve it for your children, and love it as God loves us all. One thing we know — our God is the same....Even the white man cannot be exempt from the common destiny" (Chief Sealth, Duwamish Tribe, state of Washington, from a letter written to President Franklin Pierce in 1854).

# APPENDIX
# ARCHAEOLOGICAL SITE PROTECTION POLICY STATEMENTS

The following statements or selected portions of by-laws or policy statements are reproduced with the permission of the appropriate professional organization. The editors sincerely acknowledge the cooperation and assistance of:

- The Society for American Archaeology
- The Society of Professional Archeologists
- The Advisory Council on Historic Preservation
- The American Association of Museums

## SOCIETY FOR AMERICAN ARCHAEOLOGY BY-LAWS

## Adopted April 1989

### Article II - Objective

The objectives of this Society shall be:

1. To promote and to stimulate interest and research in the archaeology of the American continents
2. To advocate and to aid in the conservation of archaeological resources
3. To encourage public access to and appreciation of the aims, accomplishments, and limitations of archaeological research
4. To serve as a bond among those interested in American archaeology, both professionals and nonprofessionals, and to aid in directing their efforts into scientific channels
5. To publish and to encourage the publication of archaeological research
6. To foster the formation and welfare of regional and local archaeological societies
7. To discourage commercialism in archaeology and to work for its elimination
8. To operate exclusively for scientific and educational purposes, including, for such purposes, the making of distributions to organizations that qualify as exempt organizations under Section 501(c)(3) of the Internal Revenue Code
9. To engage in any and all lawful activities incidental to the foregoing purposes

In the pursuit of its objectives, the Society shall promote and support all legislative, regulatory, and voluntary programs that forbid and discourage all activities that result in the loss of scientific knowledge and of access to sites and artifacts. Such activities include, but are not limited to, the irresponsible excavation, collecting, hoarding, exchanging, buying, or selling of archaeological materials. Conduct that results in such losses is declared contrary to the ideals and objectives of the Society.

299

# SOCIETY OF PROFESSIONAL ARCHAEOLOGISTS CODE OF ETHICS
## Adopted 1988

1.    The archaeologist's responsibility to the public

    1.1   An archaeologist shall
        1.   Recognize a commitment to represent archaeology and its research results to the public in a responsible manner
        2.   Actively support conservation of the archaeological research base
        3.   Be sensitive to, and respect the legitimate concerns of groups whose cultural histories are the subjects of archaeological investigation
        4.   Avoid and discourage exaggerated, misleading, or unwarranted statements about archaeological matters that might induce others to engage in unethical or illegal activity
        5.   Support and comply with the terms of the UNESCO Convention on the means of prohibiting and preventing the illicit import, export, and transfer of ownership of cultural property, as adopted by the General Conference, November 14, 1970, Paris.

    1.2   An archaeologist shall *not*

        1.   Engage in any illegal or unethical conduct involving archaeological matters or knowingly permit the use of her/his name in support of any illegal or unethical activity involving archaeological matters
        2.   Give a professional opinion, make a public report, or give legal testimony involving archaeological matters without being as thoroughly informed as might reasonably be expected
        3.   Engage in conduct involving dishonesty, fraud, deceit, or misrepre-sentation about archaeological matters
        4.   Undertake any research that affects the archaeological resource base for which she/he is not qualified

# ADVISORY COUNCIL ON HISTORIC PRESERVATION: POLICY STATEMENT REGARDING "POTHUNTING"
## Adopted September 27, 1988, Gallup, New Mexico

The council deplores the destruction caused by pothunting and applauds the efforts of Congress, the agencies, the states, and the tribes to contend with it.

The council supports, in principle, legislative and educational efforts to address the pothunting problem. However, the council also understands the desire to search out, study, appreciate, and possess artifacts and art objects, which directly or indirectly motivates pothunting.

The council expresses its strong support for, and encouragement of, efforts by the Department of Justice, and the various U.S. attorneys, and other federal and state agencies to bring to justice and prosecute to the full extent of the law all violators of federal and state laws protecting historic, archaeological, and other cultural resources. However, the council recognizes that it is unlikely that police action alone will control pothunting on federal and Indian lands, and that since pothunting occurs on other lands as well, increased enforcement on federal and Indian lands may increase pothunting elsewhere.

Accordingly, the council encourages cooperative efforts among federal agencies, states, Indian tribes, archaeologists, art and artifact dealers, artifact collectors, and other interested parties, to seek mutually agreeable means of reducing pothunting while ensuring those interested in finding, studying, enjoying, and possessing artifacts the continued opportunity to do so.

## AMERICAN ASSOCIATION OF MUSEUMS CODE OF ETHICS FOR MUSEUMS
## Approved by the AAM Board of Directors May 18, 1991

### Collections

The distinctive character of museum ethics derives from the ownership, care, and use of objects, specimens, and living collections representing the world's natural and cultural common wealth. This stewardship of collections entails the highest public trust and carries with it the presumption of rightful ownership, permanence, care, documentation, accessibility, and responsible disposal.

Thus the museum ensures that:

- collections in its custody support its mission and public trust responsibilities
- collections in its custody are protected, secure, unencumbered, cared for, and preserved
- collections in its custody are accounted for and documented
- access to the collections and related information is permitted and regulated
- acquisition, disposal, and loan activities are conducted in a manner that respects the protection and preservation of natural and cultural resources and discourages illicit trade in such materials
- acquisition, disposal, and loan activities conform to its mission and public trust responsibilities
- disposal of collections through sale, trade, or research activities is solely for the advancement of the museum's mission, and use of proceeds from the sale of collection materials is restricted to the acquisition of collections
- the unique and special nature of human remains and funerary and sacred objects is recognized as the basis of all decisions concerning such collections
- collections-related activities promote the public good rather than individual financial gain.

# INDEX

## A

Abandoned Shipwreck Act of 1987, 23–24, 42–45, 293

Accountability, joint, team approach and, 68–69

Action research, 162

*Actions for the '90s,* 273–274

Active learning, 163–165

Adams, Robert McCormick, 89

Advisory Council on Historic Preservation, 22, 84, 293

  policy statement of, regarding "pothunting", 300

Advocacy

  avocational groups and, 178–179

  children in, 143

  national model for, 143–144

Aesthetic pleasure, pothunting for, 90

Age limit, 50

  P.L. 100-555 and, 48

Agency coordination, need for improvement of, 274

Airlie House Report, 54

AkChin tribe, 220

Alarm strategies, of commercial looters, 96

Alaska

  Kodiak Island, Koniagmiut of, 220

  St. Lawrence Island, pothunting at, 86–87, 90

Amateurs

  groups of, in public education, 58–59

  in participatory archaeology, 58

American Anthropological Association, 138, 145

*American Anthropologist,* 28

American Association of Museums, Curator Code of Ethics of, 301

American Indian Religious Freedom Act, 23

American Indians, see Native Americans

Anasazi sites, 219, 220

Anthony Shoals site, signing at, 235, 242–243

Anthropology, in global curriculum, 160–161

Antidetection strategies, of commercial looters, 96

Antiquarian interest, museum experience and, 188

Antiquities, international traffic in, 87

Antiquities Act of 1906, 29–30, 33, 291

  looting and vandalism and, 94, 262

  pothunting and, 84

Anton Rygh site, pothunting at, 84

Archaeological and Historic Preservation Act of 1974, 22, 292, 293

Archaeological assessments, quality of, ensurance of, 250–251

Archaeological Conservancy, 57, 176

  site protection and, 283–287

Archaeological conservancy, 54

Archaeological fiction, 17

Archaeological Institute of America, 29

  founding of, 28

Archaeological literacy, 132–133

Archaeological materials, visibility of, signing and, 238

Archaeological public trust, 3–7

Archaeological record, 215, 221

Archaeological research

  about looting and vandalism, need for, 274

  political role of, 13

Archaeological Resource Centre, Toronto, 136–137, 139–142

Archaeological resources, defined, 4, 65

  ARPA amendments and, 48–49

Archaeological Resources Protection Act (ARPA) of 1979, 22, 47, 201, 262–263, 292, 293, see also Protection

  amendments to, 36–37, 47–49, 266–267, 268, 294

  as antecedent to cultural resource management, 31

  clearinghouses and, 194

  constituencies and, 45

  history of, 33–39

  introduction of, 42

  looting and vandalism and

    enforcement efforts, 87, 94, 243, 266

    pothunting, 83, 84, 86, 87

  native Americans and, 217, 220

  present situation and, 37–38

  prevention in, 267

  sign messages and, 238–240

  "suspension of the rules" and, 44

  team approach and, 65–69

  uniform regulations and, 35–36, 68

Archaeological Resources Protection Law seminar, 49

Archaeological sites, see Site entries

Archaeologist(s)

  benefitting students, 145–147

  as global educator, 157–165

  museum, responsibility of, 190–191

  "rogue", 97

  role of, in team approach, 66–67

  support for, 114

Archaeology, defined, 3, 103

"Archaeology and Education", 138

*Archaeology and Public Education,* 138

Archaeology for Schools Committee, Arizona Archaeological Council, teaching with archaeology and, 129–133

*Archaeology* magazine, 88, 89

Archaeology Week, 106

  LEAP and, 196

Arizona, AkChin in, 220

Arizona Archaeological Council, 145

  Archaeology for Schools Committee of, teaching with archaeology and, 129–133

Arizona Site Steward Program, 253–259

  accomplishments of, 258–259

  development of, 254–255